SERVICE SHEETS

1945 to 1958
C10-C10L
C11-C11G
C12

A Floyd Clymer Publication
Published in 2021 by VelocePress.com

INTRODUCTION

Welcome to the world of digital publishing ~ the book you now hold in your hand was printed using the latest state of the art digital technology. The advent of print-on-demand has forever changed the publishing process, never has information been so accessible and it is our hope that this book serves your informational needs for years to come. If this is your first exposure to digital publishing, we hope that you are pleased with the results. Many more titles of interest to the classic automobile and motorcycle enthusiast, collector and restorer are available via our website at www.VelocePress.com. We hope that you find this title as interesting as we do.

NOTE FROM THE PUBLISHER

The information presented is true and complete to the best of our knowledge. All recommendations are made without any guarantees on the part of the author or the publisher, who also disclaim all liability incurred with the use of this information.

TRADEMARKS

We recognize that some words, model names and designations, for example, mentioned herein are the property of the trademark holder. We use them for identification purposes only. This is not an official publication.

INFORMATION ON THE USE OF THIS PUBLICATION

This manual is an invaluable resource for those interested in performing their own maintenance. However, in today's information age we are constantly subject to changes in common practice, new technology, availability of improved materials and increased awareness of chemical toxicity. As such, it is advised that the user consult with an experienced professional prior to undertaking any procedure described herein. While every care has been taken to ensure correctness of information, it is obviously not possible to guarantee complete freedom from errors or omissions or to accept liability arising from such errors or omissions. Therefore, any individual that uses the information contained within, or elects to perform or participate in do-it-yourself repairs or modifications acknowledges that there is a risk factor involved and that the publisher or its associates cannot be held responsible for personal injury or property damage resulting from the use of the information or the outcome of such procedures.

WARNING!

One final word of advice, this publication is intended to be used as a reference guide, and when in doubt the reader should consult with a qualified technician.

BSA 'SERVICE SHEETS'

UNDERSTANDING AND INTERPRETING THE 1945 AND ONWARDS PUBLICATIONS

In 1945, after the war had ended, BSA resumed production of their civilian line of motorcycles. However, they continued their pre-war practice of publishing repair, overhaul and technical information in the form of individual 'Service Sheets'. It should be noted that BSA never intended that these service sheets would be distributed to the general public, they were 'dealer only' publications and, as such, the print quality was at times somewhat questionable. It was not until the early 1960's that BSA eventually started publishing model specific workshop manuals that were available to the general public. Consequently, these 'Service Sheets' were the only publications available for the maintenance and repair of BSA models that were manufactured through the early 1960's.

At some point in the 1930's, BSA adopted the practice of identifying their various model types by 'groups' and the models manufactured from 1945 through the mid 1960's were in Groups A, B, C, D and M. The service sheets that were associated to a particular group were identified numerically and, while there were some exceptions due to overlapping data between models, in general terms the numbers relate to a particular model group. They are as follows: The 200 series of service sheets were applicable to Group A models, the 300 series to Group B, the 400 series to Group C, the 500 series to Group D and the 600 series to Group M. In addition, there were a 700 series applicable to mechanical maintenance and an 800 series for electronic service and wiring diagrams. Both the 700 and 800 series of service sheets contained information that was not model specific but was applicable across multiple model groups. Finally, there were a 900 series for the BSA Dandy and a 1000 series for the BSA Sunbeam and Triumph Tigress scooter.

Unfortunately, as these service sheets were issued individually and at random times, the numbering sequence within any group is, at times, illogical and not necessarily consecutive. Consequently, assembling those individual sheets into a publication that serves as a model specific workshop manual is a somewhat difficult task and owners of BSA motor cycles are subjected to considerable confusion surrounding the appropriate selection from the multitude of reprints that have recently flooded the on-line marketplace. Many of the reprints found on internet websites are from 'bedroom sellers' at enticingly low prices by individuals that really have no idea what they are selling. Many are nothing more than poor quality comb-bound photocopies that are scanned and printed complete with greasy pages and thumbprints and, as such, are deceptively described as 'pre-owned', 'used' or even 'refurbished'! In addition, they are often advertised for the incorrect series and/or model years of motorcycles.

The most complete compilation of the 1945 and onwards service sheets was issued by BSA in the form of a 'dealer only' ring binder that contained all of the individual service sheets totaling to almost 500 pages, it is extremely scarce and difficult to find. It is this ring bound publication that was used to create this 'Service Sheet' manual'.

'C' GROUP SERVICE SHEET MANUALS 1945-1958

This manual contains 63 service sheets (210 pages) extracted from that 'dealer only' publication, which cover the pre-unit 1945 to 1958 rigid and spring frame C10, C10L, C11, C11G and the 1956 to 1958 swing arm C12. Please note that service sheets other than those in the 400 series that are included in this publication may also contain data that is applicable to 'other' model groups, as that was the original intention.

For additional information the reader is directed to **'The Book of the BSA 250cc, 350cc, 500cc & 600cc OHV & SV singles 1945 to 1959'** (ISBN 9781588502292) which covers the B31, B32, B33, B34, C10, C11, C11DL, M20, M21 & M33 models.

GENERAL INDEX

PAGE	SHEET	SUBJECT	PAGE	SHEET	SUBJECT
3		Supplement	98	701	Technical Data
11	209	Gearbox	100	702	Technical Data
13	308	Clutch	102	703	Technical Data
15	401	Engine	104	704	Technical Data
16	401A	Engine	106	705	General Maintenance
17	402	Engine	107	706	Front Forks
18	402A	Engine	111	708	Carburetter
19	403	Gearbox	119	708B	Carburetter
20	403A	Gearbox	120	709	Fault Diagnosis
21	403B	Gearbox	121	710	Chain
22	404	Engine	123	710X	Frames by model
27	405	Engine	140	711	Special Tools
31	406	Engine	148	711A	Special Tools
35	407	Engine	152	711B	Special Tools
37	408	Gearbox	159	712X	Flywheel
41	408A	Gearbox	161	713	Steering
45	409	Gearbox	162	714	Spokes
49	410	Hubs	166	803	Ignition
53	411	Clutch	170	804	Regulator
55	412	Hubs	174	805	Battery
57	412A	Hubs	178	806	Lights
59	412B	Hubs	181	807	Horn
63	412C	Suspension	183	808	Wiring Diagrams
64	413	Engine	185	808A	Wiring Diagrams
68	414	Engine	187	808C	Wiring
71	415	Technical Data	189	808D	Wiring
73	415A	Engine	191	809	Dynamo/Generator
75	508	Hubs	199	811	Lamps
82	509	Forks	201	813	Alternator
86	514	Suspension	209	813A	Alternator
88	603	Engine Lube	215	814	Alternator
96	612	Brakes	219	815	Battery

SUPPLEMENT

The wiring diagrams on the following pages are included as they are more legible than those in the Service Sheets. The appropriate BSA Service Sheet number is referenced on each diagram.

Reference Service Sheet 808

WIRING DIAGRAM FOR LUCAS COIL IGNITION AND DYNAMO
LIGHTING WITH COMPENSATED VOLTAGE CONTROL (1945-51)

This diagram with negative earth applied to 1937-50 and early 1951 C models (C10, C11). All internal connexions are shown dotted and the cables are identified by coloured sleeves.

1. Red	7. Red and black	20. White
2. Red and yellow	8. Yellow	22. White and brown
3. Red and blue	12. Yellow and purple	23. White and purple
4. Red and white	13. Yellow and black	28. Green and black
5. Red and green	14. Blue	33. Black
6. Red and brown	15. Blue and white	

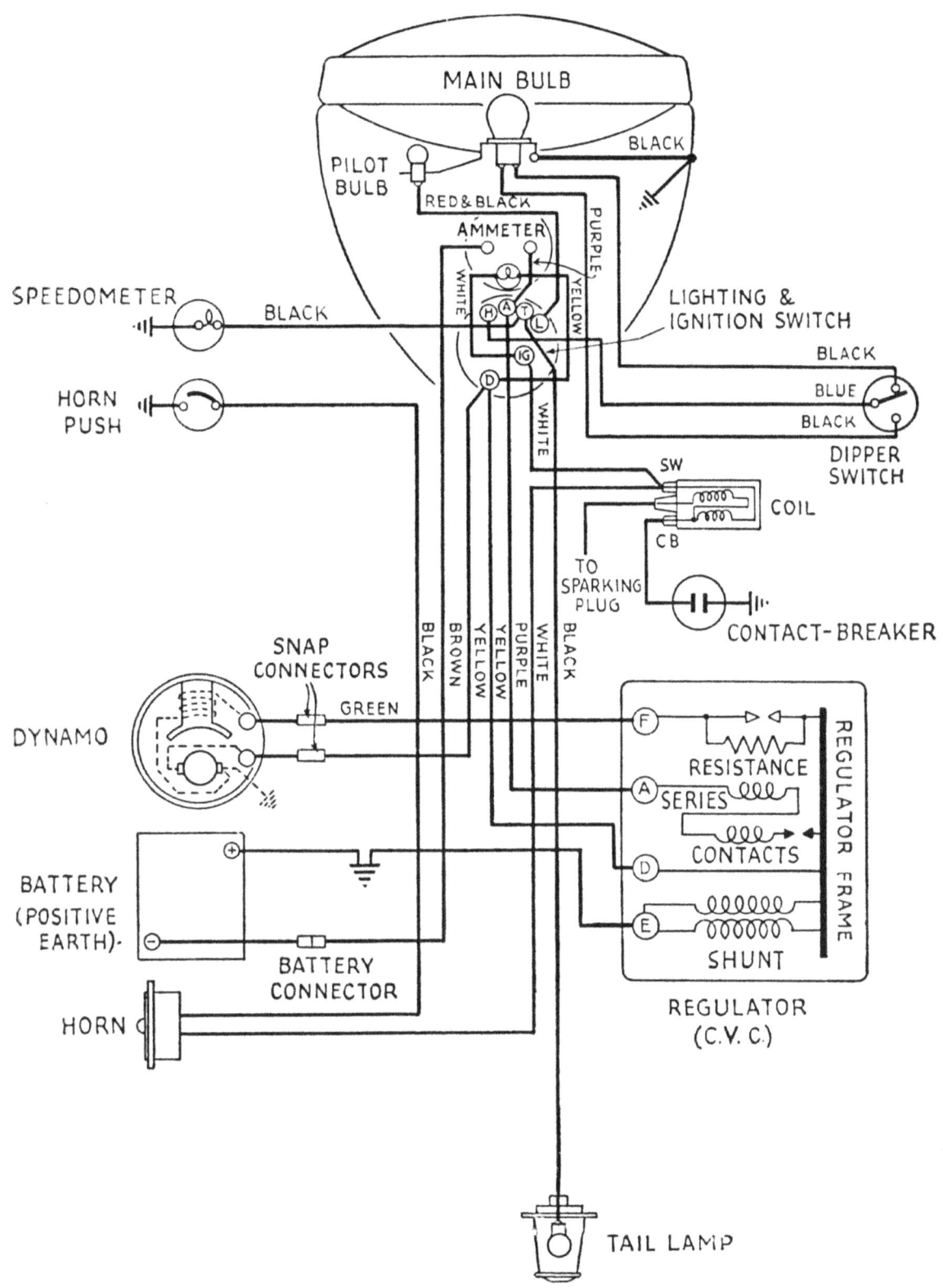

Reference Service Sheet 808A

WIRING DIAGRAM FOR LUCAS COIL IGNITION AND DYNAMO LIGHTING WITH COMPENSATED VOLTAGE CONTROL (LATE 1951 TO 1953)

This diagram with positive earth applies to late 1951 and all 1952-3 models C10, C11
A coloured cable harness is used in place of coloured sleeves for cable identification.

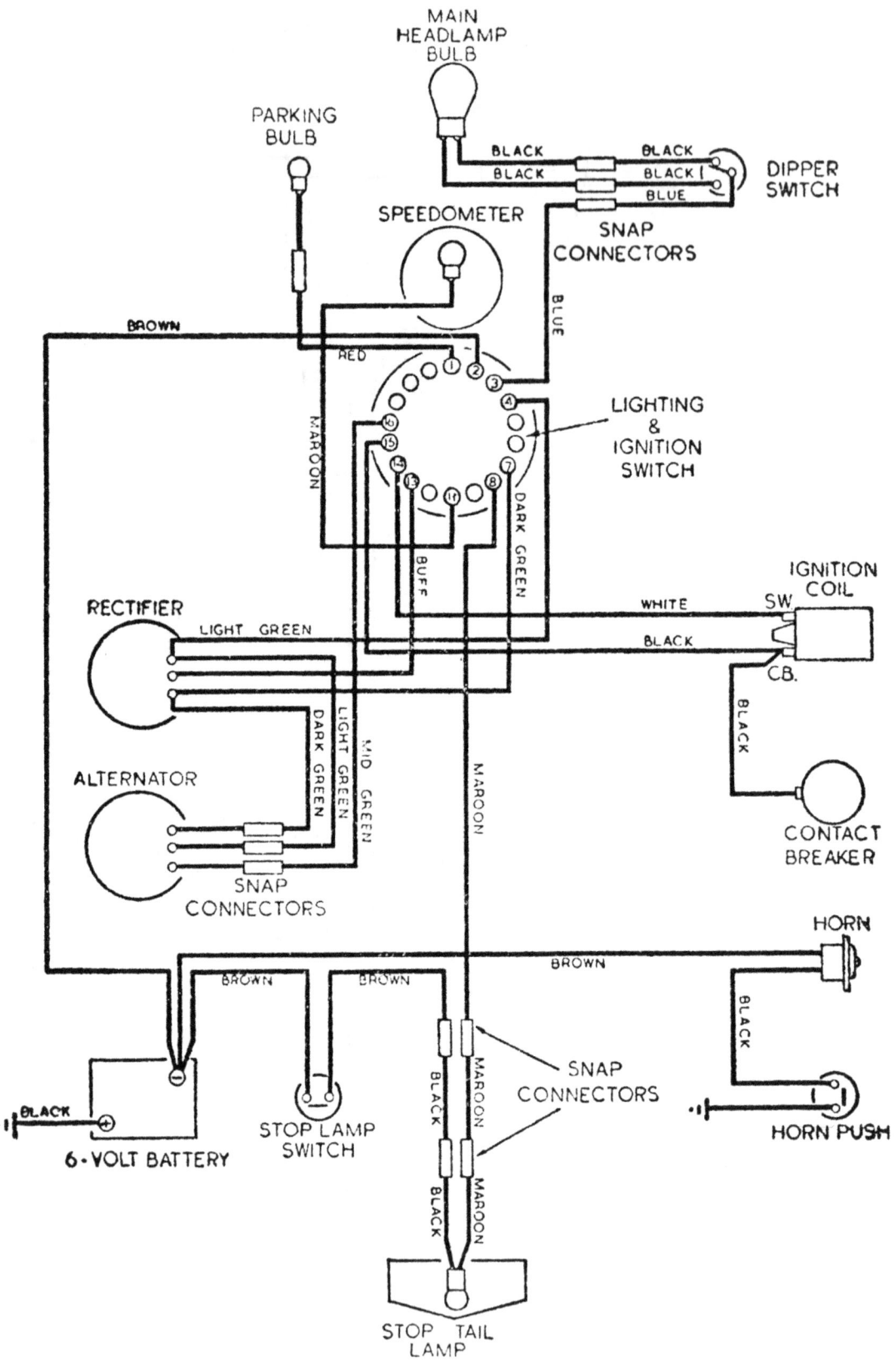

Reference Service Sheet 808C

WIRING DIAGRAM FOR MODEL C11G

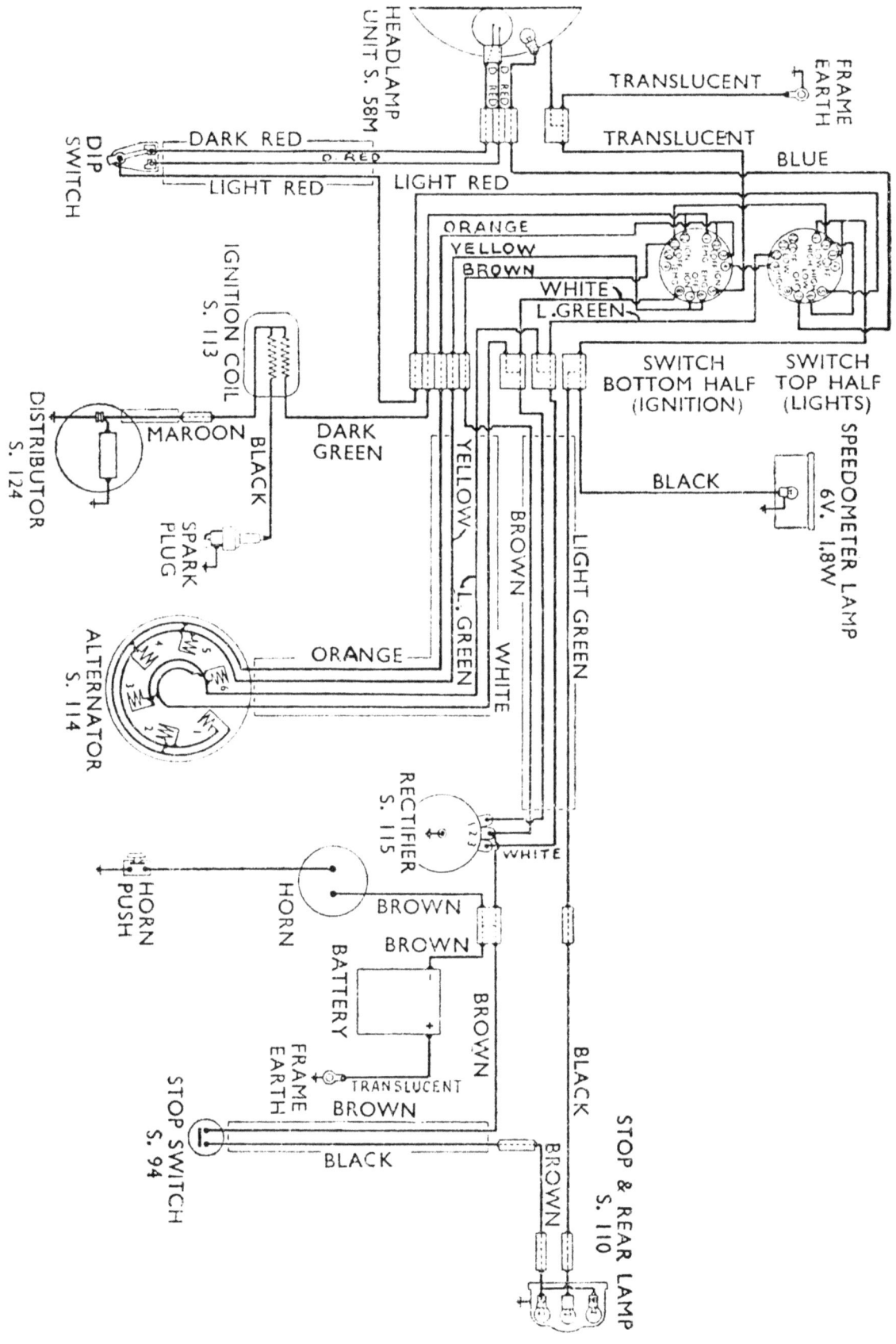

Reference Service Sheet 808C

WIRING DIAGRAM FOR MODEL C10L (1953–AUGUST 1954)

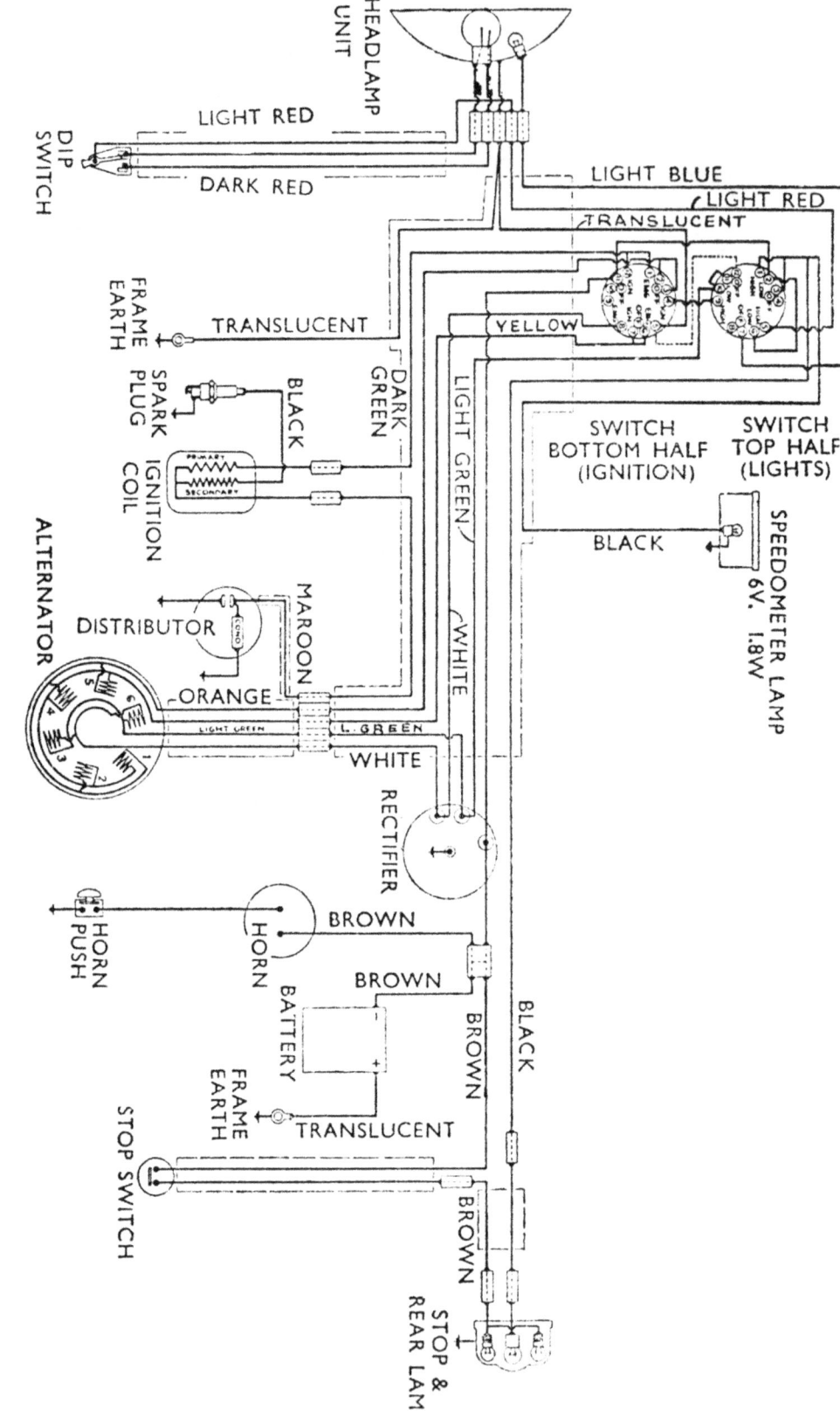

Reference Service Sheet 808C

WIRING DIAGRAM FOR MODEL C10L (OCTOBER 1954–JULY 1955)

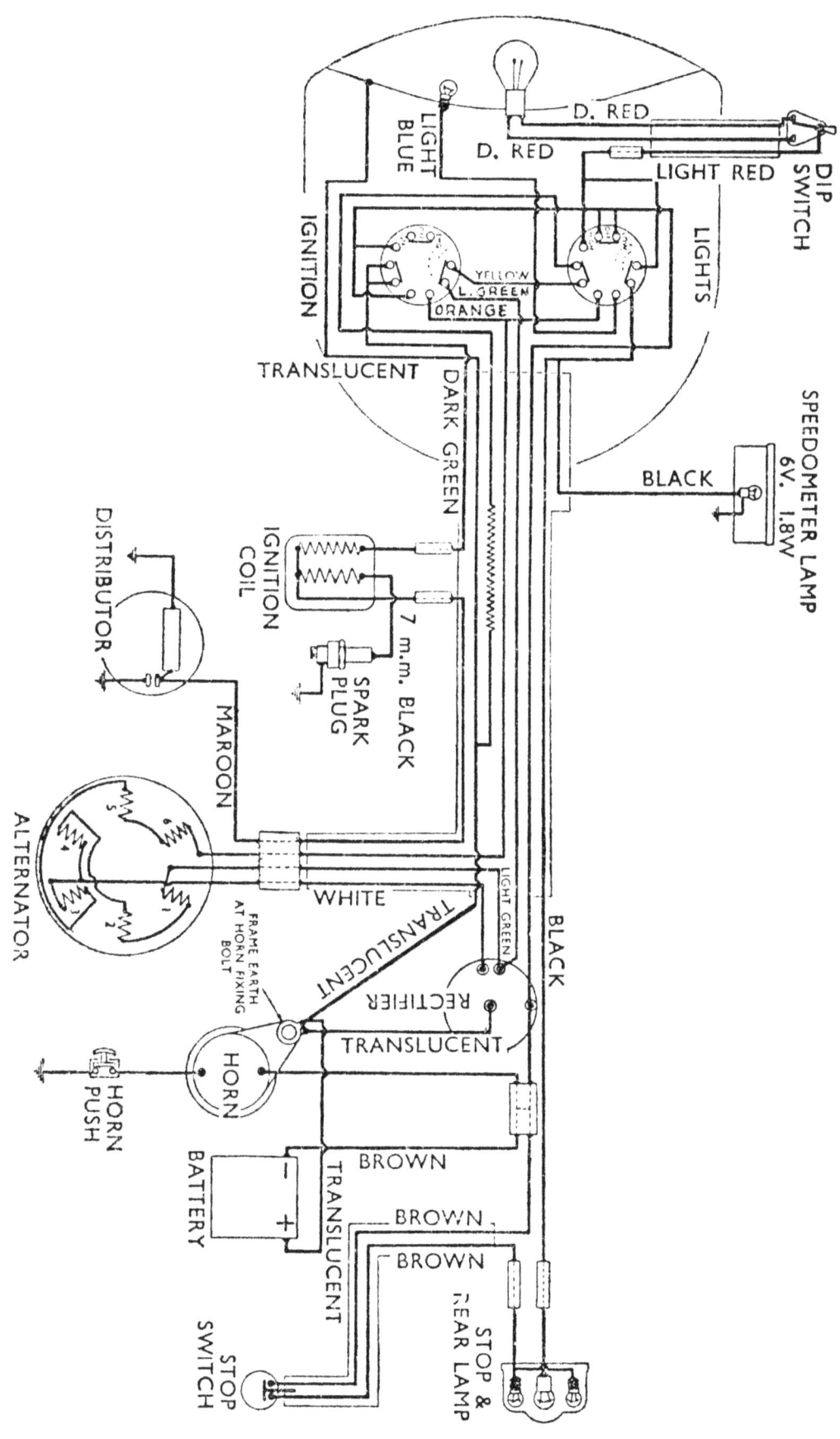

Reference Service Sheet 808D

WIRING DIAGRAM FOR MODEL C10L (AS FROM AUGUST, 1955)

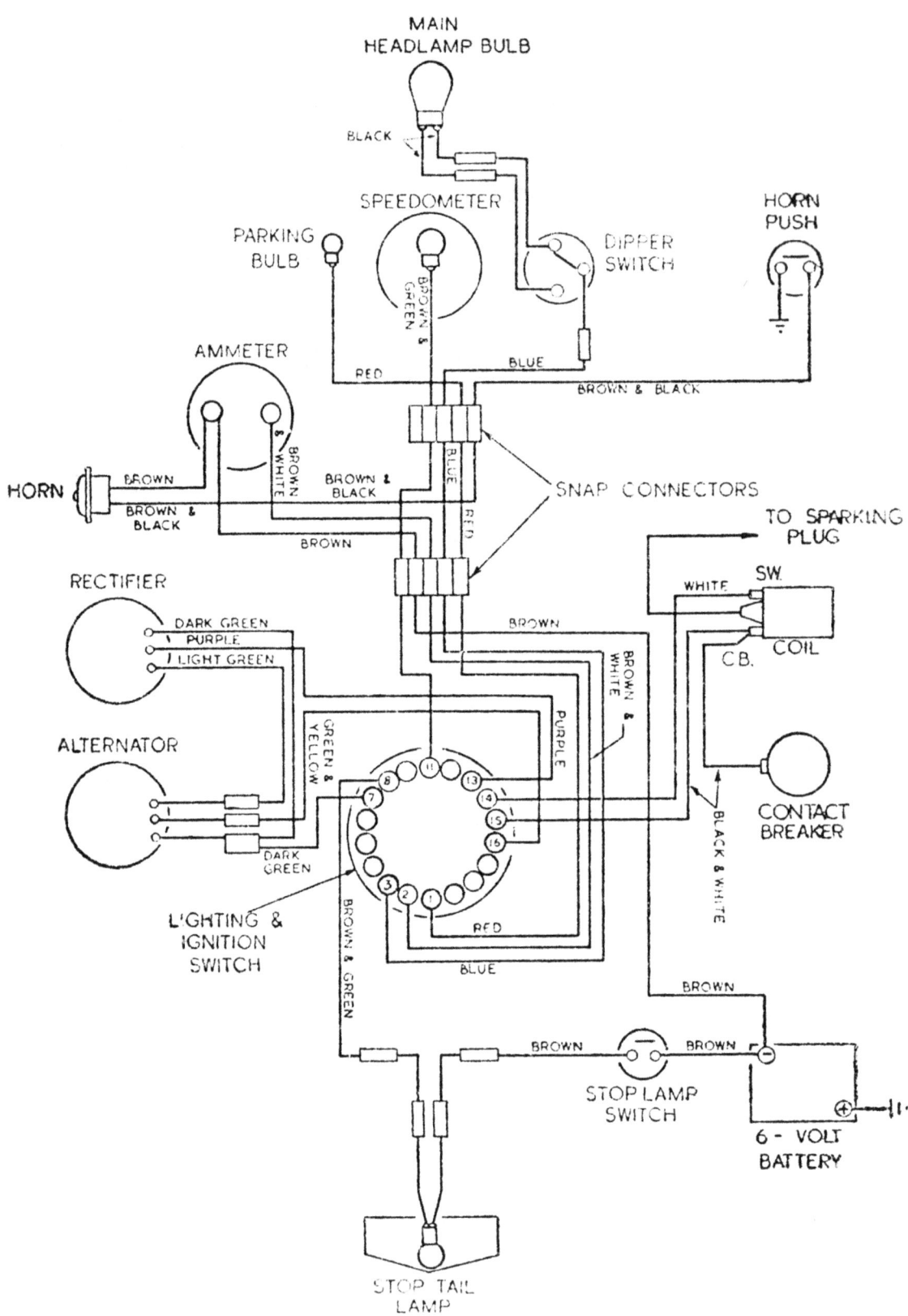

Reference Service Sheet 808D

Wiring Diagram for Model C12

BSA SERVICE SHEET No. 209

"C" GROUP, 4-SPEED (1951-57) & "A" GROUP RIGID & PLUNGER

DISMANTLING AND RE-ASSEMBLY OF GEARBOX AND GEARCHANGE

Removal

In most cases it will be found convenient to dismantle the gearbox while it is in position in the frame. If it is necessary to remove the gearbox sprocket or sleeve pinion on a "A" Group machine, the engine/gearbox unit must be removed from the frame and the gearbox separated from the crankcase (see Service Sheet No. 206). To remove the gearbox from the frame of a "C" Group machine for attention to bearings see Service Sheets Nos. 308 and 411.

Dismantling the Gearbox

Move the gears to the neutral position between first and second. Next remove the gearbox outer cover which is held in position by three screws and four nuts. The cover will come away with the kickstarter, the gearchange and the clutch lever still in position, and these need not be disturbed unless obviously requiring attention. Note that as the cover is withdrawn, the spring pressure on the kickstarter pedal is released. The clutch operating lever should be pulled out to the fullest extent, allowing the kickstarter lever to come to rest against it, thus preventing the kickstarter return spring from being released.

Pull out the clutch operating rod which passes through the centre of the mainshaft, and then release the nut on the mainshaft which holds the kickstarter ratchet pinion and spring, laying the latter aside. The gearbox partition can then be removed together with the foot gearchange rocking lever (M) Fig. A24.

The rod (G) is pressed into the gearbox shell at the clutch end and secured by a grub screw which is accessible under the gearbox. Release this grub screw and then pull out the rod. It should then be possible to withdraw the entire gear cluster complete with shafts and the two sliding forks bodily from the gearbox, although, if preferred, the components may be withdrawn separately. This may call for a certain amount of manoeuvring, but the experienced mechanic will have no difficulty. Before removing the gear selector plate (H), note the notch in which the gear control plunger engages. This is the neutral position between first and second gear, and the plate must be rotated to this position before the box can be reassembled. Unscrew the selector plunger housing locknut and remove the plunger assembly from the gearbox shell. The gear selector plate will now slide from its pivot. The layshaft bushes are a press-fit in the gearbox and if necessary must be driven out with the aid of a soft punch.

The top gear pinion sleeve is now the only part still left in the gearbox, and if the sprocket locknut is unscrewed, after suitable attention to the tab washer, the sprocket may be removed and the pinion tapped into the gearbox with the aid of a wooden mallet.

Do not disturb the ballrace unless it is suspected of being faulty. Wash it thoroughly in paraffin, to remove all traces of oil, and any play will then be immediately detected.

Examine the various parts for wear, and if the forks which actuate the sliding pinions show signs of seizure it will be advisable to replace them. Attempts to erase the seizure marks will result in excessive side play.

The fixed pinions on the layshaft and mainshaft are pressed on, and new components must be a tight fit. Examine the selector plate for worn cam grooves and for wear on the ratchet members on the boss in which the selector claw (P) engages, and replace if necessary. The selector claw should be replaced if the teeth show signs of wear as, of course, should pinions with damaged or worn teeth.

B.S.A. Service Sheet No. 209 (contd.)

Reassembly of the Gearbox and Gearbox Mechanism

If it has been decided to fit a new ballrace to the top gear pinion, remove the spring circlip and oil flinger washer with the aid of a screwdriver. In order to remove the ballrace easily, warm the gearbox shell in boiling water. If the sprocket teeth are worn hook-shaped, a new sprocket must be fitted; otherwise rapid chain wear will result. Do not forget to set the lockwasher into the grooves machined in the locknut after the latter has been tightened up. The tabs in the centre of the locknut washer must fit properly into the sprocket splines.

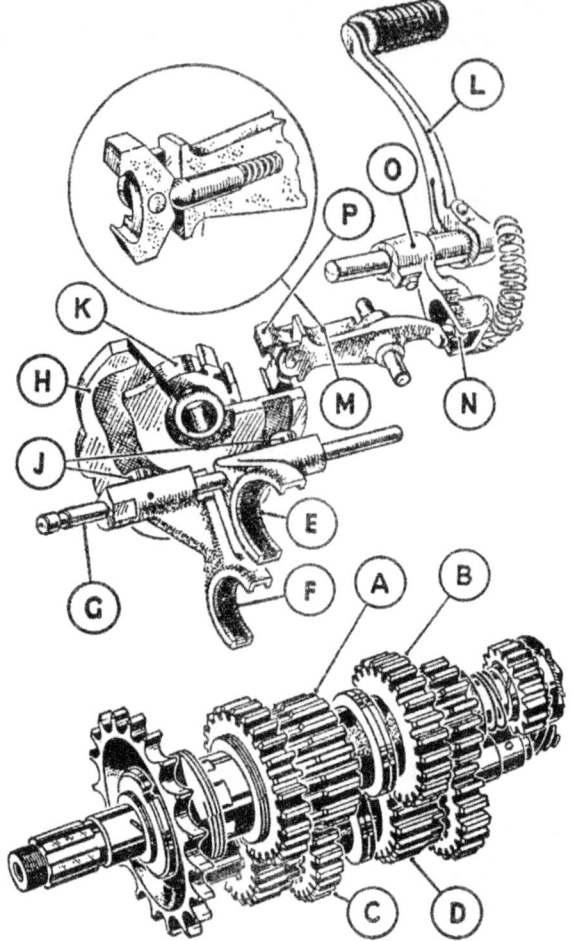

Fig. A24.

Assemble the layshaft with selector fork (F), with the exception of the low gear pinion (this is the largest on the shaft). Replace the selector plate and gear control plunger, rotating to the neutral position between first and second gears. Slide the layshaft complete with gears and selector fork into the box and engage the fork peg in the track of the cam plate.

Assemble the mainshaft pinions on the shaft and the selector fork (E), and insert the complete assembly into the gearbox shell engaging the peg of the selector fork in the cam plate. Slide the gear control shaft through the selector forks and press home into the gearbox case, replace the grub screw turning the edge of the hole over to prevent loss of the screw. Replace the thrust washer and low gear pinion on the layshaft.

The inner cover should next be assembled. Coat the paper washer between the inner cover and the gearbox shell with jointing compound, hold the gearchange rocking lever in a central position, slide the inner cover on to the four studs and push it "home". The gear selector claw must engage on the ratchet members on the selector plate boss.

The ratchet mechanism may now be fitted to the mainshaft, the parts assembling in the following order—spacing washer, sleeve bush, spring, ratchet pinion, locking washer, and nut. Tighten the nut and turn over the tab on the washer as a means of locking the nut.

The outer cover can now be replaced. Coat the paper washer with jointing compound. Take up the outer cover with the kickstart lever in the left hand and the footchange lever in the right hand. Slide the cover on to the gearbox studs and press home, entering the kickstart quadrant in the ratchet pinion and the footchange slotted lever over the ball end of the rocking lever. Replace the four nuts and three screws on the outer cover.

The unit is now ready for reassembly to the engine (see Service Sheet No. 208).

A10 and AA7 Machines

After engine numbers ZA10-1215, ZA7-11192 are fitted with a modified layshaft and gear cluster to obtain improved gear selection and the engine number should be specified when ordering spares.

B.S.A. MOTOR CYCLES LTD., Service Department, Armoury Road, Birmingham 11.

B.S.A. PRESS

BSA SERVICE SHEET No. 308

'M' GROUP, C10, C11, 'A' GROUP (S.A.), AND 'B' GROUP
(Except those engine with prefix letters G.B. or 'A' Group after engine numbers CA7-8623, CA755-8112 and DA10-13298)

DISMANTLING AND RE-ASSEMBLING THE CLUTCH

Take off the nearside footrest and then undo all the screws round the rim of the chaincase. As the outer half of the chaincase cover is taken off, careful note should be made of the positioning of the washers, etc., for replacement purposes. The joint washer should be carefully preserved.

Remove the six adjusting nuts, the springs and spring cups, and take off the clutch pressure plate so exposing the mainshaft nut which holds the clutch body in position.

The mainshaft nut is prevented from undoing by a locking washer which is turned over a flat on the nut. Flatten out the turned over edge of the washer and remove the nut. The clutch centre can now be withdrawn from the taper on the mainshaft using an extractor (part number 61-3362). Take care that the mainshaft key is not mislaid.

When the clutch is removed from the mainshaft it can be completely dismantled and the various components examined for wear. Special attention should be paid to the slots in which the clutch plates slide and any grooves should be removed with the aid of a fine file. If the grooves are very deep their removal will mean that the plates have excessive clearance and rapid wear will ensue. If the sprocket teeth are worn to a hook shape the sprocket must be replaced, otherwise rapid chain wear will result.

The steel plates should be smooth and if badly scored they should be replaced, while the fabric and cork inserts will require a thorough washing in petrol if there is any trace of oil on them. If the inserts are glazed or saturated in oil they should be replaced.

Finally, examine the balls, ball cages and tracks. If wear on the chainwheel bush or on the bearing boss of the clutch centre exceeds .0015 in. the bush or centre should be replaced (see Service Sheet No. 702 for correct dimensions).

NOTE.—When fitted to certain models this clutch is provided with additional plates, thus necessitating the use of a wider chainwheel and clutch centre, but the method of dismantling and reassembly is unaltered. C10 and C11 models have less plates than shown in the diagram but dismantling and assembly remain the same.

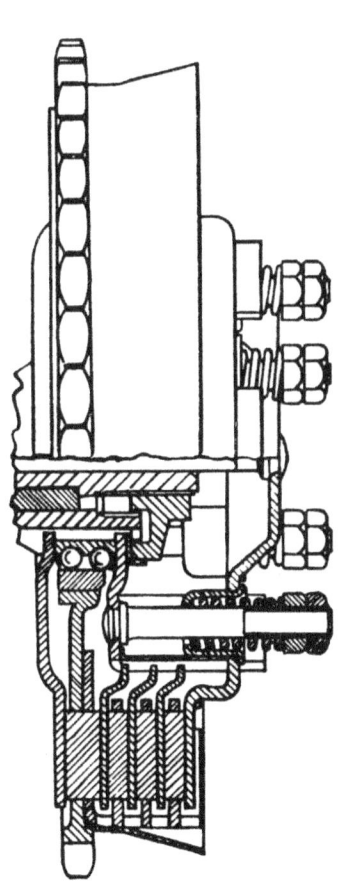

Fig. B18. *Section through clutch.*

B.S.A. Service Sheet No. 308 (contd.)

Reassembly of the Clutch
The clutch is of straightforward construction and a study of Fig. B18 will show how the parts are assembled. Do not forget the mainshaft key when replacing the clutch centre.

The plates must be fitted in their proper order as follows: drive plate (tongues on inner diameter), fabric insert plates, drive plate, etc. Before refitting the pressure plate it is advisable to smear a small quantity of grease on the centre button at the point of contact with the clutch push rod.

The clutch springs should be replaced if they have shortened appreciably. The spring retaining nuts should be tightened initially until the outer nut (A) Fig. B19, is just fully engaged on its thread.

It is most important that the clutch spring pressure is evenly distributed, and this should be checked by ensuring that the clutch pressure plate does not tilt when the clutch is withdrawn. If the plate does tilt the nuts should be adjusted until the spring pressure is even. Unequal spring pressure may cause clutch drag and noisy gearchange. When the adjustment is complete tighten the locknuts firmly.

Clutch Re-adjustment
After a considerable mileage has been covered it may be necessary to screw the spring retaining nuts in further to allow for wear on the clutch inserts. Release the locknuts (A), and tighten the nuts (B) by a few turns. After the adjustment has been carried out, check that the clutch lifts evenly and then tighten the locknuts.

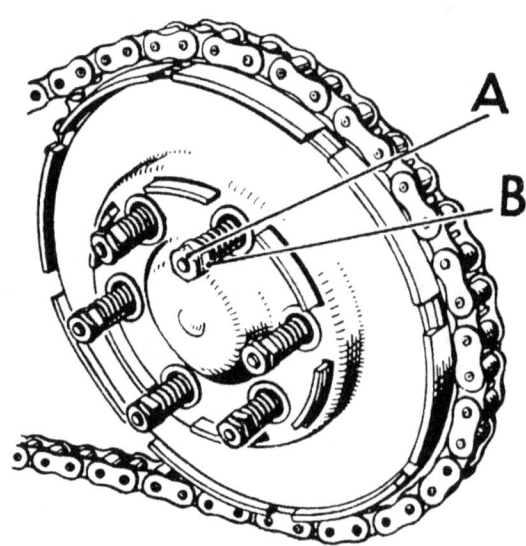

Fig. B19. *Clutch spring adjustment.*

B.S.A. MOTOR CYCLES LTD., Service Department, Armoury Road, Birmingham 11.

BSA SERVICE SHEET No. 401

Reprinted September 1959

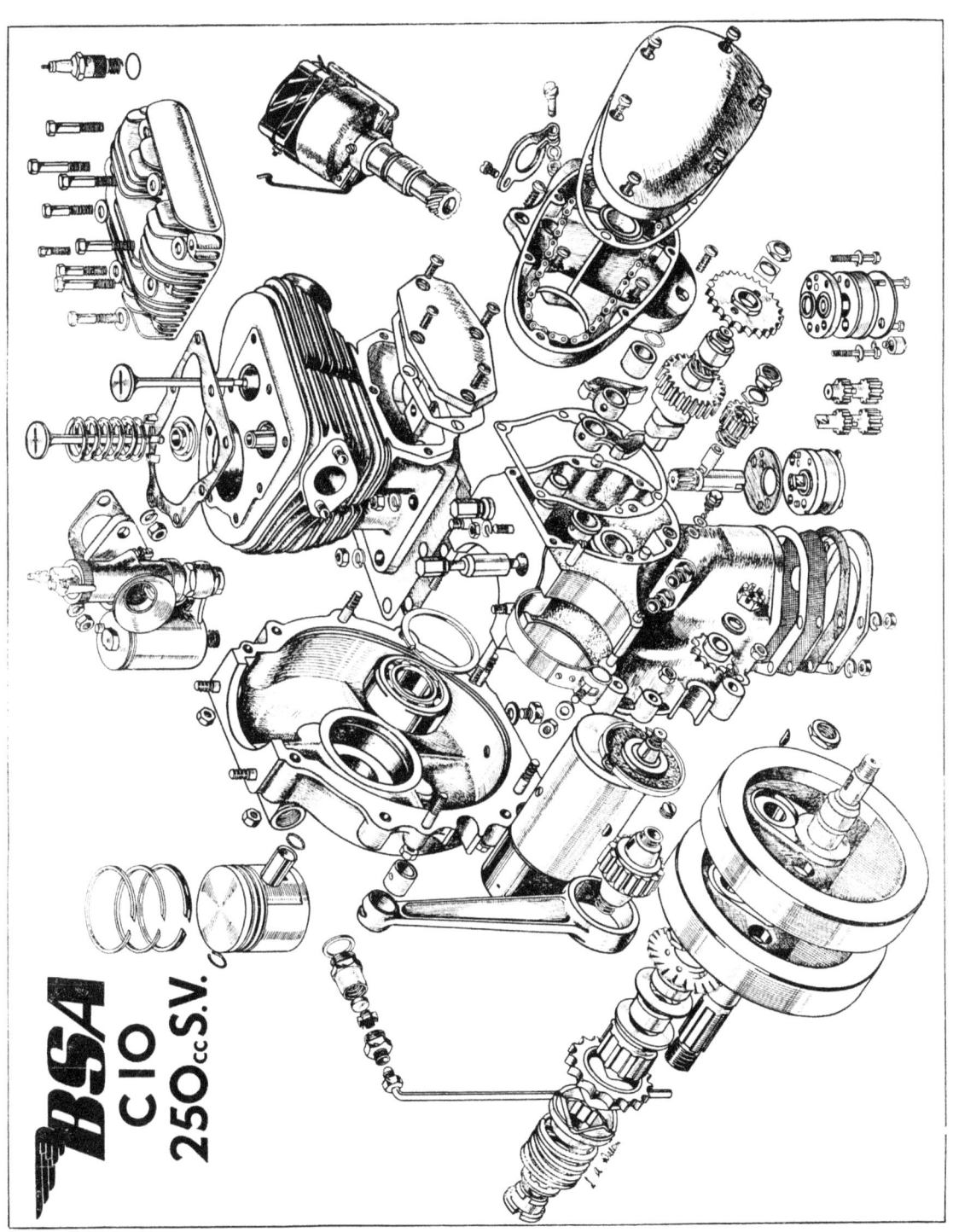

Fig. C1. The C10 Engine (Exploded View)

B.S.A. MOTOR CYCLES LIMITED, Service Dept., Waverley Works, Birmingham, 10
PRINTED IN ENGLAND

BSA SERVICE SHEET No. 401A

Reprinted March, 1955

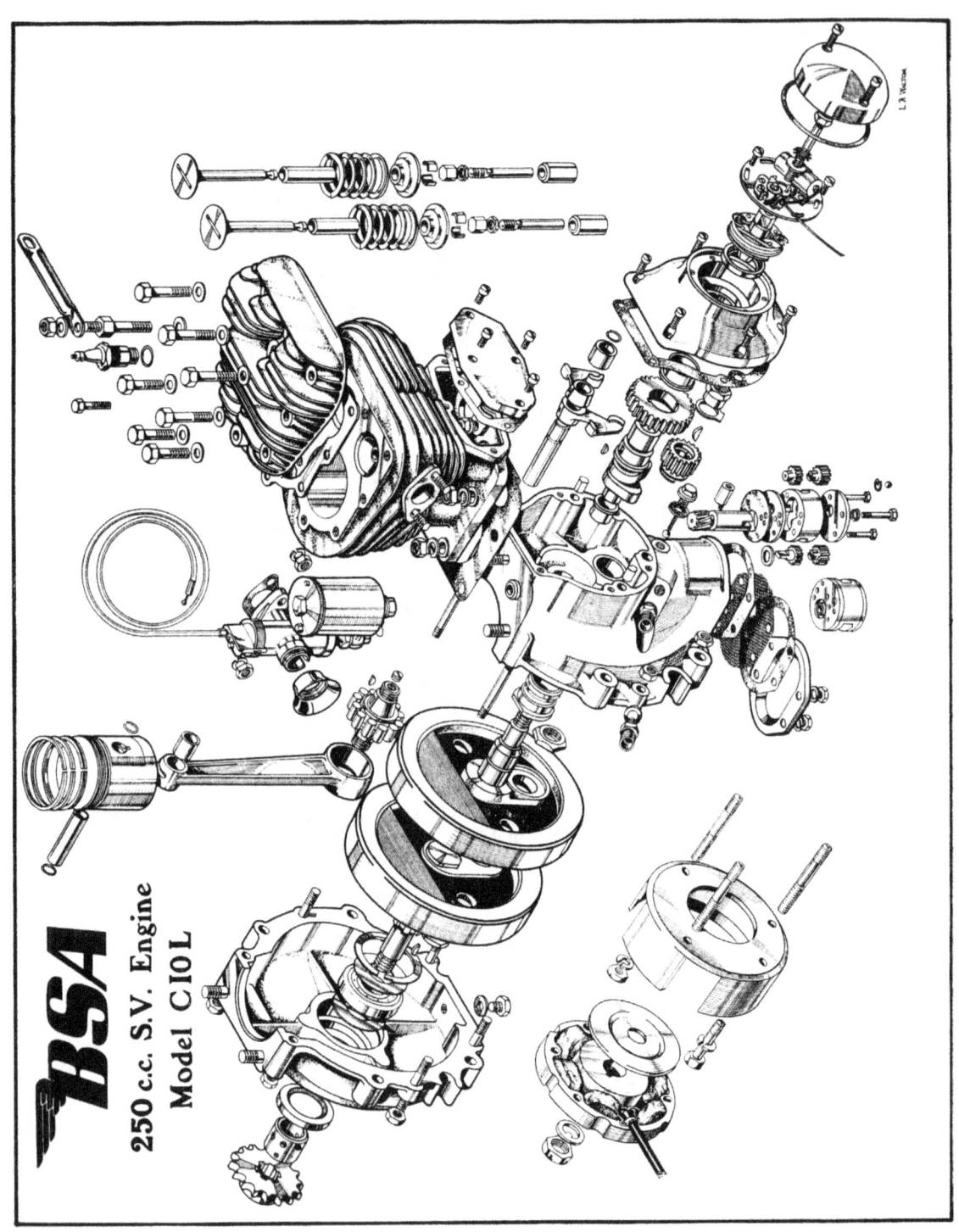

BSA 250 c.c. S.V. Engine Model C10L

B.S.A. MOTOR CYCLES LIMITED, Service Dept., Birmingham, 11.
(PRINTED IN ENGLAND)

BSA SERVICE SHEET No. 402

Reprinted July, 1962.

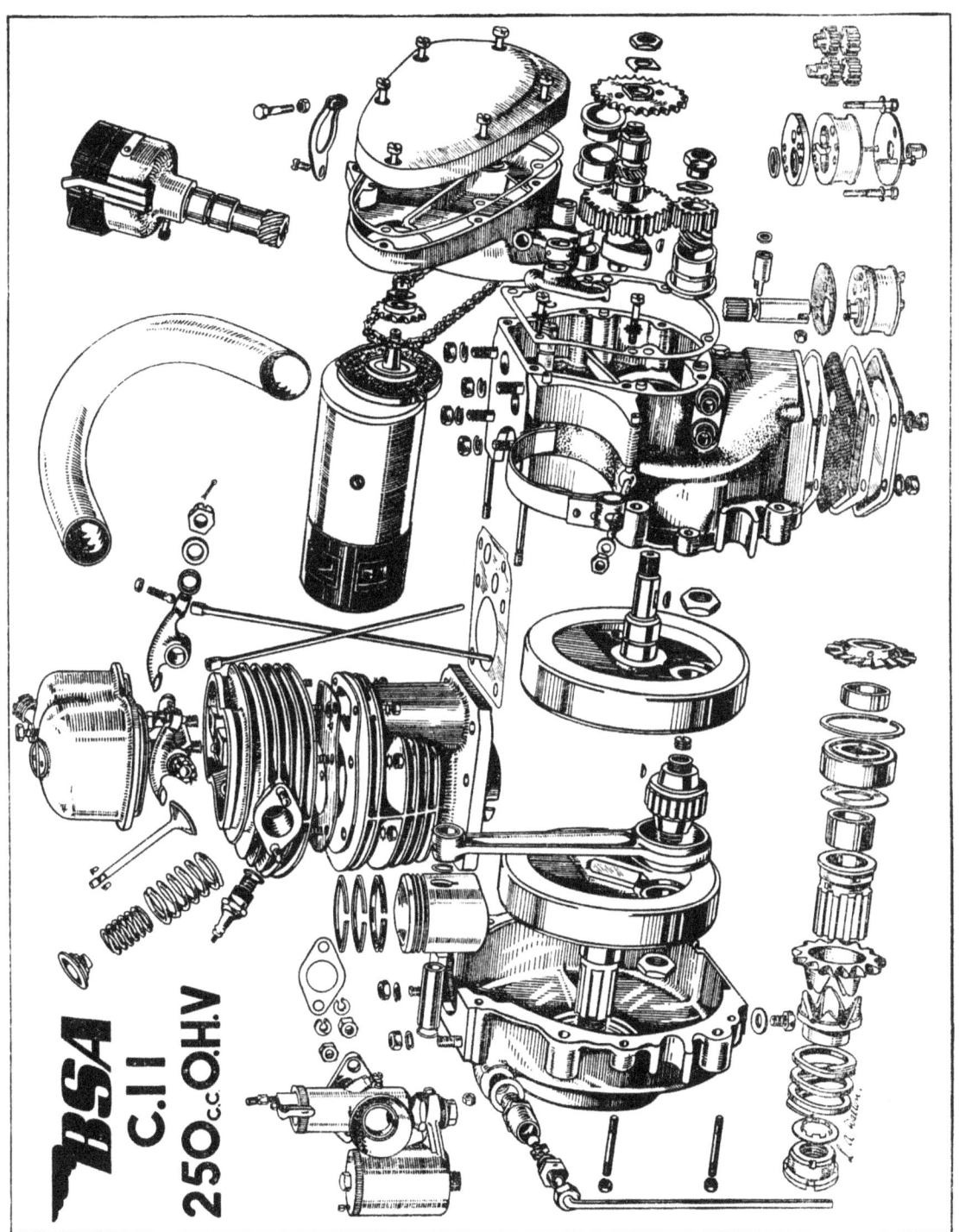

Fig. C2. The C11 Engine (Exploded View)

BSA SERVICE SHEET No. 402A

Reprinted May 1965.

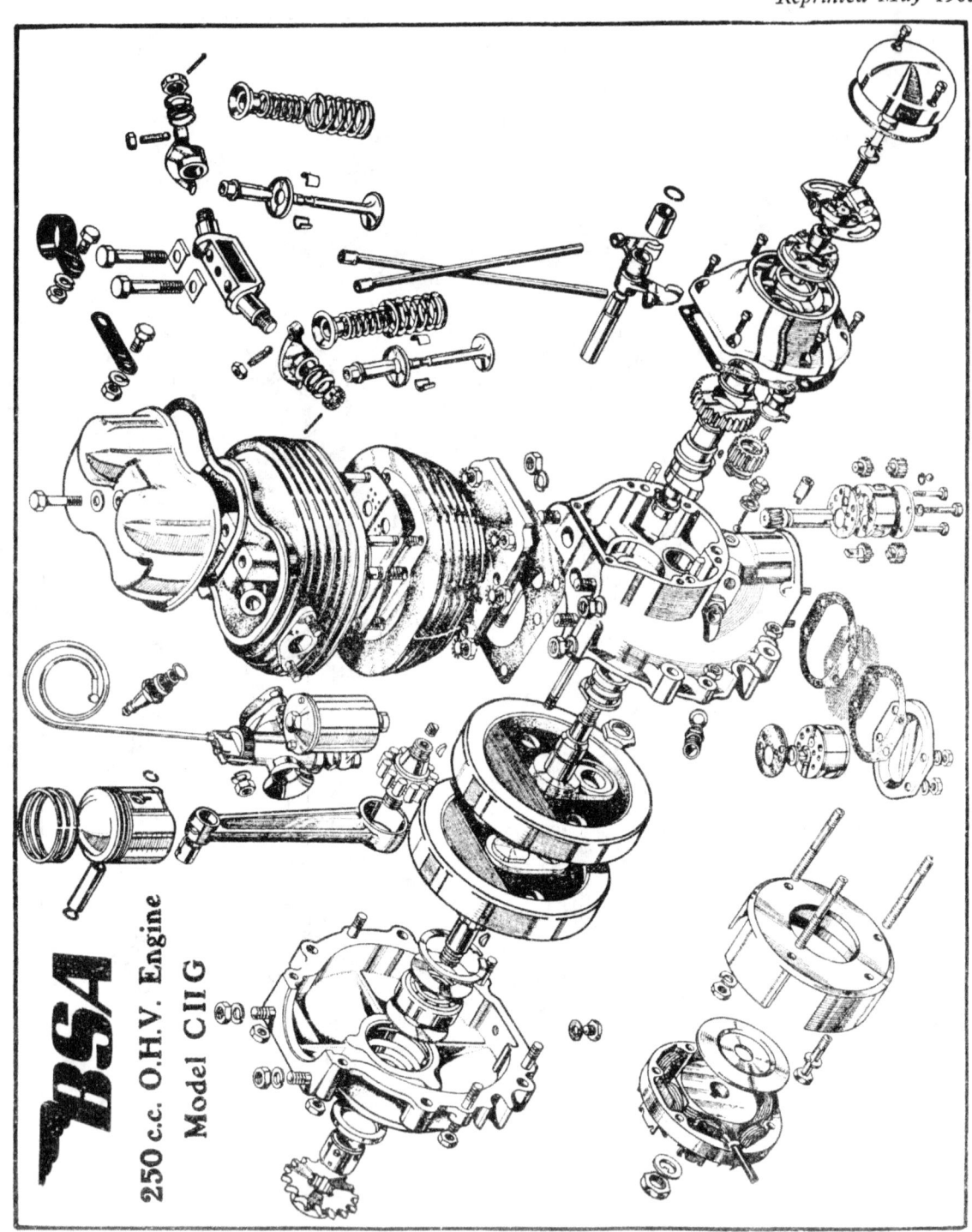

250 c.c. O.H.V. Engine Model C11G

B.S.A. MOTOR CYCLES LIMITED, Service Dept., Armoury Road, Birmingham, 11.
PRINTED IN ENGLAND

BSA SERVICE SHEET No. 403

Reprinted Sept., 1963

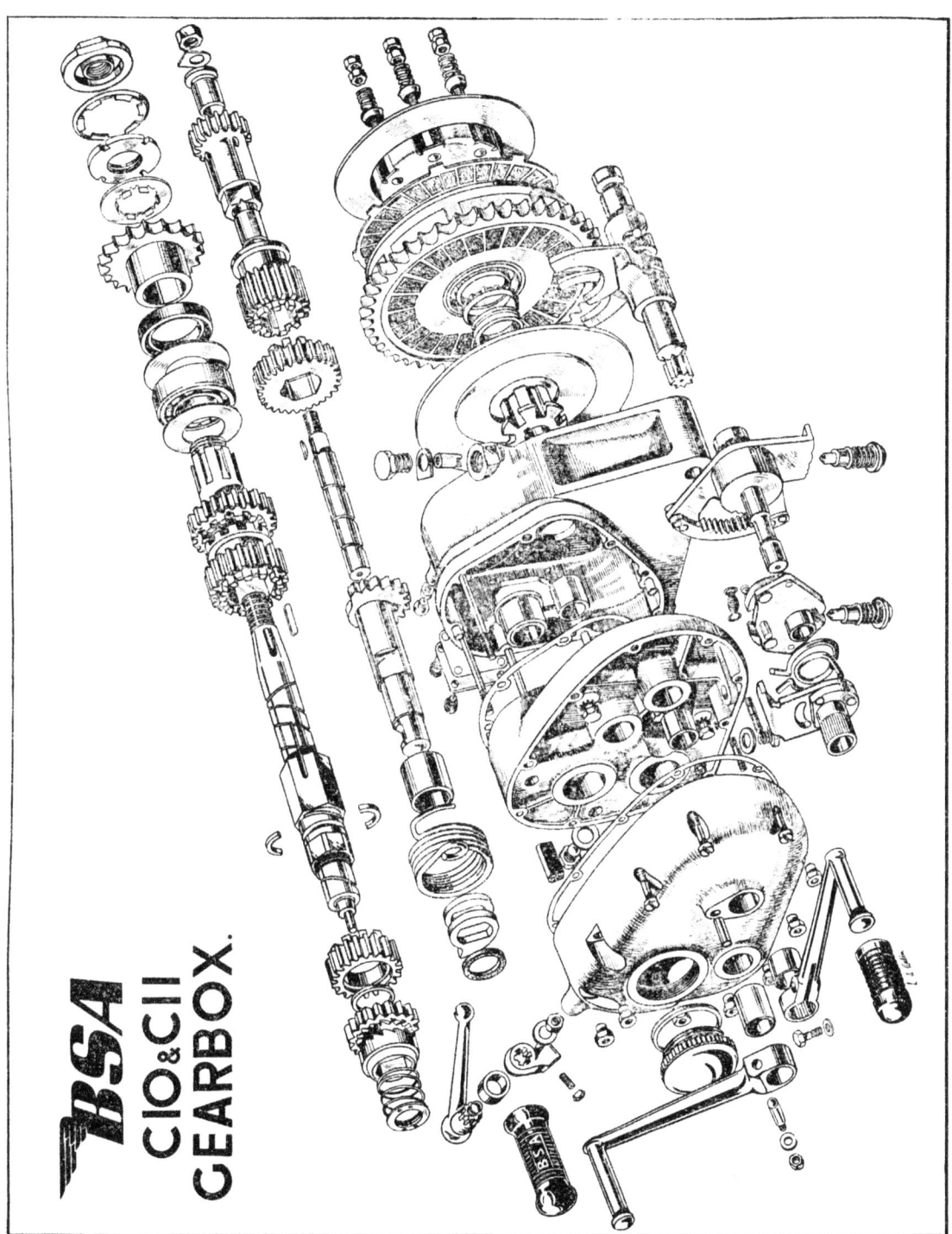

Fig. C3. The "C" Group 3-speed Gearbox (Exploded View)

B.S.A. MOTOR CYCLES LIMITED,
Service Dept., Armoury Road, Birmingham, 11.
(PRINTED IN ENGLAND)

BSA SERVICE SHEET No. 403A

Reprinted May, 1963.

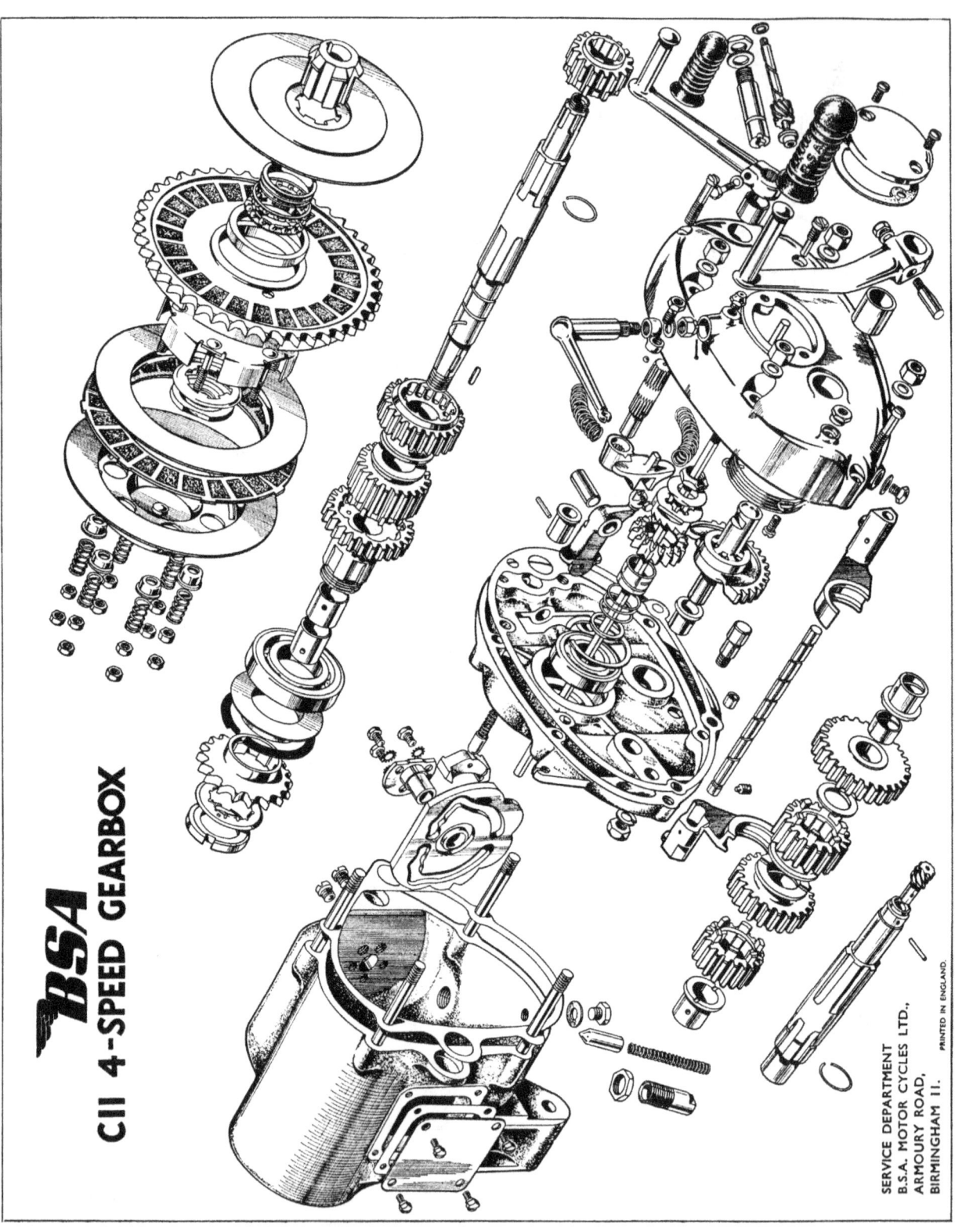

C11 Gearbox 4-Speed (Exploded View)

BSA SERVICE SHEET No. 403B

BSA Light 4 Speed Gear-box
1956 — C10L — C12

BSA SERVICE SHEET No. 404

Reprinted May 1965

"C" Group Models (except C15)
ENGINE ADJUSTMENTS WHICH CAN BE CARRIED OUT WITHOUT DISMANTLING

Oil Pressure Valves

As described under "How the Lubrication System Works", two ball valves are incorporated in the system, to prevent the transfer of oil from the tank to the crankcase.

The spring-loaded valve is located in the delivery passage between the pump and the big-end, and lies behind the hexagon-headed plug situated in the side of the crankcase just below the lowest part of the timing cover (see Fig. C4).

Should any foreign matter lodge between the ball and its seating, oil will gradually transfer from the tank when the machine is left standing, and when the engine is started up there will be a heavy discharge of smoke from the exhaust.

To rectify, remove the plug, spring and ball. The simplest way of removing the ball is to hold the hand close to the orifice and gently turn the engine over, when the ball will be forced out by oil pressure.

Clean the ball and seating, and if on replacing there is still a doubt as to whether the ball is seating properly, insert a small punch against the ball and deal it a sharp tap with a light hammer. Finally replace the spring and ball.

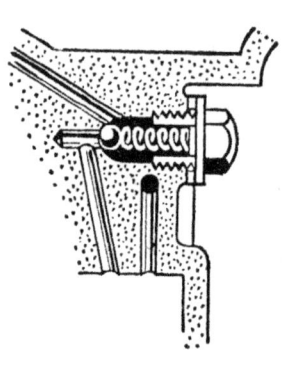
Fig. C4. *Ball valve in crankcase.*

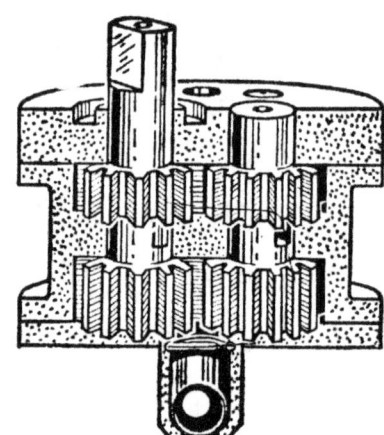
Fig. C5. *Ball valve below return pump.*

The other ball valve is located beneath the return pump (Fig. C5) and apparent failure of the return pump may be due to this ball having stuck in its seating.

B.S.A. Service Sheet No. 404 (contd.)

To rectify, remove the pump cover plate, insert a piece of wire into the orifice and lift the ball off its seating. Should the trouble keep recurring, it may be necessary to fit a new base plate to the pump.

ON NO ACCOUNT REMOVE THE OIL PUMP UNLESS IT IS ABSOLUTELY NECESSARY.

Tappet Adjustment

It is most important that tappet clearances are correctly maintained, and they should be frequently checked and adjusted if necessary, always when the engine is cold.

Before checking, make sure that the cams are in the correct position; otherwise an incorrect measurement may result.

The correct position is arrived at by turning the engine over until the piston is at the top of the compression stroke.

The simplest method is to lift the machine on to its stand and engage any gear. Then remove the compression plug in the cylinder head (on side valve models) or the sparking plug (on O.H.V. models) and with a piece of wire feel the top of the piston while rotating the engine a little in both directions by turning the rear wheel. When the piston is at the top of its stroke with both valves closed, and neither valve is opened by slight backward or forward rotation of the engine, proceed to check the clearances.

S.V. Model

Remove the tappet cover by unscrewing the four securing bolts. Check the clearance between the head of tappet base of valve stem with feeler gauge. This should be .004-in. in the case of the inlet valve and .006-in. in the case of the exhaust valve.

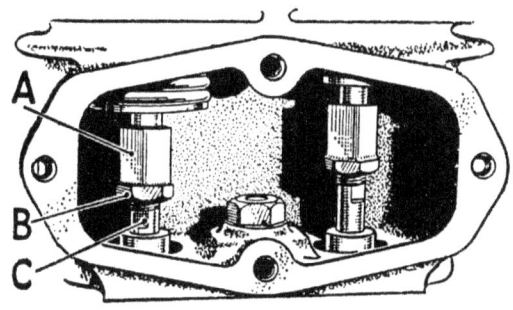

Fig. C6. Tappet adjustment.

If clearances are incorrect hold the tappet head (A) with a spanner and unscrew the locking nut (B). Now hold the stem (C), rigid with another spanner, and turn the tappet head to the right to reduce clearance, or left to increase it. When the correct adjustment is obtained, lock (B) hard against (A), and then finally check.

O.H.V. Model

Remove the rocker box cover by unscrewing the central bolt. Check the clearance by inserting a feeler gauge between the end of the rocker and the valve stem (Fig. C7). The correct clearance for both valves is .003 in. when the engine is cold. If the adjustment is incorrect, slacken locknut (B) and screw adjusting pin (A) downwards to reduce clearance and upwards to increase it.

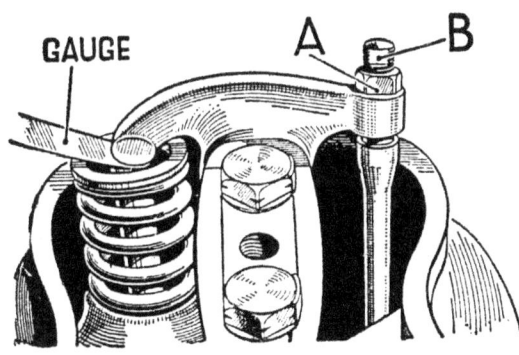

Fig. C7.

B.S.A. Service Sheet No. 404 (contd.)

When correct, tighten the locknut against the rocker, finally check the clearance and replace the rocker cover.

Tappet Adjustment (Ramp Cams)

On C10L models from engine number BC10L.3562 and C11G models from engine number BC11G.10438, ramp cams were fitted, and it is essential to adhere to the following procedure when carrying out tappet adjustment.

To check and adjust exhaust valve clearances, rotate the engine forward until the inlet valve has just closed and set the EXHAUST valve clearance to .015 in. (C10L) or .012 in. (C11G).

To check and adjust inlet valve clearance, rotate engine forward again until exhaust valve clearance is just taken up, but before the valve actually starts to lift. Set the INLET valve clearance to .012 in. (C10L) or .010 in. (C11G).

Ignition Timing (C10 and C11)

If the distributor is removed for any purpose, it will be necessary on replacement to re-time the ignition, but before doing this, the contact breaker point gap should be checked.

Turn the distributor shaft until the points are fully open and check the gap. This should be .012 in. If the gap differs from this the points should be adjusted. This is carried out by slackening the screws (B), moving the contact plate (C) until the correct gap is obtained, and finally tightening screws (B).

Ignition timing can now be carried out. Set the piston at the top of the compression stroke (as explained under "Tappet Adjustment") and insert a piece of wire through the sparking plug hole so that it is resting upright on top of the piston.

Now turn the engine backwards until the piston has descended $\frac{1}{32}$ in.

Remove the distributor cover and turn the centre spindle until there is approximately $\frac{3}{8}$ in. between the fibre pad and the start of the lift of the cam. Insert the distributor into its housing with the flat side towards the rear, and push well down on its seating, noting that as the gear meshes with the driving pinion the distributor shaft turns slightly and takes up a new position. Now rotate the distributor body until the points are just opening, and then tighten the locking screw located under the distributor body at the front.

The "C" Group of machines are fitted with an automatic advance and retard mechanism, which is housed under the contact breaker base. This mechanism requires periodical lubrication.

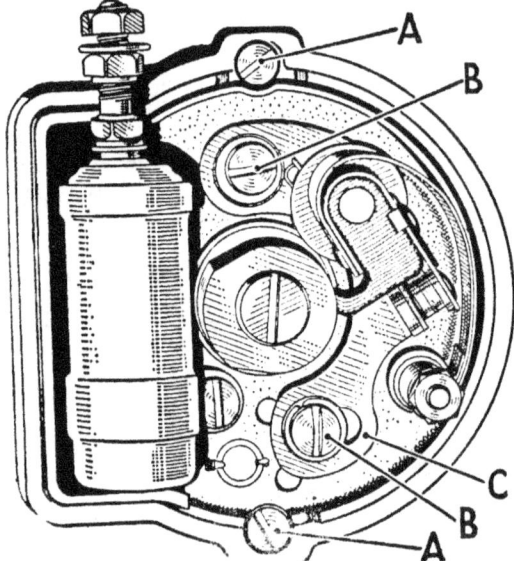

Fig. C8. The Distributor

First remove the distributor top and disconnect the low-tension lead at the side, and then unscrew the two bolts (A) (Fig. C8). The complete contact breaker unit on its base can now be removed and the advance and retard mechanism will be revealed.

B.S.A. Service Sheet No. 404 (contd.)

Lubricate with thin engine oil but do not overdo it, then replace the contact breaker base, not forgetting the low-tension lead. There is also a small lubricator below the main body for lubricating the distributor spindle. Apply a few drops of oil and be sure to close the thimble to exclude dust.

Ignition Timing (C10L and C11G)

The contact breaker mechanism is exposed by undoing the two retaining screws and removing the domed cover (A).

Before inspecting the ignition setting, the contact breaker gap should always be checked. Turn the engine over until the contact breaker gap at (B) is at its maximum, and then insert a suitable set of feeler gauges between the points. The correct gap is .015 in. and if it differs from this setting, the two screws at (D) should be slackened slightly and the contact support plate moved until the gap is correct. Tighten the screws and re-check the gap. In no circumstances must the plate be bent to alter the adjustment.

The ignition setting can best be checked in the fully retarded position. Rotate the engine until the piston is at top dead centre on the compression stroke (as described in "Tappet Adjustment").

In the case of the C11G the contact breaker points should just be opening, but when dealing with the C10L insert a piece of thin rod through the plug hole until it rests on the piston crown and rotate the engine backwards (by engaging top gear and turning the rear wheel) until the piston has descended $\frac{1}{32}$ in. (12° if using a timing disc), the points should now be just opening. This can be checked by inserting a piece of very thin paper between the points, the setting is correct when the paper is only lightly gripped. Make sure when withdrawing the paper that no particles adhere to the contact points.

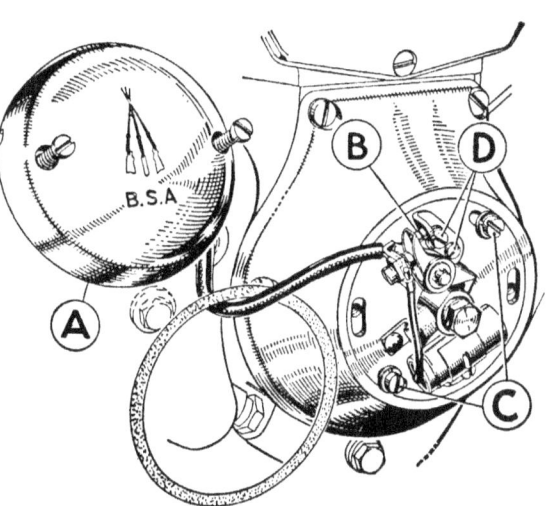

Fig. C9. Contact Breaker Mechanism

If the ignition timing is not correct, the two screws (C) (Fig. C9) should be slackened and the contact breaker back plate rotated until the points are just on the point of opening. Tighten the screws and re-check the setting.

A drop of thin oil should be applied occasionally to the felt cam lubricating pad, but over-lubrication should be avoided, as the excess oil may be thrown on to the contact breaker points.

Removal of the two screws (C) will permit the contact breaker back plate to be withdrawn, to provide access to the advance and retard mechanism, which should receive occasional lubrication with thin oil.

B.S.A. Service Sheet No. 404 (contd.)

Sparking Plug

If satisfactory performance is to be obtained, it is most important that the sparking plug is maintained in good condition. The Champion sparking plug supplied with the machine is of the non-detachable type and can only be cleaned satisfactorily by using the sand-blast type of cleaner which is standard equipment at most garages. All traces of deposit should be cleaned off the points and the inside of the plug to prevent internal shorting.

Re-set the sparking plug points gap to .018—.020 in. by bending the side contact. In no circumstances should the centre electrode be moved as this will crack the insulation. Ensure that the copper sealing washer is in good condition before replacing the plug, and make sure that the thread and plug seat in the head are clean and free from grit. When the plug has been replaced, wipe the outside of the insulation with a piece of clean rag to prevent external shorting.

If it is found that the plug requires frequent attention then the carburettor settings should be checked to ensure that the mixture is correct (see Service Sheet No. 708).

B.S.A. MOTOR CYCLES LTD., Service Department, Armoury Road Birmingham, 11.

B.S.A. PRESS

BSA SERVICE SHEET No. 405

Reprinted August 1963

"C" GROUP MODELS (EXCEPT C15)
ENGINE DISMANTLING FOR DECARBONISING

When decarbonising, it is not necessary or desirable to dismantle the cylinder barrel unless it is suspected that the valves, piston, or its rings are the cause of some trouble.

It is sufficient to remove the cylinder head and gasket, thus exposing the piston crown and valves.

Removing Cylinder Head C10 and C10L
Detach the high-tension lead to the sparking plug and remove the plug. Slacken the cylinder head bolts in the reverse order shown in Fig. C10. If, when the bolts are removed, the head is inclined to stick, a few taps with a wooden mallet low down on the vertical fins will loosen it, but be careful not to crack or break the fins.

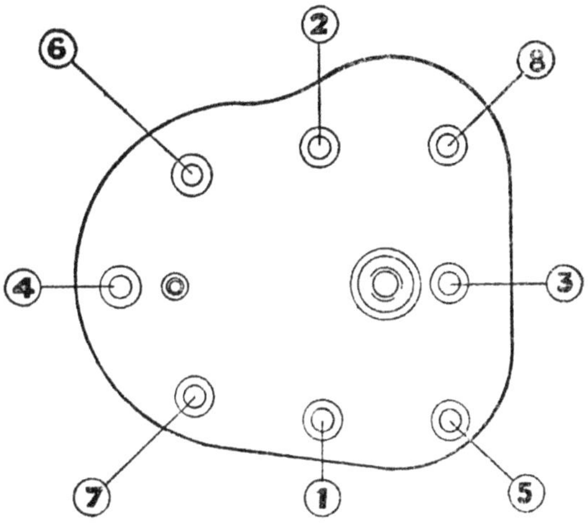

With the head removed, the piston and valves are now exposed. Set the piston at the top of its stroke and scrape off all carbon with an old blunt penknife or similar tool, taking care not to damage the piston crown.

Scrape all carbon from the cylinder head. Rotate the engine so that both valves are open and examine the seatings.

If these show a bright unbroken surface all round, leave well alone, but if they show traces of pitting, it is necessary to remove them for grinding-in. This will be facilitated if the barrel is removed.

Removing Cylinder Head C11 and C11G
It is easier to detach the cylinder head if the petrol tank is first removed. This is attached at the front to the steering head lug and at the rear to the frame top tube. Before removing the tank, turn off the petrol tap, and detach the petrol pipe. The rubber pads on which the tank is mounted should be marked so that they can be replaced in their original positions.

Fig. C10.
Order of tightening Cylinder Head Bolts (S.V.)

Detach the high-tension lead and the sparking plug. Next disconnect the petrol pipe at the carburetter and remove the carburetter. Take off the exhaust pipe. Take off the rocker box cover after removing the central bolt.

Unscrew the six nuts holding the cylinder head to the barrel. These are located between the fins at the sides of the barrel.

A gentle tap with a wooden mallet under the exhaust port will free the head, which should be raised just sufficiently at first to enable the push-rods to be freed from the rocker ballpins and the push-rods withdrawn. Then the head can be lifted right off.

Removing the Valves C10 and C10L
Stand the cylinder on a bench with valve heads downwards, and with a screwdriver or similar tool, press hard on the valve spring collars until the springs are compressed sufficiently to clear the cotters. The split cotters can then be freed, and the valves removed from the cylinder. A special spring compressor tool part number 61-3340 can be purchased from your B.S.A. dealer if desired. Scrape all carbon from the valve pockets but be careful not to damage the valve seats.

Removing the Valves C11 and C11G
Place a wooden block which will fit inside the cylinder head on a bench and then lay the head on to the block with the valve heads resting on it. Then compress the valve springs and remove collets as described for the side valve model.

Scrape all carbon from the piston and from the cylinder head and ports. The head may be polished with emery cloth, but take care not to damage the valve seats, and to remove all traces of dust before reassembly.

B.S.A. Service Sheet No. 405 (contd.)

Valve Springs

After a period of several thousand miles it may be desirable to fit new valve springs, as these tend to lose their efficiency due to heat. If the springs are renewed whilst decarbonising it will save dismantling specially to do the job at a later date.

Grinding-in Valves

Valve grinding should only be attempted if pitting is not deep. If deep pit marks appear, the valve should be refaced, as attempts at grinding in this case will cause wear of the seats and the valves may become pocketed.

Smear a small quantity of grinding compound—obtainable from any garage or accessory shop—over the face of the valve and return it to its seat. On the S.V. model a screwdriver can be used to rotate the valve, but on the O.H.V. model the stem of the valve must be gripped by the special tool provided in the tool kit.

The valve should be rotated backwards and forwards while a steady pressure is maintained, and every few strokes the valve should be lifted and turned to a new position. Continue this operation until the valve face shows a smooth polished surface all round.

It is most important that the valves should be ground-in on their correct seats, and for this reason both valves are marked, one "IN" and the other "EX".

After grinding, remove all traces of compound from both valve face and seat, and before replacing the valves, smear the stems with engine oil.

When replacing the springs make sure that the split collets are located correctly.

Removing Cylinder Barrel C10 and C10L

First turn off the petrol and detach the carburetter, which can be tied to the frame out of the way.

Next take off the exhaust pipe which is a push-fit into the cylinder and can be pulled out when the clip bolts holding it to the frame are slackened.

Now remove the five cylinder base nuts (four outside and one inside the tappet chamber), and then the cylinder barrel can be lifted off.

When removing the cylinder barrel the simplest way is to lift it up and tilt it forward into the front angle of the frame. The piston should be steadied as it emerges from the barrel to prevent possible damage. Cover the crankcase mouth with clean rag to prevent dust and grit falling in.

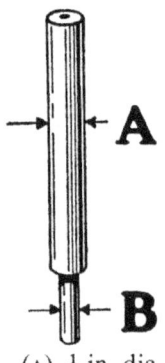

(A) ½ in. dia.
(B) .310 in. dia.
Fig. C11. *Valve Guide Fitting Punch.*
(*Service Tool 61-3264 complete with gauges for model C10. Punch only 61-3265 for C11, C12 models*).

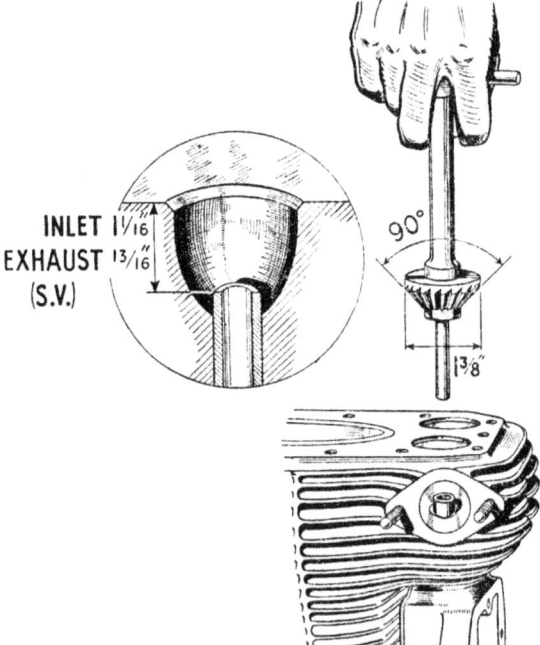

Fig. C12. *Cutting the Valve Seats.*
(*Service Tool 61-3305*).

B.S.A. Service Sheet No. 405 (contd.)

Fitting New Guides
If new guides are to be fitted, the old ones can be driven out by means of a simple punch made from a bar of steel not more than ½ in. dia. (see Fig. C11). Service Tool 61–3264 includes gauges which control the position of the guides.

The new guides can be driven in from the top using the same punch.

After fitting new guides the valve seats must be re-cut with a pilot cutter to ensure concentricity of seats and stems (Fig. C12).

Piston Rings
The gudgeon pin is located by means of wire circlips which must be removed with the tang of a file or similar tool. Withdraw the gudgeon pin, thus freeing the piston, and immediately after its removal mark the inside of the piston so that it may be reassembled in its original position.

If inspection of the piston rings shows that they are stuck, prise them out very carefully, and clean them. Remove any carbon from the grooves and rings, but before replacing them, check them in the cylinder for gap (Fig. C13). If the gaps are excessive, new rings having gaps of between .008 in. and .012 in. when in position must be fitted.

At this stage it is advisable to check the big-end bearing for wear. Turn the engine until the piston is at the top of its stroke, and resting both hands on the sides of the crankcase mouth, hold the connecting rod between fingers and thumbs, and feel for up and down play. It should be remembered that, even though there may be a little play present, it will not necessarily mean sudden failure of the bearing, though it will inevitably become worse. Where play seems excessive, and big-end noise has been noticed with the engine running, the engine should be completely dismantled, and a new big-end assembly fitted.

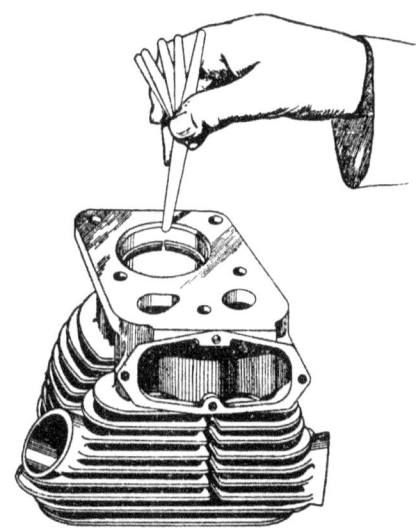

Fig. C13. *Checking Piston Ring Gaps.*

Assembly after Decarbonising
Side Valve Model.—Replace the valves and springs in the cylinder barrel, making sure that the valves are assembled on the seats from which they were removed, and take care to see that the split collets are seated correctly in their grooves in the valve stems.

Pour a little oil into the crankcase, and smear the cylinder walls liberally with oil. See that the cylinder base washer is in good condition—if damaged, replace, otherwise oil leaks will develop. Turn the engine until the crankshaft is a little past bottom dead centre, then compressing the top piston ring with the fingers, slide the cylinder barrel over the piston and top ring. Each ring must be compressed in turn as the barrel is refitted, and care is necessary to avoid breaking the rings. It is essential to see that the mouth of the crankcase is completely covered with rag before commencing to replace the cylinder, as if it is left uncovered, and a ring is broken, the pieces may drop into the crankcase and will be difficult to recover.

B.S.A. Service Sheet No. 405 (contd.)

Before trying to bolt the cylinder down, make sure that both tappets are in their lowest positions, otherwise the cylinder may not seat properly due to the pressure of the valve springs. Screw up the base nuts lightly at first, and then tighten one-quarter turn at a time, working on the outer nuts in diagonal order and then the nut inside the tappet chest.

When the cylinder is finally tightened down, replace the cylinder head gasket—first seeing that the latter is undamaged. If it is damaged, or shows sign of leakage (indicated by black patches) replace with a new one. Now fit the cylinder head, tightening the bolts one-quarter turn at a time in the order shown in Fig. C10. Check these bolts for tightness after 250 miles—particularly if a new head gasket has been fitted.

Replace the exhaust pipe, tightening the frame clips when in position, and then the carburetter. When replacing the carburetter slide take care not to damage the point of the needle. Next fit the petrol pipe.

If the sparking plug is of the detachable type, dismantle and clean it before refitting. If it is non-detachable, and obviously dirty, have it cleaned by a garage equipped for this purpose, or, failing this, fit a new one.

Finally check the tappet clearances and if necessary, adjust. Note, that if a new cylinder base washer has been fitted, it is advisable to check the nuts for tightness after 250 miles, and then again to check the tappet clearances.

O.H.V. Model.—Replace the cylinder barrel as described for the side valve model, first checking that the base washer is undamaged. Now replace the valves and springs in the cylinder head, making sure that they are on the correct seats and that the split collets are positioned correctly.

See that the cylinder head gasket is in good condition, replace it, and then fit cylinder head loosely in position. Before the head is bolted down the push-rods must be fitted. It should be noted that these are crossed, and the exhaust must be fitted first, the plain end fitting into the cup formed on the cam rocker (bottom left), and the cupped end fitting over the rocker ball end (top right). Fig. C14, shows a section illustrating how the push-rods are fitted.

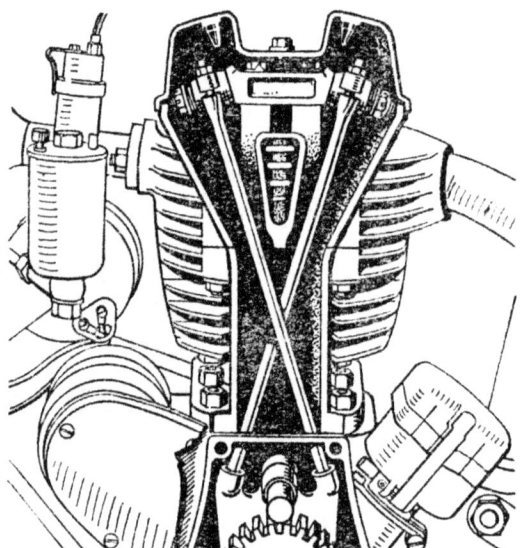

Fig. C14.
Section showing Push Rods on O.H.V. models

With the push-rods in position, the cylinder head can be bolted down. Before replacing the rocker box cover, check tappet clearances and adjust if necessary. Note that the tightness of the head should be checked after the first 250 miles, and that if the nuts are tightened at this period it will probably be necessary to re-adjust the tappets.

Next replace carburetter, taking care not to damage the needle when inserting the slide, and see that the flange washer is in good condition. Then fit exhaust pipe, and finally, replace the petrol tank and petrol pipe.

B.S.A. MOTOR CYCLES LTD., Service Department, Armoury Road, Birmingham 11.
Printed in England

BSA SERVICE SHEET No. 406

October, 1948
Reprinted June, 1963

C10 AND C11 MODELS

REMOVING ENGINE FROM FRAME AND COMPLETE DISMANTLING

The procedure for the removal of the engine and dismantling will be described from the point reached in the section on decarbonising, when the cylinder head and barrel had been removed.

The next step is to drain the oil tank or remove the oil pipes and plug the holes in the tank. Remove the oil pipes by disconnecting at the crankcase end.

Detach the leads to the dynamo (both of which are held by a small plate and single screw), and the lead to the distributor.

Removing Chaincase

The oil bath chaincase follows next. Take off the footrest and undo all the screws round the rim of the case. The nuts of the screws are welded to the rear half of the case and so cannot be lost.

When the outer case is being taken off, careful note should be made of the position of the cork washers and distance pieces to facilitate reassembly. Before removing the chain, loosen the clutch (as described in the next section), and then dismantle the engine shaft cush drive.

Tap the lock washer clear of the slot in the cush drive retaining nut and unscrew the nut. Then withdraw the spring and cam sleeve, leaving the sprocket and chain in position.

Removing Clutch

Remove the clutch actuating cap by unscrewing the spring retaining nuts and locknuts.

Tap the lock washer back, unscrew the clutch retaining nut, and withdraw the long push rod.

The clutch can then be removed with the aid of extractor 61-3362 which screws into the threads provided in the clutch hub. Now uncouple the chain, take off the clutch as a unit, and then the cush drive hub (see also section dealing with "Clutch Assembly").

The inner half of the primary chaincase is attached to the crankcase by three bolts, and it can be detached when these are removed.

Undo the engine bolts, taking great care to avoid damaging the threads, and remove the front engine mounting plates. If the rear engine and gearbox plates have been slackened sufficiently, the engine can now be withdrawn if it is tilted slightly to release it.

It is advisable to replace the various bolts and studs loosely in their respective locations to ensure correct reassembly.

B.S.A. Service Sheet No. 406 (contd.)

Dismantling the Engine

Before commencing to dismantle the engine, a simple fixture as illustrated in Fig. C15 will facilitate matters considerably.

Alternatively, clamp the engine in a vice by means of one of the mounting lugs supporting the crankcase on the bench.

Remove the crankcase drain plug and drain the oil. Take out the timing cover screws and pull off the cover. Clean it and place on one side.

Flatten the turned over end of the camshaft nut locking washer and remove the nut. Slacken the dynamo strap nut and turn the dynamo to slacken the chain.

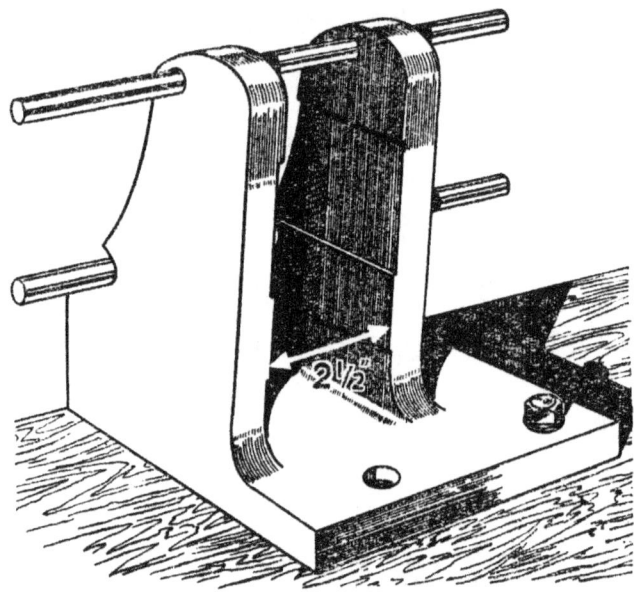

Fig. C15.   Angle Bracket for Mounting Engine.

Take off the dynamo drive sprocket (Service tool 61-3256) and chain. Remove the dynamo, clean the chain and sprocket in paraffin, and set aside.

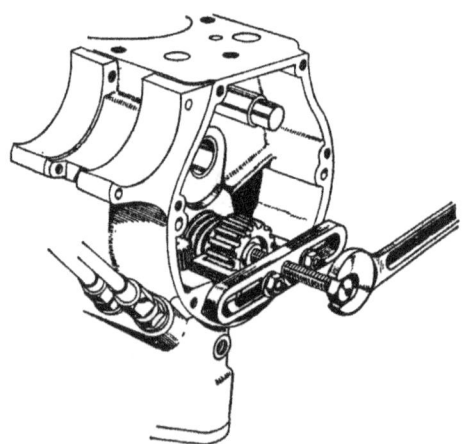

Fig. C16.   Engine Shaft Pinion Extractor (Service tool 61-3256).

B.S.A. Service Sheet No. 406 (contd.)

Slacken off the clamp nut immediately below the distributor head and withdraw the distributor complete. Take out the screws retaining the inner timing cover, noting the locations of the longer screws. Remove the cover, clean it, and set aside.

Withdraw the camshaft complete, flatten out the tab washer and remove the mainshaft nut. The mainshaft pinion can now be drawn off using Service tool 61-3256 (see Fig. C16).

The oil pump drive spindle which meshes with the mainshaft pinion is retained in position by a dowel covered by a plain washer, situated just below the mainshaft to the left, in the edge of the timing chest.

Prick out the plain washer and pull out the dowel by screwing in one of the timing cover screws. The pump spindle can now be drawn upwards into the timing chest.

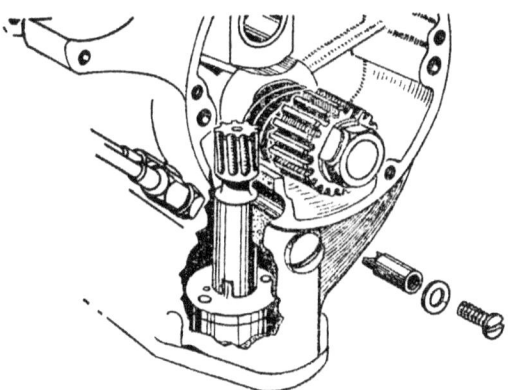

Fig. C17. Oil Pump Spindle Locking Plunger.

Remove the nuts from the crankcase studs and take out the loose studs, noting the locations. Place the engine on its side, with the thumbs on the ends of the engine shaft and, gripping the gear-side crankcase half with the fingers, pull off the gear-side half.

The halves may not separate without some persuasion, but great care is necessary if damage to the casting is to be avoided.

Lift the flywheel assembly clear of the drive-side half, and remove the distance collar and oil flinger.

Take off the four nuts and lock washers at the base of the gear-side crankcase, and remove the filter. **Do not remove the oil pump unless it requires attention.**

If new bushes and bearings are being fitted, the bushes must be reamed in position in line with the opposite bearing.

Old bushes can be driven or drawn out, but it will be necessary to heat the case in hot water to remove ball or roller bearings (see Fig. C18). The new one should then be immediately fitted while the case is warm. (See Service Sheet No. 702 for dimensions of bushes.)

It is advisable to check and if necessary correct the flywheel alignment. For procedure see the section dealing with engine reassembly.

B.S.A. Service Sheet No. 406 (contd.)

Special Note

The crankcase bearing drive-side is held in position by a spring ring, and this must be removed before attempting to remove the bearing. Careful note should also be made of the way the oil flinger is fitted to ensure correct reassembly.

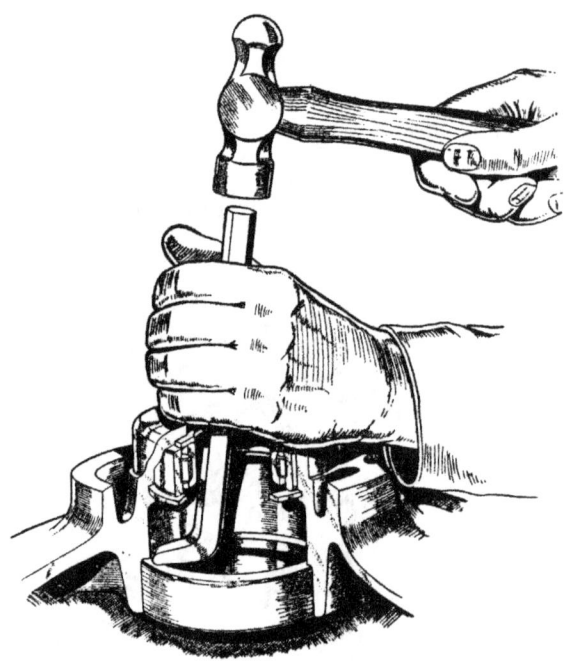

Fig. C18. Ballrace Extraction (Drive-side).

Finally, if the flywheels are to be separated they must be held securely on the bench, as extreme pressure will be required to release the crankpin nuts.

Special spanners are used, and it is usually necessary to add a piece of tubing to obtain additional leverage.

The crankpin is a taper fit in the flywheels, and can be released by a sharp blow with a mallet.

It is now only necessary to decide which parts require renewal, and the following may assist you in your decision:—

We do not advise the fitting of over-size rollers to the big-end assembly. The whole assembly, comprising crankpin, connecting rod and rollers, should be changed. All these components are carefully matched, working to one ten-thousandth part of an inch, and supplied in complete sets, ready for fitting.

If the bore of the cylinder, when measured at right angles to the gudgeon pin, shows wear to the extent of .010 in. or more, the cylinder should be rebored, and an over-size piston fitted. (Oversize pistons are available in 0.5 mm. (.020 in.) and 1 mm. (.040 in.)

Wear in mainshaft bearings or bushes will be readily apparent, and bearings showing signs of damaged balls, rollers or tracks should be replaced.

Special clearances are specified for mainshaft bearings used on B.S.A. motor cycles, and it is **not** advisable to fit other than genuine B.S.A. replacements.

B.S.A. MOTOR CYCLES LTD., Service Department, Armoury Road, Birmingham 11.
Printed in England.

BSA SERVICE SHEET No. 407

October 1948
Reprinted August 1963

C10 AND C11 MODELS

RE-ASSEMBLING THE ENGINE

The need for extreme cleanliness cannot be over-emphasised. Parts should be thoroughly cleaned, and all traces of any anti-rust preparations with which new parts may be coated must be removed.

Flywheels

If the big-end assembly is to be renewed it is as well to check the weights of the new components against those which have been removed. A slight variation in weights is inevitable, but provided that the discrepancy does not exceed 1½ ozs. no further action need be taken. This tolerance should not be exceeded since when first assembled the flywheels were balanced to suit the original parts, and the balance may be adversely affected if the weights of the new components differ considerably from those of the original ones.

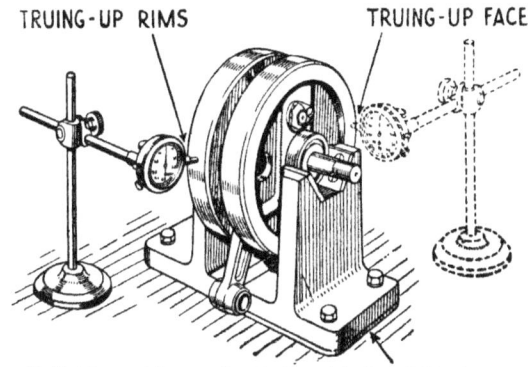

Suitable packing under timing side "vee" block to compensate for smaller diameter bearing.

Fig. C19. *Checking Flywheel Alignment.*

The driving side flywheel should now be fitted to the crankpin (this is the side with the keyway) and the nut tightened up by hand. Fit the timing side flywheel and again tighten the crankpin nut by hand.

In order to tighten the crankpin nuts properly, the whole flywheel assembly must be held rigidly. For this purpose it should be mounted in a large vice (fitted with lead clamps) with the driving side flywheel uppermost. If a large enough vice is not readily available, an alternative method is to fix two 9/16 in. diameter posts rigidly to the bench in a vertical position, the distance between their centres being 3⅞ in. Midway between the posts a hole of 1 inch diameter should be bored in the bench to receive the mainshaft. The flywheel assembly is mounted on these posts so that they pass through the holes bored in the flywheels, and the driving side flywheel should be uppermost. Tighten the crankpin nut very firmly, using a tubular extension to the spanner as when dismantling, and punch over the edge of the crankpin with a centre punch to lock the nut.

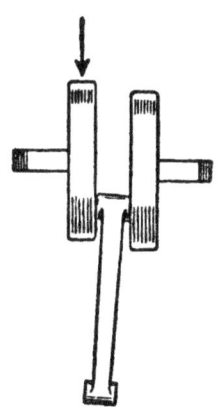 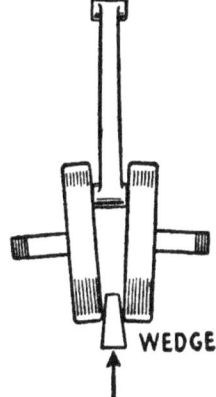 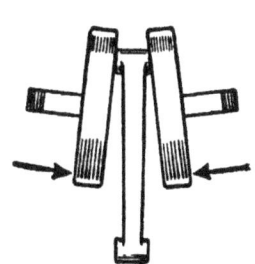

To bring shafts into line, a sharp blow with a mallet on **timing side** flywheel. (indicated by arrow)

To bring flyweels parallel when sides opposite crankpin are converging, insert wedge as shown and deal sharp blow, with mallet.

To bring flywheels parallel a sharp blow with mallet on flywheel rims on opposite side to crankpin

Fig. C20. *Method of Correcting Flywheels out of Alignment. (Note that above illustrations are exaggerated).*

B.S.A. Service Sheet No. 407 (contd.)

Now turn the assembly over, so that the gear-side flywheel is on top and tighten the crankpin nut lightly. The grub screw in the end of the crankpin must be riveted over or centre-punched to prevent its unscrewing. If it unscrews, serious damage may result to the engine. Check that the side clearance of the connecting rod in the flywheels does not exceed .012 in. and not is less than .010 in.

The flywheels will now be aligned only very approximately and further steps must be taken to ensure that the wheels are aligned as true as possible. Two of the actual (or similar) bearings to be used in the engine should be fitted to the mainshaft and the latter mounted on vee-blocks. The flywheels must be trued-up, both on faces and rims, for which purpose a dial micrometer is necessary (Fig. C19), and after the wheels are trued to within at least .005 in., tighten the timing side crankpin nut fully. A mallet or lead hammer applied to the flywheels will provide a sufficiently heavy blow for final truing, and will not harm the flywheels (Fig. C20). The shafts must not be struck. The shafts should be finally trued to within .002 in. maximum.

Fig. C21. *Valve Timing Gears.*

All parts having been cleaned, they must be perfectly free from paraffin, grit or other foreign matter, and all traces of old jointing compound and washers must be removed.

Fit the oil flinger with the boss towards the flywheel; the action of the vanes is to throw the oil away from the bearing.

Replace the distance washer between oil flinger and bearing.

Fit the drive-side crankcase half and, after coating the mating portion with jointing compound, replace the gear-side half. The two halves must be perfectly mated and the flywheels must rotate freely as the halves are bolted up.

Replace the oil pump spindle and its retaining pin. Fit the oil filter and cover plate at the base of the sump, making sure that the lockwashers are replaced under the nuts.

Having bolted up the crankcase, fit the timing pinion key and pinion, apply the lockwasher and nut and turn over the lockwasher after securing the nut.

Fit the cam followers, and also the tappets in the case of the C10, and replace the camshaft, ensuring that the mark on the camshaft pinion meshes with the mark on the timing or mainshaft pinion (Fig. C21).

Apply clean engine oil to the pinions and cams.

Now replace the small plain washer in the pump spindle locking plunger hole, and fit the inner timing cover, using a new joint washer coated with cement, and ensure that the star washers are fitted to the two long screws. Tighten the screws down a little at a time to ensure that the cover is not distorted.

Refit the dynamo, ensuring that the cork washer is in position, and replace the dynamo drive sprocket and chain.

Fit the camshaft nut washer, turning over the washer to lock the nut.

Now adjust the dynamo chain, and securely tighten the dynamo. Pack the chain housing with grease.

Refit the outer timing cover again, using a new joint washer and cement, and tighten the screws evenly.

Assembly from this point will be the same as after decarbonising.

B.S.A. MOTOR CYCLES LTD., Service Department, Armoury Road, Birmingham 11.

Printed in England

BSA SERVICE SHEET No. 408

"C" GROUP MODELS WITH 3-SPEED GEARBOX
(4-speed models, except C15, use Service Sheet No. 209)

REMOVING, DISMANTLING AND RE-ASSEMBLING OF GEARBOX AND GEAR CHANGE

To remove the gearbox from the machine proceed as for engine dismantling up to removal of the clutch (Service Sheet No. 406). Unscrew the two nuts (D) Fig. C23) and drive out the bolts. Slacken off the nuts clamping the rear engine plates and the chain stays. Take off the rear chain and guard, and the oil pipes.

It is not necessary to remove the oil tank and battery carrier, but if time permits removal of these fittings will enable the operator to raise the gearbox upwards and out of the plates more easily.

Dismantling the Gearbox

The operator should first consider carefully before attempting this operation as considerable trouble and damage can be caused by lack of experience. *If in doubt consult your Dealer.*

To assist reassembly, the positions of the various gears should be carefully studied (Fig. C22).

Fig. C22. *The Gear Cluster.*

First of all secure the gearbox in a vice or suitable fixture, with clamps on the clamping lugs. Remove the kickstarter crank (B) and footchange pedal (C) Fig. C23. The former is removed by unscrewing the nuts and extracting the cotter pin. The latter pedal can easily be taken off when the pinch bolt is released.

Next remove the outer cover by taking out the three screws and seven nuts which hold the cover in position. Unscrew plunger housing underneath the outer cover, the housing will come away complete with the plunger (L) and the plunger spring. Tap off the outer cover with a wooden mallet, at the same time holding the gear control shaft with a tommy bar so that the gear selector mechanism is retained in position.

B.S.A. Service Sheet No. 408 (contd.)

Next remove the control plunger housing (o) from the inner cover; this will release the gear selector mechanism comprising footchange operating plate (D), pawl plate and spring (G) and gear selector quadrant (H). After dismantling these the inner cover is fully exposed and the 3¼ in. (21-2889) Whitworth bolts should be unscrewed. The inner cover may now be tapped off its seating on the seven studs.

By means of a screwdriver undo the control shaft pin plug which is situated at the nearside end of the gearbox shell, and then insert a ¼ in. B.S.F. bolt or stud into the dowel to enable it to be drawn from its seating. The gear control shaft with operating forks, layshaft gear cluster, and mainshaft and sliding gear can now be taken out.

Next undo the tab washer which secures the sprocket locking nut, and remove the locking nut. Remove the locking washer and pull off the gearbox sprocket. Then tap the sleeve pinion from its seating in the bearing, using a hide or wooden mallet.

If it is necessary to remove the ballrace, a hand press is the best method, but if this is not available, warm the shell, and the ballrace can then be easily tapped from the housing.

Turn to the inner cover and the removing of the kickstarter quadrant. Unlock the quadrant from the kickstarter spring, and tap the quadrant from position through the two kickstarter return stops.

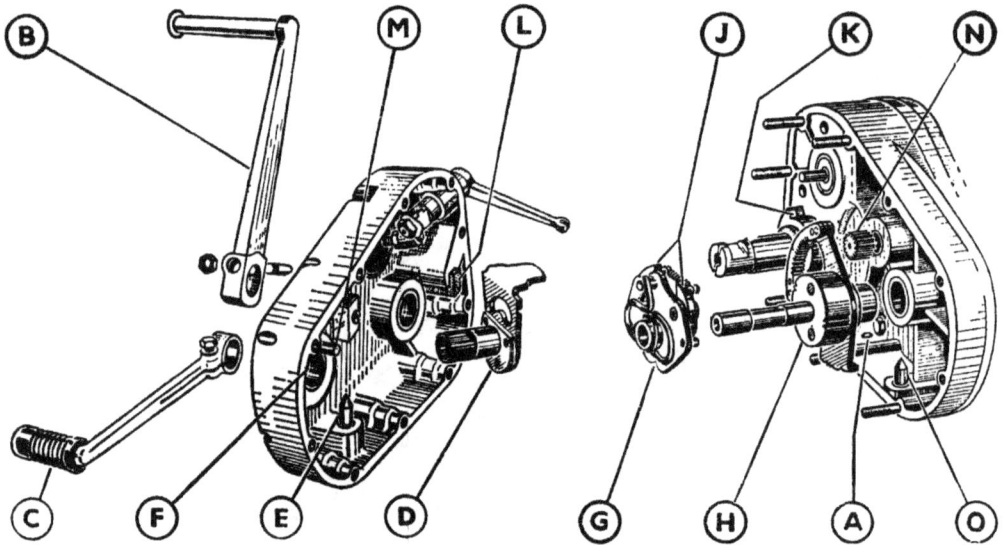

Fig. C23. *Foot Gearchange Mechanism.*

Dismantling the Gear Cluster

The sliding gear comes away easily from the mainshaft; then remove the kickstarter ratchet pinion by unscrewing the left-hand kickstarter ratchet sleeve nut. The kickstarter ratchet and shim can then be removed.

To remove the bottom gear pinion, the outer retaining ring has to be split by means of a chisel, so that the ring may be removed in two portions. Extract the two portions of the inner retaining ring with the tang end of a file, the pinion will then slide off the shaft.

B.S.A. Service Sheet No. 408 (contd.)

To dismantle the layshaft gear cluster remove the first gear pinion. This is pressed on to the layshaft pinion sleeve and can be removed by holding the gear in a vice and tapping from position with a piece of hard wood a shade larger in diameter than the phosphor bronze bearing.

To dismantle the operating forks, hold the shaft in a vice and tap out the central shaft pegs with a punch. The forks can then be removed from the shaft, but careful note should be taken of the position of the forks on the shaft before taking them off.

Reassembling

Hold the shell in a vice or suitable fixture. First of all fit the oil seal with recess inwards, the oil seal shim and the roller bearing. If the case is first warmed, the bearing can easily be pressed into its seating. Fit the sleeve pinion, ensuring that the oil retaining washer is fitted between the sleeve pinion and the ballrace. Then tap the sprocket into the splines in the sleeve pinion, securing by means of the tab washer and locknut. Ensure that the tab washer is turned over into the recesses in the locknut.

Fitting the selector forks to the shaft is the reverse operation to that for dismantling. Use new control shaft pegs.

Next replace the low gear pinion on the mainshaft, and fit the inner and outer rings to secure the pinion on the shaft. The outer ring is tapped into position and the pinion should then revolve easily on the shaft. Fit the kickstarter pinion (27-4106), and then the ratchet (27-4112), following that, the ratchet spring (27-4447). Then fit the kickstarter sleeve nut (15-0267) left-hand thread.

Fit the mainshaft sliding pinion, ensuring that the fork track is nearest the sleeve pinion. Next fit the layshaft sliding pinion on the sleeve pinion and press the layshaft first gear pinion on to the sleeve pinion (hexagon end).

Pair the layshaft and mainshaft gear clusters together, fit the operating forks, ensuring that one fork is engaging in the mainshaft sliding pinion and the other fork in the layshaft sliding pinion. Ensure that the teeth on the gear control shaft are at the reverse end to the threads on the mainshaft end.

Before entering the mainshaft and gear clusters into the gearbox shell, lubricate the gears and both shafts. Enter the clusters, locate the selector shaft and enter the retaining pin in the groove in the selector shaft. Then fit control pin plug (29-3243) and secure with the locking tab washer.

Next fit the inner cover using a new joint washer coated with jointing cement and tap into position with a wooden mallet. Secure the cover by a bolt either side, check for end-play in the layshaft and mainshaft, and if there is end-play in the former, fit shims underneath the kickstarter quadrant (.005 clearance). If there is play in the mainshaft, fit shims underneath the mainshaft bush (inner cover, 15-0268). The mainshaft must be free without end-play.

Fit the remaining ¼ in. Whitworth cover bolt.

Next fit the gear control quadrant (29-3298), ensuring that the mark on the foot gear-change selector shaft is lined up with the mark cut on the quadrant.

With the aid of a screwdriver, fit the spring to the pawl carrier plate, with the end of the right-hand coil to the left of the stud, and the end of the left-hand coil to the right of the stud.

B.S.A. Service Sheet No. 408 (contd.)

Fit the pawl carrier plate (G) Fig. C23, to the gear control quadrant, followed by the operating plate and sleeve complete (D).

The action of the footchange pedal return spring tends to throw off the operating plate, to prevent this happening a small clip should be made up from light strip and placed in position over the assembly.

Replace the two return stops on the kickstart quadrant stem followed by the cork washer.

Take up the outer cover, place a tommy bar through the operating plate sleeve bush and hold the operating plate in position as the cover is entered on its studs. Remove the clip which was placed over the footchange mechanism and still holding the operating plate with the tommy bar, push the outer cover home.

Ensure that the dowel peg in the outer cover is located between the ends of the spring on the pawl carrier plate. If this is not so positioned the footchange pedal will not return to neutral.

Secure the outer cover with fixing screws and nuts, and fit the footchange pedal (C) and kickstarter crank (B). Replace filler cap and inspection cover.

Replacement of Gearbox
The replacement of the box should not present any difficulties. When the box is in position and the fixing bolts are ready to be tightened up, make sure that the flats on the heads of the bolts register in the slots of the yoke plates, and that the chain is correctly tensioned. There should be about $\frac{3}{4}$ in. up and down play in one run of the chain when the other run is taut.

Make sure that the gearbox bolts are finally tightened before re-adjusting the rear chain, and refill the gearbox with oil to the correct level.

B.S.A. MOTOR CYCLES LTD., Service Department, Armoury Road, Birmingham 11.
Printed in England.

BSA SERVICE SHEET No. 408A

Reprinted August 1966

1956 C10L AND C12 MODELS
WITH LIGHT FOUR-SPEED GEARBOX

(1954/5 four-speed models use Service Sheet No. 209)

REMOVAL OF GEARBOX

In most cases it will be found convenient to dismantle the gearbox whilst it is in position. However, if attention to the bearings is required it may be found advisable to remove the complete gearbox. The primary transmission, clutch and chaincase must be removed (see Service Sheet No. 411).

To remove the gearbox from the frame, first detach the clutch and speedo cables. Remove the cover plates. Unscrew the gearbox holding bolts and lift the box clear.

DISMANTLING

In order to obtain access to the gearchange and kickstart mechanism the outer cover must be removed. Drain off the oil, if this has not already been done, and move the gear to neutral. Remove the three stud nuts and four screws securing the outer cover and the cover can be drawn away together with the kickstarter and gearchange levers. The internal clutch operating lever will fall away. The ratchet pinion assembly is secured by a large nut, remove this and the ratchet, ratchet pinion, bush spring and washer can be taken away.

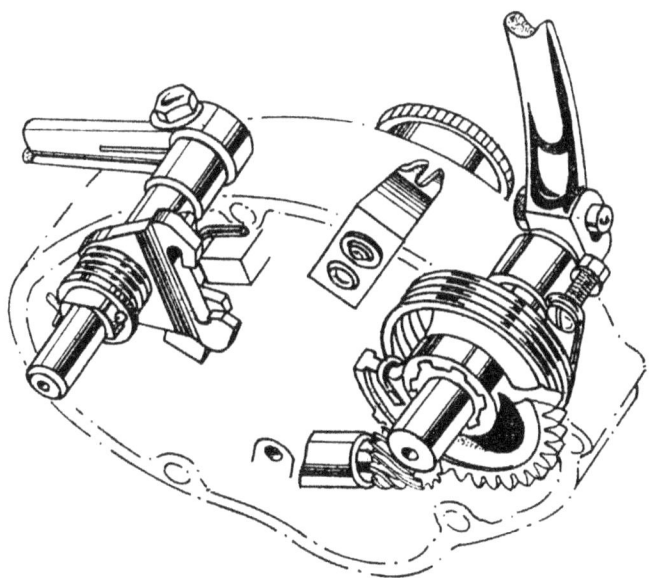

Fig. 2. C4. Kickstart and foot-change mechanism

B.S.A. Service Sheet No. 408A (contd.)

The gearchange mechanism need not be dismantled unless it needs attention. If this is the case remove the gear lever and the small circlip behind it. The spindle and gearchange mechanism can now be withdrawn.

To obtain access to the gearbox internals the gearbox inner cover must first be removed. After the ratchet assembly has been removed it will be seen that the inner cover is held in position by one nut, undo this and remove the circlip located on the end of the layshaft and adjacent to the speedo drive. The inner cover and mainshaft can now be withdrawn. If it is required to remove the gearchange control quadrant from the inner cover, press out the gearchange spindle bush and expose the end of the control quadrant spindle. The spindle is threaded ¼ in. B.S.C. and by using a suitable bolt as a draw tool the spindle can be withdrawn.

The selector shaft is secured in the gearbox shell by a grub screw which passes through the gearbox shell and engages in an annulus in the shaft. Slacken the grub screw and pull out the shaft. The gear cluster, forks and layshaft can now be withdrawn. Remove the gearbox sprocket by unscrewing the large ring nut and tap the pinion sleeve from its bearing. Lift the spring-loading selector arm and slide the cam plate from its bearing. To remove the pinion sleeve bearing take out the retaining circlip, withdraw the oil seal and warm the case before tapping out the bearing.

Should the needle roller layshaft and bearing need replacing, removal is facilitated by warming the gearbox shell.

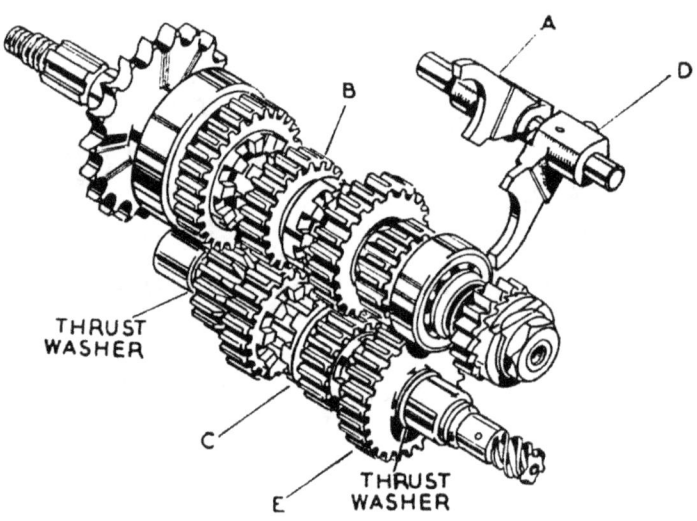

Fig. C43. Gear cluster

B.S.A. Service Sheet No. 408A (contd.)

ASSEMBLY

Lift the spring-loaded selector arm and fit the cam plate with the selector arm in the bottom gear position. If the pinion sleeve bearing and oil seal have been removed for any reason it is advisable to fit a new oil seal.

Warm the gearbox and press in the bearing. Fit the oil seal and circlip, making sure that it is correctly located. Fit the pinion sleeve.

Replace the layshaft ensuring that one of the hardened steel thrust washers is in its correct place as shown in Fig. C43. Layshaft thrust washers are available in three sizes.

Part No. 29-3645   Layshaft thrust washer   .075—.076
Part No. 29-3646   Layshaft thrust washer   .084—.085
Part No. 29-3626   Layshaft thrust washer   .092—.093

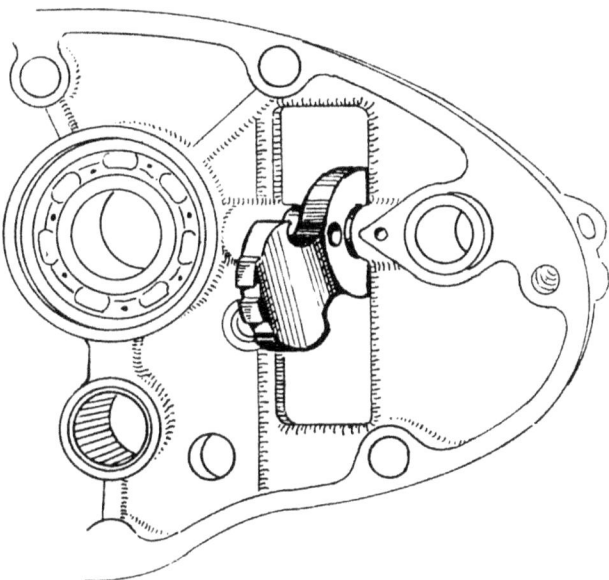

Fig. C44. Timing of gearchange operation lever

Fit the mainshaft sliding gear fork (*A*) with its peg in the cam plate slot. Correct location is assisted by sliding the selector shaft through the fork and into its position in the gearbox shell. Fit the mainshaft sliding pinion (*B*) into its place on the fork and then place the layshaft sliding pinion (*C*) on to the layshaft. Carefully remove the selector shaft. Fit the layshaft sliding pinion fork and engage the peg in the slot on the cam plate.

Slide the selector fork shaft through the two forks and into position in the gearbox shell. Tighten the small grub screw making sure that it engages in its annulus.

Slide the mainshaft into position, fit the layshaft pinion (*E*) and place the other hardened steel washer in position.

B.S.A. Service Sheet No. 408A (contd.)

Place the mainshaft and inner cover in position but before they are pushed home the operating lever must be set so that the red dot on the lever and the cover coincide in the bottom gear position. Push the cover home and fit the securing nut.

Assemble the ratchet and pinion assembly. First place in position the steel washer and then the steel bush. Fit the spring, ratchet pinion and ratchet. Finally, secure with the nut and tab washer.

Replace the outer cover, ensuring that the clutch operating lever is correctly positioned. To do this remove the inspection cap and fit the push rod in position. Moving the kickstart will prevent jamming and will assist engagement of the speedo drive.

Should the mainshaft ballbearing, located in the inner cover, need replacing it is necessary to extract the circlip, warm the cover and tap the bearing out. Refitting is self-explanatory.

Below is a list of useful part numbers:—

29-3608	Gearbox sprocket oil seal.
29-3598	27T pinion sleeve.
29-3603	Outer cover stud (long).
29-3604	Outer cover stud (short).
29-3589	Cam plate.
29-3636	Kickstart ratchet.
67-3376	Kickstart ratchet pinion.
29-3637	Kickstart ratchet pinion bush.
29-3585	Kickstart ratchet and mainshaft nut lockwasher.
29-3628	Selector fork.
29-3627	Selector fork shaft.
29-3614	Mainshaft sliding pinion 21T.
29-3621	Layshaft sliding pinion 18T.
29-3616	Layshaft complete.
29-3643	Clutch push rod.
67-3340	Footchange and stop plate return spring.
67-3174	Kickstart spring.
29-3611	Mainshaft complete.
29-3639	Layshaft bearing circlip.

B.S.A. MOTOR CYCLES LTD., Service Department, Armoury Road, Birmingham 11.

B.S.A. PRESS

BSA SERVICE SHEET No. 409

C Group Models
(EXCEPT MODEL C15)

PRIMARY TRANSMISSION

Clutch Adjustment, C10, C11, C10L 1954/5 & C11G.

Removal of the knurled filler plug from the gearbox outer cover will expose the clutch adjusting screw 'A' and locknut 'B' (Fig. C24). Loosen the locknut and turn the screw with a screwdriver until the angle between the operating lever and the cable is slightly less than a right-angle when the clutch is fully withdrawn. It will probably be necessary to alter the length of the cable by means of the adjuster 'C', to obtain the correct position for the lever. Re-tighten the locknut, and replace the filler plug.

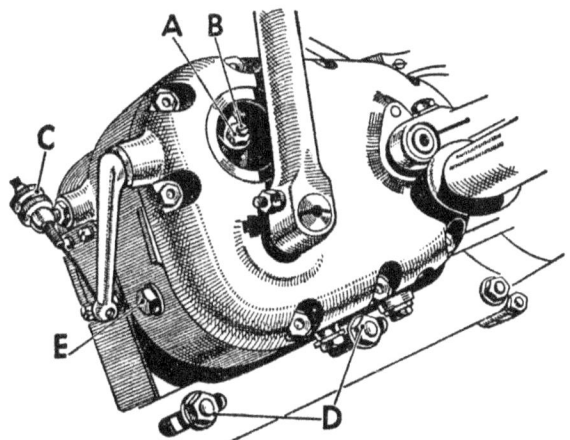

Fig. C24 Clutch and front chain adjustment.

When the clutch is engaged, it is essential that the cable has approximately $\frac{1}{8}''$ free play to avoid a constant pressure on the clutch push rod, with consequent wear and loss of efficiency.

On four-speed models, the positioning of the components is slightly different and the inspection cover is retained by two screws, but the adjustments are identical.

B.S.A. Service Sheet No. 409 (continued)

Clutch Adjustment, C10L & C12 (1956 onwards)

The main clutch adjustment consists of a screwed pin C and locknut D, Fig. C24a, on the outside of the gearbox cover. Remove the large round screwed cap to expose the end of the clutch operating lever. There should be approximately $\frac{3}{16}$ inch play between the back of the clutch lever and the inside of the cover when the clutch is released. If the clearance varies appreciably from this, the locknut must be undone and the central pin screwed in or out until the adjustment is correct. The pin is the pivot on which the operating lever rotates and, therefore, screwing the pin in reduces the clearance. Tighten the locknut and re-check the adjustment.

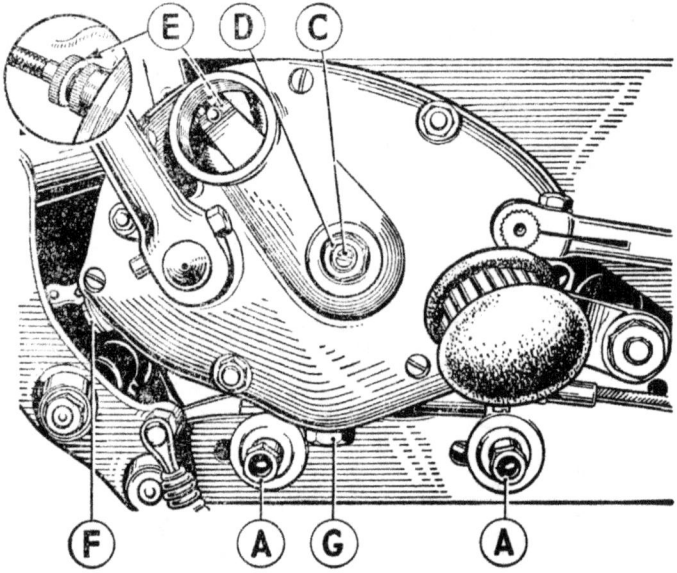

Fig. C24a. Clutch and Front Chain Adjustment.

When the adjustment has been completed the cable should be adjusted by means of the screw adjuster at the back of the gearbox inner cover E (Fig. C24a) until there is approximately $\frac{1}{8}$ inch free play at the handlebar end.

Front Chain Adjustment

The adjustment of the chain can be checked by removing the inspection cover from the chaincase. Turn the engine over slowly, and find the position in which the chain is tightest. There should be a total up and down movement of $\frac{1}{2}''$ at this point.

To adjust, slacken the two nuts ('D' Fig. C24 or 'A' Fig. C24a) and move the gearbox backwards or forwards as necessary, until the adjustment is correct. Then tighten the nuts and re-check the adjustment.

Note that, if the position of the gearbox has been altered, the rear chain will need adjusting also.

B.S.A. Service Sheet No. 409 (continued)

Chaincase Removal

Remove the drain plug from the rear of the case, and drain off the oil. Take off the left-hand footrest and undo the screws round the rim of the case, together with the two screws which secure it to the gearbox shield (when fitted). The nuts for these screws are welded on and cannot be lost. The chaincase outer cover can then be removed, taking careful note of the positions of the washers and distance pieces.

On C10 and C11 models, the engine drive shaft assembly is removed by prising back the tab of the lock washer with a screwdriver inserted between the coils of the shock absorber spring, and unscrewing the large nut on the end of the shaft. If the nut is very tight, engage top gear and apply the rear brake to prevent the engine turning. The spring and cam sleeve can then be withdrawn.

Rotate the clutch until the spring connecting link in the chain is on the top run, and in line with the recess in the back of the chaincase. Remove the spring link, followed by the chain and engine sprocket.

Take off the clutch, as described in Service Sheet No. 308, and withdraw the rear part of the chaincase after unscrewing the bolts which secure it to the crankcase.

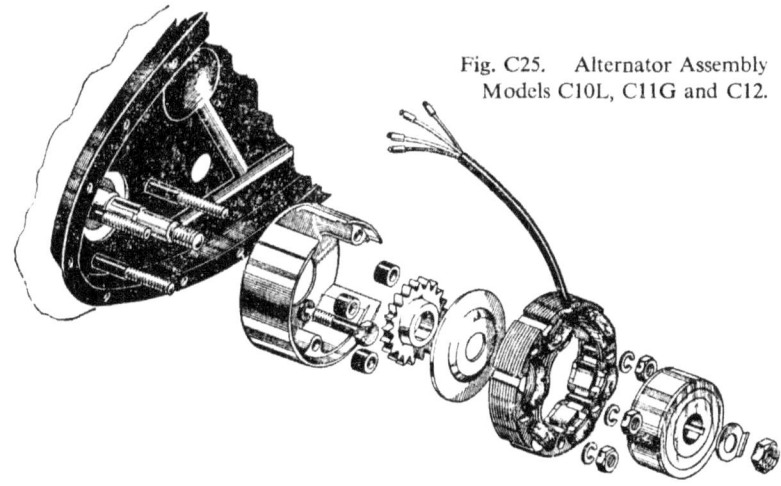

Fig. C25. Alternator Assembly Models C10L, C11G and C12.

The alternator assembly on C10L, C11G, and C12 models is dismantled by prising back the tab on the lock washer and unscrewing the large nut on the end of the engine shaft. If the nut is very tight, engage top gear and apply the rear brake to prevent the engine turning. Next take off the three nuts (four on some early models) which retain the coil assembly. Lift this off the studs and withdraw the rotor, which is keyed to the shaft, also the dished aluminium washer. Should the coil assembly prove difficult to remove, it may be gently prised off with a screwdriver, taking great care not to damage the windings.

A limited number of machines was produced employing a brass shield behind the rotor, in conjunction with a plain steel washer on the shaft, in place of the dished aluminium washer. The four stud fixing for the coil assembly was used with this arrangement.

B.S.A. Service Sheet No. 409 (continued)

Rotate the clutch until the spring connecting link is on the top run, and in line with the recess in the back of the chaincase. Remove the spring link, followed by the chain and engine sprocket.

The alternator housing can now be withdrawn, after removing the retaining bolt and the three distance pieces from the studs. On models having four studs, the housing is retained by two nuts.

Take off the clutch, as described in Service Sheet No. 411, disconnect the wires from the alternator at the push-in connectors, and withdraw the rear part of the chaincase.

Chaincase Re-assembly

Reassembly of the front chaincase is carried out in the reverse order to dismantling.

Ensure that the alternator (when fitted) is correctly assembled (see Fig. C25), and that the washer between the rotor and the engine sprocket has not been omitted. The wires from the alternator must be positioned so that they cannot foul the chain.

New lock washers should be used for the large nut on the engine shaft, and the nut must be fully tightened before the tab is bent over.

B.S.A. MOTOR CYCLES LTD., Service Department, Armoury Road, Birmingham 11.

B.S.A. PRESS

SERVICE SHEET No. 410

C10, C11 AND C11G MODELS

ADJUSTMENT, DISMANTLING AND RE-ASSEMBLY OF HUBS AND BRAKES

(For Spring Frame Rear Hub, see Service Sheet No. 412)

Front Wheel Removal and Replacement

To remove the front wheel, place a suitable support under the engine crankcase so that the wheel is held clear of the ground. Disconnect the brake cable from the brake arm clip and unscrew the wheel spindle nut which has a left-hand thread. Slacken the pinch bolt (A) Fig. C27, and pull out the spindle (B). Slide the distance bush (C) outwards to allow the wheel to drop out of the forks.

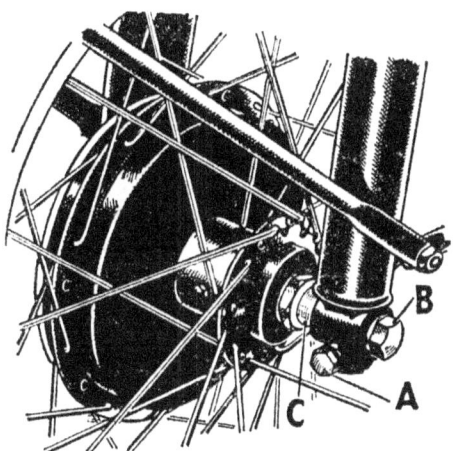

Fig. C27. Removal of Front Wheel.

The wheel is replaced in the reverse order to that for removal. It is most important that after the spindle nut has been tightened and before the pinch bolt is tightened, the forks are depressed once or twice to enable the left-hand fork end to position itself on the distance bush. If this precaution is not observed, the fork leg may be clipped out of position and the fork will not function correctly.

Rear Wheel Removal (Rigid Frame)

Disconnect the rear chain, then remove the bolt holding the brake anchor plate and the knurled brake adjuster nut on the rear brake rod. Disconnect the speedometer drive by unscrewing the nut (F) Fig. C28, then loosen the two spindle nuts and the wheel should slide out of the fork ends.

When replacing the rear wheel note that the spindle nuts are shouldered and must be correctly located in the fork ends.

B.S.A. Service Sheet No. 410 (contd.)

Rear Chain Adjustment (Rigid Frame)

The rear chain must be readjusted after the rear wheel has been replaced or when chain wear has taken place. With the spindle nuts just slack, rotate the spindle by means of a spanner on the flats at its left-hand end. Clockwise rotation will move the spindle backwards by the action of the two cams bearing on the frame stops.

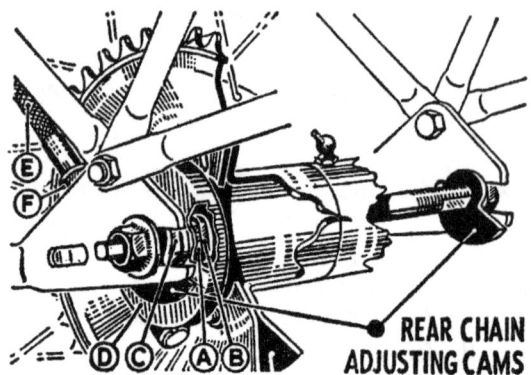

Fig. C28. Section of Hub Showing Adjustment.

The chain should be adjusted so that there is a total up and down movement of $\frac{3}{4}$ in. in the centre of the chain run and at its tightest point. Tighten the spindle nuts and check the wheel adjustment by means of a taut piece of string which should be equidistant from the front and rear of each wheel.

> Note: Where the speedometer drive gearbox is attached to the rear wheel, it must be correctly aligned so that the speedometer cable is not kinked. Slackening nut (C) Fig. C28 will permit the gearbox to be rotated, but the left-hand spindle nut must be slackened first.

Bearing Adjustment (Front Hub and Rear Hub Rigid Frame)

Both hubs are adjusted in a similar manner. Cup and cone type bearings are employed and the adjusting cone (B) Fig. C28 with its locknut (A), are on the left-hand side of the hub. Where the speedometer drive gearbox is fitted to the rear wheel it must be removed, after undoing the retaining nut and washer at (C), to gain access to the adjuster cone.

To carry out the adjustment, remove the wheel then slacken the locknut and screw the adjuster cone in or out until, with the locknut retightened, the spindle rotates freely but without any appreciable end play.

Hub Dismantling and Reassembly

With the wheel removed, undo the locknut (A) Fig. C28 and unscrew the adjuster cone (B) which will permit the brake plate, fixed cone and spindle to be withdrawn from the other side of the hub. The balls will fall free during the operation and care should be taken to prevent their loss, and to avoid the inter-mixing of one set with the other.

Removal of the retaining nut will permit the brake plate to be withdrawn from the spindle. The bearing cups can be tapped from the hubs by means of a suitable drift applied from the opposite end, and will carry with them the felt washers and their retainers. These items should only be removed if they require replacement.

B.S.A. Service Sheet No. 410 (contd.)

Reassembly is carried out in the reverse order. After the cups have been positioned insert the plain steel washer, followed by the felt washer and the felt washer retainer to complete the assembly of the oil seal for each bearing. Pack the cups with grease and insert the ball bearings. The front hub should have eleven 5/16 in. balls in each cup and the rear hub ten 5/16 in. balls.

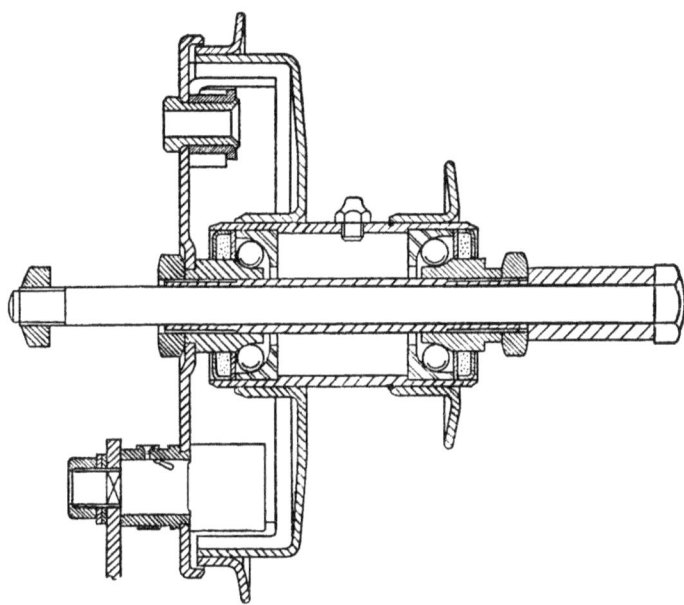

Fig. C29. Front Hub (Section View).

If the non-adjustable cone has been removed from its spindle or spindle sleeve it should be screwed into position again, noting that it screws on to the shorter thread of the rear spindle.

Replace the spindle in the hub and screw the adjustable cone and locknut into position to secure the spindle. Replace the brake plate and its retaining nut or distance piece and adjust the bearings as described in the earlier paragraph. The brake plate should rotate freely without binding.

Brake Relining

To remove the brake shoes lay the drum cover plate flat on a bench and lever the shoes upwards. They can then be drawn over, and free of the cam and fulcrum pin. If the cam pads show excessive wear the brake shoes should be removed.

When the brake shoes are removed the linings can be replaced as described in Service Sheet No. 612.

B.S.A. Service Sheet No. 410 (contd.)

Chainwheel Replacement

The rear chainwheel is of the bolted-on type and can be simply replaced after removing the rear wheel and the speedometer drive gearbox. Make sure that the retaining bolts are quite tight as, if they are allowed to work loose, fracture is likely.

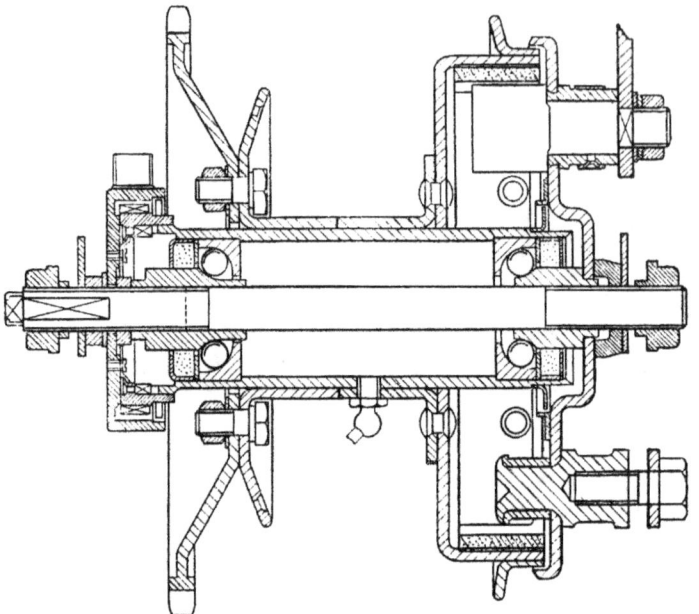

Fig. C30. The Rear Hub (Section View).

B.S.A. MOTOR CYCLES LTD., Service Department, Armoury Road, Birmingham 11.
B.S.A. Press

BSA SERVICE SHEET No. 411

October, 1948
Reprinted May, 1964

C10L, C11G and C12 MODELS
CLUTCH

Dismantling

Remove the nearside footrest and then undo the small screws round the rim of the chaincase. As the outer half of the chaincase is taken off, careful note should be made of the positioning of the distance pieces and washers, etc., for replacement purposes. The joint washer should be carefully preserved.

Remove the three spring retaining nuts and withdraw the springs, spring cups and distance pieces. The spring pressure plate and other clutch plates can then be removed, and if only attention to these items is required the clutch need not be dismantled further. The steel plates should be smooth, and if badly scored must be replaced, while the cork inserts will require washing in petrol if there is any trace of oil on them. If the inserts are burnt or glazed they should be replaced.

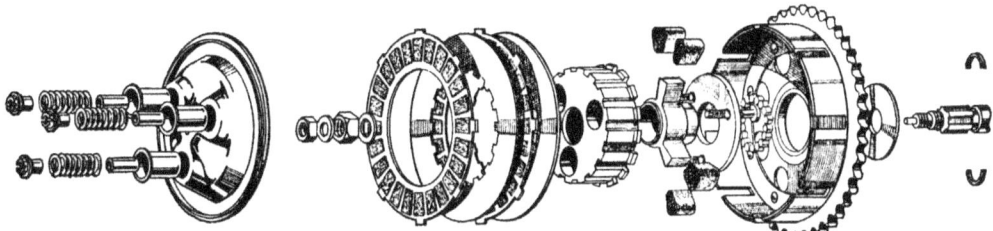

Fig. C31. Exploded View of Clutch.

To dismantle the remainder of the clutch, remove the outer mainshaft nut, which has a left-hand thread. Remove the washer and unscrew the inner nut, which has a right-hand thread. The complete clutch can then be withdrawn from the mainshaft, making sure that the rollers do not fall out from between the clutch centre and the chainwheel. The clutch thrust washer and its split circlip will probably remain in position on the mainshaft, but can easily be withdrawn.

Lift the chainwheel from the clutch centre and remove the 18 rollers. The three bolts and the cover plate from the clutch centre can also be removed to expose the vane and shock absorber rubbers. If the rubbers require attention, the vane must be pushed out with the aid of a suitable drift.

Reassembly

Before commencing reassembly examine the roller tracks on the chainwheel bush and clutch centre, and if the wear on either of these components exceeds .0015 in. it should be replaced.

If the chainwheel teeth are worn to a hook shape, the chainwheel must be replaced or rapid wear on the chain will result.

To reassemble the vane into the clutch centre, first replace the vane and the three thicker rubbers which should be on the left-hand side of each vane arm (A) Fig. C32. Hold an old gearbox mainshaft in a vice and position the vane centre on it to prevent it rotating.

B.S.A. Service Sheet No. 411 (contd.)

Rotate the clutch centre so as to compress the rubbers and slip the remaining three rubbers into position. The clutch centre can best be gripped with the aid of a plain clutch plate. Replace the clutch centre cover plate (B) and the three bolts.

The remainder of the clutch assembly is quite straightforward. Ensure that the split circlip is properly located on the mainshaft before the clutch thrust washer is positioned against it. A dab of grease will serve to hold them in place. Position the 18 rollers carefully on the clutch centre before sliding the chainwheel over them. Re-position the remainder of the clutch on the shaft and replace the two nuts and washers, noting that the inner nut has a right-hand thread and the outer a left-hand. Make sure that the inner nut is fully tightened before the outer is replaced.

Replace the clutch plates ensuring that the thick plain back plate is put in first. When the spring assemblies have been replaced the retaining nuts should be tightened down firmly on to the distance pieces.

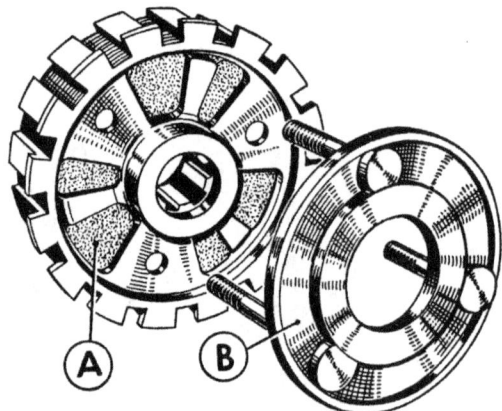

Fig. C32. Vane Assembly.

B.S.A. MOTOR CYCLES LTD., Service Department, Armoury Road, Birmingham 11.

THE B.S.A. PRESS

BSA SERVICE SHEET No. 412

Models C10, C11 and C11G (with Plunger Type Rear Suspension)

ADJUSTMENT, DISMANTLING AND RE-ASSEMBLY OF REAR HUB AND BRAKE

Wheel Removal

Undo the spring link of the rear chain and allow the chain to hang down. A piece of clean paper should be placed below the machine so that the chain does not pick up grit.

Remove the brake rod adjuster (D) Fig. C33, and loosen the nuts (E). On three-speed models the speedometer drive cable must also be detached. The wheel can then be moved to the rear and withdrawn from the machine.

When replacing the rear wheel ensure that the slot in the brake torque plate is located on the extended head

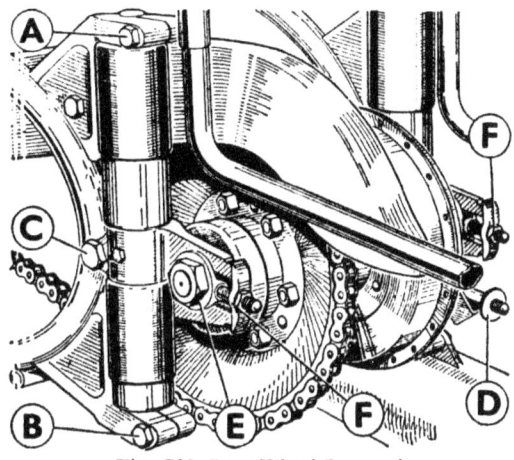

Fig. C33. Rear Wheel Removal

of the pinch bolt on the right-hand rear suspension lug, and that the wheel alignment has not been disturbed.

Hub Dismantling and Reassembly

After unscrewing its retaining nut (D) Fig. C34, withdraw the brake plate complete with brake shoes.

Removal of the sleeve nut (C) will permit the spindle, complete with speedometer drive or dust cover, to be pulled out of the hub from the chainwheel end.

Prise off the dust cap and remove the felt oil seal from the brake drum end of the hub. Then with the aid of a suitable soft drift unscrew the bearing retaining ring (A) which has a left-hand thread. Displace the central distance piece (J) in the hub and drive out the bearing (E) with the aid of a suitable drift. As the bearing comes away it will carry with it the oil seal, oil seal holder and oil seal retaining washer.

Remove the distance piece and drive out the other bearing. Unscrewing the nut (H) will permit the speedometer drive or dust cover to be withdrawn, to leave only the short distance collar (F) and its retaining nut (G) on the spindle. The chainwheel can be detached after bending back the lockwashers and undoing the retaining nuts.

Reassembly is carried out in the reverse order to that for dismantling. Both bearings should be greased before reassembly. Position the distance collar (L) in the brake drum side of the hub and insert the bearing (B) until it is firmly against the collar. Replace the flat oil seal washer and then screw in the bearing retaining collar (A) which has a left-hand thread. Ensure that this collar is quite tight before replacing the felt oil seal and its retaining dust cap.

The centre distance piece (J) can then be replaced, followed by the chainwheel side bearing and its oil seal assembly. Pass the spindle through the two bearings and the central distance piece and lock the assembly up tight with the sleeve nut (C). Replace

B.S.A. Service Sheet No. 412 (contd.)

the speedometer drive gearbox (three-speed models) making sure that the dogs on the inside of the gearbox sleeve engage in the two notches on the end of the hub. Ensure that the washers fitted one on either side of the speedometer drive or dust cover are not omitted.

Replace the brake plate and secure with the aid of the spigot nut (D). This completes the reassembly.

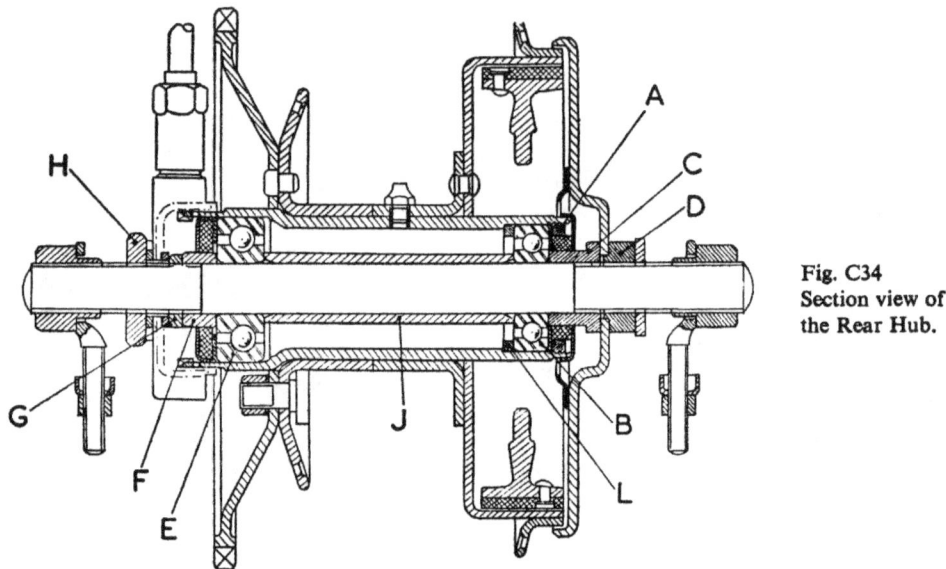

Fig. C34
Section view of the Rear Hub.

Brake Shoe Re-lining

When the brake plate is removed from the drum it should be laid on a bench, shoes uppermost. Insert two small levers under the edge of the shoes and lever them up and away from the plate. They can then be drawn over and free of the cam and fulcrum pin. The operating cam and fulcrum pin should be inspected but it is unlikely that more than greasing will be necessary. If the cam pads on the brake shoes show excessive wear then new shoes should be fitted. To replace the shoes, attach the springs and push the shoes over the cam and pivot by reversing the dismantling procedure.

For instructions on removing and replacing the brake shoe linings see Service Sheet No. 612.

Rear Chain Adjustment

First place the machine on its centre stand so that the rear wheel is clear of the ground. The wheel must be at its lowest point in the suspension when the adjustment is made. Slacken the two nuts (E) Fig. C33, then draw the wheel rearwards by means of the two chain adjusters (F) to tighten the chain. Turn each nut by an equal number of turns so that the wheel alignment is not altered. The chain should be adjusted so that there is a total up and down movement of ½ in. at its tightest point. Tighten the nuts (E) and check the adjustment.

The wheel alignment can be checked by means of a taut piece of string which should be equidistant from the front and rear of each wheel. Note that the rear brake may need adjusting when the chain adjustment has been altered.

B.S.A. MOTOR CYCLES LTD., Service Department, Armoury Road, Birmingham 11

B.S.A. PRESS

BSA SERVICE SHEET No. 412A

C Group Models
(Except C15)

ADJUSTMENT, DISMANTLING AND RE-ASSEMBLY OF FRONT HUB AND BRAKE (7 in. Brake)

Wheel Removal and Replacement

To remove the front wheel, first disconnect the brake cable, then slacken the pinch bolt *A* (Fig. C33a). Insert a tommy bar in the hole in the head of the spindle at *B* and unscrew the spindle, noting that it has a left hand thread and therefore unscrews in a clockwise direction. Support the wheel as the spindle is withdrawn, and when it is clear the wheel can be pulled away from the right hand fork leg and removed from the machine.

After removal do not let the wheel fall on to the bush which projects from the brake drum side of the hub. Although the bush is pressed in, it may, if subjected to a sharp blow, be forced back into the hub. If this should happen the bush can be retrieved and re-positioned with the aid of the wheel spindle.

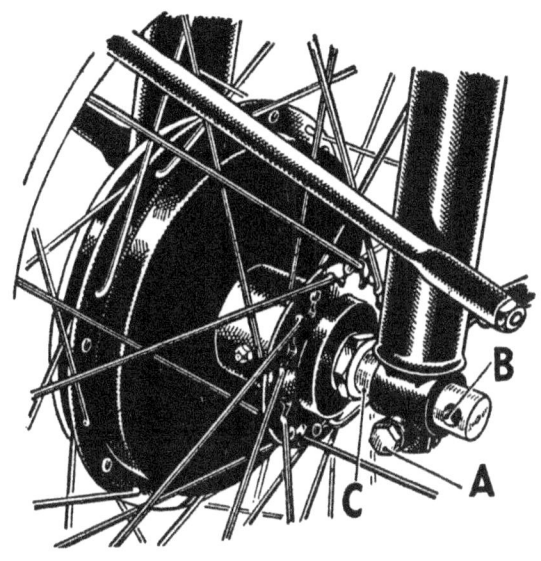

Fig. C33a. Wheel Removal

The wheel is replaced in the reverse order to that for removal. It is most important that after the spindle has been tightened and before the pinch bolt is tightened, the forks are depressed once or twice to enable the left hand fork end to position itself on the spindle shank. If this precaution is not observed, the fork leg may be clipped out of position and will not function correctly.

Dismantling and Re-assembly of the Hub

Withdraw the brake plate which is a push fit on the bush *B* (Fig. C34a). Remove the locking split pins and unscrew the bearing retaining collars *C* and *D*, which have normal right hand threads. Replace the spindle and drive out the brake side ballrace *E* together with the bush *B* by striking the end of the spindle with a hide mallet. Only the ball race *F* now remains in the hub and can be removed with a suitable soft drift.

Before commencing re-assembly make sure that the hub distance collar behind each bearing is in position. Press the bearings in as far as they will go and secure with the screwed collars.

Before replacing the bearing retaining collars ensure that the rubber oil seals in them are in good condition. The collars should be done up quite tight and if necessary fresh holes should be made for the locking split pins.

B.S.A. Service Sheet No. 412A (cont.)

Brake Relining

To remove the brake shoes lay the drum cover plate flat on a bench and lever the shoes upwards. They can then be drawn over, and free of the cam and fulcrum pin. If the cam pads show excessive wear the brake shoes should be renewed.

When the brake shoes are removed the linings can be replaced as described in Service Sheet No. 612.

When new linings or new shoes have been fitted, the brakes must be centralised after refitting the wheel. To do this, replace the brake cover plate, complete with shoes, fulcrum pin and cam in the brake drum. Slacken the fulcrum pin nut, and turn the cam so as to open the brake shoes in the normal manner. The fulcrum pin will then move in its slot until both shoes are pressing equally on to the drum. Tighten the fulcrum pin nut firmly and release the brake.

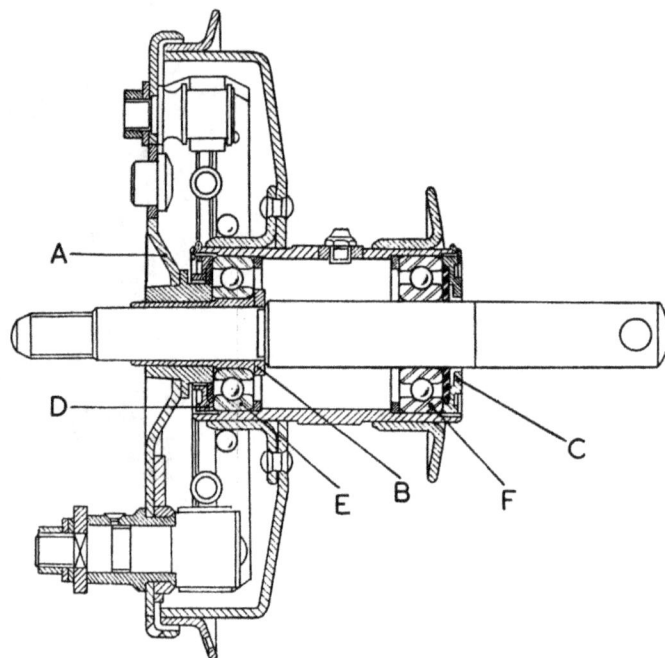

Fig. C34a. Section of Front Hub (7 in. Brake)

B.S.A. MOTOR CYCLES LTD.
Service Dept., Armoury Road,
Birmingham, 11
Printed in England.

SERVICE SHEET No. 412B

Reprinted February, 1965

C12 Model

ADJUSTMENT, DISMANTLING AND RE-ASSEMBLY OF HUBS AND BRAKES

Wheels

Both wheels are fitted with ball forward bearings which require no adjustment. The bearings are packed with grease during assembly and should last until the machine is overhauled. The brakes are provided with knurled finger adjusters and should not be adjusted too closely as any 'rubbing' will generate heat which may distort the drum and melt the grease in the hub.

Front Wheel Removal

Place the machine on the stand with the front wheel clear of the ground. Disconnect the brake cable and slacken pinch bolt 'A' (Fig. C42), insert a tommy bar in the wheel Spindle 'B' and unscrew the spindle which has a left-hand thread. Support the wheel and withdraw the spindle. The wheel can be pulled away from the right-hand fork leg and removed from the machine.

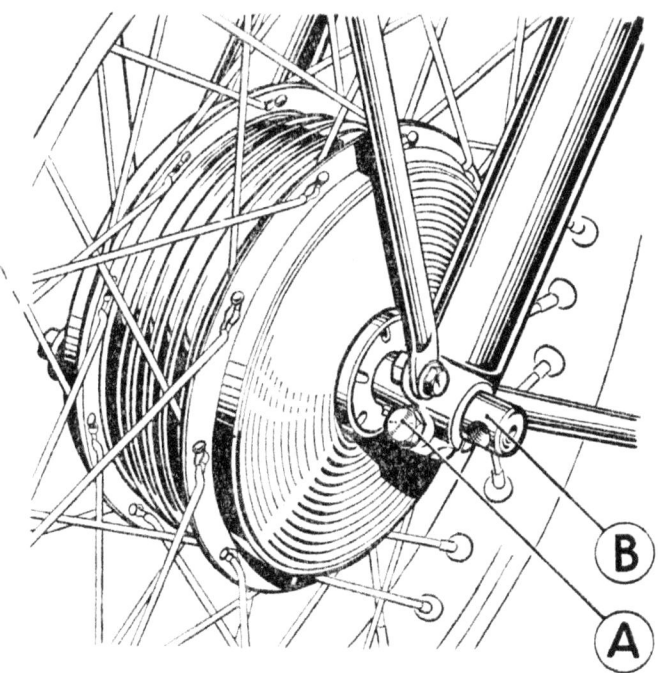

Fig. C42. Front Wheel Removal.

B.S.A. Service Sheet No. 412B (cont.)

After removal take care that the wheel is not allowed to fall on to the bush which projects from the brake drum side of the hub or it may be forced back on to the hub. If this should happen the bush can be retrieved and repositioned with the aid of a wheel spindle.

The wheel is replaced in the reverse order. After the spindle has been tightened and *before* the pinch bolt is tightened, depress the forks several times with the wheel on the ground to enable the left-hand fork end to position itself in the spindle shank otherwise the fork leg may be clamped out of position.

Rear Wheel Removal

Place the machine on the stand and remove the rear chain. Do not allow the chain to unwind itself from the gearbox sprocket. Undo the knurled brake adjuster and slacken the two spindle nuts 'B' (Fig. C43). The wheel can now be withdrawn to the rear and removed from the machine under one side of the rear mudguard.

The wheel is replaced in the reverse order. Ensure that the slot in the brake plate is engaged on its locating peg and that the chain adjusters are up against the fork ends.

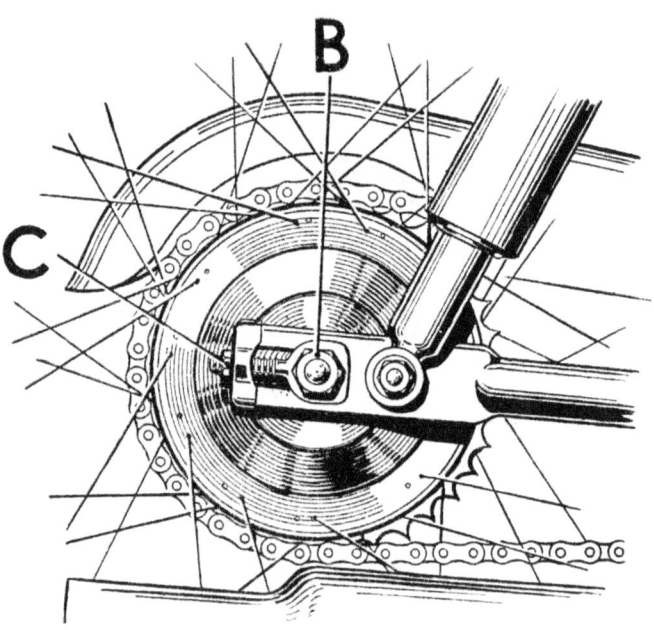

Fig. C43. Rear Wheel Removal and Chain Adjustment.

B.S.A. Service Sheet No. 412B (cont.)

Rear Chain Adjustment

The rear chain must be adjusted when the machine is on the stand and the suspension is at its lowest point. Rotate the wheel and find the tightest point on the chain. The total up and down movement at this point should be $1\frac{1}{8}''$ measured at the centre of the chain run. If it varies from this the chain must be adjusted by moving the rear wheel. Slacken the spindle nuts 'B' and screw the adjusters 'C' in or out as required. When the chain tension is correct tighten the spindle nuts and recheck. Finally, ensuring that the adjusting nuts are tight.

Wheel Alignment

During chain adjustment it is important to see that the wheel alignment remains correct. If the adjusters are moved an equal amount alignment will not be disturbed assuming that it was originally corrected, but it is wise to check it occasionally by means of a long straight edge placed along the sides of the wheels. The straight edge should touch the front and rear walls of both tyres. Where different sizes of tyres are used allowance must be made.

Dismantling Front Hub

This should not be necessary unless it is intended to renew the bearings. Withdraw the brake plate, which is a push fit on the bush 'B' (Fig. C44). After removing the locking cotters unscrew the bearing retaining collars 'C' and 'D' which have right-hand threads. Replace the spindle and drive out the brake side ballrace 'E' together with bush 'B' by striking the spindle with a soft mallet. Ballrace 'F' can now be removed with a suitable drift.

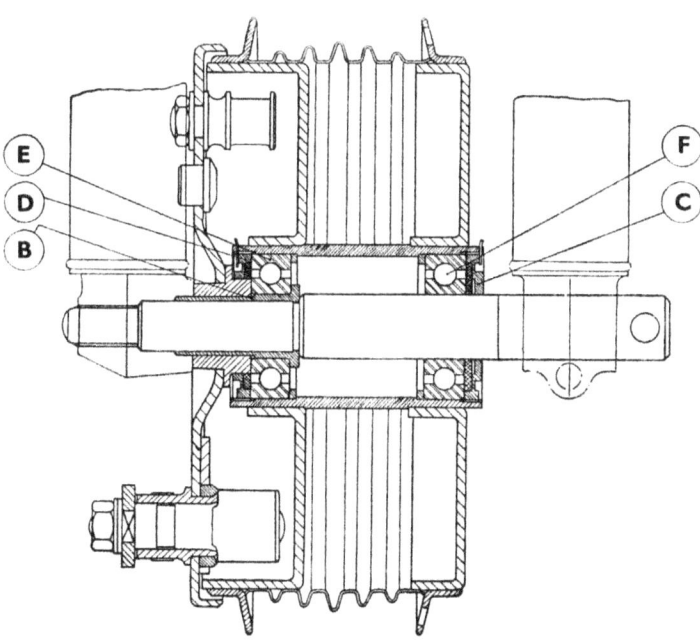

Fig. C44. Front Hub.

B.S.A. Service Sheet No. 412B (cont.)

Re-assembly

Ensure that the hub distance collar located behind each bearing is in position. Press in the bearings until they are fully home and screw in the retaining collars making sure that the oil seals are serviceable lock the collars up tight. It may be found necessary to drill fresh holes for the split pins.

If the brakes have been relined or new shoes fitted it will be necessary to centralise the brakes. Replace the brake cover plate complete with shoes, cam and fulcrum pin into the drum. Slacken the fulcrum pin nut and turn the cam so as to operate the shoes in the normal way. The fulcrum pin will move in the slot until the shoes press equally on to the drums. The fulcrum pin should be fully tightened and the brake cam can then be released.

Dismantling Rear Hub

Remove the retaining nut 'A' (Fig. C45) and left of the brake plate and shoes. The spindle nut 'B' is now exposed, remove this and tap the spindle through until it can be withdrawn. Prise off the dust caps 'C' and felt washers 'D'. Unscrew the locking ring 'E' (Note:- this has a left-hand thread.) Drive out the ballraces using a suitable drift inserted through the hub.

Re-assemble in the reverse order. Grease the bearings thoroughly and ensure that the bearings are up against the distance collar. Tighten the locking ring fully.

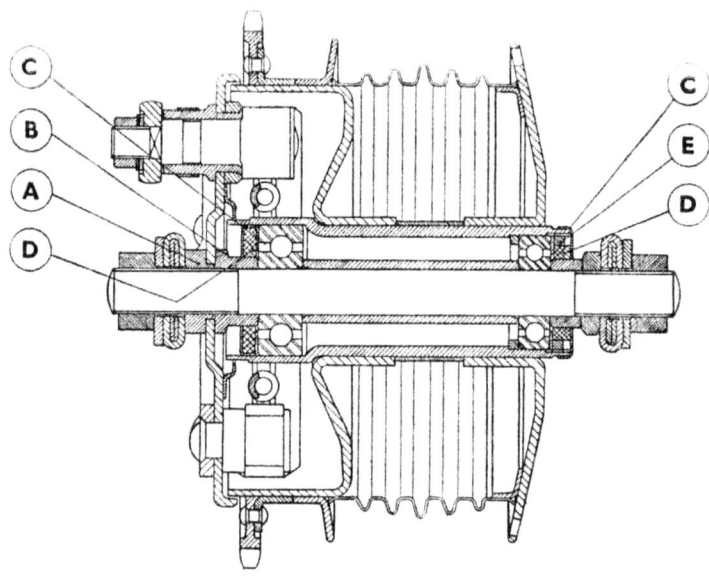

Fig. C45. Rear Hub.

B.S.A. MOTOR CYCLES LTD.
Service Dept., Armoury Road,
Birmingham, 11
Printed in England.

JU/B6269

BSA SERVICE SHEET No. 412C

D3, D5, D7, C12, C15 and B40 SWINGING ARM MODELS
REAR SUSPENSION

FRAME

The silent bloc bushes fitted to the rear suspension swinging arm are unlikely to need replacement for some considerable time. If it is found necessary to renew them, first remove the suspension units by detaching the top pivot bolts and the bottom retaining nuts.

Remove the rear wheel and chainguard. Undo the fork spindle nut and tap out the spindle, using a suitable drift.

Lift the rear fork until it is clear of the side plates; it can then be turned and pulled away from the rear.

After the central distance piece has been displaced the bushes can be removed with a suitable drift.

DISMANTLING THE SUSPENSION UNITS

Early C12 models were fitted with a damper spring of 100 lb./inch rate, this was later increased to 124 lb./inch.

The 124 lb./inch spring, part number 29-4570 can be fitted to early machines where it is considered necessary.

The spring is retained by circlips fitted at its base and a service tool, part number 61-5064 has been introduced to facilitate removal.

The tool is assembled as shown in Fig. C46 and when the nut is screwed down sufficiently the spring is compressed thus releasing the circlips. The circlips can be extracted through the apertures in the tool and the spring comes away when the tool is removed.

Reassembly is in the reverse order.

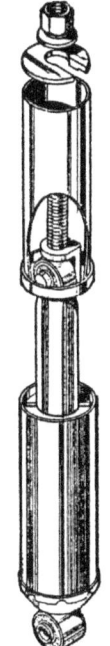

Fig. C46.

B.S.A. MOTOR CYCLES LTD., Service Department, Armoury Road, Birmingham 11.

Printed in England at the B.S.A. Press

BSA SERVICE SHEET No. 413

March, 1960
Reprinted August, 1964

C10L AND C11G MODELS

REMOVING ENGINE FROM FRAME AND COMPLETE DISMANTLING

Engine Removal

The procedure for removal and dismantling of the engine will be described from the point reached in Service Sheet No. 405 on decarbonising, when the cylinder head and barrel have been removed.

Remove the primary chaincase as described in Service Sheet No. 409 on primary transmission.

Remove the contact breaker cover and disconnect the lead from the terminal. Undo the retaining bolt and place the crankcase and gearbox shield on one side.

Drain the oil tank and disconnect the oil pipes from the crankcase unions.

Remove the nuts securing the front engine plates and the rear crankcase fixing studs. Remove the front engine plates and slacken the frame and gearbox nuts clamping the rear engine plates, as these tend to hold the engine in position. Withdrawal of the rear crankcase securing studs will permit the engine to be lifted from the frame.

Engine Dismantling

Whilst working on the engine, a simple fixture as illustrated in Fig. C35 will facilitate matters considerably. Alternatively, clamp the engine in a vice by one of the mounting lugs, supporting the engine on a bench.

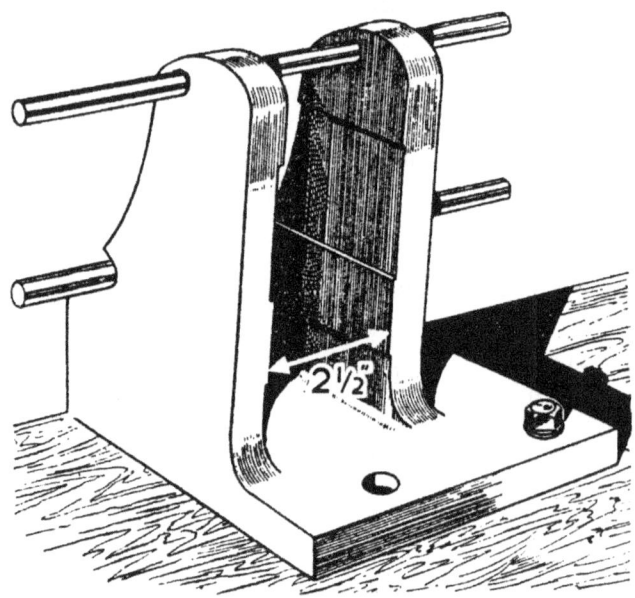

Fig. C35. Angle bracket for mounting engine.

B.S.A. Service Sheet No. 413 (contd.)

Undo the two screws and withdraw the contact breaker back plate. Then remove the advance and retard mechanism by undoing the central bolt. Resistance will be felt after a few turns of the bolt and further rotation will pull the shaft from its taper.

Early models did not have this self-extracting device, but an effective extractor can be simply made. Remove the retaining bolt and pass a piece of $\frac{3}{16}$ in. steel rod down the bolt hole as far as it will go. Mark the rod at a point flush with the end of the shaft, then remove the rod and cut it off $\frac{3}{8}$ in. short of this mark. Replace the rod and screw a $\frac{5}{16}$ in. C.E.I. bolt into the end of the shaft. As this is tightened down on to the rod it will pull the mechanism from its taper.

Take out the timing cover screws and pull off the cover. Clean it and place on one side. If the oil seal requires replacing, it can be prised from the cover with the aid of a screwdriver.

Withdraw the camshaft complete, then flatten out the tab washer and remove the mainshaft nut. The mainshaft pinion can now be drawn off with the aid of Service Tool, Part No. 61-3256 (see Fig. C36).

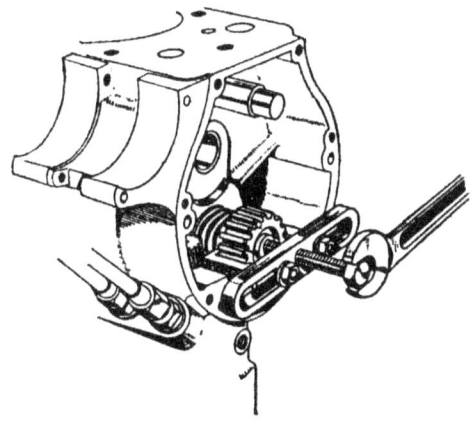

Fig. C36. Engine shaft pinion extractor (Service Tool 61-1735)

The oil pump driving spindle is located by a dowel situated in the bottom left-hand edge of the timing chest. Screw one of the timing screws into the dowel and use it to pull the dowel from the crankcase. The pump driving spindle can then be drawn upwards into the timing chest (Fig. C37). In some instances the dowel will be found to be covered by a small washer which must be removed before the screw can be inserted.

Before parting the crankcase halves remove any distance washers from the drive-side crankshaft and withdraw the sleeve which projects through the crankcase oil seal.

Remove the nuts from the crankcase studs and take out the free studs, noting their locations. The halves may now be separated. This may be somewhat difficult but a little care will allow them to be parted without damage. A few careful blows with a hide mallet will serve to break the joint if the jointing compound prevents separation.

B.S.A. Service Sheet No. 413 (contd.)

Pull the gear-side crankcase half away from the flywheel assembly, then lift the flywheel assembly from the other crankcase half, taking care not to lose the oil retaining washer which lies between the flywheel and the mainshaft ball bearing.

Take off the four nuts and lockwashers at the base of the gear-side crankcase, and remove the base plate and filter.

The two bolts retaining the pump can be unscrewed to permit the pump to be withdrawn, but it should not be removed unless it requires attention. The bolts retaining the pump in position can be identified by the spring washers underneath their heads.

If the drive-side ballrace requires replacing, remove the retaining circlip and after heating the case in a degreaser or hot water, the bearing should be driven out with a suitable drift applied from the outside of the case. The new bearing should be fitted while the case is still warm, and the drift used should fit the outer race of the bearing. Do not omit the oil retaining washer behind the bearing.

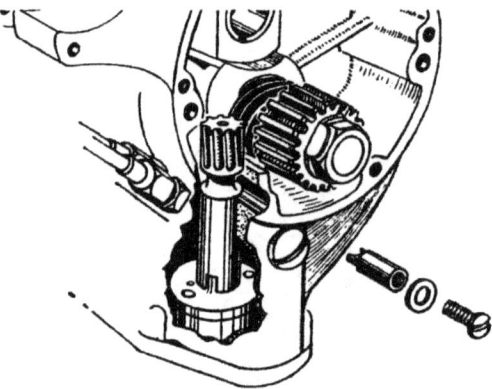

Fig. C37. Oil pump spindle locking plunger.

The case should also be heated before attempting to remove any of the bushes in the timing-side crankcase or timing cover.

The cam pinion spindles should also be inspected for wear and, if necessary, removed while the case is hot.

Finally, if the flywheels are to be separated they must be held securely on the bench, as extreme pressure will be required to release the crankpin nuts.

Special spanners are used, and it is usually necessary to add a piece of tubing to obtain additional leverage.

The crankpin is a taper fit in the flywheels, and can be released by a sharp blow with a mallet.

It is now only necessary to decide which parts require renewal, and the following may assist you in your decision.

B.S.A. Service Sheet No. 413 (contd.)

We do not advise the fitting of over-size rollers to the big-end assembly. The whole assembly, comprising crankpin, connecting rod and rollers, should be changed. All these components are carefully matched, working to one ten-thousandth part of an inch, and supplied in complete sets, ready for fitting.

If the bore of the cylinder, when measured at right angles to the gudgeon pin, shows wear to the extent of .010 in. or more, the cylinder should be rebored, and an oversize piston fitted. (Oversize pistons are available in 0.5 mm. (.020 in.) and 1 mm. (.040 in.).

Wear in mainshaft bearings or bushes will be readily be apparent, and bearings showing signs of damaged balls, rollers or tracks should be replaced.

Special clearances are specified for mainshaft bearings used on B.S.A. motor-cycles, and it is *NOT* advisable to fit other than genuine B.S.A. replacements.

B.S.A. MOTOR CYCLES LTD., Service Department, Armoury Road, Birmingham 11.
B.S.A. PRESS

BSA SERVICE SHEET No. 414

August, 1954
Reprinted June, 1963

MODELS C10L AND C11G

RE-ASSEMBLING THE ENGINE

The need for absolute cleanliness cannot be over-emphasized. Parts should be thoroughly cleaned, and all traces of any anti-rust preparation with which new parts may be coated must be removed. All bearings should be smeared with fresh engine oil before reassembly.

Flywheels

If the big-end assembly is to be renewed it is as well to check the weight of the new components against those which have been removed. A slight variation in weight is inevitable, but if it does not exceed $1\frac{1}{2}$ ozs. no action need be taken; otherwise the flywheel assembly should be re-balanced. This tolerance should not be exceeded since, when first assembled, the flywheels were carefully balanced to suit the original parts, and the balance may be adversely affected if the weights of the new components differ considerably from those originally fitted.

Fit the flywheels to the crankpin, making sure that the key on the drive-side is properly engaged in its keyway, and tighten the crankpin nuts by hand.

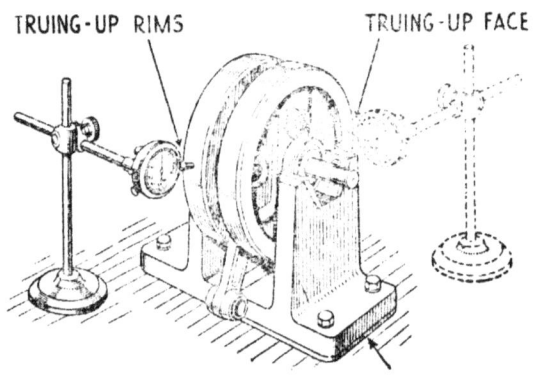

Suitable packing under timing side 'vee'block to compensate for smaller diameter bearing.

Fig. C38. Checking Flywheel Alignment.

In order to tighten the crankpin nuts properly, the whole flywheel assembly must be held rigidly, preferably with the aid of a flywheel bolster. Alternatively, fix two 9/16-in. diameter posts rigidly to the bench with their centres $3\frac{7}{8}$-in. apart. Midway between these posts a hole of 1-in. diameter should be bored to receive the mainshaft. The flywheel assembly can be mounted on these posts so that they pass through the holes bored in the flywheels. Tighten the drive-side crankpin nut very firmly, using a tubular extension piece on the spanner, and punch over the edge of the crankpin with a centre punch to lock the nut.

Now turn the assembly over, so that the gear-side flywheel is on top and tighten the crankpin nut lightly. The grub screw in the end of the crankpin must be riveted over or centre-punched to prevent it unscrewing. If it unscrews, serious damage may result to the engine. Check that the side clearance of the connecting rod in the flywheels does not exceed .012-in. and is not less than .010-in.

The flywheels will now be aligned only very approximately and further steps must be taken to ensure that the wheels are as true as possible. Two of the actual (or similar) bearings to be used in the engine should be fitted to the mainshaft and the latter mounted on

B.S.A. Service Sheet No. 414 (contd.)

vee-blocks. The flywheels must be trued up, both on faces and rims, for which purpose a dial micrometer is necessary (Fig. C38), and after the wheels are trued to within at least .005-in., tighten the timing side crankpin nut fully. A mallet or lead hammer applied to the flywheels will provide a sufficiently heavy blow for final truing, and will not harm the flywheels (Fig. C39). The shafts should be finally trued to within .002-in. maximum. The shafts must not be struck.

All parts must be thoroughly clean and free from paraffin, grit or other foreign matter, and all traces of old jointing compound should be removed. If any bushes have been replaced then they must be reamered out to the correct dimensions.

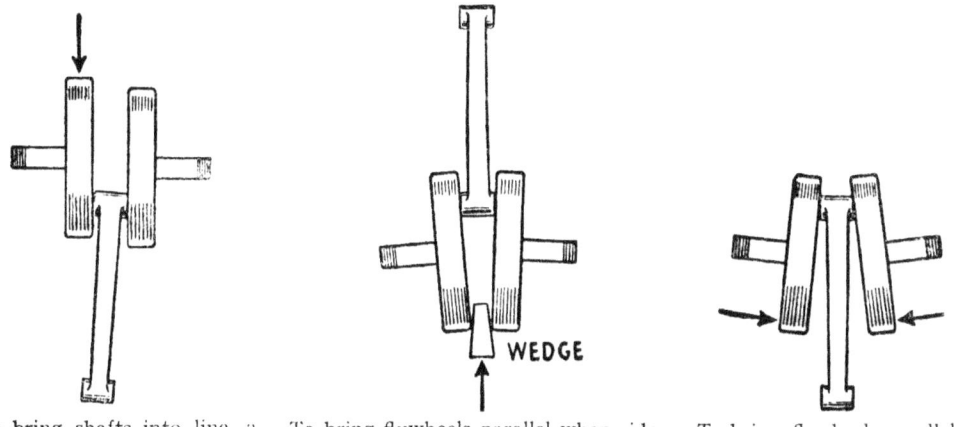

To bring shafts into line, a sharp blow with a mallet on **timing side** flywheel (indicated by arrow)

To bring flywheels parallel when sides opposite crankpin are converging, insert wedge as shown and deal sharp blow with mallet

To bring flywheels parallel a sharp blow with a mallet on flywheel rims on opposite side to crankpin

Fig. C39. Method of Correcting Flywheels Out of Alignment.
(Note that above illustrations are exaggerated).

Place the oil flinger washer on the drive-side mainshaft and push the flywheel assembly into position in the drive-side crankcase half. Thinly coat the mating faces of the crankcase with jointing compound and slide the gear-side half into position. The two halves must be perfectly mated and the flywheel assembly must rotate freely when the halves are bolted firmly together.

Replace the oil pump and bolt it into position making sure that the spring washers beneath the bolt heads are not omitted. Slide the pump driving spindle into position and retain it with its pin. Make sure that the blade of the pin is fully engaged in the spindle groove, and if necessary a small washer should be placed over the end of the pin to prevent its moving away from the spindle, but ensure that it does not force the pin too tightly into the groove when the timing cover is replaced.

Replace the key and push the small timing pinion into position on the mainshaft. Tighten the retaining nut and turn over the lockwasher.

Fit the cam followers, also the tappets in the case of the C10L, then replace the cam-

B.S.A. Service Sheet No. 414 (contd.)

shaft, ensuring that the mark on the camshaft gear coincides with the marked tooth on the mainshaft pinion (see Fig. C40).

Apply clean engine oil to the pinions and cams, then replace the timing cover using a new joint washer. Make sure that the oil seal passes easily over the shaft, or if a new oil seal is to be fitted, it can be pushed into position after the timing cover has been replaced.

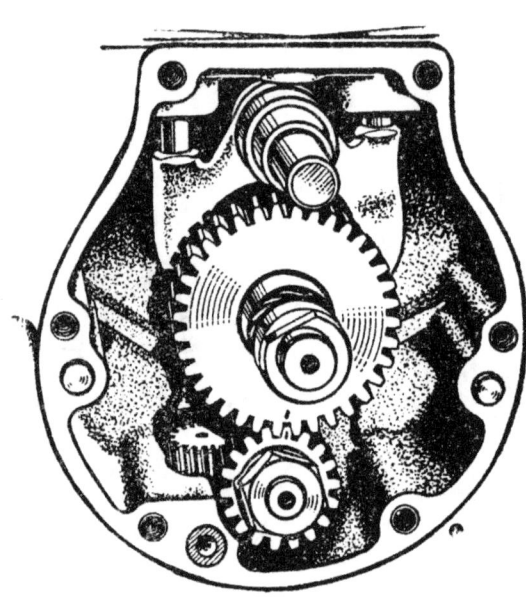

Fig. C40. Timing Gear Marks.

Replace the advance and retard mechanism, making sure that, as the taper is engaged, the peg on the advance and retard spindle locates in the groove in the camshaft, then tighten down the retaining bolt.

Finally time the engine as described in Service Sheet No. 404.

Assembly from this point is the same as after decarbonising. Replace the engine in the frame and tighten the engine and gearbox plate stud nuts.

Replace the primary chaincase as indicated in Service Sheet No. 409. Make sure that the ported mainshaft sleeve which passes through the drive-side oil seal is correctly positioned with the ports nearest the flywheel. It is immaterial which of the mainshaft grooves engages with the peg on the inside of the sleeve.

B.S.A. MOTOR CYCLES LTD., Service Department, Armoury Road, Birmingham 11.

BSA SERVICE SHEET No. 415

September, 1954
Revised July, 1962
Reprinted Aug., 1966

Models C10L and C11G
USEFUL DATA

	C10L	C11G & C12
Cylinder bore (mm.)	63	63
Engine stroke (mm.)	80	80
Engine capacity (c.c.)	249	249
Standard compression ratios	5–1	6.5–1
1954 Camshaft, Part No.	29–1993	29–2025
Tappet clearance, Inlet	.004 in.	.003 in.
Exhaust	.006 in.	.003 in.
Valve timing, Inlet opens before T.D.C.	25°	25°
Inlet closes after B.D.C.	70°	70°
Exhaust opens before B.D.C.	70°	70°
Exhaust closes after T.D.C.	25°	25°
1955–56 Camshaft, Part No.	29–2075	29–2076
Tappet clearance, Inlet	.012 in.	.010 in.
Exhaust	.015 in.	.012 in.
Valve timing, Inlet opens before T.D.C.	29°	29°
Inlet closes after B.D.C.	84°	84°
Exhaust opens before B.D.C.	80°	80°
Exhaust closes after T.D.C.	28°	28°
Piston ring gap, Compression	.010 in.	.010 in.
Oil control	.010 in.	.010 in.
Piston ring side clearance	.002 in.	.002 in.
Piston clearance at base of skirt	.0045/.0065 in.	.0035/.0055 in.
Contact breaker gap	.015 in.	.015 in.
Ignition setting, Fully advanced before T.D.C.	$\frac{5}{32}$ in.	$\frac{1}{4}$ in.
Fully retarded before T.D.C.	$\frac{1}{32}$ in.	T.D.C.
Plug type, Champion	N8B	L10S
Plug gap	.018/.020 in.	.018/.020 in.
Carburetter, Standard type	274BT/3EG	274BU/1EH
Choke size	$\frac{13}{16}$ in.	$\frac{13}{16}$ in.
Throttle slide	4/4	4/4
Needle position	2	3
Needle jet	.1055	.1065
Main jet	90	80
Carburetter, Monobloc type	375/2	375/4
Choke size	$\frac{13}{16}$ in.	$\frac{13}{16}$ in.
Throttle slide	375/3½	375/3½
Needle position	2	3
Needle jet	.1055	.1055
Main jet, without air cleaner	120	140
Main jet, with air cleaner	85	100

B.S.A. Service Sheet No. 415 (contd.)

	C10L	C11G & C12
Petrol tank capacity (galls.)	2½	2½
Oil tank capacity (pints)	4	4
Gearbox capacity (pints) 1954–55	½ (3 speed)	½ (3 speed)
		1 (4 speed)
Standard gear ratios 4th	—	6.2
3rd	6.6	6.2 7.6
2nd	9.8	9.25 11.1
1st	14.5	14.1 16.15
Gearbox capacity (pints) 1956 4 speed	½	½
Standard gear ratios, 4th	6.6	6.26
3rd	8.0	7.64
2nd	11.7	11.1
1st	17.1	16.15
Engine sprocket	16T	17T
Clutch sprocket	43T	43T
Gearbox sprocket	19T	17T (C12 19T)
Rear wheel sprocket	47T	42T (C12 47T)
Primary chain size	½ × .305 in.	½ × .305 in.
No. of links	69	69 (C12 70)
Rear chain size	½ × .205 in.	½ × .305 in.
No. of links, Rigid frame 1954–55	—	104
No. of links, Spring frame 1954–55	110	107
No. of links, Spring frame 1956	111	115
Front fork movement, 1954–55	3¾ in.	6 in.
Front fork movement, 1956	6 in.	6 in.
Rear suspension movement	2 in.	2 in. (C12 2¾ in.)
Front fork capacity (engine oil) 1954–55	Grease	¼ pint (142 c.c.)
Front fork capacity (engine oil) 1956	¼ pint (142 c.c.)	¼ pint (142 c.c.)
Front brake size, 1954	5½ × 1 in.	5½ × 1 in.
Front brake size, 1955–56	5½ × 1 in.	7 × 1⅛ in.
Rear brake size	5 × ⅝ in.	5½ × 1 in.
Rim sizes	WM1 × 19	WM1 × 19
Standard tyre sizes	2.75 × 19	3.00 × 19
Tyre pressures, p.s.i. Front	18	18
Rear	27	26
Wheelbase	52½ in.	53½ in. (C12 54 in.)
Ground clearance	5 in.	4½ in. (C12 4 in.)
Saddle height	29½ in.	29½ in.
Dry weight (Rigid frame) 1954	—	301 lbs.
(Spring frame) 1954	256 lbs.	316 lbs.
(Spring frame) 1955	256 lbs.	304 lbs.
(Spring frame) 1956	260 lbs.	312 lbs.

B.S.A. MOTOR CYCLES LTD.,
Service Dept., Armoury Road, Birmingham 11.
Printed in England

BSA SERVICE SHEET No. 415A

July, 1955
Revised Nov. 1957

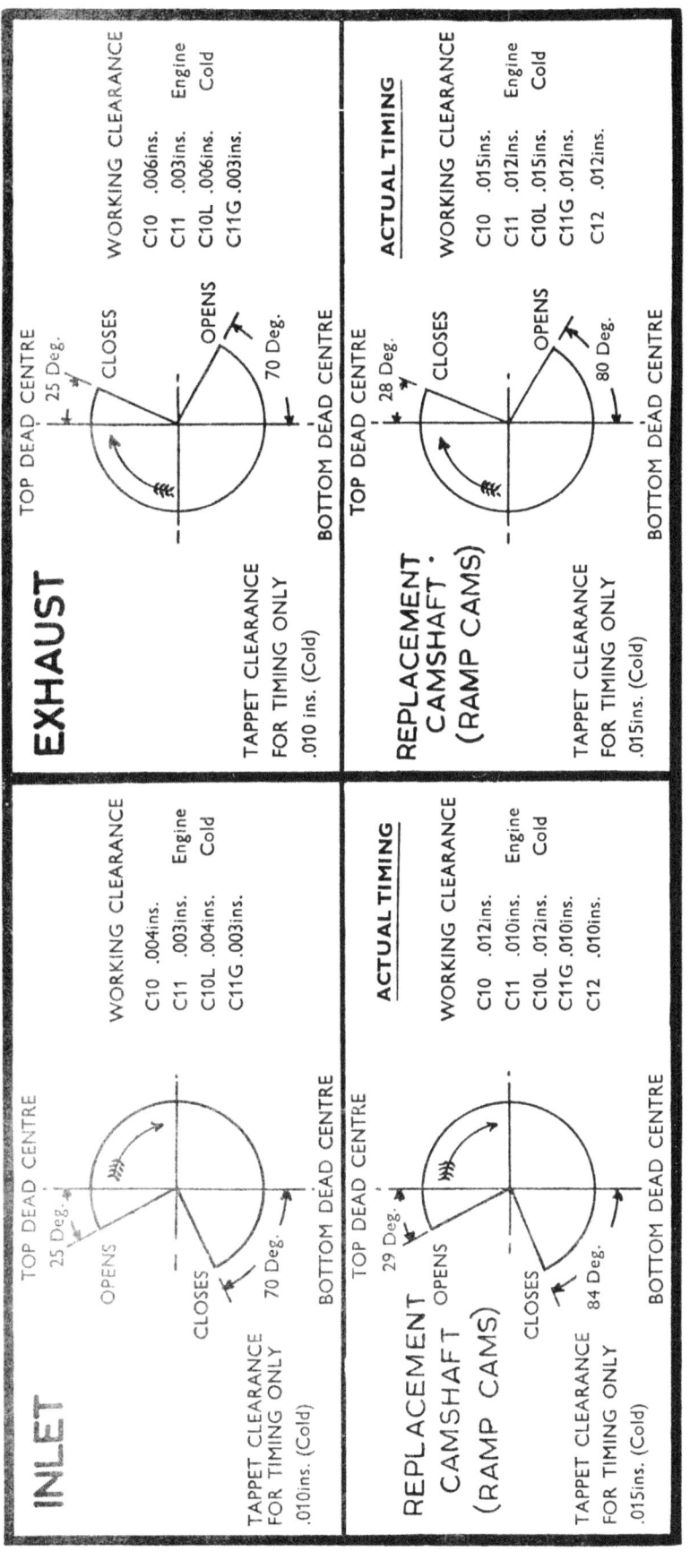

Fig. 1. 'C' GROUP MODELS VALVE TIMING CHART

B.S.A. Service Sheet No. 415A (cont.)

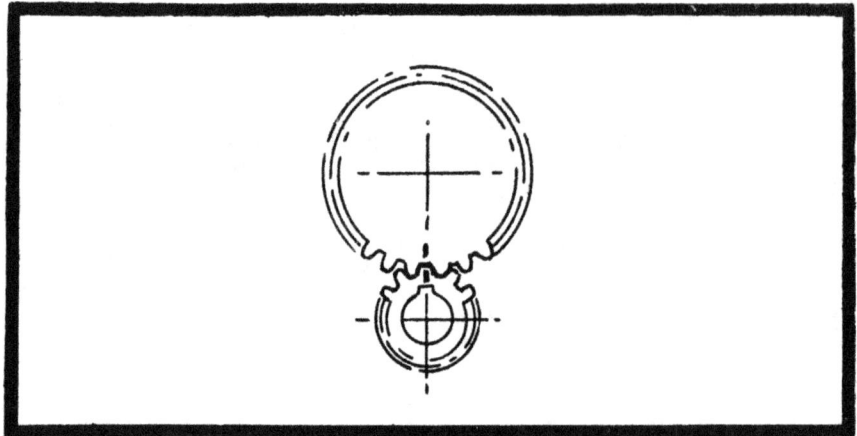

Fig. 2. VALVE TIMING MARKS

B.S.A. MOTOR CYCLES LTD.
Service Dept., Birmingham, 11
Printed in England.

BSA SERVICE SHEET No. 508

MODELS D1, D3, D5 AND C10L

DISMANTLING AND RE-ASSEMBLY OF THE HUBS AND BRAKES

FRONT WHEEL

To remove the front wheel from the forks, disconnect the brake cable at the brake arm on the cover plate, by removing the ¼ in. diameter round head bolt and nut holding the "U" shaped cable clip. Unscrew the cable adjuster, withdraw the cable and place it out of the way.

Unscrew the two spindle nuts, using the plug spanner, and remove the three mudguard stay bolts on the left-hand fork end bracket. (The latter is not necessary on earlier models, where the mudguard is attached to the outer fork tubes). Lift the left-hand lower fork leg away from the spindle, and pull the wheel away from the right-hand leg, so that the brake anchor plate clears it. The wheel will then drop out.

FRONT BRAKE

Unscrew and remove the spindle nut securing the cover plate. The plate can now be withdrawn and the brake shoes examined. It is not advisable to remove the shoes from the cover plate unless the linings require renewal.

If it is necessary to remove the shoes, first take off the brake lever (A) Fig. D22, and tap in the cam (B) until the cam plate clears the shoes. Insert a screwdriver between the brake shoes adjacent to the fulcrum pin (C) and twist the screwdriver. Place a small lever, (D) between the shoe and the anchor plate and lever the shoe upwards until the spring tension is released. The shoes can then be lifted from the cover plate.

If the shoes require re-lining, see Service Sheet No. 612.

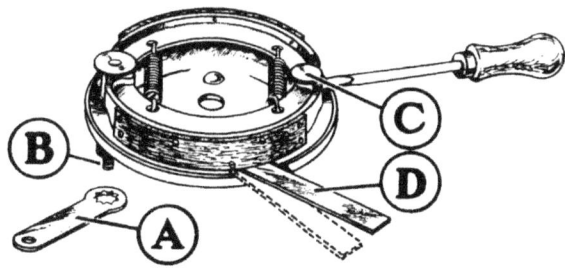

Fig. D22.

B.S.A. Service Sheet No. 508 (contd.)

FRONT WHEEL BEARINGS (Standard Model)

If it is necessary to remove the bearings for examination or cleaning, unscrew the locknut (L) and spindle nut (A) Fig. D23, and tap the spindle right through, using a hide mallet and soft drift to prevent damage to the threads.

The dust caps (B) can be prised off with the aid of a screwdriver between the cap and the edge of the spoke flange. Care should be taken to work the caps off a little at a time, to avoid distortion. Next unscrew the lock ring (G) securing the outer ring of the ball journal on the brake side. This ring has a left-hand thread.

Take out the felt washers (C) and (H) and the plain steel washers (D).

The ball journals can now be inspected, but they should not be removed unless new ones are required.

If it is necessary to renew the journals the hub should be supported at the brake drum end. With the aid of a suitable soft drift applied to the inner ring of the ball journal,(E) Fig. D23, drive the journal in towards the centre of the hub. This will cause the brake drum side journal to be driven out. When it is clear of the hub, take out the distance piece (F) and pass a drift through the hub until contact is made with the other journal, in order to drive it out.

Note:—This procedure is possible only on machines after engine number YD-2850. Earlier models have no deep counterbore in the hub and the journals must be driven out from opposite ends after the distance piece (F) has been displaced slightly to allow a soft drift to be applied to the inner ring of the race.

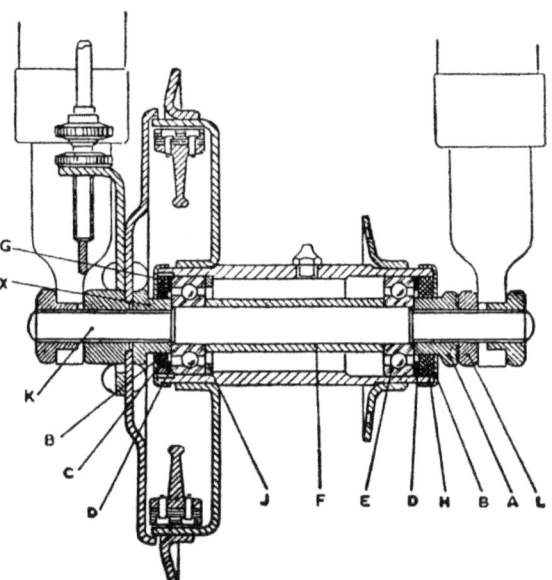

Fig. D23.

B.S.A. Service Sheet No. 508 (contd.)

COMPETITION MODELS

The front hubs are fitted with adjustable taper-roller bearings as illustrated in Fig. D23a, but instructions for removing the wheel and dismantling the brake are identical with those for standard machines.

To dismantle the bearings, unscrew the two locknuts (M) and (N), remove the brake plate washer (P) and bearing distance piece (R), prise off the dust caps (S), and take out the felt washers (T). The spindle may now be withdrawn from the brake drum side, leaving only the bearings, felt retaining cups (U) and bearing abutment rings (V) and (W) in the

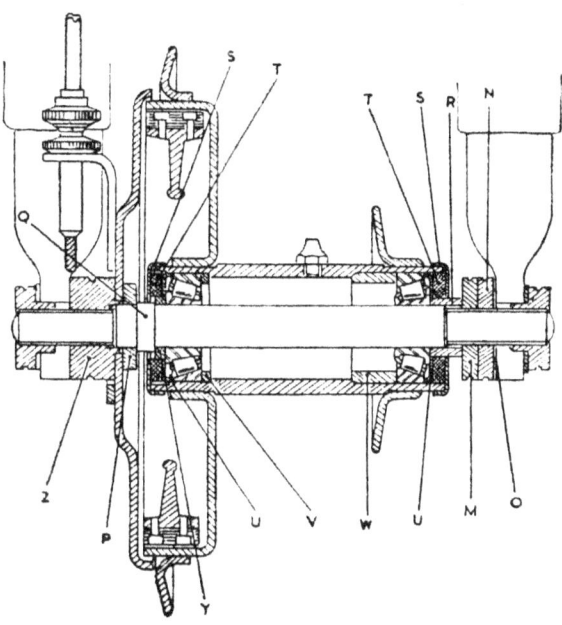

Fig. D23a.

hub. With the hub suitably supported at the brake drum end and a soft drift applied against the abutment ring (V), the ring itself, the bearing and the retaining cup (U) may be driven out in one operation, during which the drift should be moved around the circumference of the abutment ring to ensure even extraction. The hub may now be turned over and the same procedure adopted for removal of the corresponding parts in the other side of the hub.

Note:—The front spindle assembly of the early competition models differed slightly in that the spindle itself had no fixed collar (Q), brake plate washer (P) or bearing thrust washer (Y). These parts replace a shaped nut which was screwed along the brake drum side threaded end of the spindle, tight against the spindle shoulder. Also, a shaped nut was used in the place of the existing distance piece (R) and nut (M). These points should be borne in mind when dismantling and reassembling, but the procedure otherwise is the same as for the current type hub described.

B.S.A. Service Sheet No. 508 (contd.)

REAR WHEEL

To remove the rear wheel from the frame, disconnect the brake rod by unscrewing the knurled adjusting nut and lift the rod out of the way.

Uncouple the chain at the connecting link, and run the chain off the sprockets after first placing a clean piece of paper or other suitable material underneath the machine to protect the chain from road or floor grit.

Disconnect the speedometer drive by unscrewing the locknut on the speedometer gearbox.

Slacken off the spindle nuts sufficiently to draw the wheel out of the fork ends. Lean the machine over and draw the wheel out under the left-hand chainstay.

REAR BRAKE

The brake cover plate and shoes are identical with those of the front wheel, and the instructions given for removal will apply equally to the rear brake.

REAR BEARINGS

The rear wheel hub is identical with that in the front wheel except that a speedometer drive gearbox is fitted to the offside. This is held in position by a plain washer and an additional locknut; after removing the locknut the gearbox can be drawn straight off the hub barrel. The instructions given for removal of the front hub bearings will apply equally to the rear hub, except that on spring frame models the inner locknut (corresponding to "L" on Fig. D23) is replaced with a plain distance collar.

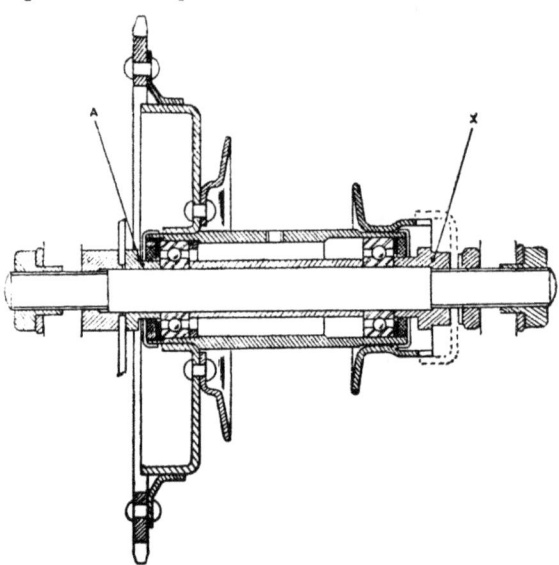

Fig. D23b.

Note:—On later spring frame models (1958 onwards) the distance collar is omitted; correct positionig of the speedometer gearbox allowed for by the shape of the spindle nut (x), Fig. D23b.

B.S.A. Service Sheet No. 508 (contd.

The rear hub spindle assembly is also different in other respects, but removal of the wheel and dismantling of the brake is the same as for earlier models, as also is the procedure for removing the speedometer gearbox. After these operations have been carried out, the spindle can be tapped through from the brake drum side, as the part (A) Fig. 23b, is merely a distance piece; which will then fall away. From this stage, dismantling is again the same as for earlier models.

REASSEMBLY OF THE HUBS

The following applies to all hubs, except the front hub on competition models, and refer to the illustration Fig. D23, unless otherwise stated. If new ball journals are to be fitted first place the distance piece (J) in position in the hub barrel, brake drum side, and press in the hub journal, taking care to see that it is square to the housing. Insert one plain steel washer (D) and then screw in the lock ring (G). This has a left-hand thread. Reverse the hub, insert the inner distance sleeve (F), and push the spindle (K) through the bearing and distance sleeve. At this stage, if the hub has been cleaned out, it should be re-packed with grease. Place the second journal in position and press it into the housing until the inner distance sleeve is firmly gripped, and remove the spindle. Replace the other plain washer (D), felt washers (C) and dust caps (B), and re-insert the spindle so that the "fixed" nut is on the brake drum side, except on the rear hubs of the later spring frame models; where it should be on the opposite side.

The "fixed" nut is marked (X) on both illustrations, Fig.s D23 and D23b, and has been left undisturbed on the spindle throughout all the previously mentioned operations. If, for any reason, it has been slackened; it should be retightened firmly against the shoulder of the spindle. The "fixed" nut is located on the longer-threaded end of the spindles fitted to all front wheels and the later type spring frame rear wheel. On the rear wheels fitted to pre-1953 spring frame models and all rigid frame rear wheels the "fixed" nut is located on the shorter-threaded end of the spindle.

The spindle nut (A) may now be replaced and thoroughly tightened, except on the later spring frame rear hub where it is necessary to replace the distance collar (A) Fig. D23b, and the brake cover plate complete with shoes, before finally tightening down with the brake cover plate nut. In each case the tightening of the nut will lock together the spindle, the inner rings of the journals, and the sleeve (F). This assembly should rotate freely in the ball races if the journals have been pressed in squarely. On the ohter wheels, the brake cover plate and its nut should now be replaced, and the nut sequrely tightened. It should be noted that in each case the brake cover plate nut has a spigot which must be correctly located in the centre hole of the brake plate before the nut is tightened. The locknut (L) should now be replaced and tightened against the spindle nut (A) — front hub and rigid frame rear hub only.

Refitting of the speedometer drive gearbox will now complete the reassembly. This may be placed straight over the wheel spindle on the rigid frame models and on the lates spring frame models, making sure the driving dogs are located correctly in the recesses in the end of the hub barrel. The plain washer and the outer locknut should then be replaced and tightened securely. On earlier spring frame models the plain distance collar must be replaced before the speedometer drive gearbox is refitted.

Where a speedometer is not fitted, a plain hub-end cap (part number 90-6029) should be fitted in place of the speedo gearbox.

B.S.A. Service Sheet No. 508 (contd.)

REASSEMBLY (Competition Front Hub)

All references will be to Fig. D23a.

Place the distance piece (v) in position in the brake drum side of the hub barrel and press the outer ring only of the taper-roller race firmly and squarely up to it. Reverse the hub, place in the distance piece (w) and press in the outer ring of the other race in the same manner.

Take the hub bearing thrust washer (y) and slide it along almost the full length of the spindle, up to the spindle shoulder. Place the remainder of the brake drum side bearing (inner ring complete with cage and rollers) in position, backing it up to the thrust washer. Insert the spindle into the hub from the brake drum side, re-pack the hub with grease and slide into position the remainder of the other bearing. Press in the felt retainers (u), followed by the felt grease seals (t), and press on the dust caps (s). Owing to the "fixed" nut used on early spindles, the brake side bearing and oil seal assembly must be positioned in the hub before the spindle is inserted. Refit the bearing distance piece (r) and screw on to the spindle the nuts (m) and (n), locking them together when the correct bearing adjustment is obtained. Over-tightening of the hub bearings will cause rapid wear and when the wheel is refitted into the forks, just perceptible play (about 1/32 in.) should be felt at the rim.

Replace the brake plate washer (p) and the brake cover plate and its nut (z), the spigot of which must be correctly located through the hole in the centre of the brake cover plate, before tightening securely.

SPECIAL NOTE (All Front Wheels)

The dimension over the front hub locknuts, inside the fork ends, must be maintained between 4.910—4.920 in. To adjust, use shims part number 90-5545 as required, between locknut and bearing abutment nut. On competition models the shims can be interposed at point (o) Fig. D23a, to avoid disturbing the bearing adjustment. It will be necessary to add shims periodically, as bearing wear progresses, and after each re-adjustment.

REPLACING THE WHEELS

Reassembly of the wheels is the reverse procedure to removal, except that care must be taken to locate the brake plate anchorages correctly, over the lower fork sliding member in the case of the front wheel, and over the fork end stud in the case of the rear wheel. Care must also be taken to see that the speedometer gearbox is lined up to the cable. Sharp bends in the cable will result in fracture of the inner wire.

Couple up the brakes and chain, adjust the wheels in the fork ends, lock securely, and finally adjust the brakes by means of their respective knurled thumb screws.

REAR CHAIN ADJUSTMENT

The rear chain is adjusted by means of screw adjusters in the fork ends behind the wheel spindle. Slacken off the nuts (a) Fig. D23c, and screw the adjusters (b) in or out until the chain tension is correct with an up and down movement of three-quarters of an inch (2 cm.). Make sure that the adjustment is equal on both sides of the wheel so that the latter is in correct alignment in the frame. This can be done either by glancing along the line of both wheels when the front wheel is set straight, or by means of a long straight-edge or the edge

B.S.A. Service Sheet No. 508 (contd.)

of a plank placed along the sides of the wheels. The straight-edge should touch both walls of both tyres.

After adjusting retighten the nuts (A).

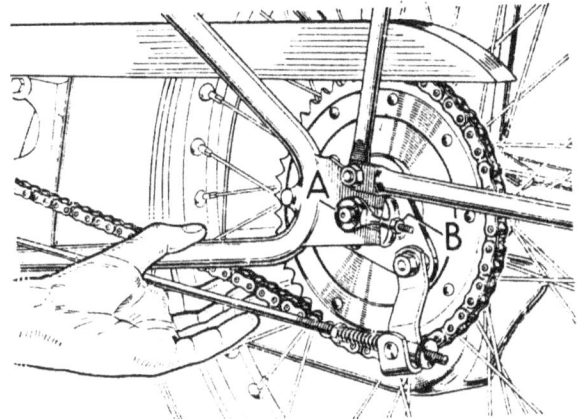

Fig. D23c.

On spring frame machines the rear chain should be adjusted when the machine is on its stand and the rear wheel in its lowest position. The adjustment should the be made so that the chain has a total up and down movement of ½ in. in the centre of the chain run at its tightest point.

In the case of the D3 and D5 swinging arm models, the movement should be ¾ in. (2 cm.) again with the machine on its stand.

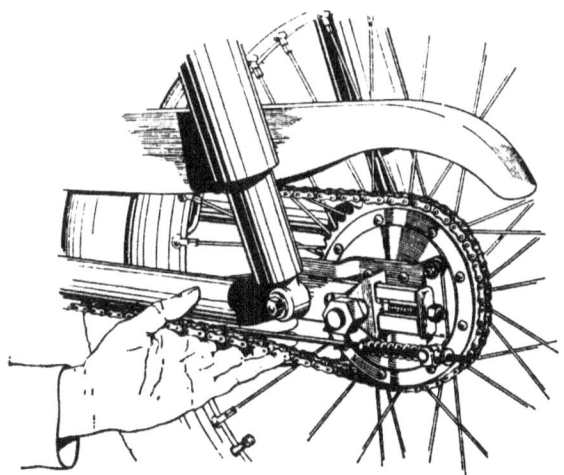

Fig. D23d.

B.S.A. MOTOR CYCLES LTD., Service Department, Armoury Road, Birmingham 11.
Printed in England
B.S.A. PRESS

BSA SERVICE SHEET No. 509

Models D1, D3, D5 and C10L — up to 1956
(for C10L 1956 onwards, please see Service Sheet No. 706)

REMOVAL AND DISMANTLING OF THE FRONT FORKS AND STEERING HEAD

Remove the front wheel as described in Service Sheet No. 508.

If only attention to the sliding members and bushes is required it is not necessary to dismantle the top part of the fork assembly but the mudguard must be unbolted from the lower fork members. On early D1 models the mudguard is attached to the upper fork tubes and removal is only necessary if the forks are to be completely dismantled.

Free the top end of the telescopic gaiters from the oil seal holders (B) Fig. D25, and slide the gaiters down the lower tubes. Remove the locking clips engaging in the top groove of the oil seal holders, which can then be unscrewed. On early models these clips are secured by the mudguard stay studs and later by the grease nipples which are screwed into the outer fork tube. Very early D1 models have no locking clips and the fork bushes on these models are non-detachable.

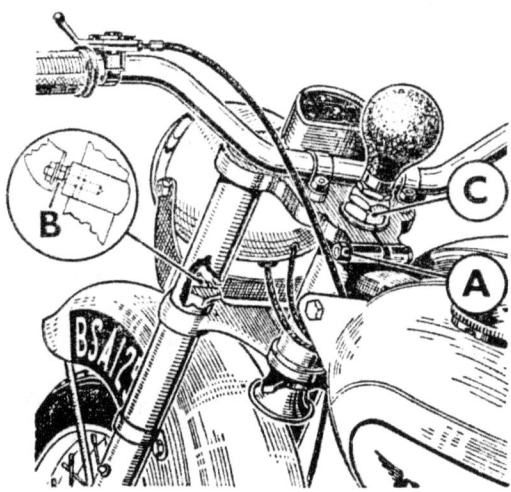

FIG. D24. *Front fork and steering head.*

Remove the two small nuts (A) Fig. D25, from the top of the two large nuts in the top yoke. On D3 and C10L models the small domed caps must first be removed. They should be levered up with the tang of a file inserted in the small hole in the edge of the dome. The sliding members complete with their springs can then be withdrawn from the bottom of the fixed tubes.

To detach the springs, hold the lower leg in a vice, as shown in Fig. D26, and using a small punch tap the spring from its thread. The spring can be removed from its upper end housing in a similar manner. Some models have a rubber tube fitted inside the spring to increase the resistance of the fork, and this can only be removed if one end of the spring is detached.

With the sliding tubes removed the lower fork bushes can be withdrawn. Removal of the grease nipples in the side of the outer legs will allow the fork bush distance piece

B.S.A. Service Sheet No. 509 (contd.)

and top bush to be pulled out of the fork outer tube with the aid of a spoke or other similar tool. On D1 models before frame No. YD1-57331 the fork bushes are non-detachable and if they show signs of wear then the fork outer tubes complete must be replaced by the later type.

Detach the clutch cable from the handlebar lever and remove the headlamp switch handlebar lever, when fitted. Removal of the four nuts beneath the fork top yoke which retain the handlebar clips or aluminium cover plate will allow the handlebars to be lifted away from the top yoke. If a bulb type horn is fitted in the steering head this should be removed before the handlebars.

From this point onwards the dismantling procedure for the D1 fork is slightly different from that for the other models and will be described first.

Remove the two nuts (D) Fig. D27, together with washers (E) and the two locknuts (C). Remove the headlamp from its bracket and lower it to the full extent of the wiring harness. This will allow access to the underside of the top yoke so that the speedometer cables can be disconnected and the instrument removed.

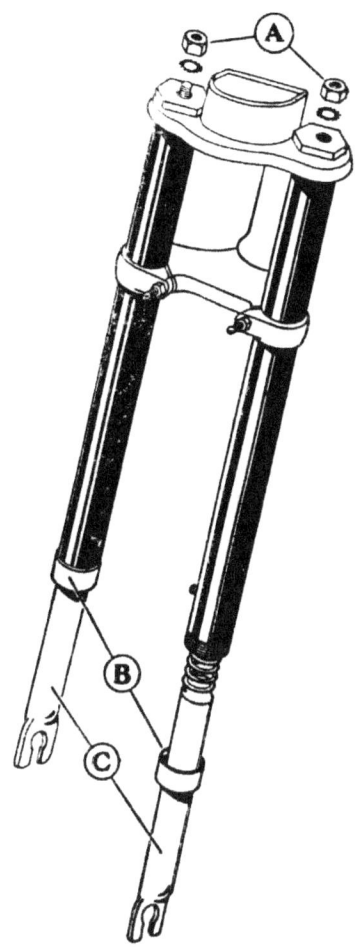

Fig. D25.

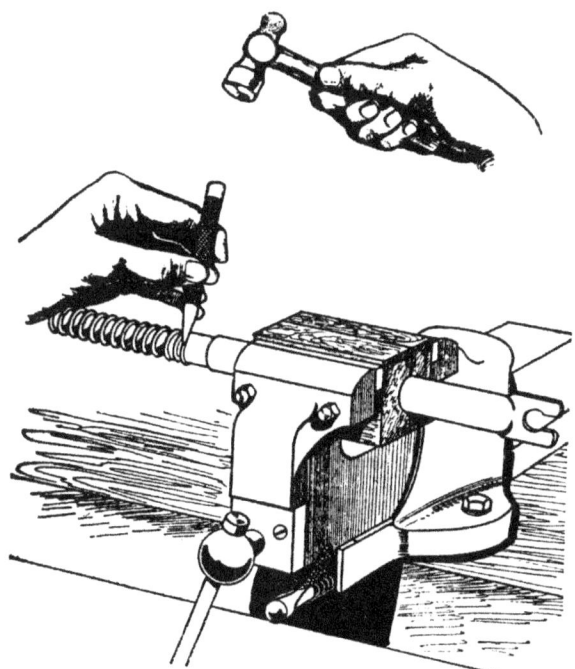

FIG. D26. *Removing the front fork springs.*

Slackening off the pinch bolt at the back of the top yoke will permit the yoke to be removed and placed aside, noting that it will be necessary to hold the lower part of the fork in position to prevent the balls of the lower head bearing dropping away. Pull the headlamp cowl assembly (when fitted) off the fork outer tubes and lift the headlamp over the forks so that it is resting securely on the petrol tank. As the remainder of the fork is withdrawn from the frame head a piece of clean rag should be held underneath the bottom yoke to catch any ball bearings which may escape.

B.S.A. Service Sheet No. 509 (contd.)

To remove the outer fork tubes place the assembly on a bench and slacken the pinch nuts (A) Fig. D28, in the bottom yoke. Expand the slots in the yoke by inserting a screwdriver as shown in Fig. D28 and draw the tubes down until they are resting on the large washers. Replace the nuts (D) and tap gently to remove the washers. The fork outer tubes can now be withdrawn.

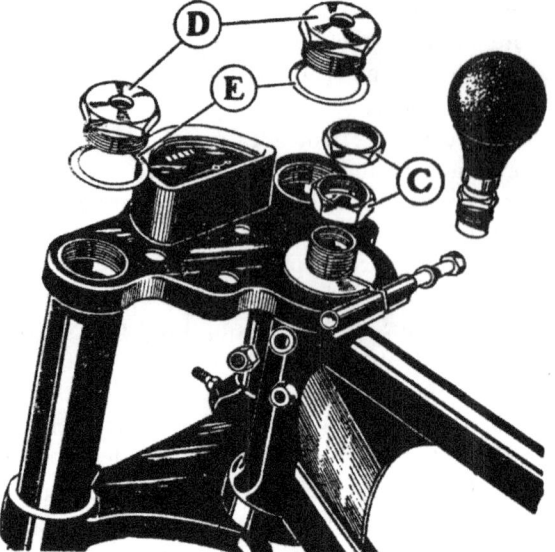

The trumpet part of the horn (when fitted) can be removed by unscrewing the slotted collar (B) Fig. D28.

On D3, D5 and C10L models the outer tubes are a taper fit in the top yoke and they should be freed by undoing the pinch nuts (A) Fig. D28, in the lower yoke and slackening the top nuts (D) Fig. D27, by about two turns. A sharp tap on the head of the nut with a hide mallet will free the tube and dismantling can then proceed as for the D1.

Fig. D27.

To remove the top yoke it is not necessary to undo the castellated sleeve nut on the fork stem and this will hold the lower part of the fork in position until it is ready to be removed.

When the forks have been dismantled the bearing cups can be removed from the frame head by screwing in Service Tool 61-3060 and driving them out from the opposite end with a suitable punch. Do not disturb the cups unless they are pitted or otherwise damaged.

Reassembly

New cups in the steering head should be driven in carefully and squarely to avoid damage and obtain correct alignment. This can best be done with a hide mallet. Grease the cups and place twenty-four $\frac{3}{16}$ in. balls in each cup.

Assembly can then be carried out in the reverse order to dismantling. Do not forget the rubber washers at the bottom of the headlamp cowl tubes (when fitted), the washers on top of the main fork tubes (D1 models), and the dust cover over the top bearing.

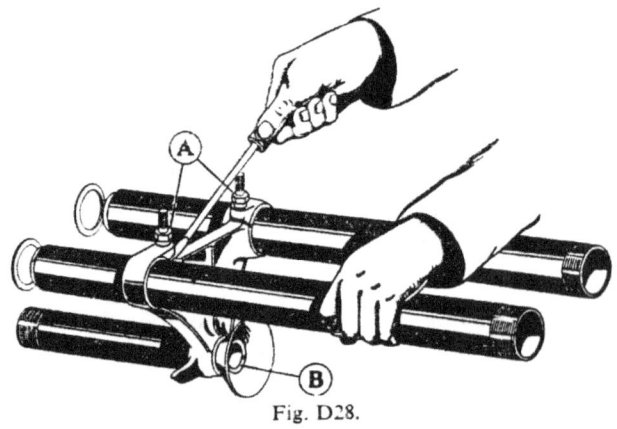

Fig. D28.

B.S.A. Service Sheet No. 509 (contd.)

On D1 models, when replacing the nuts (C) Fig. D27, ensure that the thicker of the two nuts is at the bottom with its recess facing downwards.

D1 Steering Head Adjustment

The method of adjusting the steering head bearings on the D1 models is different to that for the other models. The forks should be completely assembled but only the large nuts (D) Fig. D27, should be tightened, after ensuring that the mudguard stay studs on the fork outer tubes are facing each other and in line. Where the mudguard is attached to the sliding tubes, the two grease nipples should be facing outwards. Tighten down the lower of the two nuts (C) Fig. D24, until the forks rotate freely but have no up and down play. Secure the lower nut by means of the locknut and then check to ensure that the bearing is not over-tightened. A "lumpy" feeling as the forks are turned indicates that the adjustment is too tight. When this adjustment is completed the top yoke clamp nut (A) Fig. D24, and the lower clamp nuts (B) should be tightened securely.

D3 and C10L Steering Head Adjustment

The fork can be completely assembled and all the nuts fully tightened before the steering head adjustment is carried out. The fork should be assembled so that the headlamp cowl tubes are held firmly between the top and bottom fork yokes, with the rubber washers at the lower end of the tubes and the steel washers on top. The fork nuts can then be fully tightened with the exception of the stem nuts and the pinch bolt at the rear of the top yoke. The castellated sleeve nut (B) Fig. D29, should then be screwed down with the aid of Service Tool, part number 61-3002, or other similar tool until the forks rotate freely but without up and down play. Tighten the pinch bolt nut (C) to secure the sleeve nut and replace the top cap (A).

Fig. D29.

Check that the bearing adjustment is still correct and replace the handlebar assembly.

Sliding Tube Reassembly (all models)

Place the upper bushes in the outer tubes and push them up as far as they will go with the aid of the distance tube. Line up the holes in the distance tubes with the grease nipple holes in the outer tubes and screw in the nipples. Position the telescopic gaiters on the lower tubes together with the oil seal holders and lower fork bushes. Take care that the oil seals are not damaged as they pass over the springs. Grease the springs and sliding members, then pass them up into the outer tubes. Position the lower bushes and screw up the oil seal holders. Secure the upper end of the springs in position by means of the nuts (A) Fig. D25, making sure that the fork ends are correctly positioned to receive the wheel spindle, before tightening the nuts. When the oil seal holders are fully tightened they should be secured by the small locking tabs which engage in the top groove of the holders. Make sure that the curved portion of the tab engages properly in the groove before it is tightened down.

B.S.A. MOTOR CYCLES LTD., Service Department, Armoury Road, Birmingham 11

B.S.A. PRESS

BSA SERVICE SHEET No. 514

This Sheet supersedes No. 814

"D" and "C" Group Models
PLUNGER TYPE REAR SUSPENSION

DISMANTLING

First remove the rear wheel, see Service Sheet number 410 for "C" Group models and number 508 for "D" Group models. "C" Group part numbers are shown in brackets where they differ from "D" Group part numbers.

Disconnect the rear mudguard stays, and take out the pinch bolts at the top and bottom of the rear suspension columns. The centre column, part number 90–4117, Fig. D27, can now be driven out using a soft drift so as to avoid damage to the end of the column.

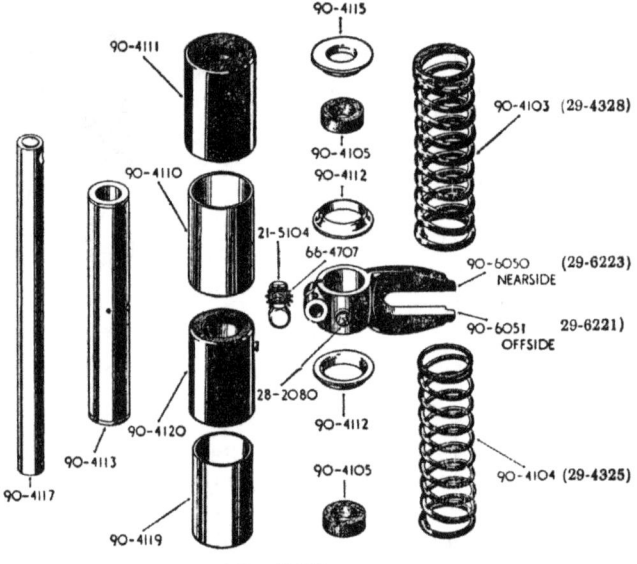

Fig. D27.

Grip the upper and lower shrouds firmly with both hands, compress the springs and lift out the suspension assembly.

Remove the shroud and springs from the sliding member, part number 90–4113. Carefully note the position of the steel washers and rubber bushes for subsequent assembly.

The bushes in the sliding member can now be examined for wear. If they require renewal, the tube complete with bushes must be replaced.

Unscrew the pinch bolt locknut, part number 21–5104, and take out the bolt. Insert a screwdriver into the slot, in the fork end 90–6051 (29–6221), the tube can then be withdrawn.

When replacing the tube ensure that the hole in the side of the tube lines up with the grease nipple in the fork end.

Note that the nearside fork end carries an anchor lug for the brake cover plate. On "C" Group models the head of the right-hand fork end clamping bolt is employed to secure the brake cover plate.

REASSEMBLY

Replace the shroud and springs on the sliding member in the reverse order to that of dismantling.

Take up the assembly and place the lower shroud in the frame lug. Press down on the upper shroud to compress the springs, and slide the assembly between the lugs Fig. D28).

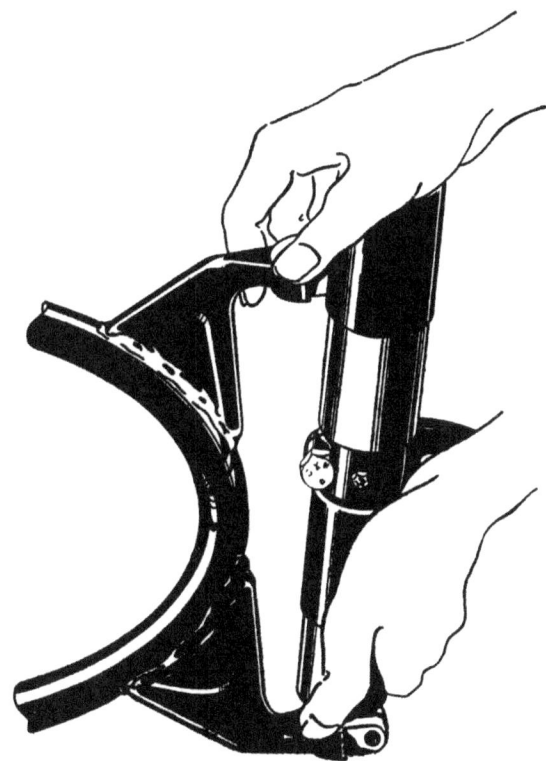

Fig. D28.

Use the champher on the lower end of the centre column to locate the assembly correctly in the frame top and bottom lugs. Insert the column from the top, ensuring that the slots are in line with the pich bolt hole.

Replace the pinch bolts, mudguard stays and rear wheel, couple up the brake and adjust.

Finally, check over all nuts and bolts for tightness.

B.S.A. MOTOR CYCLES LTD., Service Department, Armoury Road, Birmingham 11.
B.S.A. Press

BSA SERVICE SHEET No. 603
"B" "C" and "M" Group Models

THE LUBRICATION SYSTEM

The engine lubrication system is of the dry sump type operated by a double gear pump, situated in the bottom of the crankcase on the right-hand side. The only external oilways are the supply and return pipes to the tank and the rocker feed and drainage pipes on the "B" Group. The oil drawn from the oil tank to the supply side of the pump first passes through a close mesh filter. This filter is not fitted to "M" Group machines as a felt filter is incorporated in the oil return pipe.

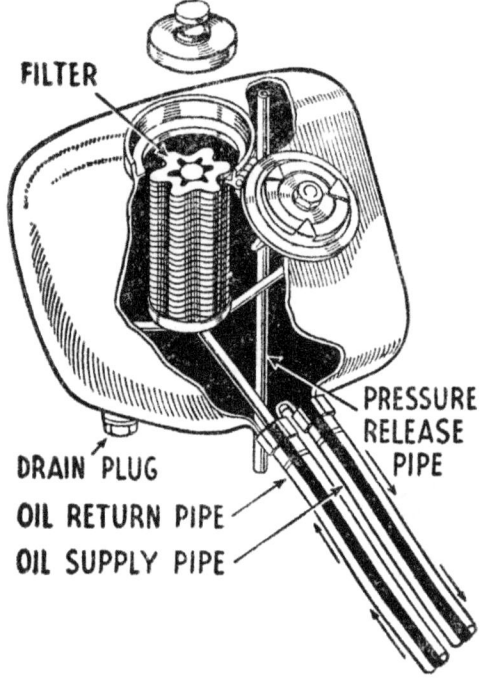

Fig. M3. *The Lubrication System* (models M20 and M21)

From the supply side of the pump the oil passes through a ball valve (A) and is then transferred to the hollow drive side mainshaft to supply the big-end roller bearing. On "B" and "M" models the transfer is made via a nozzle fitted in the timing cover which projects into the end of the drilled mainshaft and additional oilways in the timing cover provide positive lubrication to the cam pinion spindles. In the case of the "C" Group models, the oil passes through a hole in the main bearing bush, round an annular groove in the journal and thence via a radial drilling to the hollow centre of the shaft. (See Fig. M4). On C10L and C11G models a fine bleed hole from the main bearing meters a supply of oil to the camshaft and cam followers.

B.S.A. Service Sheet No. 603 (contd.)

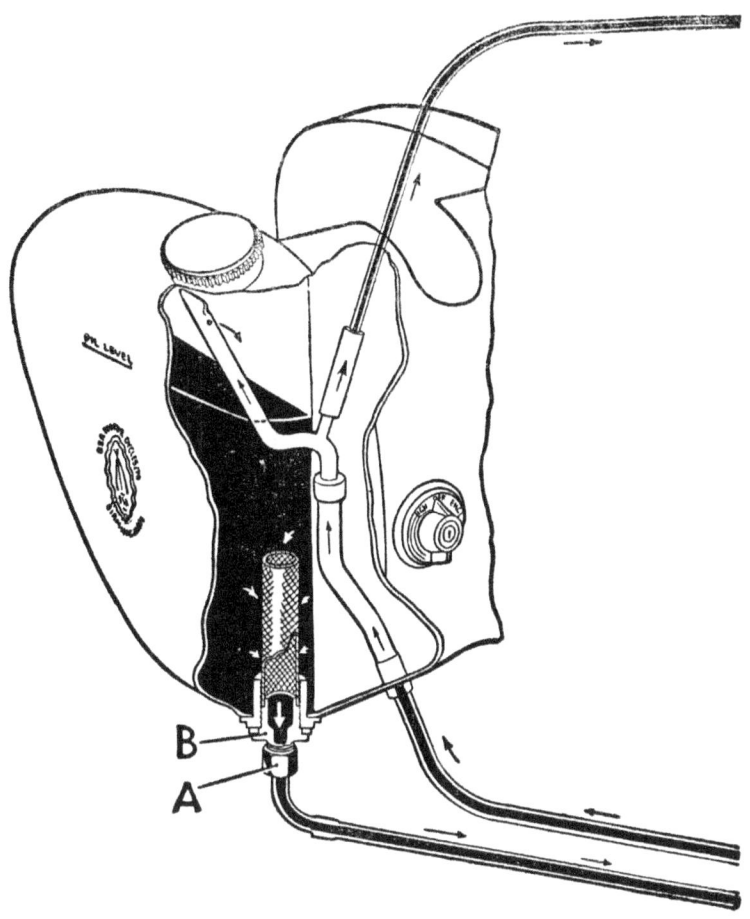

The Oil Tank C15.

MODEL C15

The lubrication system is of the dry sump type and is operated by a double gear pump situated in the bottom of the crankcase on the right-hand side. The oil tank capacity is four pints and oil is drawn from the oil tank to the supply pump (top set of gears). It is then pumped past the non-return valve (A), and along the hollow mainshaft to the big-end.

After lubricating the engine the oil flows down through a filter to the bottom of the crankcase from which it is drawn by the return pump (lower set of gears) past the non-return oil valve (C), and delivered up the return pipe to the tank. At the junction of the return pipe to the tank a by-pass pipe leads a supply of oil to the rockers, push-rods end, etc.

B.S.A. Service Sheet No. 603 (contd.)

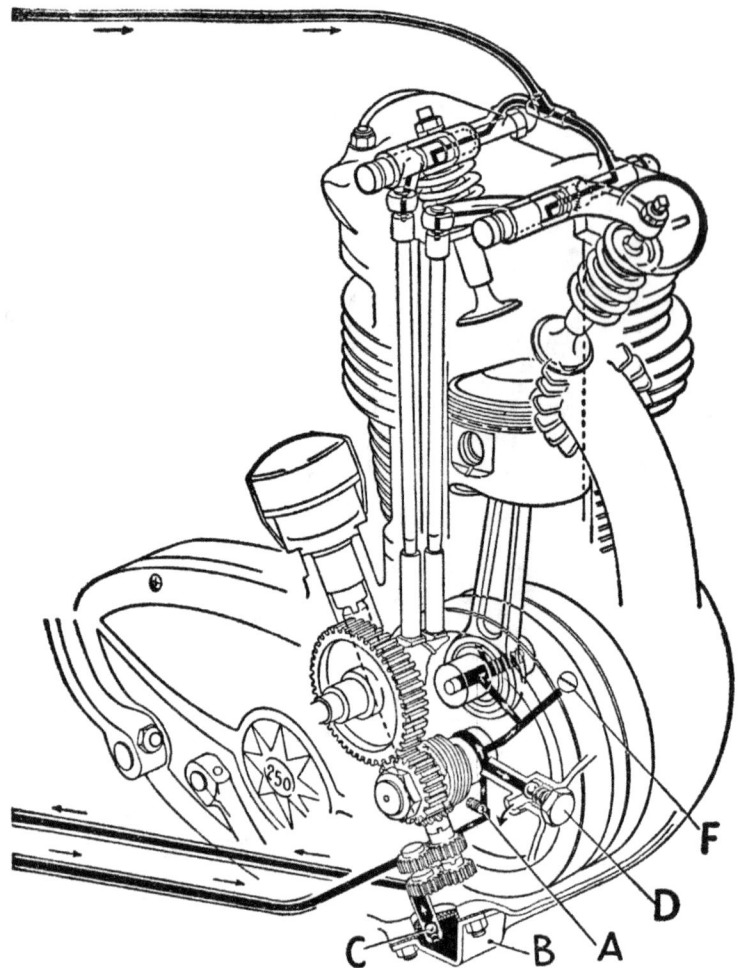

Lubrication System C15.

The valve (A) prevents oil transfer from the tank to the crankcase while the machine is standing, and together with the sludge trap (F), does not require attention until such time as the engine is completely dismantled.

A by-pass valve (D) ensures a constant pressure in the system. Surplus quantities of oil are discharged into the crankcase.

If the ball valve (C) should be stuck in its seating there will be no return of oil to the tank. In this event remove the cover plate (B) below the pump, insert a piece of wire into the valve orifice and lift the ball off its seating to free it.

B.S.A. Service Sheet No. 603 (contd.)

THE CRANKCASE BREATHER VALVE

The crankcase air release valve is of similar construction on all models although its position in the crankcase is dependant on the model and the year of manufacture.

On all "C" Group models the breather is situated on the left-hand side of the crankcase behind the primary chaincase. 1946 and 1947 "B" and "M" machines have the breather positioned at the rear of the drive-side bearing boss. Later "B" and "M" Group models have the breather positioned in the lower edge of the timing chest cover.

In each case its purpose is to allow free release of air from the crankcase as the piston descends, and to prevent air being drawn back into the crankcase as the piston ascends. A crankcase breather valve which is faulty, or partially blocked, will result in oil leakage from the engine.

Before the breather valve can be withdrawn the air release pipe must be removed by unscrewing the union nut. The complete breather valve can then be unscrewed from the crankcase. To dismantle the breather, undo the large hexagon on the outer end of the valve, the valve retaining collar can then be unscrewed with the aid of a large screwdriver thus allowing the fibre disc valve to fall free. Before reassembling, wash the components thoroughly in petrol to free them from any oil residue that may cause the valve to stick.

Before replacing the breather valve on "C" Group models the movement of the disc valve should be checked to ensure that it does not exceed .010 in. If excessive clearance is found and the disc valve is undamaged the face of the retaining collar should be ground so as to reduce the depth of the recess in which the disc valve lies. Take care not to grind too much away so that the disc valve has no clearance.

If the breather valve is fitted into the timing case cover, ensure that it is positioned so that the hole drilled in the side of the pipe inside the cover is facing towards the cover and slightly towards the rear. Failure to observe this precaution may result in excessive oil loss. Correct positioning of the hole may be effected by varying the thickness of the fibre washer fitted between the air release valve and the timing case cover.

MODELS C10L AND C11G

Instead of the pressure operated clack valve, a mechanically timed breather is employed. This takes the form of a hollow drive-side engine mainshaft with a radial drilling which, at the appropriate piston position, is brought in line with a drilled port in the crankcase thus allowing the gases to exhaust freely to the atmosphere. The engine sprocket distance sleeve, which fits over the portion of the mainshaft with the radial drilling, has six transfer ports so that it is immeterial which of the six spline-grooves locates the internal peg of the sleeve.

This type of breather is completely automatic and requires no adjustment or other maintenance whatsoever.

B.S.A. Service Sheet No. 603 (contd.)

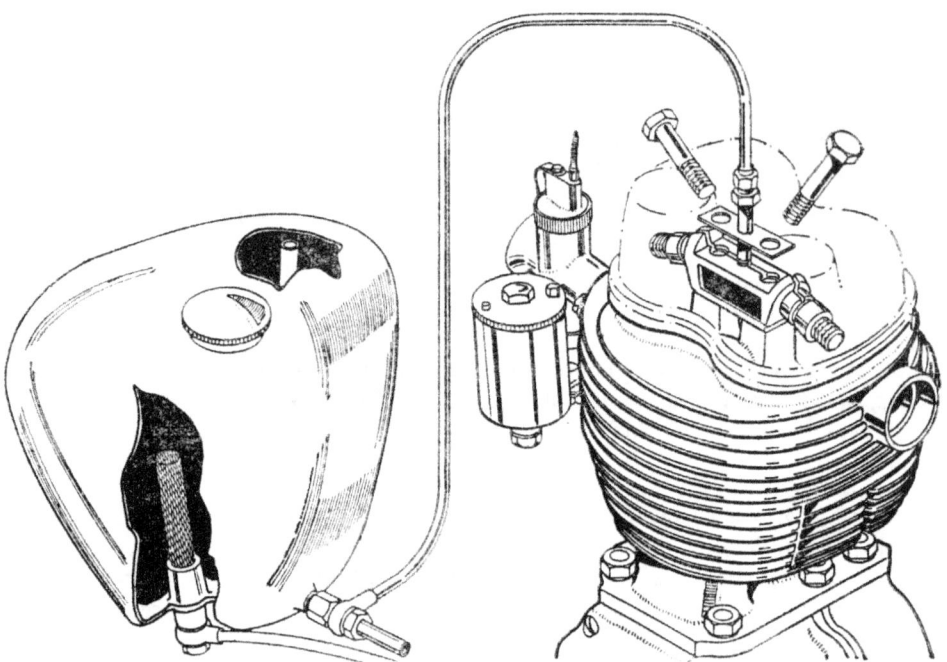

Rocker Gear Lubrication C12 (1956).

Parts required for conversion of C11 and C11G engines:—

Part No.	Description
29–2086	Rocker Oil Feed Pipe.
29–2091	Rocker Trunnion.
29–2092	Bolt.
45–2454	Locking Plate.
65–8420	Connection.
65–8421	Washer.
65–8424	Nut.

MODEL C12, 1956

The model C12 engine is identical with the C11G model. However, the lubrication system has been modified to provide positive lubrication to the valve rocker gear. The take off is from the oil tank return pipe, as on the "B" Group plunger models and the oil is fed through a rocker feed pipe to the rocker cover securing bolt which is drilled to allow the oil to pass to the trunnion. This trunnion incorporates oil grooves direct to each rocker fulcrum. After lubricating, the oil drains to the sump down the push rod tunnel, providing extra lubrication for the cams and cam followers in the process.

This modification can be adopted on the C11 and C11G engines at very low cost. The parts required are listed above, and they can be obtained through your dealer.

B.S.A. Service Sheet No. 603 (contd.)

After lubricating the big-end and circulating throughout the engine in the form of oil mist, the oil drains down, through a filter to the bottom of the crankcase from which it is drawn by the return pump past ball valve (C) and delivered up the return pipe to the tank.

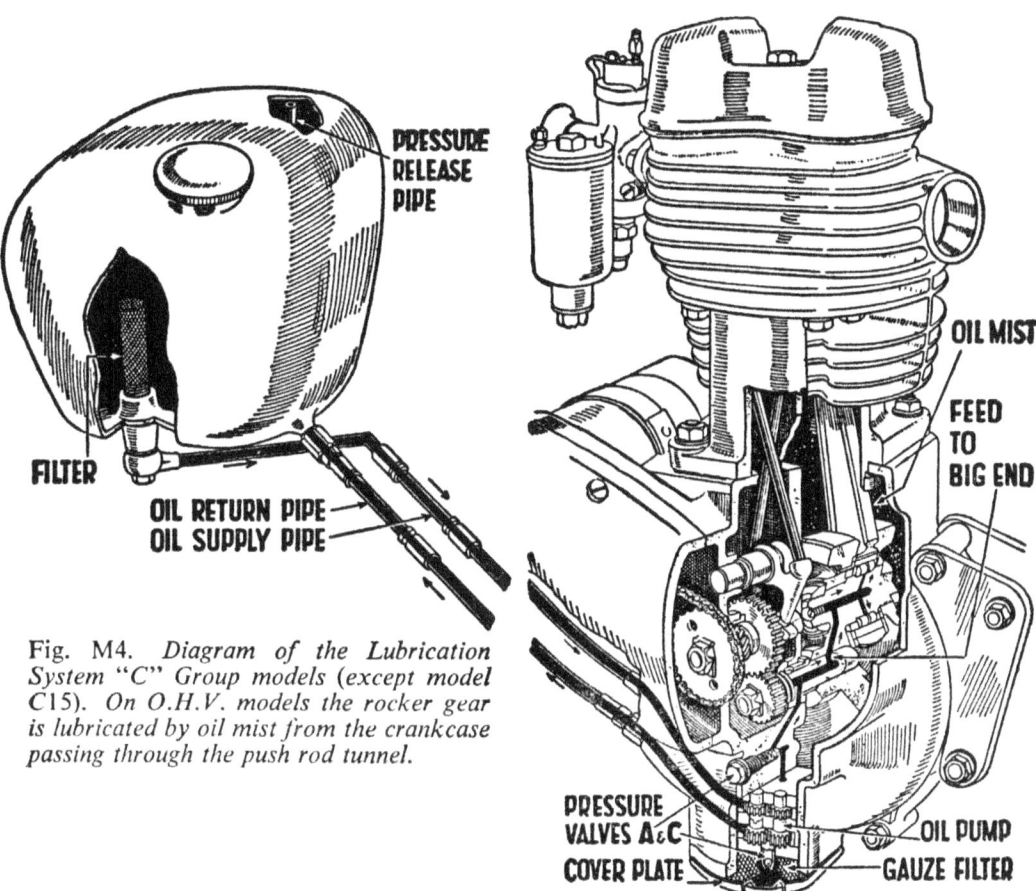

Fig. M4. *Diagram of the Lubrication System "C" Group models (except model C15). On O.H.V. models the rocker gear is lubricated by oil mist from the crankcase passing through the push rod tunnel.*

On "B" Group machines oil is fed through a union situated in the pipe between the return pump and the tank, to the rocker spindles, and after lubricating the rockers and enclosed valves, is returned to the crankcase through an external oil pipe attached to the base of the inlet valve spring housing (see Fig. M5). An internal oilway connects the two valve spring wells.

Incorrect seating of the ball valve (A) will allow oil to transfer from the tank to the engine, whilst the machine is stationary. In this event, unscrew the plug over the valve, and remove spring and ball. Clean the ball and its seating and replace. If the ball valve (C) should get stuck in its seating, there will be no return of oil to the tank. To correct, remove the cover plate below the pump and insert a piece of wire into the valve orifice, and lift the ball off its seating to free it. To check the flow of oil in the lubricating system, remove the tank filler cap whilst the engine is running. Oil should be seen issuing from the return pipe from the crankcase. The tank and crankcase should be drained periodically, and replenished with clean oil (see "Periodical Maintenance").

B.S.A. Service Sheet No. 603 (contd.)

Any restriction in the pressure release pipe in the tank will cause an increase in pressure inside the oil tank, and will result in leakage of oil at the filler cap. This can be put right by inserting a length of flexible wire into the pipe at its lower end (just in front of the rear mudguard) and pushing the wire right up the pipe, thus clearing obstruction.

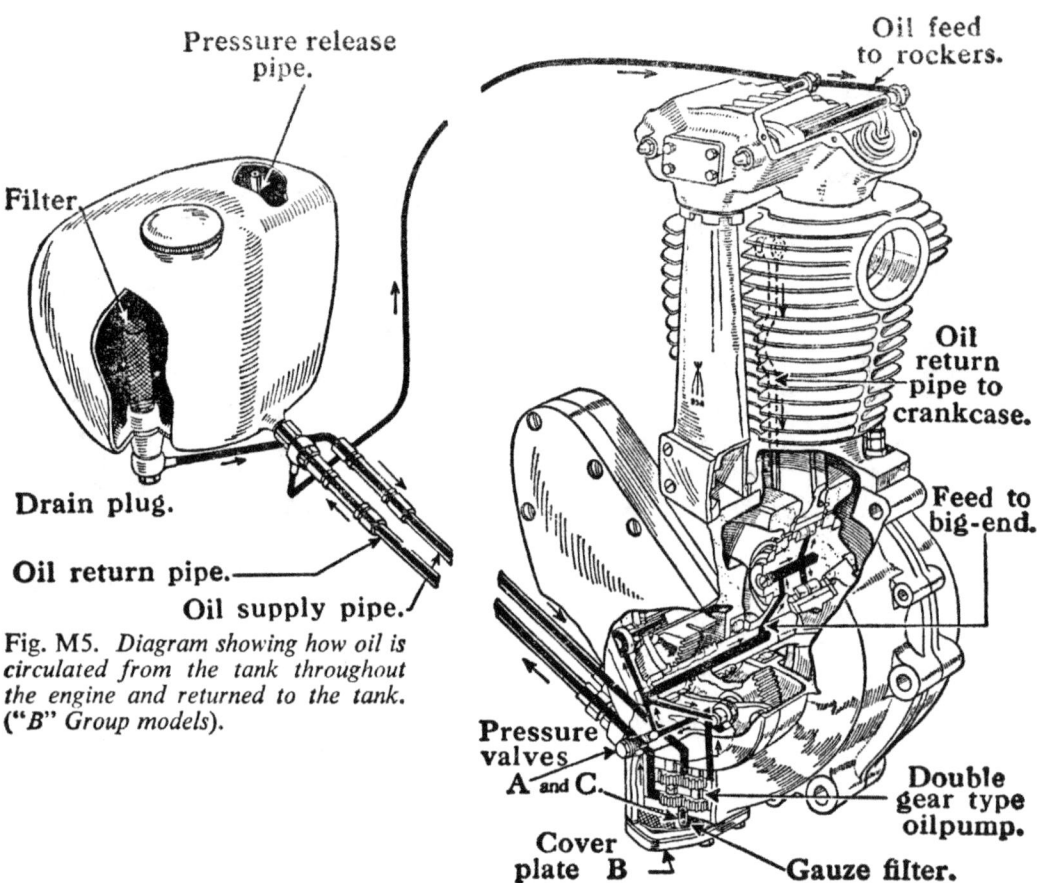

Fig. M5. *Diagram showing how oil is circulated from the tank throughout the engine and returned to the tank. ("B" Group models).*

To remove the "B" and "C" Group oil tank filter for cleaning, remove the oil pipe banjo union plug at the bottom of the tank. The filter will come out with the plug.

On models with the swinging arm type frame the oil tank is of slightly different construction but the system is the same. The oil tank filter is attached to the large hexagon nut in the outside of the tank and its removal does not entail interfering with the oil pipes.

To remove the "M" Group filter for cleaning, release the tank filler cap, release the filter cap thus exposed, and lift the filter out. In all cases the filter should be placed in a can big enough to cover it with petrol, and thoroughly washed. Before replacing make sure that it is quite dry of petrol.

The pump filter can be withdrawn after removing the cover plate (B) and should be thoroughly washed with petrol, dried and replaced.

On no account try to remove the oil pump unless it requires attention (see Service Sheet on complete "Dismantling of Engine").

B.S.A. Service Sheet No. 603 (contd.)

Crankcase Breather C15

The breather is mechanically timed as on the C10L and C11G models but takes the form of a hollow camshaft with a radial drilling which, at the appropriate piston position, is brought in line with a drilled port in the inner timing cover, this port has its outlet inside the outer timing cover. Pressure is then released through a small radial cut-away at the rear end of the outer cover joint face.

Changing the Oil C15

This should preferably be done immediately after running, so that the oil is warm and will, therefore, flow more freely. Disconnect the oil pipe union nut (A), at the base of the tank and collect the old oil in a suitable receptacle.

Filters

Remove the oil tank and crankcase filters for cleaning at regular intervals, this can be carried out in conjunction with the change of oil. After releasing the oil pipe at (A), unscrew the hexagon plug (B), which carries the filter in the tank, and wash thoroughly in petrol. Make sure that all the petrol has evaporated before replacing. Refill with the correct grade of oil.

The pump filter can be withdrawn after removing the crankcase cover plate and should be thoroughly washed with petrol, dried and replaced. The oil pump is extremely reliable and it is most unlikely that it will give trouble therefore it should not be disturbed unnecessarily. The pump is held in position by three bolts. The two other bolts hold the sections of the pump together.

B.S.A. MOTOR CYCLES LTD., Service Department, Armoury Road, Birmingham 11.
B.S.A. Press

BSA SERVICE SHEET No. 612

Reprinted Sept. 1960

All Models

BRAKE RELINING

Brake Shoe Removal and Replacement

After the brake plate has been removed from the wheel, the brake cam lever A (Fig. M40) should be detached and the cam spindle B pushed in slightly to allow the shoes to clear the brake plate. Insert a screwdriver between the brake shoes at the fulcrum pin C and twist the screwdriver.

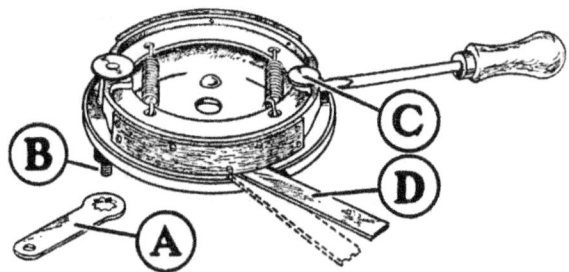

Fig. M40. Removing the Brake Shoes

Place a small lever D between one of the shoes and the cover plate and lever the shoe away from the cover plate until the spring pressure is released. Both shoes can then be lifted from the brake plate.

The shoes can be replaced by the reverse procedure. Hook the springs on to the shoes and place the ends of the shoes in position on the fulcrum pin and cam lever. Then push the shoes outwards until the springs pull them into their correct position.

NOTE: The brake shoe springs are quite strong and care should be taken that the fingers are not trapped by the brake shoes during these operations.

Brake Shoe Relining

With the shoes removed the linings can best be removed by drilling away the heads of the rivets and punching the shanks out to the inside of the shoe with a suitable drift.

New linings are die pressed to suit the curvature of the shoes, but will require drilling and counter-boring for the rivets. Position the lining and hold it in place at one end by means of clamps. Using the holes in the shoes as guides, drill holes of the correct size for the rivets adjacent to the clamp. Turn the shoe over, and counterbore the holes just drilled sufficiently deep so that the rivet heads will stand below the lining surface; this is important, since the rivets will otherwise score the brake drum.

B.S.A. Service Sheet No. 612 (continued)

Insert the rivets into the holes and rivet them over on the inside of the shoe. This is easily accomplished by holding in a vice a short length of rod, whose diameter is equal to that of the rivet head, and using it as an anvil upon which to rest the rivet head while hammering the shank over. (See Fig. M41.) This will also make sure that the rivets do not stand proud of the lining.

Move the clamps to the next pair of holes, taking care that the lining is kept in firm contact with the shoe the whole time, and repeat the above procedure. When the lining is finally riveted down, bevel off the ends of the linings and file off any local high spots.

Precautions to be observed when fitting the relined shoes to the hubs are given in the Service Sheet on Hubs and Brakes.

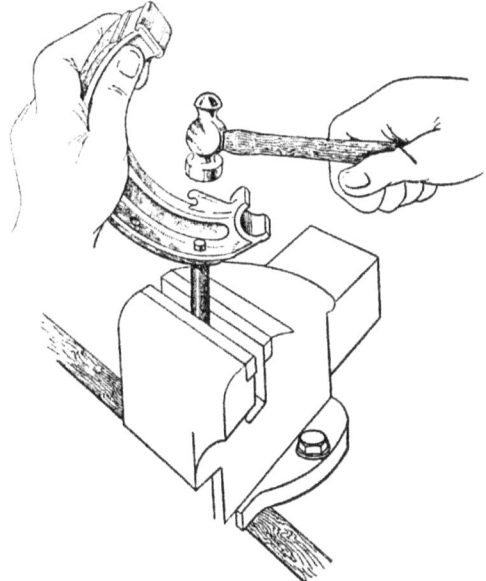

Fig. M41. Riveting the Linings

Works reconditioned brake shoes can be obtained through the medium of your Dealer from the B.S.A. Exchange Replacement Service.

B.S.A. MOTOR CYCLES LTD.
Service Dept., Waverley Works, Birmingham 10
Printed in England.

U/B5305

BSA SERVICE SHEET No. 701

ALL MODELS — USEFUL DATA

MODEL	C10	C11	C12	C15 Std.	B31	B32	B33	B34	M20
Engine bore (mm.)	63	63	63	67	71	71	85	85	82
Engine stroke (mm.)	80	80	80	70	88	88	88	88	94
Engine capacity (c.c.)	249	249	249	249	348	348	499	499	496
Petrol tank capacity (galls.)	2½	2½	2¾	2½	3	3	3	3	3
Oil tank capacity (pints)	4	4	4	4	4	4	4	4	5
Gearbox capacity (pint)	*½	*½	½	½	1	1	1	1	1
Tappet clearance cold:									
inlet (in.)	.004	.003	.010	.008	.003	.003	.003	.003	.010
exhaust (in.)	.006	.003	.012	.010	.003	.003	.003	.003	.012
Tyres—front	3.00×19	3.00×20†	3.00×19	3.25×17	3.25×19	2.75×21	3.25×19	2.75×21	3.25×19
Tyres—rear	3.00×19	3.00×20†	3.00×19	3.25×17	3.25×19	4.00×19	3.25×19	4.00×19	3.25×19
Piston ring gap:									
plain (in.)	.010	.010	.010	.010	.010	.010	.010	.010	.010
oil control (in.)	.010	.010	.010	.010	.010	.010	.010	.010	.010
Piston ring side clearance (in.)	.002–.004	.002–.004	.002–.004	.002–.004	.002–.004	.002–.004	.002–.004	.002–.004	.002–.004
Piston clearance:									
bottom of skirt	.0045–.0065	.0035–.0055	.0035–.0055	.0025–.004	.0040–.0055	.0040–.0055	.0045–.0065	.0045–.0065	.0040–.0060
Gear ratios:									
Top	6.6	6.6	6.26	5.98	5.6	7.1	5.0	5.6	5.3
third	—	—	7.64	7.65	7.3	9.2	6.5	7.4	7.0
second	9.8	9.8	11.1	10.54	11.1	14.2	10.0	11.5	10.9
first	14.5	14.5	16.15	15.96	15.9	20.2	14.2	16.8	15.8
Ignition setting (in. before T.D.C.):									
fully advanced	—	—	—	11/32	7/16	7/16	7/16	7/16	7/16
fully retarded	1/32	1/32	T.D.C.	—	—	—	—	—	—
Carburetter:									
jet	90	80	140	—	150	150	200	200	170
with air cleaner	90	80	100	140	150	150	170	170	—
Sparking plug:									
C.I. cylinder head	L.10	L.10S	L.10S	—	L.10S	L.10S	L.10S	L.10S	—
Al. alloy cylinder head	N.8	—	—	N.5	—	NA.8	—	NA.8	N.8
Compression ratio	5.1 : 1	6.5 : 1	6.5 : 1	7.25 : 1	6.5 : 1	6.5 : 1	6.8 : 1	6.8 : 1	4.9 : 1
Valve timing—inlet (deg.):									
opens before T.D.C.	25	25	34	26	25	25	25	25	25
closes after B.D.C.	70	70	78	70	65	65	65	65	65
Valve timing—exhaust (deg.):									
opens before B.D.C.	70	70	74	61½	65	65	65	65	65
closes after T.D.C.	25	25	38	34½	25	25	25	25	25
Distributor points gap (in.)	.012	.012	.015	.012	—	—	—	—	—
Magneto points gap (in.)	—	—	—	—	.012	.012	.012	.012	.012
Plug points gap (in.)	.015–.018	.015–.018	.018–.020	.020–.025	.015–.018	.015–.018	.015–.018	.015–.018	.015–.018
Tyre pressures:									
front (lb. per sq. in.)	20	20	18	16	16	—	16	—	17
rear (lb. per sq. in.)	28	28	26	22	20	—	17	—	22

For Swinging Arm and other models not listed see appropriate series.

*Four-speed gearbox, 1 pint.   †3.00 × 19 on later models.

B.S.A. SERVICE SHEET No. 701 (contd.)

MODEL	M21	M33	A7 (up to Eng. No. ZA7-11192)	A7 ST 2 carburetters)	A7 (on (and after Eng. No. AA7-101)	A7 S/T & S/S (on & Eng. No. AA7S-101)		A10	R/R & S/R
Engine bore (mm.)	82	85	62	62	66	66		70	70
Engine stroke (mm.)	112	88	82	82	72.6	72.6		84	84
Engine capacity (c.c.)	591	499	495	495	497	497		646	646
Petrol tank capacity (galls.)	3	3	3	3½	3½	3½		4¼	2 or 4
Oil tank capacity (pints)	5	5	4	4	4	4		4	5½
Gearbox capacity (pint)	1	1	1	1	1	1		1	14 fl. oz.
Tappet clearance—cold:									
inlet (in.)	.010	.003	.015	.015	.010	.008		.010	.008
exhaust (in.)	.012	.003	.015	.015	.016	.012		.016	.008
Tyres—front	3.50×19	3.25×19	3.25×19	3.25×19	3.25×19	3.25×19		3.25×19	—
Tyres—rear	3.50×19	3.50×19	3.50×19	3.50×19	3.50×19	3.50×19		3.50×19	—
Piston ring gap:									
plain (in.)	.010	.010	.013	.013	.013	.013		.013	—
oil control (in.)	.010	.010	.011	.011	.011	.011		.011	—
Piston ring side clearance	.002-.004	.002-.004	.002-.004	.002-.004	.002-.004	.002-.004		.002-.004	.002-.004
Piston clearance:									
bottom of skirt (in.)	.0040-.0060	.0045-.0065	.0030-.0050	.0030-.0050	.0030-.0050	.0030-.0050		.0030-.0050	.0030-.0050
Gear ratios:						S/T	S/S		
Top	5.9	4.8	5.1	5.1	5.1	5.0	5.28	4.42	4.53
third	7.8	6.3	6.2	6.2	6.2	6.05	6.38	5.36	5.48
second	12.2	9.9	9.0	9.0	9.0	8.8	9.28	7.77	7.96
first	17.8	14.3	13.2	13.2	13.2	12.9	13.62	11.41	11.68
Ignition setting (in. before T.D.C. fully advanced)	7/16	7/16	3/8	3/8	5/16	3/8		11/32	3/8
Carburetter:									
jet	170	200	—	110	—	—		—	250
with air cleaner	—	170	140	—	140	160		170	240
Sparking plug:									
C.I. cylinder head	L.10	L.10S	L.10S	L.10S	L.10S	L.10S		L.10S	NA.10
Al. alloy cylinder head	N.8	—	—	—	—	—		—	—
Compression ratio	5 : 1	6.8 : 1	6.6 : 1	7 : 1	6.6 : 1	7.25 : 1		6.5 : 1	R/R 8 : 1 S/R 8.26:1
Valve timing—inlet (deg.):									
opens before T.D.C.	25	25	24	24	30	42		30	42
closes after B.D.C.	65	65	65	65	70	62		70	62
*Valve timing—exhaust (deg.):									
opens before B.D.C.	65	65	60	60	65	67		65	67
closes after T.D.C.	25	25	21½	21½	25	37		25	37
Distributor points gap	—	—	—	—	—	—		—	—
Magneto points gap (in.)	.012	.012	.012	.012	.012	.012		.012	.012
Plug points gap (in.)	.015-.018	.015-.018	.015-.018	.015-.018	.015-.018	.015-.018		.015-.018	.018-.020
Tyre pressures:									
front (lb. per square inch)	16	17	17	17	17	17		17	17
rear (lb. per square inch)	18	18	18	18	18	18		18	19

*NOTE.—Standard A7's after engine number CA7-5232 and Standard A10's after engine number DA10-1647 have the same camshaft as the S/S and R/R machines and valve timing is therefore the same.

B.S.A. MOTOR CYCLES LTD., Service Department, Armoury Road, Birmingham 11.
PRINTED IN ENGLAND—B.S.A. PRESS

BSA SERVICE SHEET No. 702

Reprinted June, 1959.

ALL MODELS

WORKSHOP DATA

ENGINE, BUSH AND SHAFT DIAMETERS

(All Dimensions in Inches, after Reaming or Grinding).

	D1	C10, C11	B31, B32	M33 B33, B34	M20, M21	A7 Up to Engine No. ZA7 11192	A7 On and After Engine No. AA7 101	A10
Overhead Rocker Arm	— —	.569 .567 C10 only	.562 .563	.562 .563	— —	.4995 .5005	.4995 .5005	.4995 .5005
Inlet Valve Guide	— —	.313 .314	.313 .314	.3525 .3515	.3525 .3515	.313 .314	.313 .314	.313 .314
Exhaust Valve Guide	— —	.313 .314	.352 .353	.3785 .3795	.3525 .3535	.313 .314	.313 .314	.313 .314
Inlet Tappet Guide	— —	.3125 .3135 C10 only	.3745 .3755	.3745 .3755	.3745 .3755	.3125 .3135	— —	— —
Exhaust Tappet Guide	— —	.3125 .3135 C10 only	.3745 .3755	.3745 .3755	.3745 .3755	.3125 .3135	— —	— —
Cam Pinion Bush	— —	— —	.6255 .6245	.6255 .6245	.6255 .6245	— —	— —	— —
Cam Shaft Bush	— —	.687 .688	— —	— —	— —	.7485 .7495	.7485 .7495	.7485 .7495
Idler Pinion Shaft Bush	— —	— —	— —	— —	— —	.7485 .7495	.7485 .7495	.7485 .7495
Idler Pinion Bush	— —	— —	.7505 .7495	.7505 .7495	.7505 .7495	.7485 .7495	.7485 .7495	.7485 .7495
Cam Shaft Bush T/Cover	— —	1.0005 .9995	— —	— —	— —	— —	— —	— —
Crankshaft Bush G/S	— —	.983 .982	— —	— —	— —	1.375 1.3745	1.375 1.3745	1.375 1.3745
Conrod Big End	— —	— —	1.7704 1.7702	1.7704 1.7702	1.7704 1.7702	1.4495 1.4500	1.4495 1.4500	1.4495 1.4500
Gudgeon Pin Bush	.4697 .4692	.6255 .625	.7506 .7503	.7506 .7503	.7506 .7503	.6881 .6878	.6881 .6878	.7506 .7503

B.S.A. Service Sheet No. 702 (Contd.).

GEARBOX—BUSH DIAMETERS

(All Dimensions in Inches, after Reaming or Grinding)

	D Group	C Group	B Group 1945/48	M Group 1945/48	A Group	B & M 1949 on
Pinion Sleeve Bush	.4975 .4965	—	.7505 .7495	.8755 .8745	.812 .813	.8755 .8745
Layshaft Bush (Shell)	.501 .500	—	.687 .688	.687 .688	.687 .688	.687 .688
Mainshaft Bush (I/Cover)	—	.751 .752	.687 .688	—	—	—
Layshaft Bush (K/S Quadrant)	—	—	—	.687 .688	.7495 .7505	.687 .688
Layshaft 1st Gear Bush	—	—	.8125 .8135	.8765 .8755	.7495 .7505	.8765 .8755
Layshaft Pinion/s Bush	—	.562 .563	—	—	—	—
M/Shaft 3rd L/Shaft 2nd Gear Bush	—	—	.9375 .9385	1.0005 1.0015	—	1.0005 1.0015
K/S Quadrant Bush I/Cover	—	.9995 1.0005	1.1245 1.1255	—	.561 .563	—
K/S Quadrant Bush O/Cover	—	.812 .813	.812 .813	1.187 1.188	.7495 .7505	1.187 1.188
Control Shaft Bush (Shell)	—	—	.562 .563	.562 .563	—	.562 .563
Control Shaft Bush (I/Cover)	—	.689 .688	—	.562 .563	—	.562 .563
Control Quadrant Bush (I/Cover)	—	—	—	.562 .563	—	.562 .563
Pedal Spindle Bush (I/Cover)	—	.7495 .7505	.6245 .6255	.6245 .6255	.467 .468	.6245 .6255
Pedal Spindle Bush (O/Cover)	—	.7495 .7505	.8745 .8755	.8745 .8755	.6245 .6255	.8745 .8755
Speedo Spindle Small Bush	—	—	.218 .219	—	.218 .219	.218 .219
Speedo Spindle Long Bush	—	—	.281 .282	—	.281 .282	.281 .282
Clutch Push Rod Bush	—	.257 .258	—	—	—	—

B.S.A. MOTOR CYCLES LTD., Service Dept., Waverley Works, Birmingham, 10.   *Printed in England.*

BSA SERVICE SHEET No. 703

Revised Dec. 1958.

All Models
WORKSHOP DATA (BEARINGS) 1956

B.S.A. Part No.	Hoffman No.	Skefko No.	Ransome & Marles No.	British Timkin No.	Fischer No.
24–722	RM.9L	CFM7/C2	MRJA.$\frac{7}{8}$	—	RFM.9
24–724	R.325L	402454.B	MRJA.25	—	MFM.25
24–732	325	6305	MJ.25	—	6305
24–4065	135	6207	LJ.35	—	6207
24–4217	L.S.8	RLS.6	LJ$\frac{3}{4}$	—	LS.8
24–6860	—	2K.1178X 2K.1130N1	—	1178X 1130.N1	—
27–261	MS.9	RM.S7	MJ.$\frac{7}{8}$	—	MS.9
27–4027	LS.11	RL.S9	LJ.$1\frac{1}{8}$	—	—
29–3857	130	6206	LJ.30	—	6206
29–6211	MS.7	RM.S5	MJ.$\frac{5}{8}$	—	MS.7
42–5819	120	—	—	—	—
65–1388	RMS.11	CRM.9	MRJ.$1\frac{1}{8}$	—	RMS.11
65–2045	125	6205	LJ.25	—	6205
65–5883	LS.9	RLS.7	LJ.$\frac{7}{8}$	—	LS.9
67–670	R.130L	NFL.30	LRJA.30	—	NFL.30
89–3022	LS.10	RLS.8	LJ.1	—	LS.10
89–3023	LS.8	RLS.6	LJ.$\frac{3}{4}$	—	LS.8
90–10	117	6203	LJ.17	—	6203
90–11	LS.7	RLS.5	LJ.$\frac{5}{8}$	—	LS.7
90–12	S.9	EE.8J	KLNJ.$\frac{7}{8}$	—	EE.8
90–5525	112	6201	LJ.12	—	6201
90–5559	—	—	—	A.2126	—
90–6063	115	6202	LJ.15	—	6202

B.S.A. SERVICE SHEET No. 703 (continued)

LOCATION OF BEARINGS

Model	Crankcase Roller Bearing Driveside	Crankcase Ball Bearing Driveside	Crankcase Roller Bearing Gearside	Crankcase Ball Bearing Gearside	Crankcase Ball Bearing (Small)	Crankcase Ball Bearing (Large)	Gearbox Pinion Sleeve Ball Bearing	Gearbox Mainshaft Ball Bearing	Front Hub Ball Bearing	Rear Hub Ball Bearing	Rear Hub Brake Drum and C/Wheel Ball Bearing
Dandy	—	—	—	—	90-6063	24-4217	90-6063 (Output shaft)	90-6063 (Input shaft)	—		
D1, D3 & D5					90-10	24-4217	90-12	90-11	90-5525	90-6063	
D1, D3 (Comp.)									90-5559		
C10L		24-732					29-3857	90-11		90-6063	
C12		24-732					29-3857	90-11	65-5383	90-11 O/S 29-6211 N/S	
C15		24-782					29-3857		90-10	90-10 O/S 42-5819 N/S	
B31 S/A	24-724	65-2045	24-722				24-4065	24-4217	89-3022	89-3022	89-3022
B31 S/A (1958)									42-5819	42-5819	89-3022
B32 Comp. Rigid	24-724	65-2045	24-722				24-4065	24-4217	65-5883	65-5883	65-5883
B32/34 Gold Star	65-1338	65-2045	24-722				24-4065	24-4217	65-5883	65-5883	65-5883
B33 S/A	24-724	65-2045	24-722				24-4065	24-4217	89-3022	89-3022	89-3022
B33 S/A (1958)									42-5819	42-5819	89-3022
B34 Comp. Rigid	24-724	65-2045	24-722				24-4065	24-4217	65-5883	65-5883	65-5883
M21 Rigid	24-724	65-2045	24-722	27-261			24-4065	24-4217	65-5883	24-6860 (Tapered Roller)	
M21 Plunger	24-724	65-2045	24-722	27-261			24-4065	24-4217	65-5883	65-5883	89-3022
M33	24-724	65-2045	24-722				24-4065	24-4217	65-5883	65-5883	89-3022
A7 and Shooting Star	67-670						24-4065	24-4217	89-3022	89-3022	89-3022
A7 & S/S (1958)									42-5819	42-5819	89-3022
A10 S/A	67-670						24-4065	24-4217	89-3022	89-3022	89-3022
A10 S/A (1958)									42-5819	42-5819	89-3022
A10 Plunger	67-670						24-4065	24-4217	65-5883	65-5883	89-3022
A10 Road Rocket	67-670						24-4065	24-4217	65-5883	89-3022	89-3022
A10 Super Rocket	67-670						24-4065	24-4217	42-5819	42-5819	89-3022

Printed in England B.S.A. MOTOR CYCLES LTD., Service Dept., Birmingham 11.

BSA SERVICE SHEET No. 704

ALL MODELS
PISTON CLEARANCES

To avoid the possibility of seizure or piston tap, pistons must be fitted with adequate but not excessive clearance.

The following are the recommended total clearances between the bottom of the piston and the cylinder wall.

MODEL			Tolerances
Dandy 70		7.25 : 1	.003—.004"
D1			.0027—.0045"
D3, C15			.0025—.004"
D5, D7			.003—.005"
C10, C10L			.0045—.0065"
C11, C11G, C12			.0035—.0055"
C15	(Star Group)	6.4 : 1 to 10 : 1	.0017—.0033"
B31			.004—.0055"
B31	(Split skirt)		.0005—.0016"
B32A			.002—.004"
BB32	Gold Star	8 : 1	.003—.0045"
		6.5 : 1	.004—.0055"
		7.5 : 1	.002—.004"
		9 : 1	.003—.0045"
CB32	Gold Star	6.5 : 1	.002—.004"
		8 : 1	.003—.0045"
		8.5 : 1	.003—.0045"
		9 : 1	.003—.0045"
		12.25 : 1	.004—.0055"
		13 : 1	.004—.0055"
DB32	Gold Star	7.25 : 1	.0025—.004"
		8 : 1	.003—.0045"
		9 : 1	.003—.0045"
B40	(Star Group)	7.0 : 1 to 8.7 : 1	.0015—.003"
B33			.0045—.0065"
B33	(Split skirt)		.0006—.00275"
B34A			.0045—.0065"
BB34	Gold Star	7.5 : 1 Standard	.0045—.0065"
		8 : 1	.0025—.0045"
		9 : 1	.0025—.0045"
		6.8 : 1	.0045—.0065"
		11.1	.0025—.0045"
CB34	Gold Star	7.25 : 1	.003—.0045"
		8 : 1	.003—.0045"
		9 : 1	.003—.0045"
DB34	Gold Star }	8 : 1	.003—.0045"
DBD34	Gold Star	8.75 : 1	.003—.0045"

B.S.A. Service Sheet No. 704 (contd.)

MODEL			Tolerances
M20			.004—.006″
M21			.004—.006″
M33			.0045—.0065″
M33	(Split skirt)		.0006—.00275″
A7		6.7 : 1	.002—.004″
	(Split skirt)	6.7 : 1	.0011—.0031″
		7.25 : 1	.002—.004″
	(Split skirt)		.0011—.0031″
A7	(Star Twin)		.002—.004″
A7	(Split skirt)	(Star Twin and Shooting Star)	.001—.0031″
A7	(Shooting Star)	8 : 1 (after Engine No. CA7SS-4501)	.0035—.005″
A50	(Star Twin)	8.0 : 1 to 9.0 : 1	.0011—.0025″
A10	(Golden Flash)	6.5 : 1	.003—.0045″
	(Split skirt)	6.5 : 1	.0025—.0045″
	(Split skirt)	7.25 : 1	.0025—.0045″
A10	(Super Flash and Road Rocket)	8 : 1	.003—.0045″
A10	(Golden Flash)	7.5 : 1 (after Engine No. DA10-651)	.0035—.005″
A10	(Super Rocket)	8.5:1 (after Engine No. CA10R-6001)	.004—.0055″
A10	(Rocket Gold Star)	8.75 : 1	.001—.0025″
A65	(Star Twin)	7.5 : 1 to 9.0 : 1	.0012—.0027″

B.S.A. MOTOR CYCLES LTD., Service Department, Armoury Road, Birmingham 11

B.S.A. PRESS

BSA SERVICE SHEET No. 705

All Models
October, 1948
Reprinted April, 1960

PERIODICAL ATTENTIONS.

HUBS.   **Every 1,000 miles.**

Inject grease through the nipples located in the centres of the hubs. Do not overdo this, otherwise grease will penetrate to the brake linings and cause ineffective brakes. Three or four strokes of the gun should be ample. Where no grease nipple is provided the bearings should be removed and packed with grease when the machine is in need of complete overhaul.

BRAKE CAM SPINDLES.

Grease sparingly. Two or three strokes of the gun only, or if no grease nipple is provided, apply a few drops of engine oil between the brake arm and the spindle.

SPEEDOMETER DRIVE.

Grease well. Three or four strokes of the gun regularly.

ENGINE OIL.   **Every 2,000 miles (except 2-stroke models).**

The oil tank and sump should be drained (preferably when the engine is warm after a longish run), and the tank refilled with fresh oil.

In case of new or re-conditioned engines, the oil should be drained and renewed after the first 250 miles, and again after 1,000 miles.

REAR CHAIN.

Remove the rear chain, clean thoroughly in paraffin, and soak in engine oil or molten grease and graphite.

CONTACT BREAKER (except A and C Group Models).

A very small quantity of thin oil should be injected into the lubrication wick, and the face cam smeared with oil. The wick is accessible after removing the spring contact arm (held by the round-headed screw at the opposite end to the contact point) and is located in the hollow end of the round-headed screw which is revealed when the spring arm is removed.

When replacing the arm, it is important that the small curved backing spring is refitted correctly, i.e., with the bent portion facing outwards.

DYNAMO ARMATURE BUSH (A and C Group Models fitted with lubricator).

A few drops of oil injected through the lubricator are sufficient.

Every 5,000 miles.

Drain the gearbox and refill with new oil up to the level of the filler plug.

Drain the telescopic forks and refill each leg with correct amount of new oil.

In the case of new or re-conditioned gearboxes, change the oil after the first 1,000 miles.

New Machines.

CYLINDER HEAD BOLTS (except B and M O.H.V. engines).

Examine the cylinder head joint daily, and if leakage becomes apparent, tighten the bolts, working diagonally so as to pull the head down evenly. Do not over-tighten otherwise there is a possibility of distortion or bolt stretch.

CYLINDER BASE NUTS (except B and M O.H.V. engines).

There are five of these—one at each of the four corners outside, and one inside the tappet chest on the single cylinder models. A Group Models have eight cylinder base nuts and Model C11 six nuts. Tighten after the first 100 miles.

CYLINDER BARREL AND HEAD FIXING (B and M O.H.V. engines).

The barrel and head are both secured to the crankcase by four long bolts coupled to bushes screwed into the latter. Apply a spanner to the upper hexagon for tightening. These bolts have right-hand threads, and, being inverted, are tightened by turning the spanner to the right.

B.S.A. MOTOR CYCLES LTD.,
Service Dept., Waverley Works, Birmingham, 10

(PRINTED IN ENGLAND)

BSA SERVICE SHEET No. 706

TELESCOPIC FORKS

'A', 'B' AND 'M' GROUP, C10, C11G AND C12 MODELS

Of robust design B.S.A. telescopic forks require the minimum of maintenance it being necessary only to replenish the oil occasionally between major overhauls.

For normal use each fork leg should contain a quarter pint of oil (142 c.c.) or three-eighths of a pint (213 c.c.) according to model as detailed below.

Quarter-pint Capacity
Models C10, C10L (1956 onwards), C11, C11G, C12, B31-33 (up to 1956), B32-34 and Gold Stars (up to 1952), M20, M21, M33, 'A' Group (up to 1952).

Three-eighth Pint Capacity
Models B31-33 (1956 onwards), B32-34 and Gold Stars (1952 onwards), 'A' Group (1952 onwards).

Oil Changes
To replenish the oil remove the drain plugs at the base of the fork tubes and remove the fork top nuts. Allow the oil to drain off. Replace the plugs and pour either a quarter or three-eighths pint of oil into the hollow tubes revealed when the top plugs are removed.

Dismantling
Before beginning to overhaul the forks have the following tools and replacement parts available in case they are required:—

61-3001	Fork top nut spanner.
61-3003	Fork plug spanner.
61-3005	Oil Seal holder assembly tool.
61-3006	Oil seal extractor.
61-3007	Oil seal assembly tool.
61-3350	Fork leg assembly and removal tool.
29-5334	Packing shim (.005 in.).
29-5335	Packing shim (.010 in.).
29-5336	Packing shim (.020 in.).
29-5337	Packing shim (.030 in.).
65-5424 (2)	Fork top bush ('A' and 'B' Group).
29-5347 (2)	Fork bottom bush ('A', 'B', C11G and C12).
29-5346 (2)	Fork top bush (C10L, C11G and C12).
29-5313 (2)	Fork oil seal (all models).
	Number 5 twine (approx 18 in.).

B.S.A. Service Sheet No. 706 (contd.)

Remove the front wheel and front mudguard. Take out the fork top cap (*A*) Fig. X1, screw service tool part number 61-3350 into the thread at the top of the fork shaft using the larger of the fine threads.

Slacken off the pinch bolt (*B*) Fig. X1.

Take a firm grasp of the lower fork sliding tube and strike the top of the tool smartly with a hammer. This will release the shaft from its taper and the complete fork leg can be drawn down and removed from the machine.

Repeat the operation on the other leg.

To dismantle the lower section of the fork hold the fork sliding tube by gripping the wheel spindle lug in a soft-jawed vice and lift off the spring (see Fig. X2).

Enter service tool part number 61-3005 until the dogs on the tool engage in the slots at the bottom of the oil seal holder (*D*) Fig. X2. Pressing the tool down and turning at the same time unscrew the oil seal holder. Slide the holder up the shaft until it becomes tight on the tapered section of the shaft. Do not use excessive force or the oil seal may be damaged.

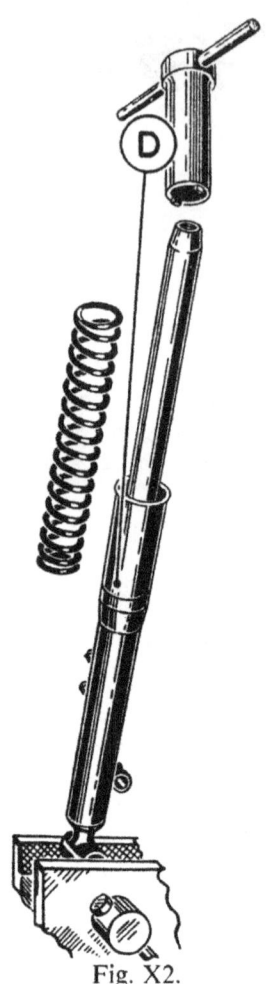

Fig. X2.

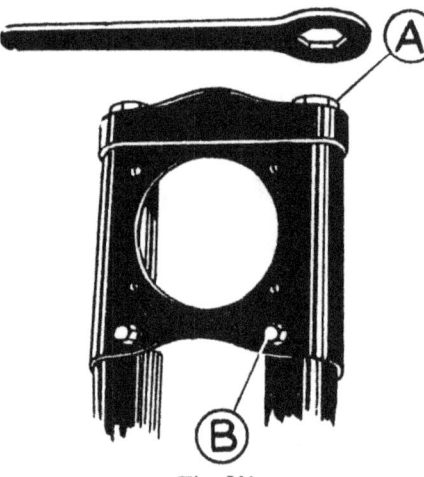

Fig. X1.

The top fork bearing is retained in the fork leg by a circlip (*E*) Fig. X3, which can be prised out with a sharp tool such as the tang end of a file. There may be a number of shims fitted between the circlip and the top bearing. These must be replaced if the bushes are not renewed when assembling.

Grip the shaft in a vice using soft-jaw clamps on the unground portion of the shaft and unscrew the gland nut (*F*) Fig. X4. Service tool part number 61-3003 is designed for this purpose. Remove the gland nut which secures the lower bearing and both bearings, shims, circlip and oil seal holder will then slide off the shaft.

B.S.A. Service Sheet No. 706 (contd.)

If it is necessary to remove the oil seal place the lower edge of the holder on a soft wooden block and enter service tool part number 61-3006 into the top of the holder. Give this tool a sharp tap with a hammer and the oil seal will be driven out.

Reassembly

Reassembly is carried out in the reverse order. Cleanliness is essential and before attempting to reassemble clean all parts thoroughly and clean down the bench on which the forks have been dismantled.

If the oil seal is to be replaced care must be taken that the feather edge of the seal is not damaged. Enter the oil seal (*I*) Fig. X6 into the holder, metal part first, and drive home using B.S.A. service tool part number 61-3007 (*H*) Fig. X6. Place the oil seal holder over the shaft and pass it up the shaft until it is firmly held on the tapered section. Do not use excessive force or the oil seal may be damaged. Place the circlip over the shaft followed by the shims and top bearing and then the bottom bearing. Place the steel washer over the thread of the gland nut, screw up the gland nut and holding the shaft firmly in a soft-jawed vice as described in dismantling procedure firmly tighten the gland nut.

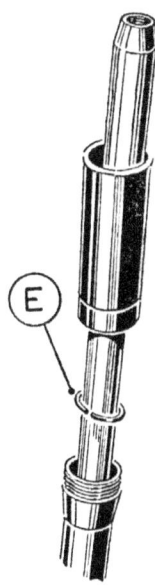

Fig. X3.

Place the lower sliding tube in a vice and enter the fork shaft with parts assembled into the lower sliding tube. Fit the circlip and check for up and down movement on the

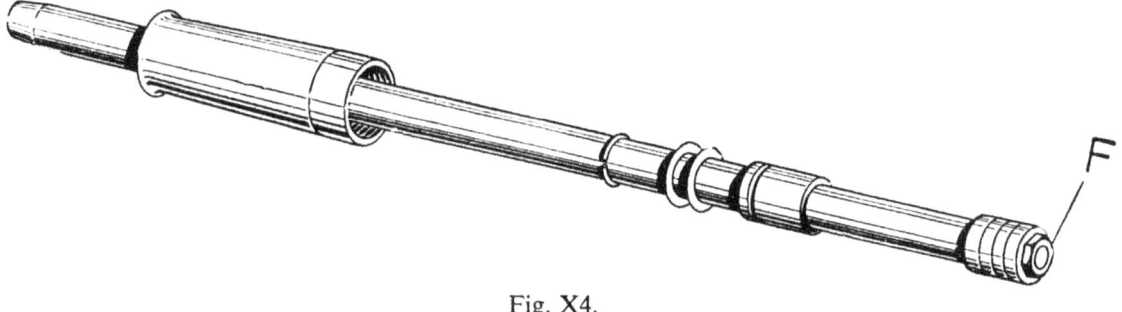

Fig. X4.

top bush. If a new bush has been fitted it may be necessary to add to, or take from, some of the existing shims. Packing shims are available in the following sizes:—

.005 in.   Part Number 29-5334
.010 in.   Part Number 29-5335
.020 in.   Part Number 29-5336
.030 in.   Part Number 29-5337

B.S.A. Service Sheet No. 706 (contd.)

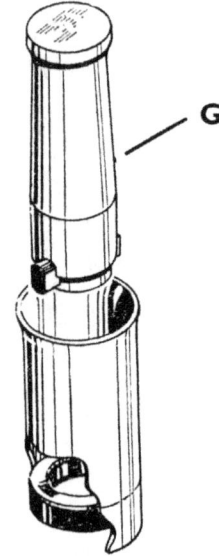

Fig. X5.

If the bush is not properly shimmed a tapping noise may be heard when the machine is ridden.

Having shimmed up the bush correctly and fitted the circlip firmly in position, screw down the oil seal holder and take one turn of number five twine around the base of the thread to provide an additional seal. Screw down the oil seal firmly using B.S.A. service tool part number 61-3005.

To fit the main tubes to the fork yokes screw B.S.A. service tool part number 61-3350 into the top of the tube and pass it up through the two yokes, then fit the collar and nut and draw the tube firmly home into the yokes. When the tube is fully home the pinch bolts on the lower yoke should be tightened. The tool may then be removed and after filling the legs with the correct amount of oil the top plugs can be replaced and fully tightened. Finally slacken the pinch bolt. position the top outer shroud centrally over the lower leg Check that the top nuts are completely tight and retighten the pinch bolts.

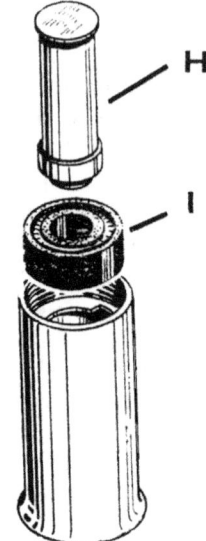

Fig. X6.

B.S.A. MOTOR CYCLES LTD., Service Department, Armoury Road, Birmingham 11.
PRINTED IN ENGLAND — B.S.A. PRESS

BSA SERVICE SHEET No. 708

ALL MODELS

CARBURATION. Monobloc and Seperate Float Chamber Type

How the Carburetter Works

The function of the carburetter is to atomise the petrol and proportion it correctly with the air drawn in through the intake on the induction stroke. The action of the float and needle in the float chamber maintains the level of fuel at the needle jet, and when the engine is stopped and no further fuel is being used the needle valve cuts off the supply.

The twist-grip controls, by means of a cable, the position of the throttle slide and the throttle needle and so governs the volume of mixture supplied to the engine.

The mixture is correct at all throttle openings, if the carburetter is correctly tuned.

The opening of the throttle brings first into action the mixture supply from the pilot jet, then as it progressively opens, via the pilot by-pass the mixture is augmented from the needle jet. Up to three-quarter throttle this action is controlled by the tapered needle in the needle jet, and from three-quarters onwards the mixture is controlled by the main jet.

The pilot jet (J), which in the older type of carburetter is embodied in the jet block, has been replaced in the Monobloc carburetter by a detachable jet (9) Fig. X5, assembled in the carburetter body and sealed by a cover nut.

The main jet does not spray directly into the mixing chamber, but discharges through the needle jet into the primary air chamber and goes from there as a rich petrol/air mixture through the primary air choke into the main air choke.

Although the maintenance and tuning instruction contained in this Service Sheet apply equally well to the Monobloc and separate float chamber types of carburetter, the new instrument has been designed with a view to giving improved performance, and certain constructional changes have been made.

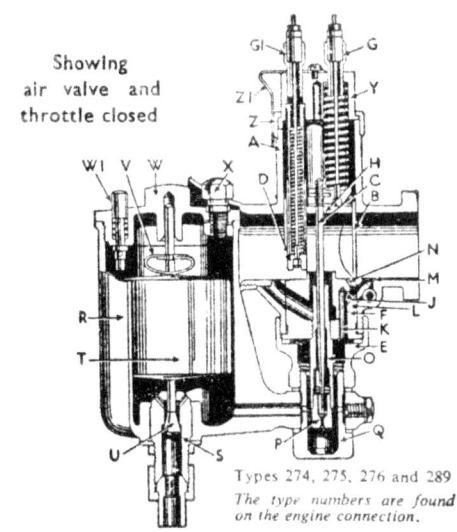

Showing air valve and throttle closed

Types 274, 275, 276 and 289
The type numbers are found on the engine connection.

A. Mixing Chamber.
B. Throttle Valve.
C. Jet Needle and Clip above.
D. Air Valve.
E. Mixing Chamber Union Nut.
F. Jet Block.
G/G1. Cable Adjusters.
H. Jet Block Barrel.
J. Pilot Jet.
K. Passage to Pilot.
L. Pilot Air Passage.
M. Pilot Mixture Outlet.
N. Pilot by-pass.
O. Needle Jet.
P. Main Jet.
Q. Float Chamber Holding Bolt.
R. Float Chamber.
S. Needle Valve Seating.
T. Float.
U. Float Needle Valve.
V. Float Needle Clip.
W. Float Chamber Cover.
W1. Tickler.
X. Float Chamber Lock Screw.
Y. Mixing Chamber Top Cap.
Z. Mixing Chamber Lock Ring.
Z1. Mixing Chamber Security Spring.

Fig. X4. *A sectioned illustration of Needle Jet Carburetter.*

B.S.A. Service Sheet No. 708 (contd.)

The float chamber is a drum-shaped reservoir, die cast in one piece with the mixing chamber. The material used being zinc-alloy. The float is designed to pivot instead of rising and falling, as in the separate float chamber type, and as it does so, it impinges on a nylon needle controlling the inflow of fuel.

Variations of up to 20° in the angle of the carburetter when fitted, do not affect the working of the float, therefore it lends itself to use for down draught carburation and is not so greatly effected by the degree of lean when cornering. Access to the float (Fig. X6) is gained by removing a plate held in place by three screws.

Compensation for over-rich mixture which results from snap throttle openings, is provided by bleed holes in the needle jet (Fig. X5). A compensatory air bleed is provided, this is the larger of the two holes at the mouth of the air intake, which leads to the space around the needle jet (Fig. X5).

The pilot intake is the smaller of the two holes, and operates in conjunction with the detachable pilot jet (Fig. X5). This pilot mixture is adjusted as before, by an adjusting screw (Fig. 8a).

Hints and Tips—Starting from Cold
Flood the carburetter by depressing the tickler and close the air control, set the ignition say, half-retarded. Then open the throttle about $\frac{1}{8}$ in., then kick-start. If the throttle is too far open, starting will be difficult.

Starting—Engine Hot
Do not flood the carburetter, but it may be found necessary with some engines to close the air lever, set the ignition to half-retarded, the throttle to $\frac{1}{8}$ in. open and kick-start. If the carburetter has been flooded and won't start because the mixture is too rich—open the throttle wide and give the engine several turns to clear the richness, then start again with the throttle $\frac{1}{8}$ in. open, and air valve wide open. Generally speaking it is not advisable to flood at all when an engine is hot.

Starting—General
By experiment, find out if and when it is necessary to flood, also note the best position for the air lever and the throttle for the easiest starting. Excessive flooding, particularly when the engine is hot, will make starting more difficult. It is necessary only to raise the level of petrol in the float chamber, by depressing the tickler.

Starting—Single Lever Carburetters
Open the throttle very slightly from the idling position and flood the carburetter more or less according to the engine being cold or hot respectively.

B.S.A. Service Sheet No. 708 (contd.)

SECTIONAL ILLUSTRATIONS OF CARBURETTERS. Types 375, 376 and 389

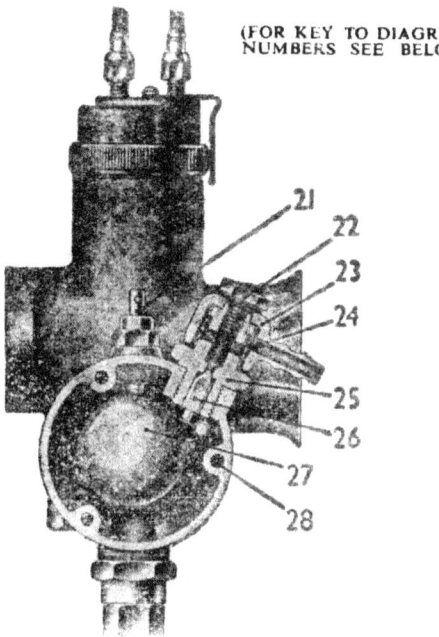

(MONOBLOC)
Fig. X6. *Section through Float Chamber.*

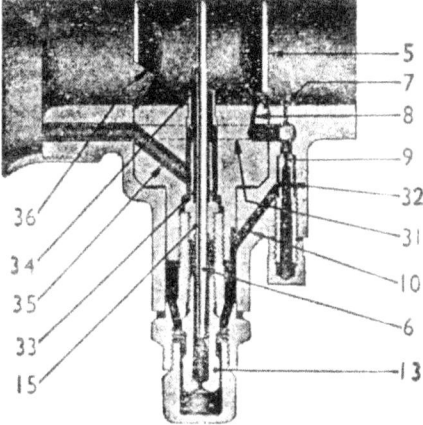

Diagrammatic section of Carburetter showing only the lower half of the throttle chamber with the throttle a little open—and the internal primary air passages to the main jet and pilot system.

FOR KEY TO DIAGRAM NUMBERS SEE BELOW
Fig. X5.

1. Mixing Chamber Top.
2. Mixing Chamber Cap.
3. Carburetter Body.
4. Jet Needle Clip.
5. Throttle Valve.
6. Jet Needle.
7. Pilot outlet.
8. Pilot by-pass.
9. Pilot Jet.
10. Petrol Feed to Pilot Jet.
11. Pilot Jet Cover Nut.
12. Main Jet Cover.
13. Main Jet.
14. Jet Holder.
15. Needle Jet.
16. Jet Block.
17. Air Valve
18. Mixing Chamber Cap Spring.
19. Cable Adjuster (air).
20. Cable Adjuster (throttle).
21. Tickler.
22. Banjo Bolt.
23. Banjo.
24. Filter Gauze.
25. Needle Seating.
26. Needle.
27. Float.
28. Side Cover Screws.
31. Air to Pilot Jet.
32. Feed Holes in Pilot Jet.
33. Bleed Holes in Needle Jet.
34. Primary Air Choke.
35. Primary Air Passage.
36. Throttle Valve Cut-away

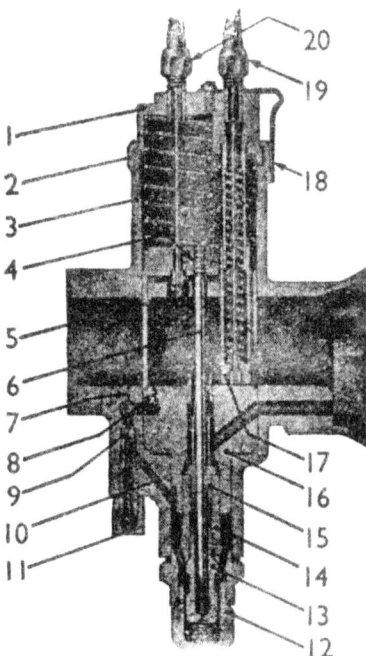

Fig. 7. *Section through Mixing Chamber, showing Air Valve and Throttle closed.*

29. PILOT AIR ADJUSTING SCREW
This screw regulates the strength of the mixture for "idling" and for the initial opening of the throttle. The screw controls the depression on the pilot jet by metering the amount of air that mixes with the petrol.

30. THROTTLE ADJUSTING SCREW
Set this screw to hold the throttle open sufficiently to keep the engine running when the twist-grip is shut off.

B.S.A. Service Sheet No. 708 (contd.)

Cable Controls

See that there is a minimum of backlash when the controls are set back and that any movement of the handlebar does not cause the throttle to open; this is done by the adjusters on the top of the carburetter. See that the throttle shuts down freely.

Petrol Feed

Verification. Detach petrol pipe union at the float chamber end; turn on petrol tap momentarily and see that fuel gushes out. Avoid petrol pipes with vertical loops as they cause air-locks. Flooding may be due to a worn or bent needle or a leaky float, but nearly all flooding with new machines is due to impurities (grit, fluff, etc.) in the tank—so clean out the float chamber periodically till the trouble ceases. If the trouble persists the tank might be drained, swilled out, etc. Note that if the carburetter, either vertical or horizontal, is flooding with the engine stopped, the overflow from the main jet will not run into the engine but out of the carburetter through a hole at the base of the mixing chamber.

Fixing Carburetter and Air Leaks

Erratic slow running is often caused by air leaks, so verify there are none at the point of attachment to the cylinder or inlet pipe—check by means of oil placed around the joint, if there are leaks the oil will be sucked in, and eliminate by new washers and the equal tightening up of the flange nuts. Also in old machines look out for air leaks caused by a worn throttle or worn inlet valve guides.

Explosions in Exhaust

May be caused by too weak a pilot mixture when the throttle is closed or nearly closed— also, it may be caused by too rich a pilot mixture and an air leak in the exhaust system; the reason in either case is that the mixture has not fired in the cylinder and has fired in the hot silencer. If the explosion occurs when the throttle is fairly wide open the trouble will be ignition—not carburation.

Excessive Petrol Consumption

On a new machine may be due to flooding, caused by impurities from the petrol tank lodging on the float needle seat and so preventing its valve from closing. If the machine has had several years use, flooding may be caused by a worn float needle valve. Also excessive petrol consumption will be apparent if the throttle needle jet (o) Fig. X4. or (15) Fig. X5, has worn; it may be remedied or improved by lowering the needle in the throttle, but if it cannot be, then the only remedy is to get a new needle jet.

Air Filters

These may affect the jet setting, so if one is fitted afterwards to the carburetter the main jet may have to be smaller. If a carburetter is set with an air filter and the engine is run without it, take care not to overheat the engine due to too weak a mixture; testing with the air control will indicate if a larger main jet and higher needle position are required.

B.S.A. Service Sheet No. 708 (contd.)

Faults

The trouble may not be carburation; if the trouble cannot be remedied by making mixtures richer or weaker with the air control, and you know the petrol feed is good and the carburetter is not flooding, the trouble is elsewhere.

Fault Finding

There are only *two* possible faults in carburation, either *richness* of mixture or *weakness* of mixture, so in case of trouble decide which is the cause, by:—

1. Examining the petrol feed ...
   - Verify jets and passages are clear.
   - Verify ample flow.
   - Verify there is no flooding.

2. Looking for air leaks ...
   - At the connection to the engine.
   - Or due to leaky inlet valve stems.

3. Defective or worn parts ...
   - As a slack throttle-worn needle jet.
   - The mixing chamber union nut not tightened up, or loose jets.

4. *Testing with the air control* to see if by richening the mixture the results are better or worse.

Indications of

Richness:	Weakness:
Black smoke in exhaust.	Spitting in carburetter.
Petrol spraying out of carburetter.	Erratic slow running.
Four strokes, eight-stroking	Overheating.
Two strokes, four-stroking.	Acceleration poor.
Heavy, lumpy running.	Engine goes better if:—
Heavy petrol consumption.	Throttle not wide open, or air control is partially closed.
? If the jet block (F) is not tightened up by washer and nut (E) richness will be caused through leakage of petrol.	? Has air cleaner been removed.
? Air cleaner choked up.	? Jets partially choked up
? Needle jet worn large.	Removing the silencer or running with a racing silencer requires a richer setting and large main jet.
Sparking plug sooty.	

Note

Verify correctness of fuel feed, stop air leaks, check over ignition and valve operation and timing. *Decide by test whether richness or weakness is the trouble and at what throttle position.* See throttle opening diagrams, Fig. X6.

B.S.A. Service Sheet No. 708 (contd.)

Procedure

If at a particular throttle opening you partially close the air control, and the engine goes better, weakness is indicated; or on the other hand the running is worse, richness is indicated. *Then you proceed to adjust the appropriate part as indicated for that position.*

Fault at Throttle Positions indicated on Fig. X9

To Cure Richness:		To Cure Weakness:
Fit smaller main jet.	1st	Fit larger main jet.
Screw out pilot air screw.	2nd	Screw pilot air screw in.
Fit a throttle with larger cut-away.	3rd	Fit a throttle with smaller cut-away.
Lower needle one or two grooves.	4th	Raise needle one or two grooves.

Notes

It is not correct to cure a rich mixture at half-throttle by fitting a smaller main jet because the main jet may be correct for power at full throttle: the proper thing to do is to lower the needle.

Information on throttle slides and needle position is given in paragraphs (*f*) and (*e*) respectively in the next section entitled "Tuning".

Changing from Standard Petrols to Special Fuels.

Such as alcohol mixtures will, with the same setting in the carburetter, certainly cause weakness of mixture and possible damage from overheating.

TUNING

(*a*) Figs. X8 and 8a are two diagrammatic sections of the carburetter to show:
1. The throttle stop screw.
2. The pilot air screw.

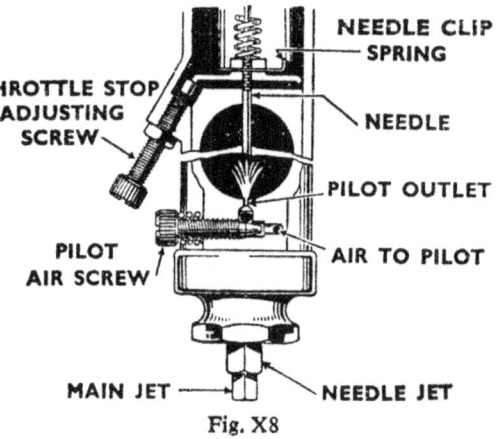

Fig. X8

(*b*) **Throttle Stop Screw**

Set this screw to prop the throttle open sufficiently to keep the engine running when the twist-grip is shut off.

(*c*) **Pilot Air Screw**

This screw regulates the strength of the mixture for "idling" and for the initial opening of the throttle. The screw controls the suction on the pilot petrol jet by metering the amount of air that mixes with the petrol.

NOTE:—The air for the pilot jet may be admitted internally or externally according to one or other of the designs, but there is no difference in tuning.

(*d*) **Main Jet**

The main jet controls the petrol supply when the throttle is more than three-quarters open, but at smaller throttle openings although the supply of fuel goes through the main jet, the amount is diminished by the metering effect of the needle in the needle jet.

Each jet is calibrated and numbered so that its exact discharge is known and two jets of the same number are alike.

B.S.A. Service Sheet No. 708 (contd.)

Never reamer a Jet out, get another of the right size
The bigger the number the bigger the jet. Spare jets *are sealed*.

To get at the main jet, undo the float chamber holding bolt (Q) Fig. X4, or main jet cover number 12 (Fig. X7). The jet is screwed into the needle jet so if the jet is tight, hold the needle jet also carefully with a spanner whilst unscrewing the main jet.

(e) Needle and Needle Jet

The needle is attached to the throttle and being tapered either allows more or less petrol to pass through the needle jets as the throttle is opened or closed throughout the range, except when idling or nearly full throttle. The needle jet is of a defined size and is only altered from standard when using alcohol fuels.

The taper needle position in relation to the throttle opening can be set according to the mixture required by fixing it to the throttle with the needle clip spring in a certain groove (see illustration above), thus either raising or lowering it. Raising the needle richens the mixture and lowering it weakens the mixture at throttle openings from quarter to three-quarter open (see illustration, Fig. X9).

(f) Throttle Valve Cut-away

The atmospheric side of the throttle is cut away to influence the depression on the main fuel supply and thus gives a means of tuning between the pilot and needle jet range of throttle opening. The amount of cut-away is recorded by a number marked on the throttle, viz.: 6/3 means throttle type 6 with number 3 cut-away; larger cut-aways, say 4 and 5, give weaker mixtures, and 2 and 1 richer mixtures.

(g) Air Valve

Is used only for starting and running when cold, and for experimenting with, otherwise run with it wide open.

(h) Tickler

A small plunger located in the float chamber lid. When pressed down on the float, the neddle valve is pushed off its seat and so "flooding" is achieved. Flooding temporarily enriches the mixture until the level of the petrol subsides to normal.

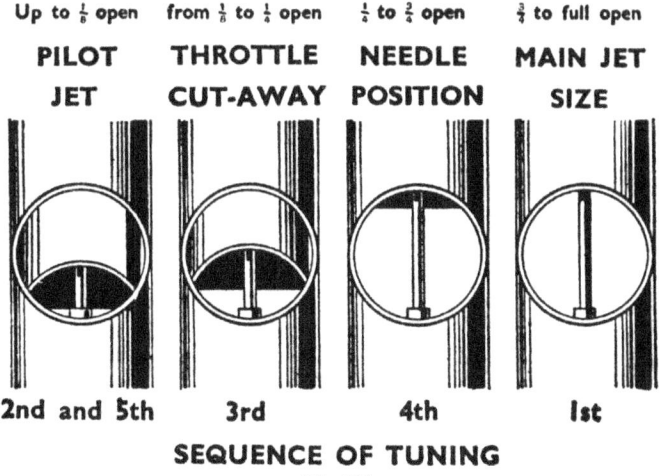

Phases of Amal Needle Jet Carburettor Throttle Openings

Fig. X9

B.S.A. Service Sheet No. 708 (contd.)

Sequence of Tuning

Tune up. In the following order only, by so doing you will not upset good results obtained.

NOTE.—The carburetter is automatic throughout the throttle range—the air control should always be wide open except when used for starting or until the engine has warmed up. We assume normal petrols are used.

Read remarks on "Fault Finding" and "Tuning" for each tuning device and get the motor going perfectly on a quiet road with a slight up gradient so that on test the engine is pulling.

1st Main Jet with Throttle in position

Test the engine for full throttle; if when at full throttle, the power seems better with the throttle less than wide open or with the air valve closed slightly the main jet is too small. If the engine runs "heavily" the main jet is too large. If testing for speed work note the jet size is rich enough to keep engine cool, and to verify this, examine the sparking plug by taking a fast run, declutching and stopping engine quickly. If the plug body at the end has a bright black appearance, the mixture is correct; if sooty, the mixture is rich; or if a dry grey colour, the mixture is too weak and a larger jet is necessary.

2nd Pilot Jet with Throttle in positions 2 and 5

With engine idling too fast with the twist-grip shut off and the throttle shut down on to the throttle stop screw, and ignition set for best slow running: (1) Loosen stop screw nut and screw down until engine runs slower and begins to falter, then screw the pilot air screw in or out to make engine run regularly and faster. (2) Now gently lower the throttle stop screw until the engine runs slower and just begins to falter, then lock the nut lightly and begin again to adjust the pilot air screw to get best slow running; if this second adjustment makes engine run too fast, go over the job again a third time. Finally, lock up tight the throttle stop screw nut without disturbing the screw's position.

3rd Throttle Cut-away with Throttle in position

If, as you take off from the idling position, there is objectionable spitting from the carburetter, slightly richen the pilot mixture by screwing the air screw in about half a turn, but if this is not effective, screw it back again and fit a throttle with a smaller cut-away. If the engine jerks under load at this throttle position and there is no spitting, either the throttle needle is much too high or a larger throttle cut-away is required to cure richness.

4th Needle with Throttle in position 4

The needle controls a wide range of throttle opening and also the acceleration. Try the needle in as low a position as possible, viz., with the clip in a groove as near the end as possible; if acceleration is poor and with air valve partially closed the results are better, raise the needle by two grooves; if very much better try lowering needle by one groove and leave it where it is best.

NOTE:—If mixture is still too rich with clip in groove number 1 nearest the end—the needle jet probably wants replacement because of wear. The needle itself never wears out.

5th Finally go over the idling again for final touches.

B.S.A. MOTOR CYCLES LTD., Service Department, Armoury Road, Birmingham 11.
Printed in England   B.S.A. Press.

BSA SERVICE SHEET No. 708B

ALL MODELS

CARBURATION AT HIGH ALTITUDES

The carburetter settings of all B.S.A. motor cycles are designed to give the best all round performance at altitudes of a few thousand feet.

At greater altitudes the air becomes rarefied with the result that the mixture is incorrect.

To overcome this difficulty it is necessary to reduce the size of the main jet, the reduction depending on the altitude at which the machine is mainly used.

The table below shows the percentage of reduction at given altitudes, but it must be emphasised that while the alteration to jet size will correct the mixture, it will not replace the lost power. This can only be corrected by "blowing" or super-charging.

It may also be advisable to re-tune the carburetter for smaller throttle openings this should be done in accordance with Service Sheet 708.

Altitude.	Percentage of reduction in jet size.
3,000 feet	5%
6,000 feet	9%
9,000 feet	13%
12,000 feet	17%

B.S.A. MOTOR CYCLES LTD., Service Dept., Armoury Road, Birmingham 11.

B.S.A. Press.

BSA SERVICE SHEET No. 709

ALL MODELS
FAULT FINDING

No adjustments should be made, or any part tampered with, until the cause of the trouble is known. Otherwise adjustments which are correct may be deranged.

Engine Stops Suddenly:
    Petrol shortage in tank, or choked petrol supply pipe or tap.
    Choked main jet, or water in float chamber.
    Oiled up or fouled sparking plug.
    Water on high-tension pick-up or on sparking plug.

Engine Fails to Start, or is difficult to start:
    Lack of fuel, or insufficient flooding if cold.
    Excessive flooding, allowing neat petrol to enter the cylinder.
    Oil sparking plug, or stuck-up valve or valve stem sticky.
    Weak valve spring, or valve not seating properly.
    Throttle opening too large, or pilot jet choked.
    Contact points dirty, or gap incorrect.
    Flat battery, if coil ignition, or faulty electrical connections in ignition circuit.

Loss of Power:
    Valve, or valves, not seating properly.
    Weak valve spring or springs, or sticking valve.
    No tappet clearance, or excessive clearance.
    Lack of oil in tank.
    Brakes adjusted too closely.
    Badly fitting or broken piston rings.
    Punctured carburettor float.
    Incorrect ignition timing.

Engine Overheats:
    Lack of proper lubrication.
    Weak valve springs, or pitted valve seats.
    Worn piston rings, or late ignition setting.
    Carburettor setting too weak, or partly choked petrol pipe.

Engine Misses Fire:
    Weak valve spring.
    Defective or oiled sparking plug, or oil on contact points.
    Incorrectly adjusted contact points or tappets.
    Faulty condenser.
    Defective sparking plug or high-tension cable.
    Loose sparking plug terminal.
    Carburettor flooding, due to stuck or defective float.
    Partly choked main jet.
    Choked vent hole in petrol tank filler cap.

Excessive Oil Consumption:
    Stoppage, or partial stoppage, in pipe returning oil from engine to tank.
    Clogged, or partially clogged, filter in sump, or oil tank.
    Badly worn or stuck-up piston rings, causing high pressure in engine crankcase.
    High crankcase pressure, caused by release valve (breather) action.
    Air leak in dry sump oiling system.
    Non-return valve in system not seating.
    Ball valve in oil pump stuck on its seat.

B.S.A. MOTOR CYCLES LTD., Service Department, Armoury Road, Birmingham 11

B.S.A. PRESS

BSA SERVICE SHEET No. 710

ALL MODELS
CHAIN ALTERATIONS AND REPAIRS

A chain rarely breaks if it is kept properly lubricated and adjusted. Usually it is worn out long before it reaches breaking point. The rear chain is the most heavily stressed and is therefore the one most likely to give trouble. Spare parts should be carried to enable the rider to carry out a repair on the road with the aid of a chain rivet extractor (see Fig. X7). The front chain will probably be worn out before it requires shortening.

How to use the Chain Rivet Extractor

First press down lever (A) Fig. X7 to open the two jaws (B). Insert the link to be removed so that the jaws grip the roller and support the uppermost inner side plate. The punch (C) is then screwed on to the rivet head until the rivet is forced through the outer plate.

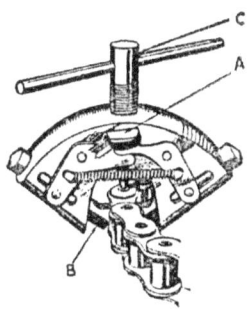

Fig. X7.

To shorten a worn Rear Chain

After a big mileage, the rear chain may have stretched so that no further adjustment is possible by the usual method. In this case it is possible to shorten the chain by one link or pitch, so increasing its useful life. First remove the single connecting spring link (A) securing the two ends of the chain, Fig. X8. If the chain terminates in two ordinary links as in Fig. X8 (in which case the chain will be an even number of pitches) extract the third and fourth rivets (B) from the end and replace the detached three pitches by a single connecting link (C). The connection is made with an additional spring link (D). If one end of the chain has a double cranked link, Fig. X9—in which case the chain will have an odd

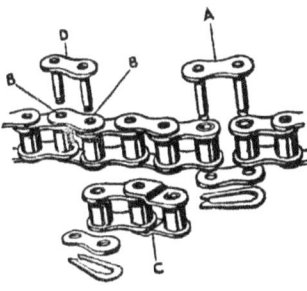

Fig. X8.

Printed in England

B.S.A. Service Sheet No. 710 (contd.)

number of pitches—extract the second and third rivets (A), releasing the cranked link unit complete, which can be retained for further use. Replace with one inner link (B) and again connect up with an additional single connecting link (C).

To repair a damaged Chain

If a roller or link has been damaged (X) Fig. X9, remove rivets (D), take out the damaged link and replace with one inner link, secured by two single connecting links.

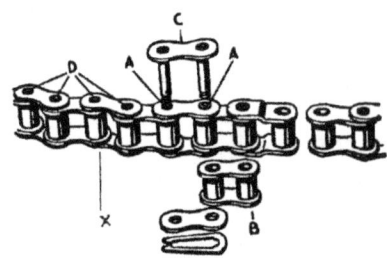

Fig. X9.

It is important that the spring clip fastener should always be put on so that the *closed* end faces the direction of travel of the chain—i.e. when clip is on top run of chain, closed end is toward front of machine—when clip is on bottom run, closed end is towards rear of machine.

It should be noted that once a rivet has been extracted it must not be used again, so that it is important to check that the correct rivet is being removed before actually removing it. In the case of double cranked links, the complete unit comprises an inner link and the cranked outer link—three rollers in all—and these must never be separated.

Fitting Rear Chain

To fit a new rear chain, turn wheel until the spring link of the old chain is located on rear sprocket. Disconnect, and allow the lower run to drop down. Join the top run of the old chain to the new chain by means of the connecting link, and then by pulling on the bottom run of the old chain the new one will be carried round the gearbox sprocket. Then the old chain can be disconnected and the ends of the new one joined together.

When the rear chain breaks and falls from its sprockets, the new or repaired chain can be replaced without taking off the chainguards. One end of the chain must be fed (from the rear) under the front end of the rear top chainguard on to the gearbox sprocket A long bladed screwdriver or a piece of stiff wire may assist this operation When the chain has located on the sprocket teeth, engage a gear and gently turn gearbox over with the kickstarter This will feed chain round gearbox sprocket When sufficient length of chain is hanging below sprocket, disengage gear and chain can then be pulled round until both runs can be fed inside rear chainguard and engaged on rear wheel sprocket.

B.S.A. MOTOR CYCLES LTD., Service Department, Armoury Road, Birmingham 11.

SERVICE SHEET No. 710x

MARCH, 1969

FRAME REPAIRS

ALL MODELS

Frame repairs must not be attempted unless adequate workshop facilities are available.

The information given in this sheet is intended for the use of Dealers who are unable to take advantage of the B.S.A. repair service and who have frame repair facilities.

Spotting points to enable frame trueing to be carried out can be determined by making use of the dimensions given.

B.S.A. Motor Cycles Ltd., Armoury Road Birmingham 11.

PRINTED IN ENGLAND

IT IS DIFFICULT TO UNDERSTAND WHY B.S.A. ISSUED THE FOLLOWING FRAME DRAWINGS IN VARYING SCALES AND AT SUCH SMALL SIZES - MAKING SOME OF THE DIMENSIONS ALMOST IMPOSSIBLE TO READ. HOWEVER, THEY ARE INCLUDED FOR THE SAKE OF COMPLETENESS

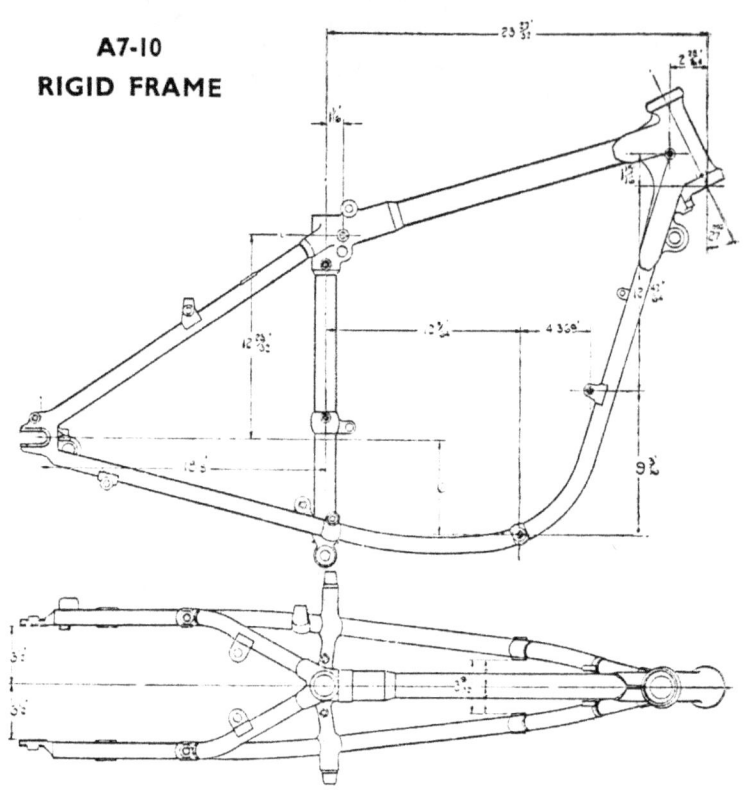
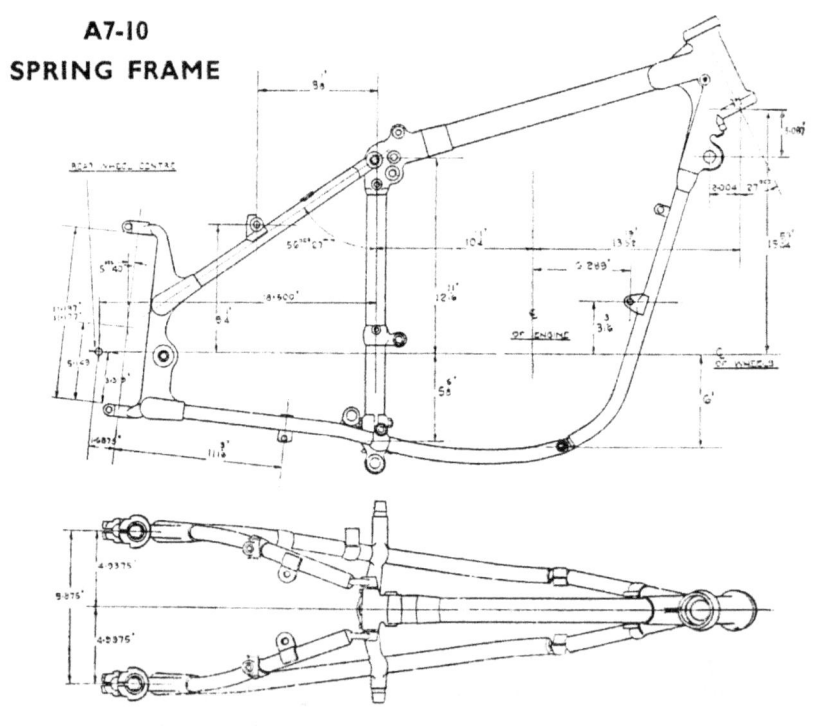

1953 SUPER FLASH SPRING FRAME

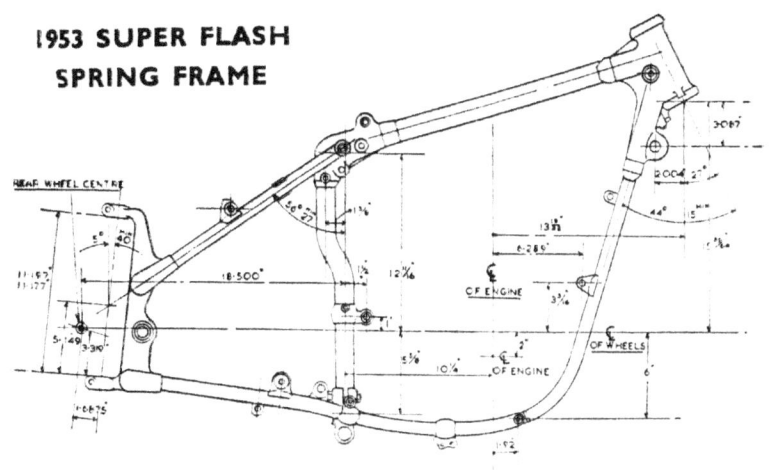
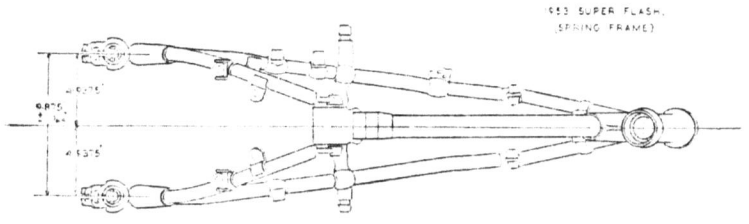

M20, M21 and M33 RIGID FRAME
1945 - 1948

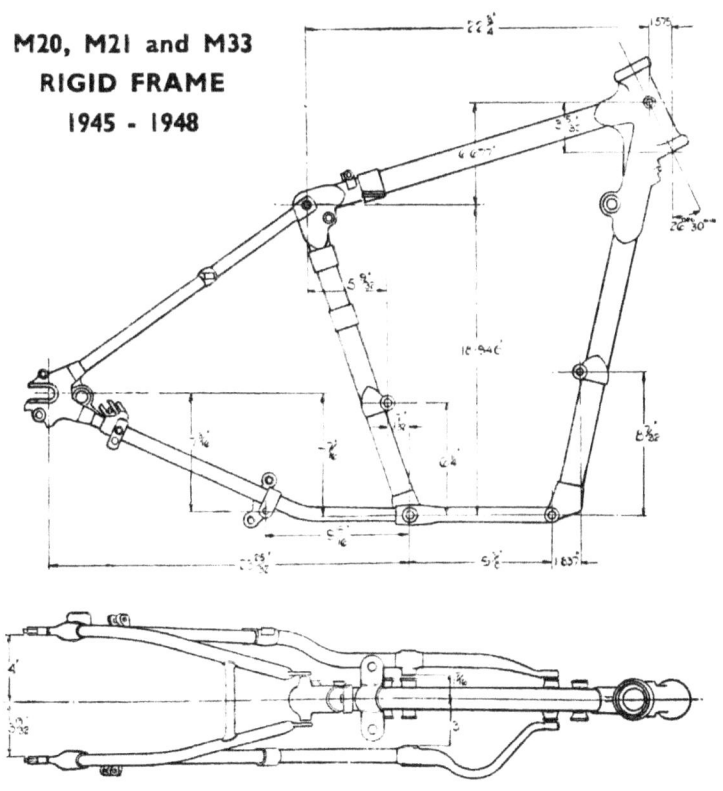

M20, M21 and M33 RIGID FRAME 1949 onwards

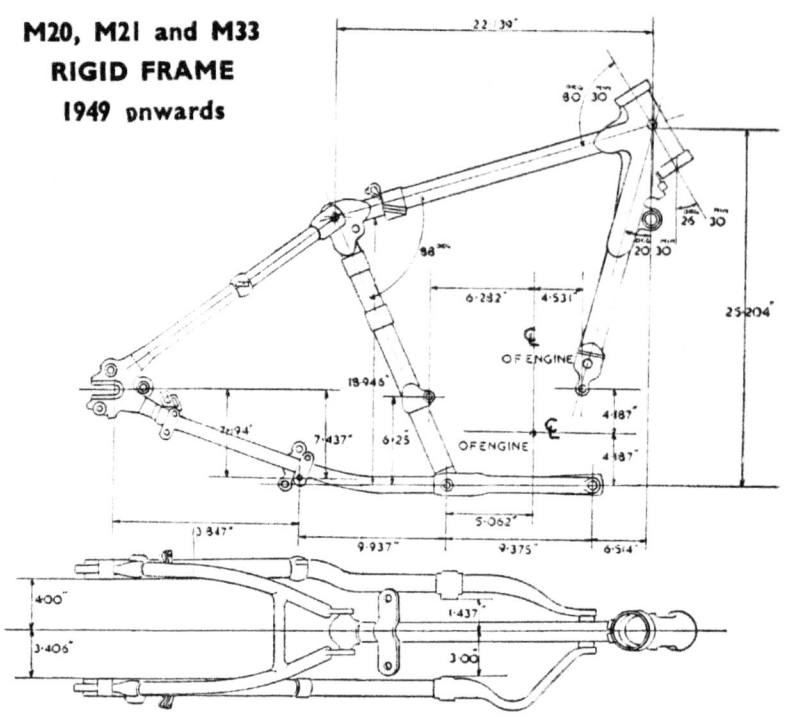

M20, M21 and M33 SPRING FRAME

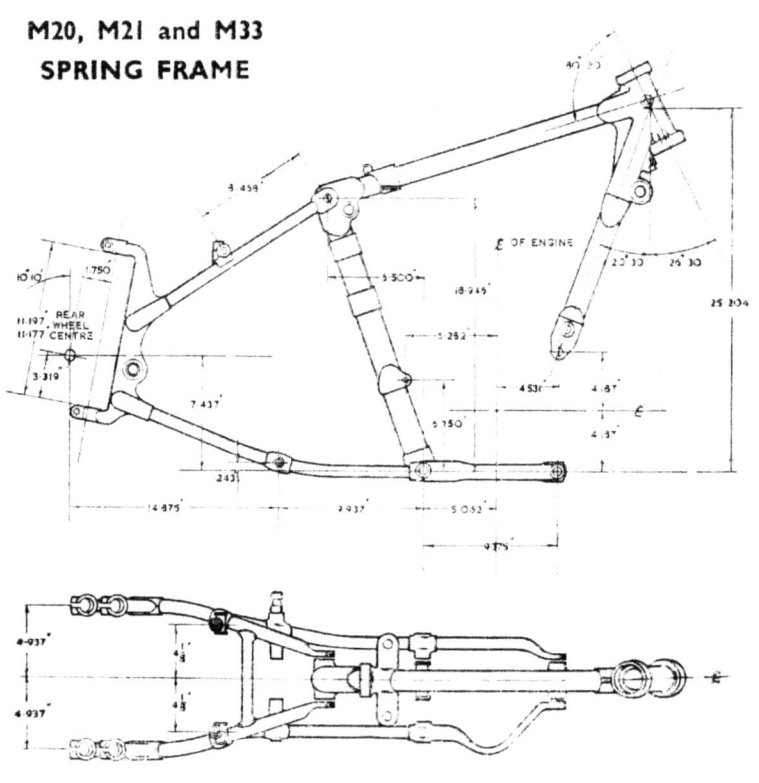

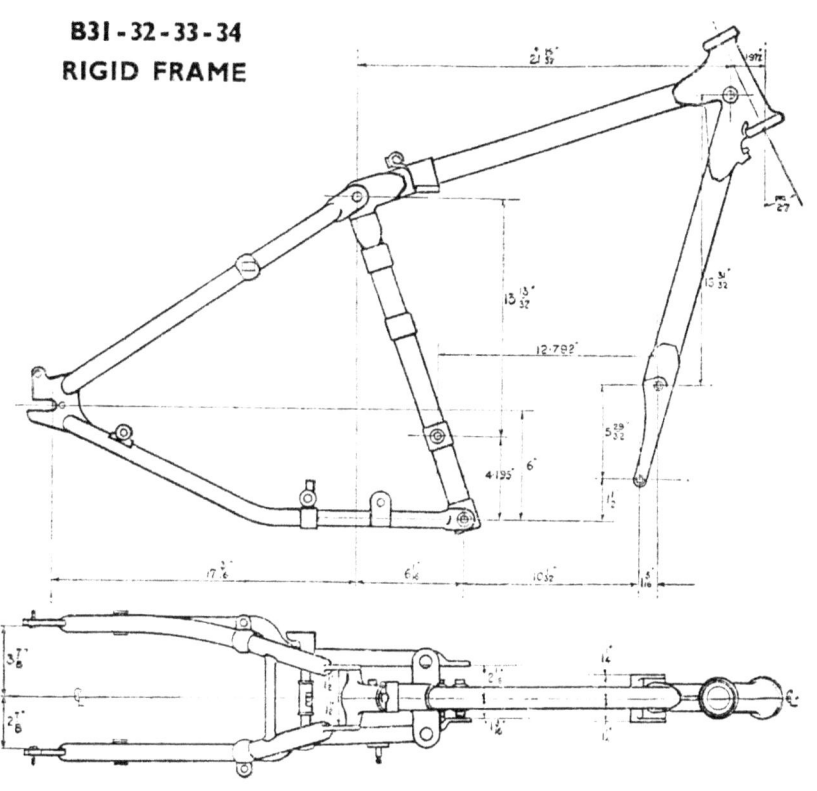

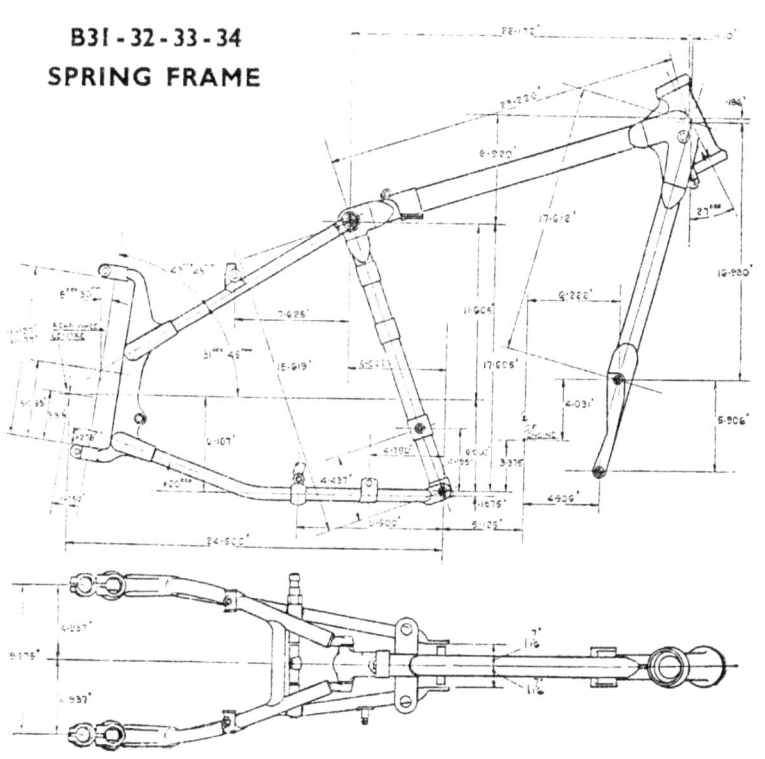

D1 and D3
RIGID FRAME

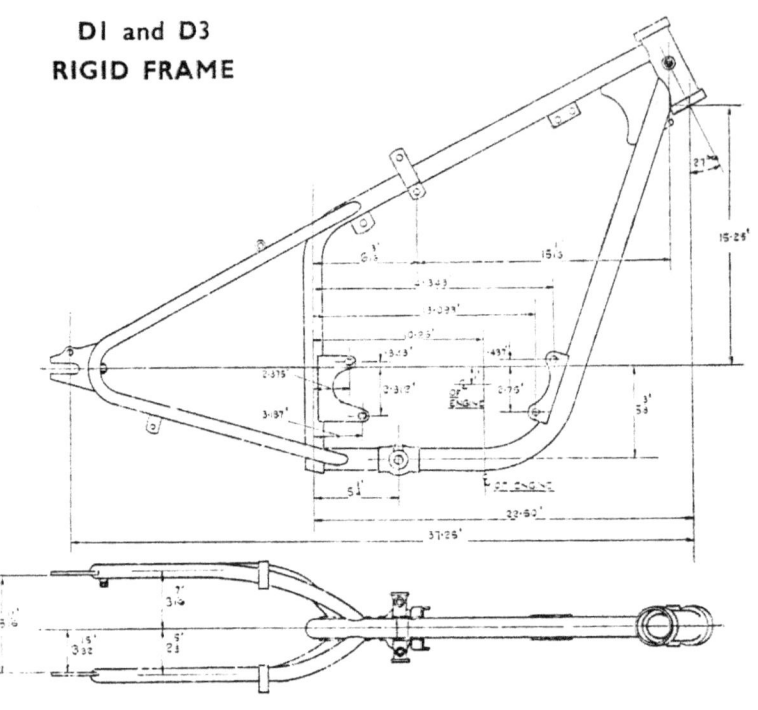

D1 and D3
SPRING FRAME

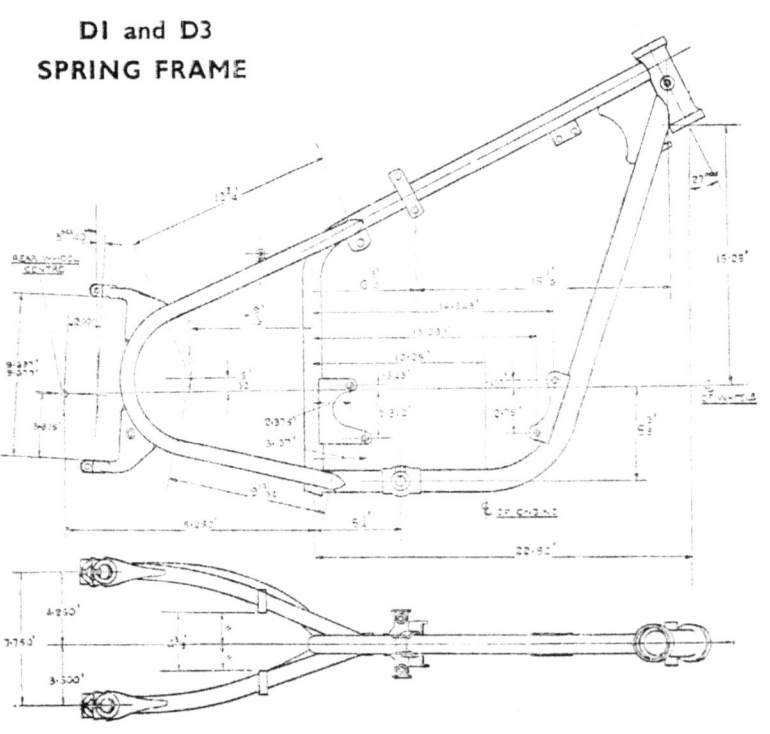

C10L SPRING FRAME

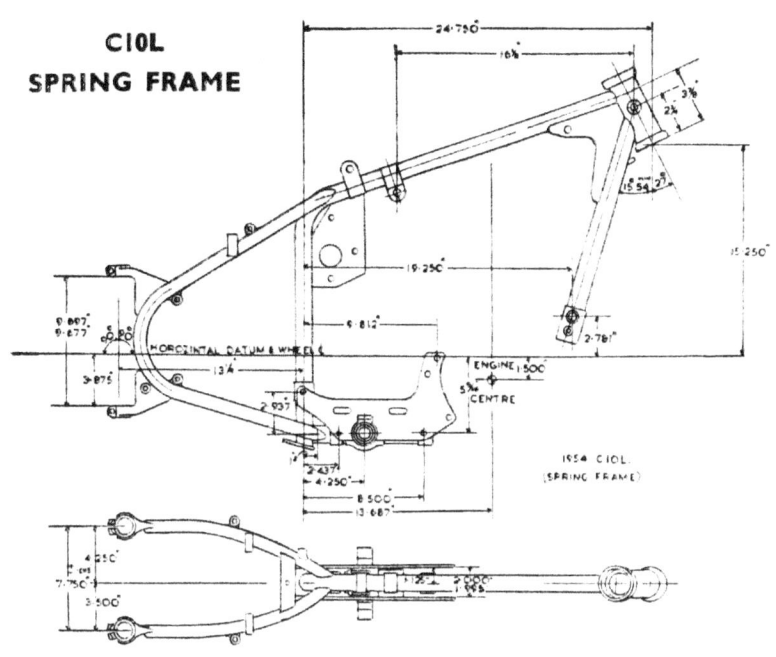

C10, C11, C11G RIGID FRAME

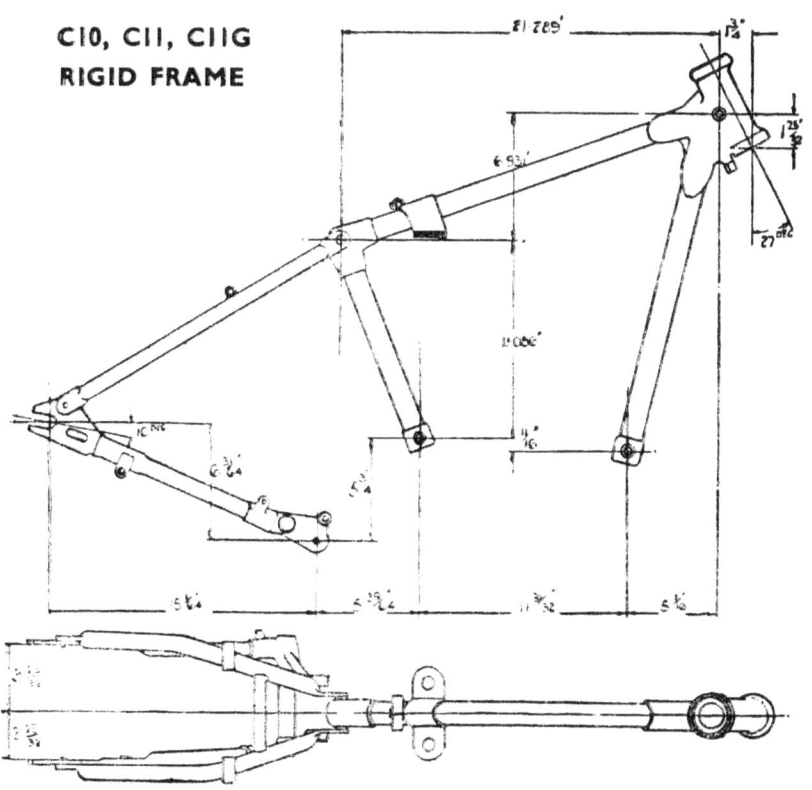

C10, C11, C11G SPRING FRAME 3 SPEED GEARBOX

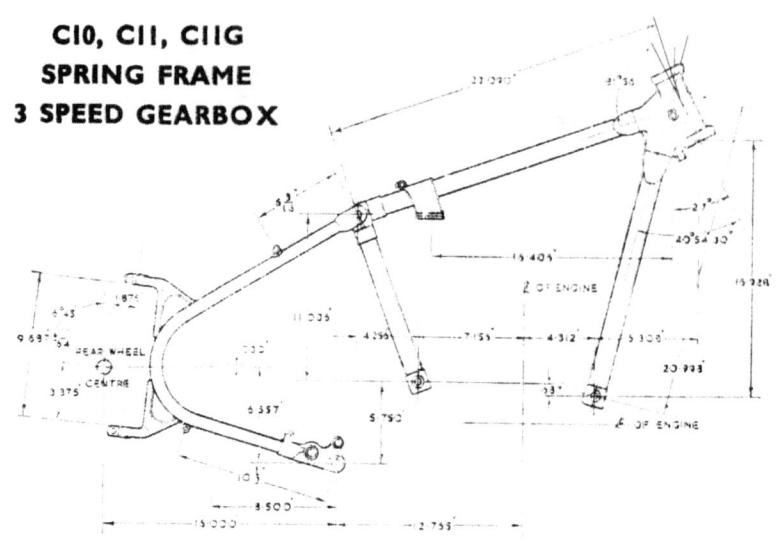
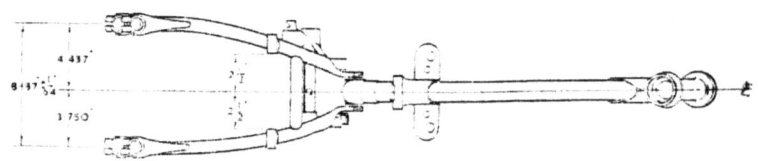

C10, C11, C11G SPRING FRAME 4 SPEED GEARBOX

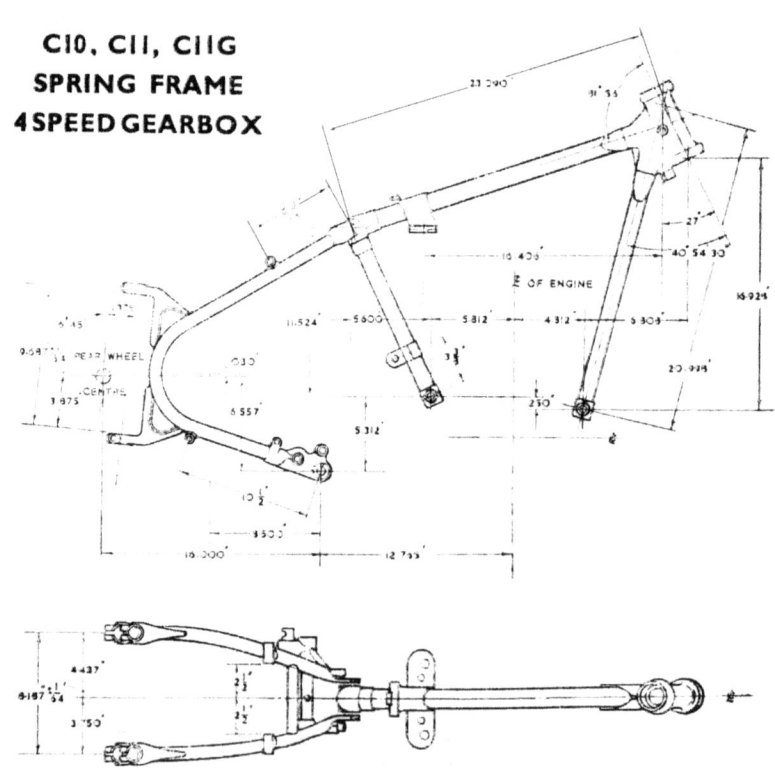

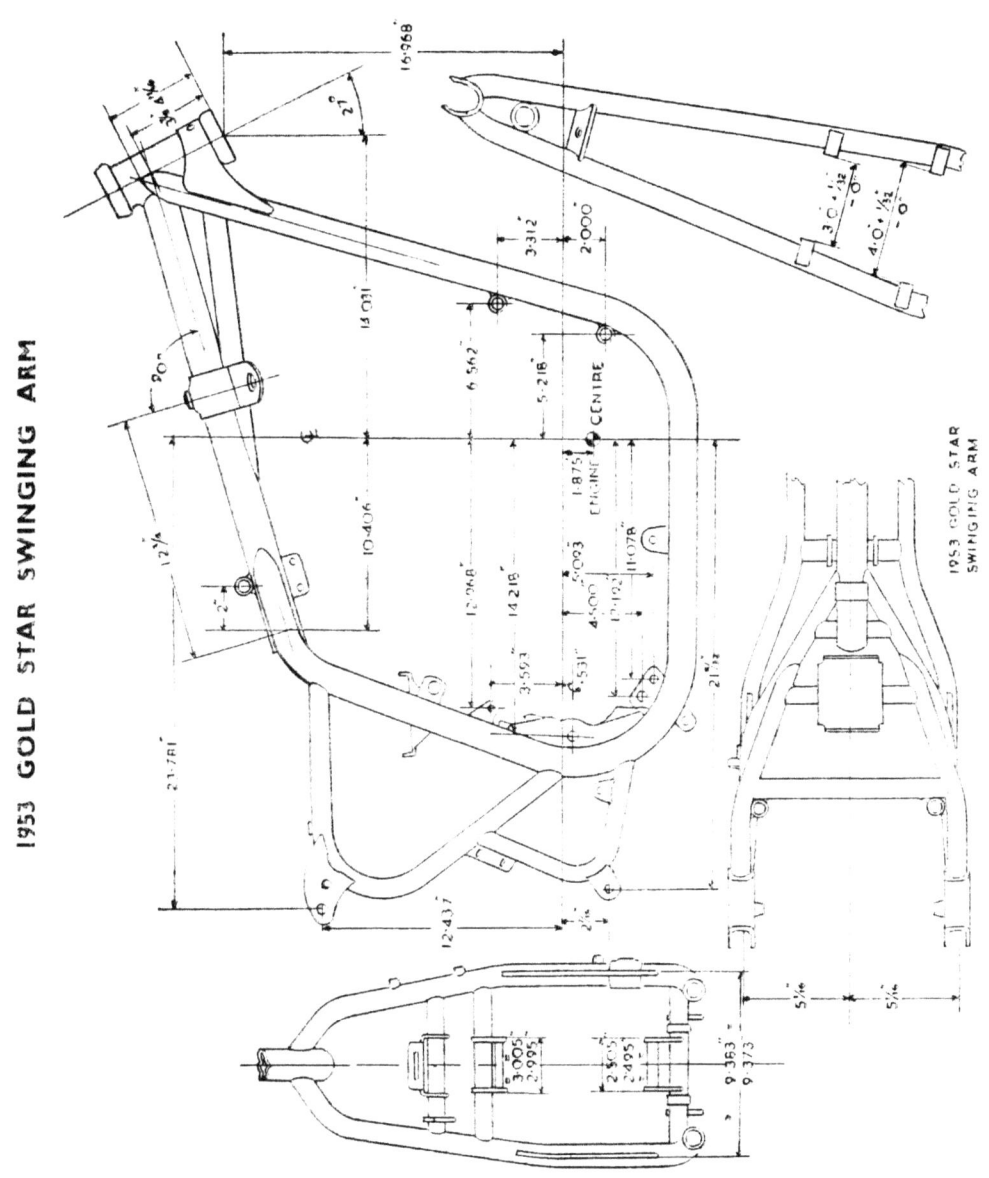

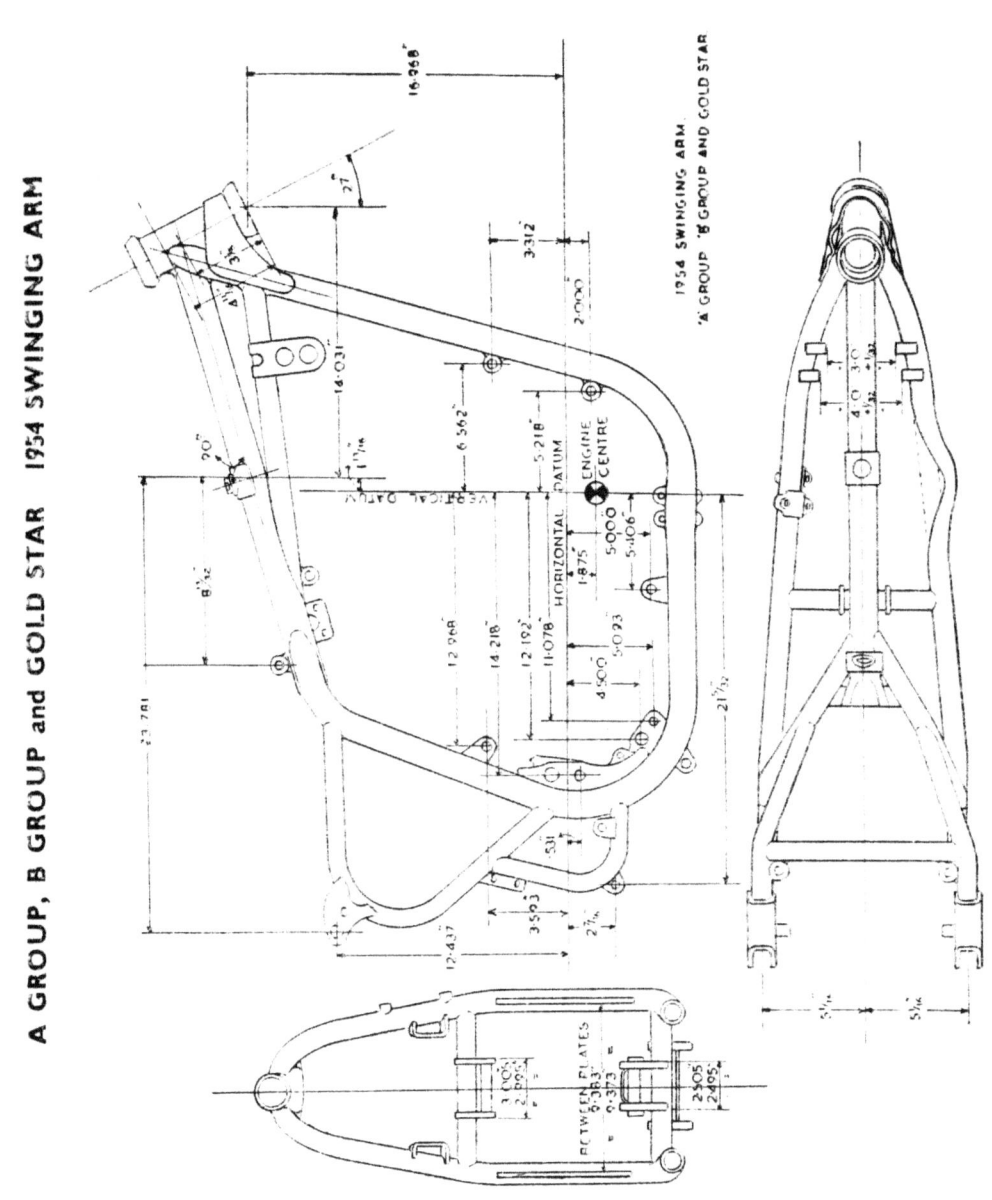

B32 and B34
1954 RIGID FRAME

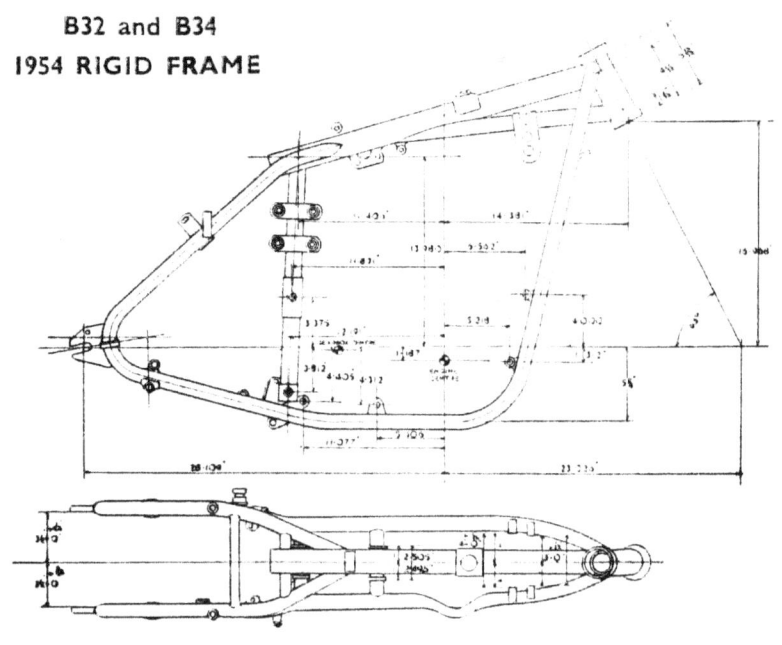

D3 SWINGING ARM

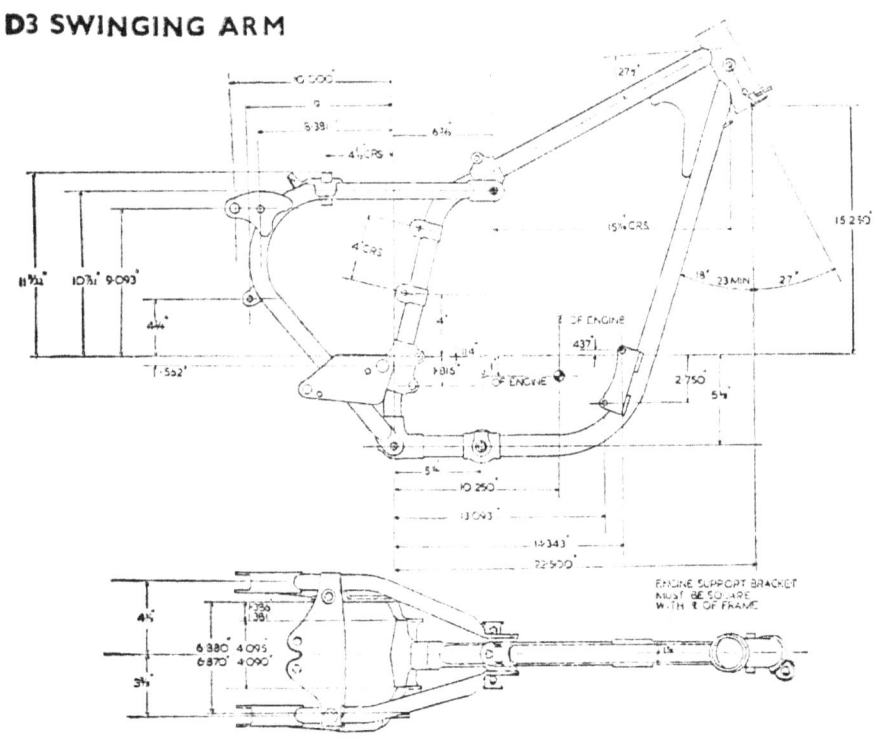

C12 SWINGING ARM

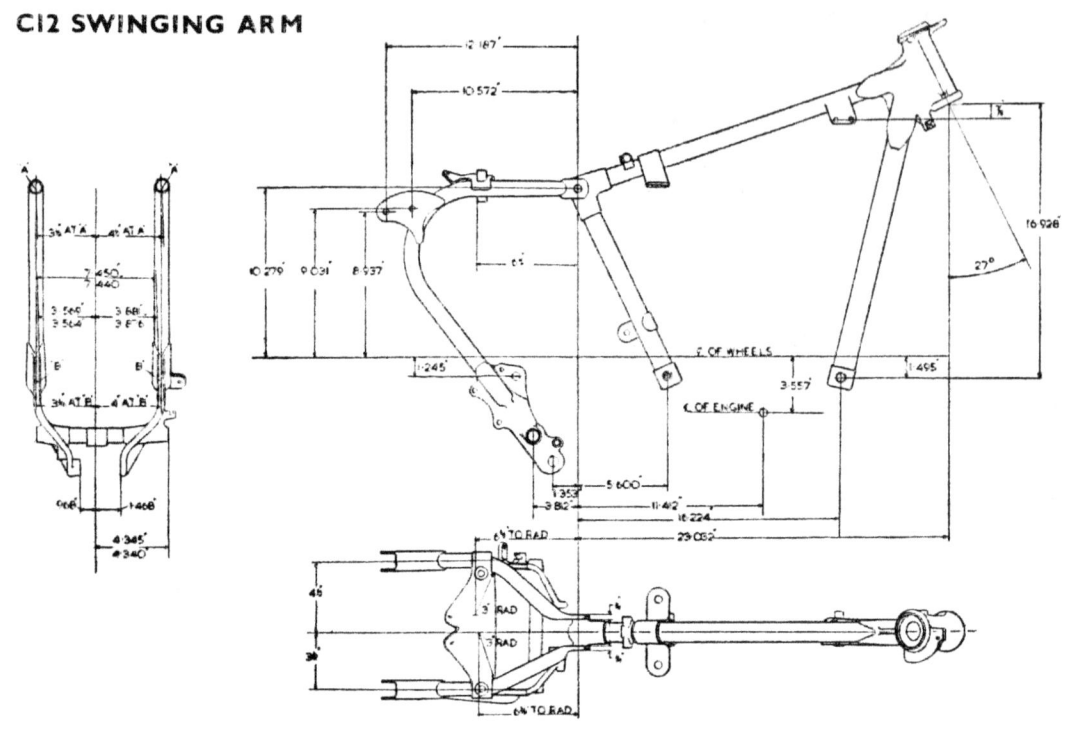

D5 SWINGING ARM

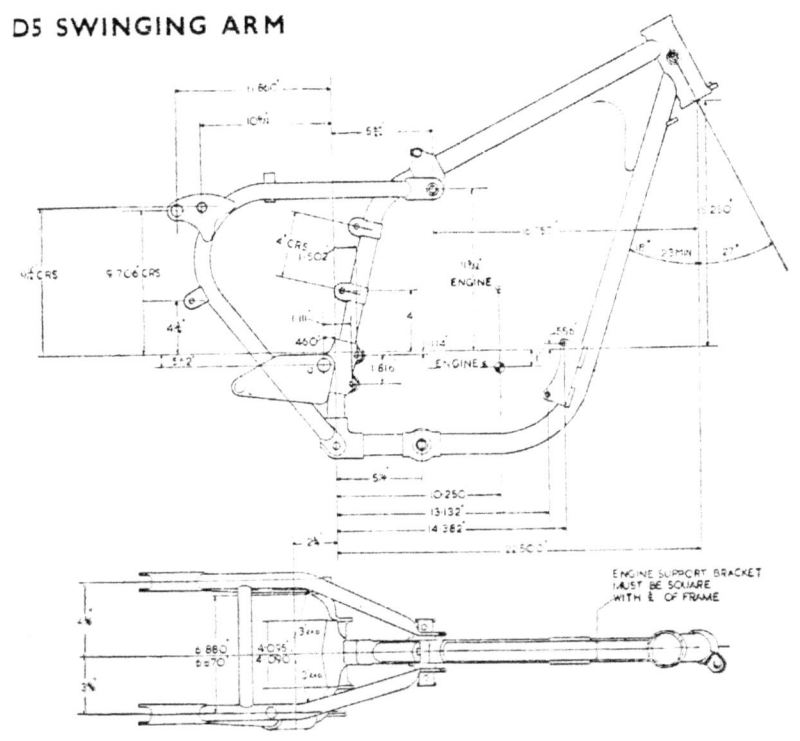

D7 SWINGING ARM

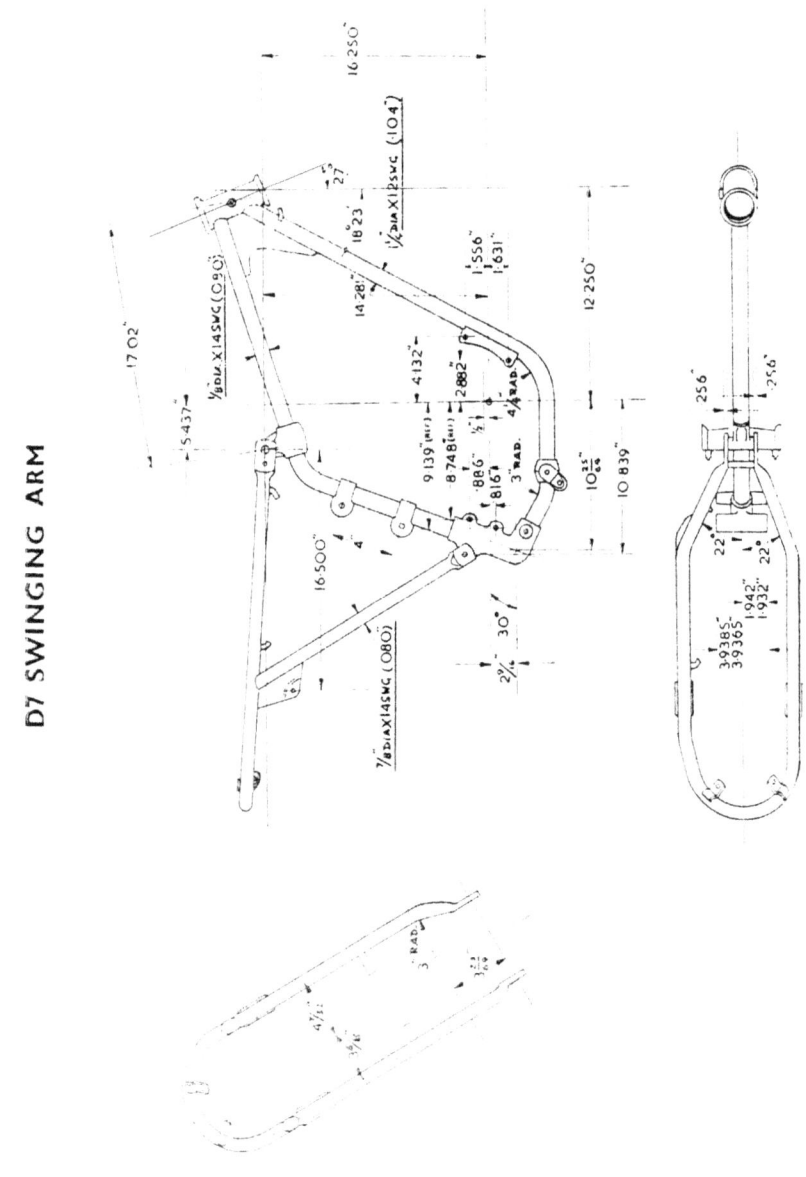

C15 STAR AND C15 SPORTS STAR

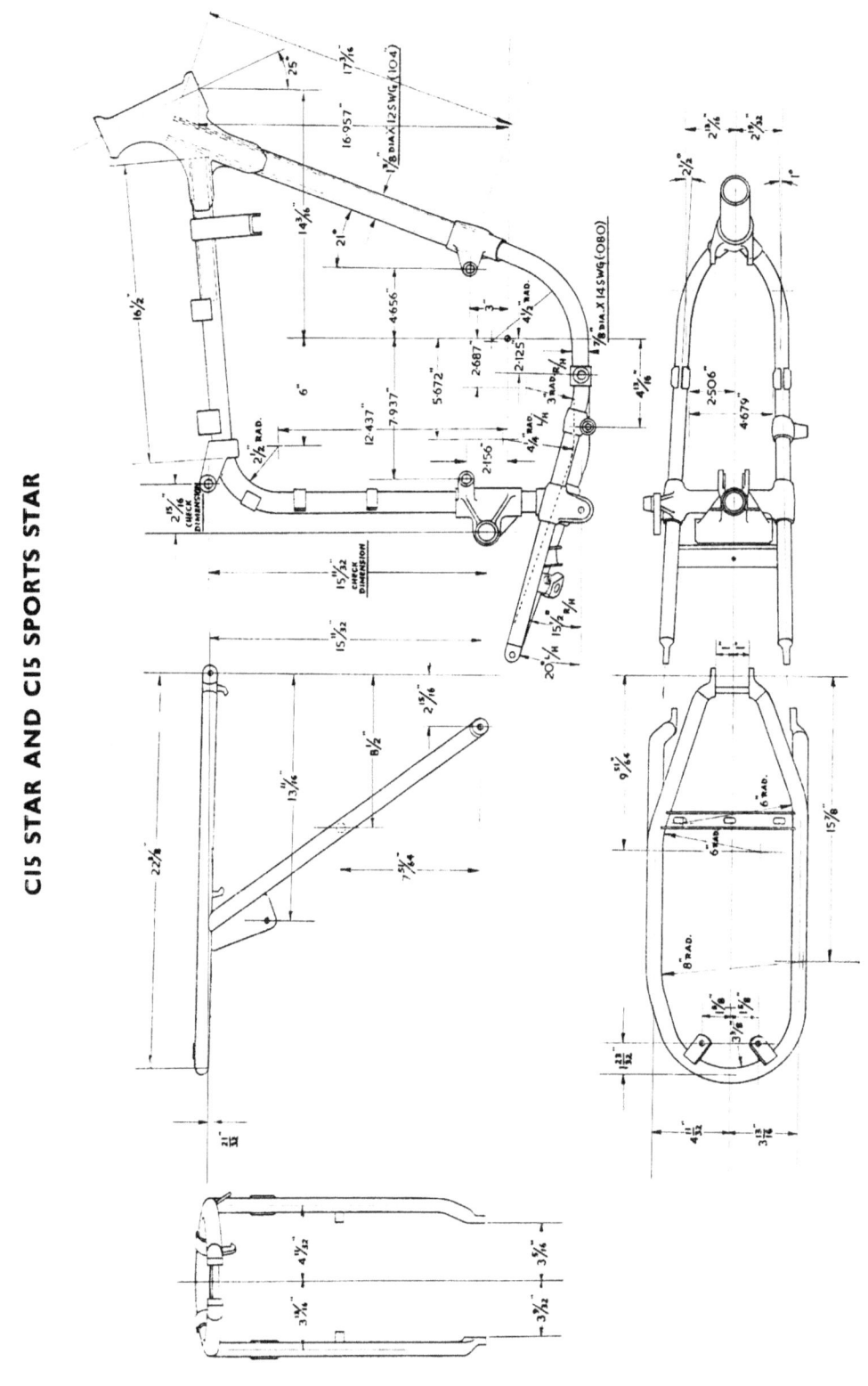

C15 TRIALS AND C15 SCRAMBLES

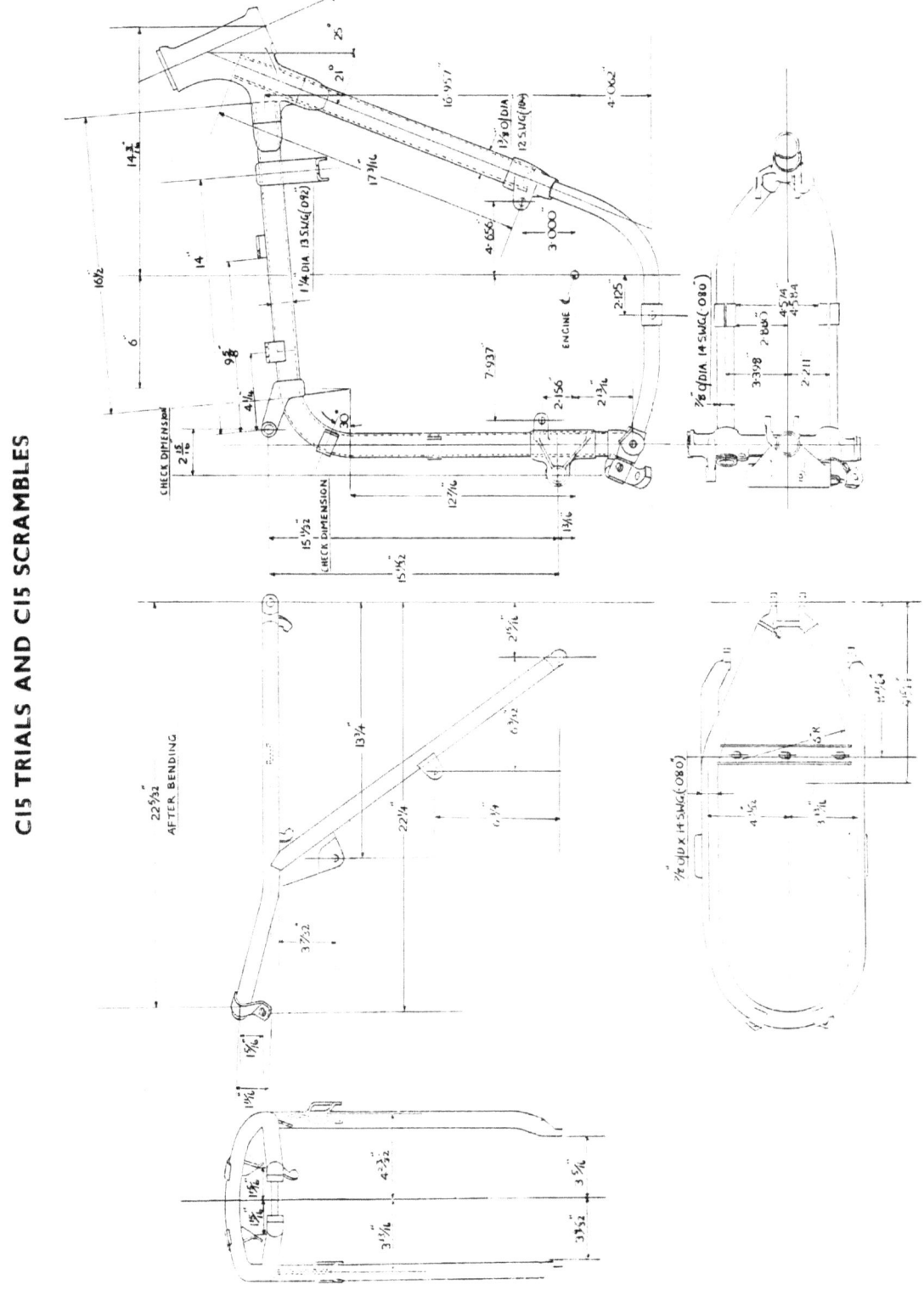

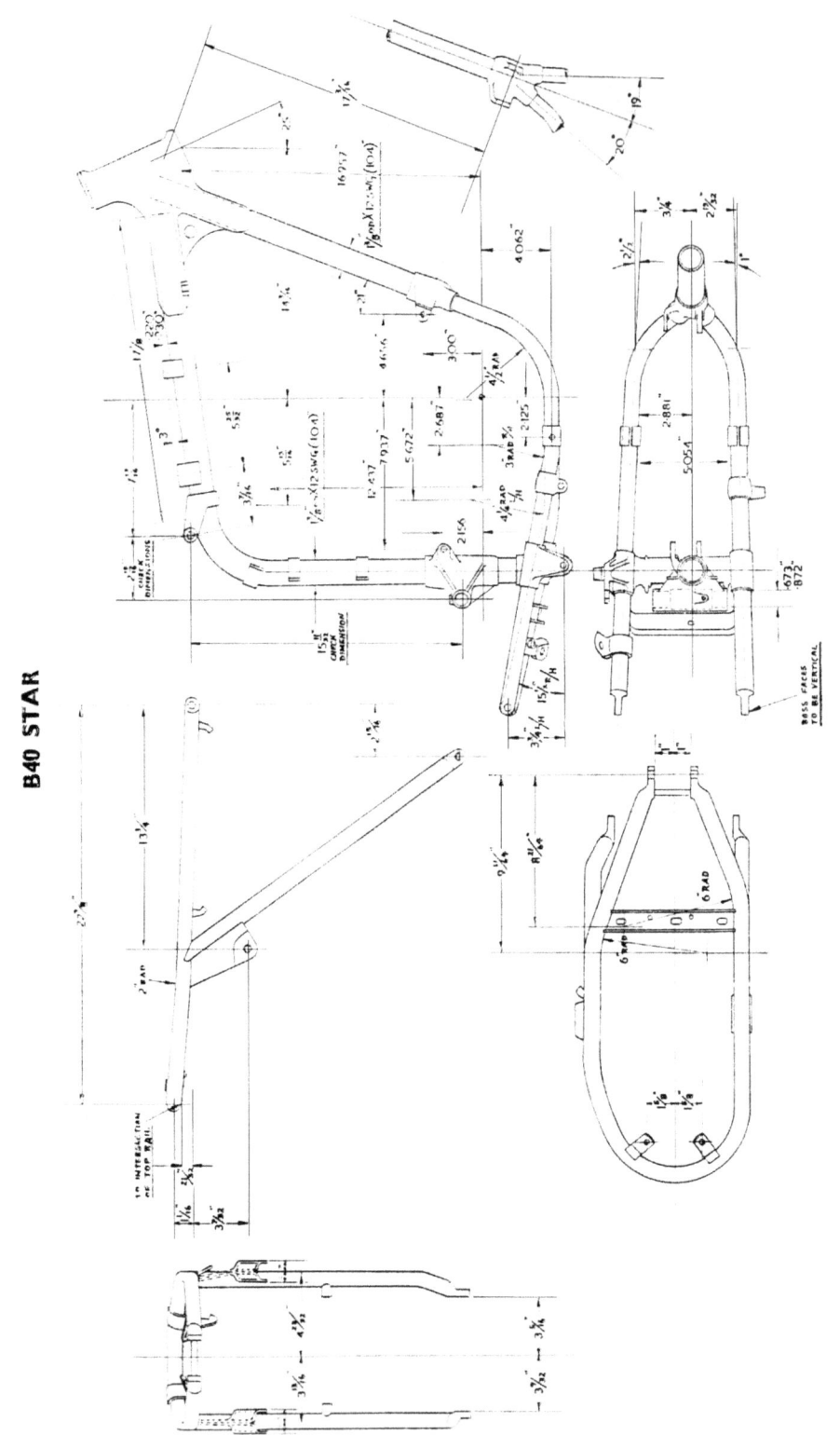

500 c.c. STAR AND 650 c.c. STAR MODELS A50 AND A65

B.S.A. Service Sheet No. 711

Revised Sept. 1958.

SERVICE TOOLS

for all

MOTOR CYCLES

1946 to 1958 Inclusive

Use in conjunction with
Service Sheet No. 711A
For Details of Models and Prices.

BSA SERVICE SHEET No. 711

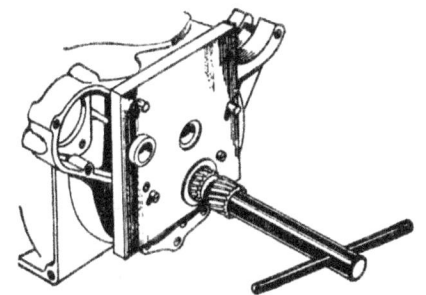

61-3281 Reaming Jig (mainshaft and camshaft gear bushes)
61-3275 Reaming Jig (mainshaft and camshaft gear bushes)

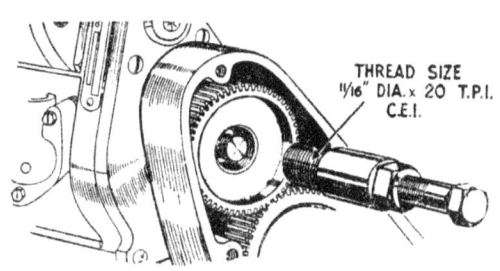

61-1903 Magdyno Driving Pinion Extractor Tool complete.
For Models fitted with Magdyno Lighting Equipment.

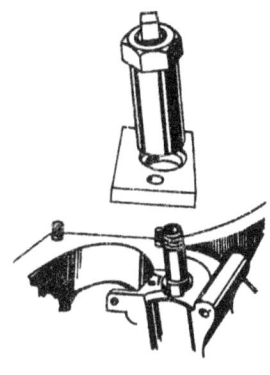

61-3069 Inlet Tappet Guide Extractor

61-3284 Mainshaft Bush Reamer
61-3285 Pilot for Jigs 61-3275
61-3286 Pilot for Jigs 61-3281
61-3287 Shell Reamer Holder
61-3288 Tommy Bar for 61-3287

61-3167 Reamer for use with 61-3162 61-3281 and 61-3275

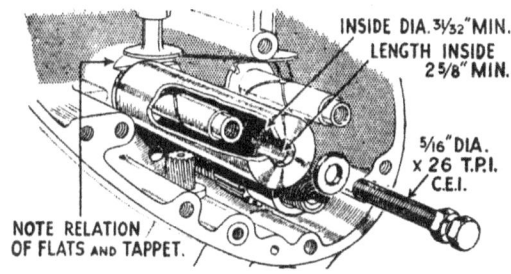

61-691 Cam Pinion Post Extractor

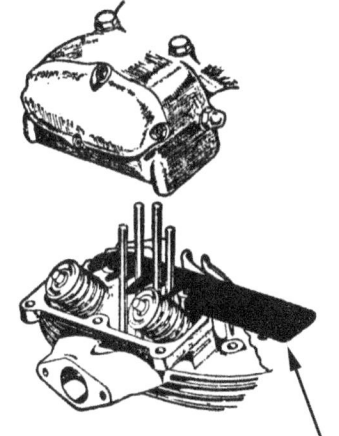

67-9114 Push Rod Assembly Tool

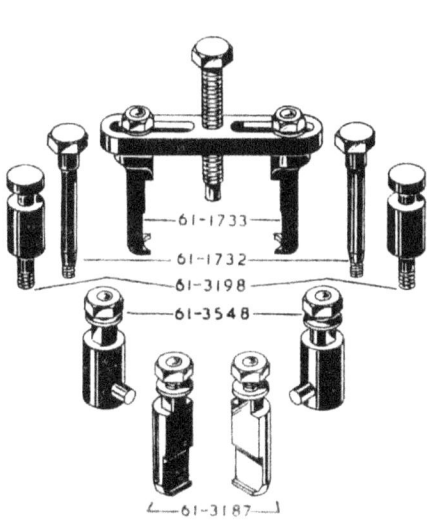

61-3256 Extractor Set Complete

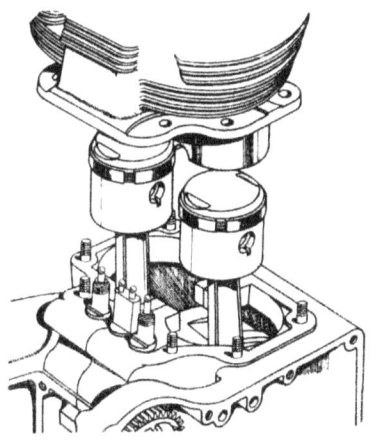

61-3061 Piston Ring Slipper
61-3334 Piston Ring Slipper,
61-3262 Piston Ring Slipper,
(2 per set)

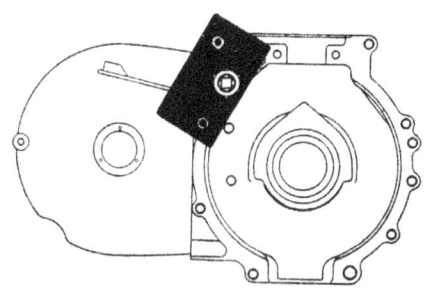

61-3159 Camshaft Bush Extractor

B.S.A. SERVICE SHEET No. 711—*continued*

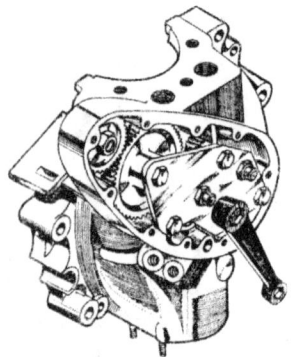

15-832 Mainshaft Nut Spanner

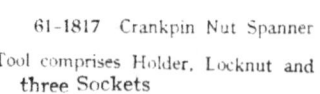

61-1817 Crankpin Nut Spanner

Tool comprises Holder, Locknut and three Sockets

Sockets for 61-1817
61-1754
61-1755
61-3228

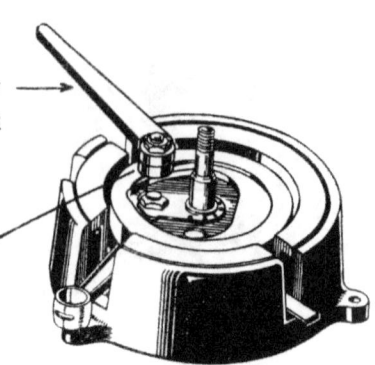

61-1751 Flywheel Bolster
61-1750 "   " Gauge Rod
61-1747 "   " Ring
61-1749 "   " "

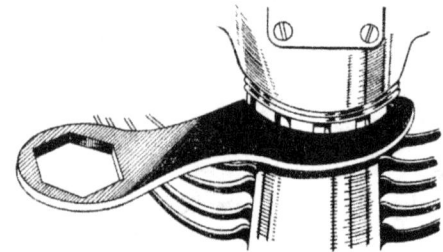

65-9243 C Spanner and Fork Top Nut Spanner

61-658 Gudgeon Pin Bush Extractor comprising Spindle with various size bushes.

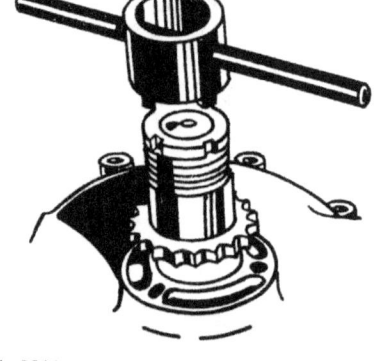

61-3220 Cush Drive Nut Tube Spanner

61-3305 Valve Seating Tool complete

Comprising Tommy Bar 61-3291
Holder 61-3290

Cutters
61-3298 .. 1 7/16" × 45° × 20°
61-3299 .. 1 1/2" × 45° × 20°
61-3300 .. 1 5/8" × 45° × 20°
61-3301 .. 1 3/4" × 45° × 20°
61-3302 .. 1 7/8" × 45° × 20°

Pilots
61-3293 .. 5/16"
61-3294 .. .350"
61-3295 .. 3/8"

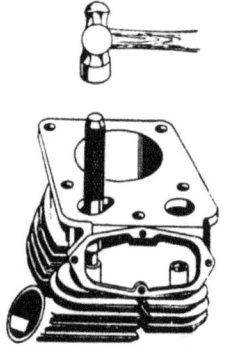

61-3263 61-3264 61-3265 61-3267 61-3268
Valve Guide fitting and extracting punches

65-9240 Valve Grinding Tool

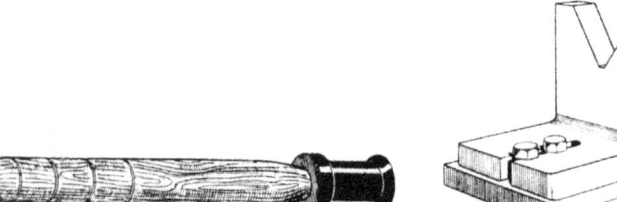

61-692 Vee Block and Base Plate

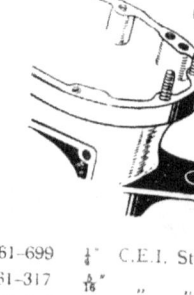

61-699 1/4" C.E.I. Stud Boxes
61-317 5/16"   "   "   "
61-545 3/8"   "   "   "

B.S.A. SERVICE SHEET No. 711—continued

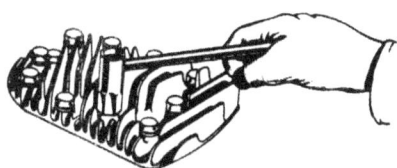

61-3049 Cylinder Head Spanner

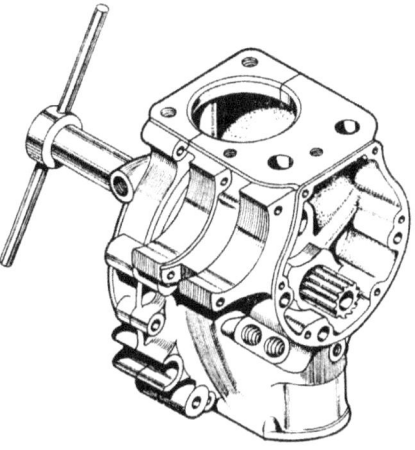

61-1932 Reamer and Holder complete (mainshaft bush)
61-1922 Reamer for 61-1932

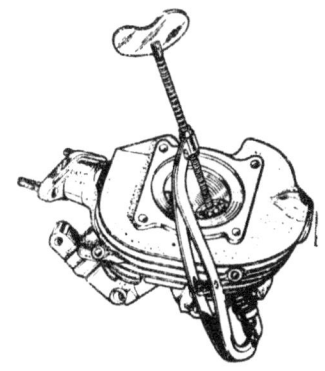

61-3340 Valve Spring Compressor with Adaptor
Models M33
"B" Group, "A" Group, and Sunbeam

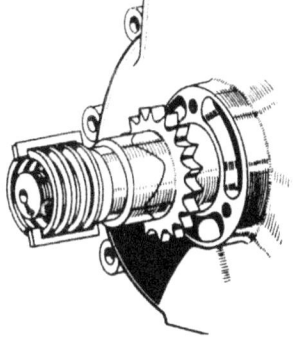

61-1822 Cush Drive Spring Assembly Tool
For holding Spring compressed whilst fitting Lockring.
(2 per set)

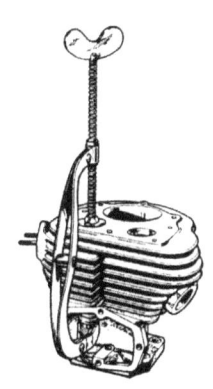

61-3340 Valve Spring Compressor
Models C10, C11, M20, M21
(Use without adaptor)

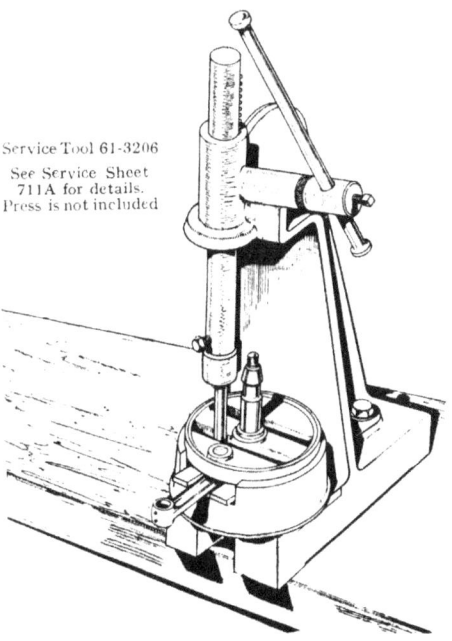

Service Tool 61-3206
See Service Sheet 711A for details.
Press is not included

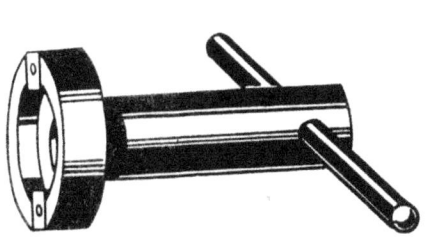

61-3052 Cylinder Base Nut Spanner

61-3257 Gearbox Sprocket Locknut Spanner,
61-3258 Gearbox Sprocket Locknut Spanner,

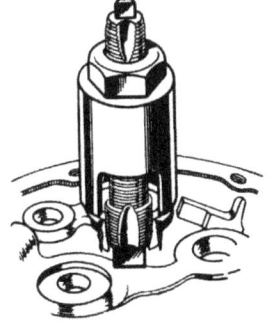

61-3185 Bush Extractor

61-3246 Gudgeon Pin Bush Reamer (.4687")
61-3367 Gudgeon Pin Bush Reamer (.625")
61-3556 Gudgeon Pin Bush Reamer (.6875")
61-3366 Gudgeon Pin Bush Reamer (.750")
61-3580 Gudgeon Pin Bush Reamer (.4375")
61-3581 Gudgeon Pin Bush Reamer (.5625")

B.S.A. SERVICE SHEET No. 711—continued

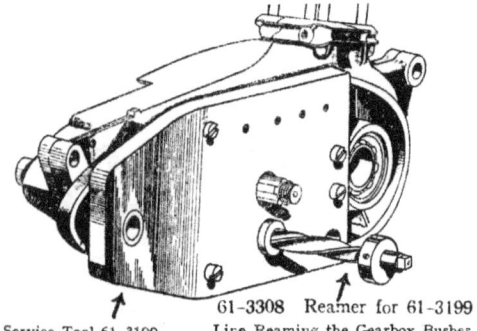

Service Tool 61-3199. 61-3308 Reamer for 61-3199
Line Reaming the Gearbox Bushes

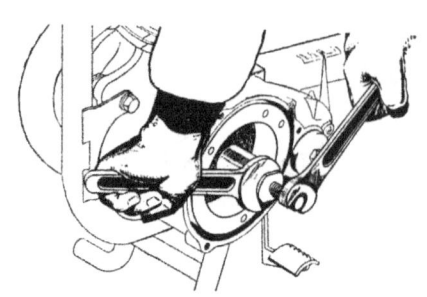

61-3188 Generator Flywheel Removal Tool (Wico Pacy)
90-297   Generator Flywheel Removal Tool (Lucas)

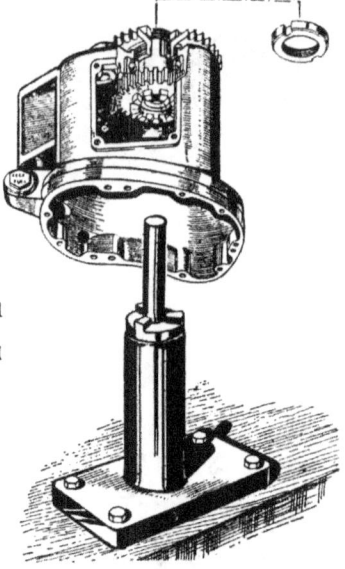

61-3064 Pinion Sleeve Extractor

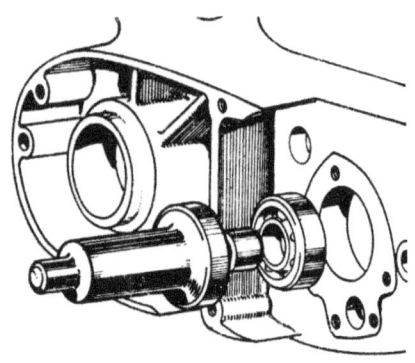

61-3214 Ballrace Pilot (gearbox pinion bearing)
61-3215 Ballrace Pilot (gearbox mainshaft bearing)

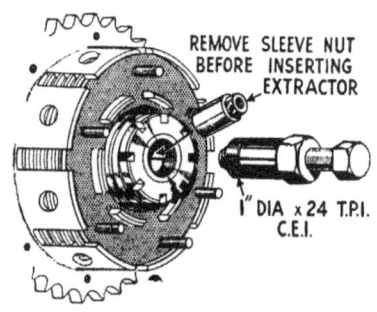

61-1912 Clutch Extractor Tool

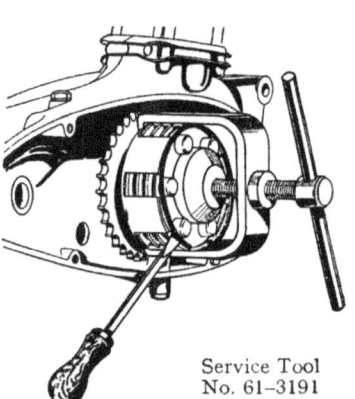

Service Tool No. 61-3191
Removing the Clutch Plate Circlip

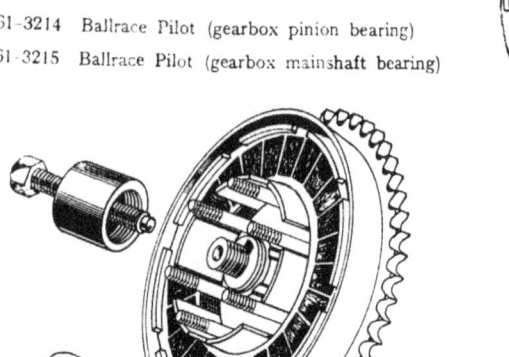

61-3362 Clutch Extractor Tool

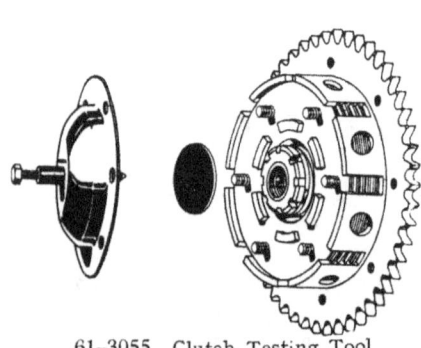

61-3055 Clutch Testing Tool

61-3212 Ballrace Pilot for large engine bearing
61-3213 Ballrace Pilot for small engine bearing

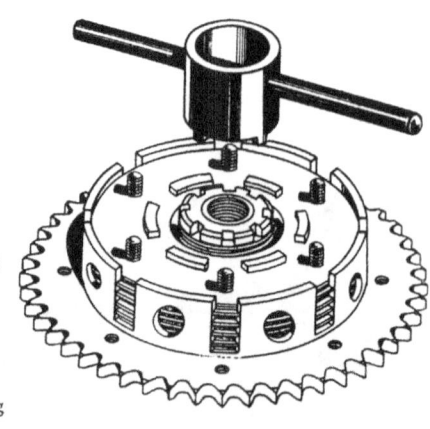

61-1915 Clutch Spring Nut Tube Spanner.

144

B.S.A. SERVICE SHEET No. 711—continued

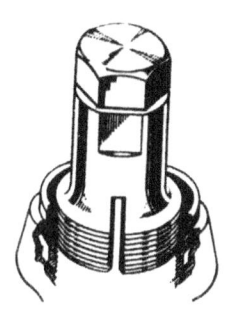

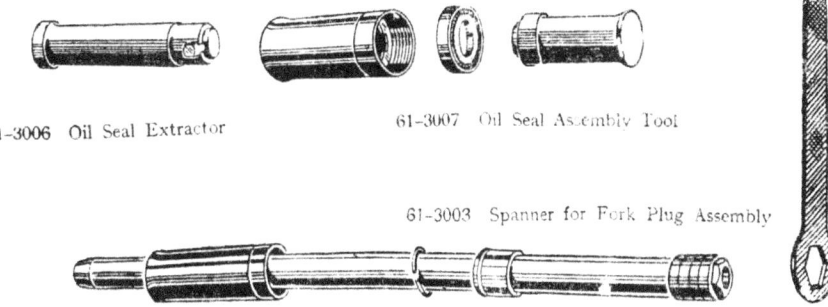

61-3006 Oil Seal Extractor

61-3007 Oil Seal Assembly Tool

61-3003 Spanner for Fork Plug Assembly

61-3060 Ballrace Extractor (steering head) for all 3/16" balls

61-3063 Ballrace Extractor (steering head) for all 1/4" balls

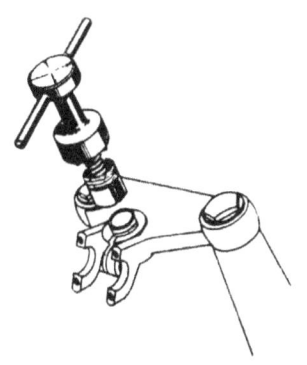

61-3002 Assembly Tool for Adjuster Sleeve
61-3008 Assembly Tool for Adjuster Sleeve

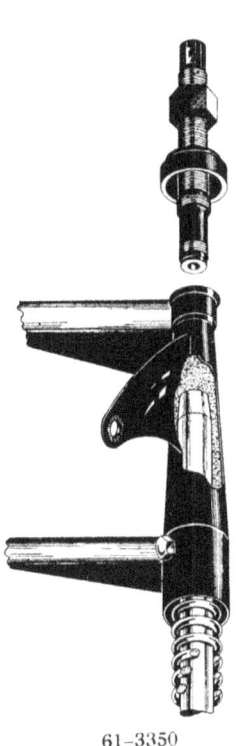

61-3350 Fork Shaft Dismantling and Assembly Tool

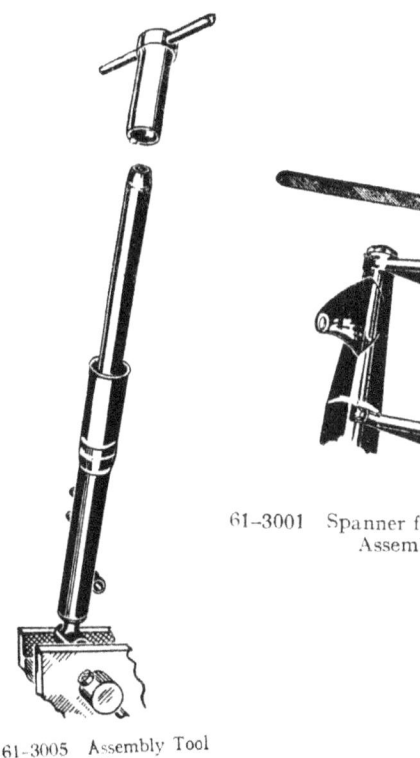

61-3005 Assembly Tool for Oil Seal Holder

61-3001 Spanner for Fork Top Nut Assembly

61-3222 Rear Suspension Strip and Assembly Tool

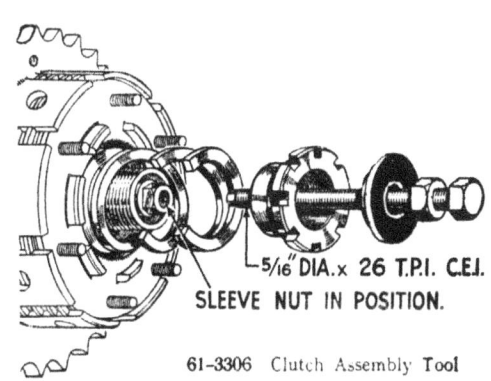

5/16" DIA. x 26 T.P.I. C.E.I. SLEEVE NUT IN POSITION.

61-3306 Clutch Assembly Tool

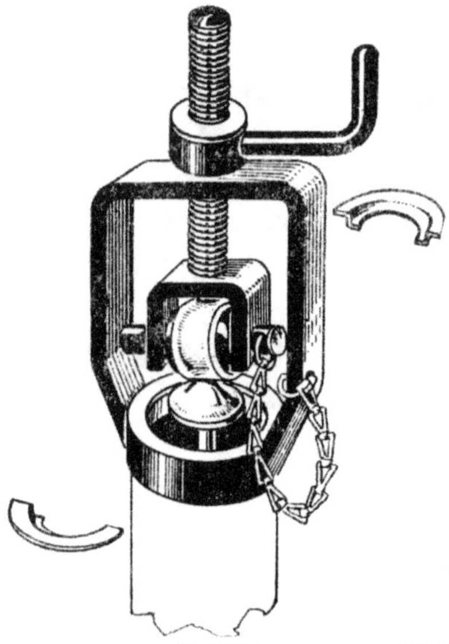

B.S.A. SERVICE SHEET No. 711—*continued*

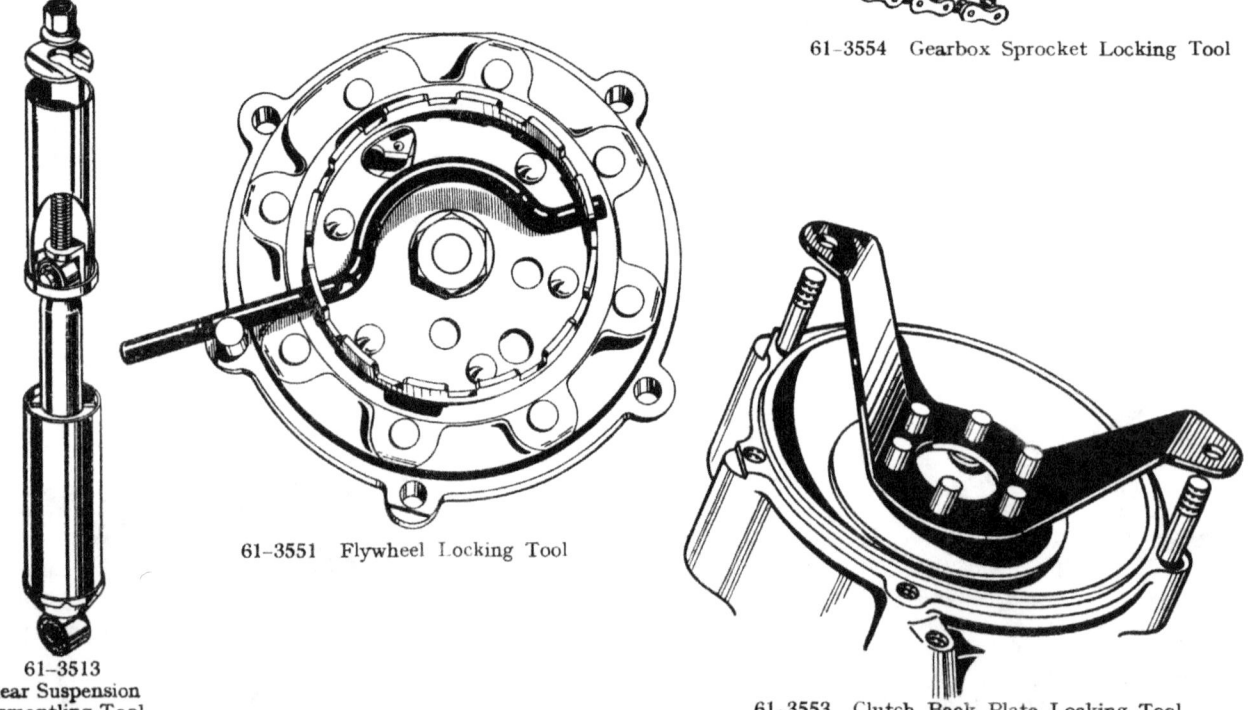

61-3503 Rear Suspension Dismantling Tool

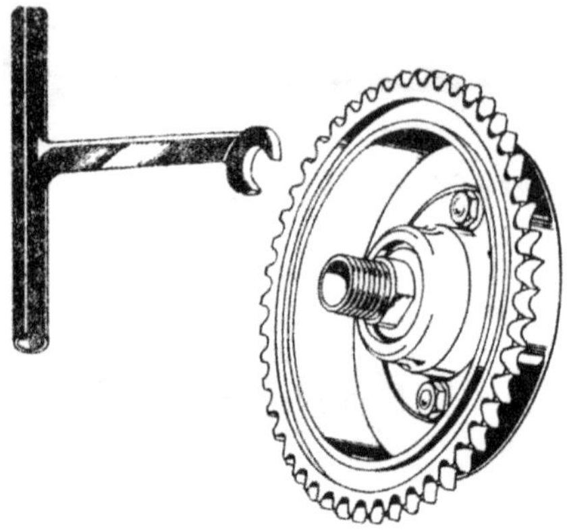

61-3217 Spanner for rear chain sprocket

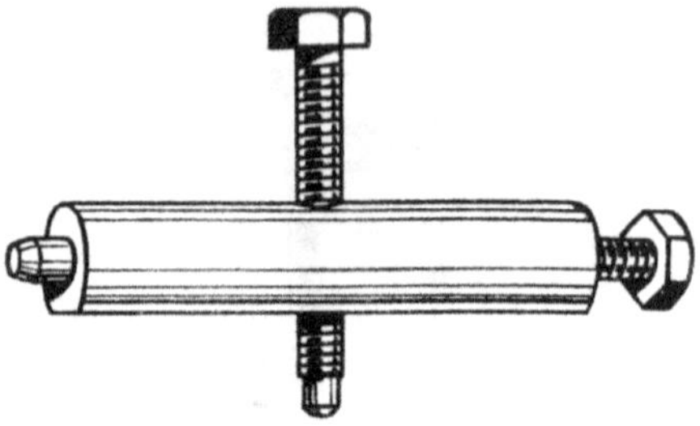

61-3540 Flywheel Removal Tool

61-3542 Wheel Bearing Nut Peg Spanner

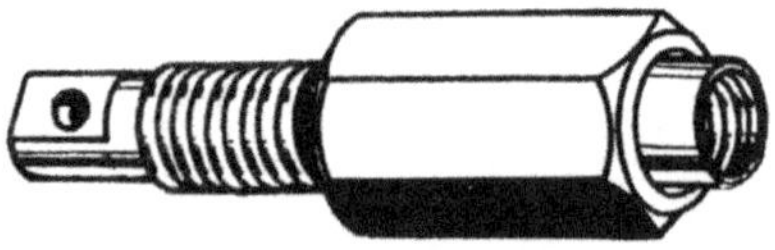

61-3536 Flywheel Assembly Tool

61-705 Spoke Nipple Key. (10 and 12 gauge)
61-773 Spoke Nipple Key (8 and 10 gauge)

61-3552 Starter Ratchet Circlip Assembly Tool

61-3554 Gearbox Sprocket Locking Tool

61-3513 Rear Suspension Dismantling Tool

61-3551 Flywheel Locking Tool

61-3553 Clutch Back Plate Locking Tool

B.S.A. SERVICE SHEET No. 711—*continued*

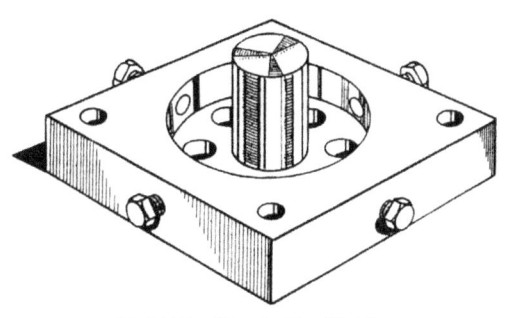
61-3499 Bench Die Holder

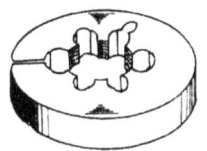
61-3483 Die

Tap

Die Nut

Part No.	Description	For
61-3574	Tap and Die Set in wooden case comprising tools listed below except 61-3483	General Workshop use
61-3575	Tap and Die Set in wooden case comprising all tools listed below	General Workshop use

TAPS.

Part No.	Taps.		For
61-3461	3/8" x 19 TPI B.S.P.	(R/H)	Petrol Tap Hole.
61-3462	3/8" x 20 TPI B.S.F.	(L/H)	Sunbeam Dynamo.
61-3463	7/16" x 20 TPI C.E.I.	(R/H)	General.
61-3464	1/2" x 20 TPI C.E.I.	(R/H)	General.
61-3502	9/16" x 20 TPI C.E.I.	(R/H)	General.
61-3465	9/16" x 20 TPI C.E.I.	(L/H)	Front Fork Spindle Hole.
61-3466	5/8" x 20 TPI C.E.I.	(R/H)	General.
61-3467	3/4" x 20 TPI C.E.I.	(R/H)	General.
65-3468	3/4" x 20 TPI B.S.W.	(R/H)	General.
61-3469	3/4" x 12 TPI B.S.F.	(L/H)	Sunbeam Rear Spindle Hole.
61-3470	7/8" x 20 TPI B.S.W.	(R/H)	Rear Suspension Shaft.
61-3471	1-1/16" x 20 TPI C.E.I.	(R/H)	Fork Shaft Top.
61-3472	1 1/8" x 28 TPI B.S.W.	(R/H)	Fork Shaft Bottom.
61-3473	1 1/2" x 20 TPI B.S.W.	(R/H)	Filler Caps.
61-3531	14 mm. x 1.25 mm.	(R/H)	14 mm. Spark Plug Hole
61-3533	1.250" x 20 TPI B.S.W.	(R/H)	Bantam Fork Tube (90-5021)

DIES.

Part No.	Dies.		For
61-3474	7/16" x 20 TPI C.E.I.	(R/H)	General.
61-3475	1/2" x 20 TPI C.E.I.	(R/H)	General.
61-3476	9/16" x 20 TPI C.E.I.	(R/H)	Gearbox Mainshaft.
61-3477	9/16" x 20 TPI C.E.I.	(L/H)	"A" Group Mainshaft.
61-3478	5/8" x 20 TPI C.E.I.	(R/H)	General.
61-3479	3/4" x 20 TPI C.E.I.	(R/H)	General.
61-3480	3/4" x 12 TPI B.S.F.	(L/H)	Sunbeam Rear Spindle.
61-3481	1" x 24 TPI C.E.I.	(R/H)	Fork Stem.
61-3482	1.120" x 24 TPI C.E.I.	(R/H)	Fork Stem.
61-3483	1 7/8" x 28 TPI WHIT.	(R/H)	Fork Sliding Tube Top.
61-3499	Bench Die Holder (for use with 61-3483)		

B.S.A. MOTOR CYCLES LTD.
Service Dept., Birmingham 11
Printed in England

B.S.A. Service Sheet No. 711A

Revised Sept., 1958

PRICE LIST
for
SERVICE TOOLS
1946 to 1958 Inclusive

Use in conjunction with Service Sheet No. 711

Part No.	Description	Used on Model	Retail Price Per Unit £ s. d.
15-832	Rear Hub Nut Spanner	A, B, C and M	4 5
61-317	Stud Box 5/16" c.e.i.	General	3 0
61-545	Stud Box 3/8" c.e.i.	General	3 0
61-658	Gudgeon Pin Bush Extractor	All Models	10 6
61-691	Cam Pinion Post Extractor	B and M	4 6
61-692	Flywheel "V" Blocks (used with 61-1821)	B, C and M	2 5 4
61-696	Socket Nut (used with 61-1817)	B, C and M	1 5
61-698	Crankpin Nut Spanner only (used with 61-1817)	B, C and M	1 1 0
61-699	Stud Box 1/4" c.e.i.	General	3 0
61-705	Nipple Key (10 and 12 gauge)	General	3 10
61-773	Nipple Key (8 and 10 gauge)	General	3 10
61-1747	Flywheel Bolster Ring	C Group	4 1 3
61-1749	Flywheel Bolster Ring	B and M 500 c.c.	4 1 3
61-1750	Flywheel Bolster Gauge Rod (2 per set)	B, C and M	7 7
61-1751	Flywheel Bolster	B, C and M	3 11 9
61-1754	Crankpin Nut Socket (used with 61-1817)	C Group	8 0
61-1755	Crankpin Nut Socket (used with 61-1817)	B and M	8 0
61-1817	Crankpin Nut Spanner complete	B, C and M	2 7 6
	Comprising:—		
	61-696 Socket Nut		1 5
	61-698 Spanner		1 1 0
	61-1754 Socket	C Group	8 0
	61-1755 Socket	B and M	8 0
	61-3228 Socket	Gold Star	9 1

BSA SERVICE TOOLS

Part No.	Description	Used on Model	Per Unit Retail Price
			£ s. d.
61-1821	"V" Block Base Plate (used with 61-692)	B, C and M	1 10 3
61-1822	Cush Drive Spring Assembly Tool (2 per set)	A, B, C and M	4 6
61-1903	Magdyno Drive Pinion Extractor	B and M	3 0
61-1912	Clutch Extractor	M to 1948	6 0
61-1915	Clutch Spring Nut Tube Spanner	M to 1948	4 6
61-1922	Reamer (used with 61-1932) (mainshaft bush)	C Group	3 5 0
61-1932	Reamer and Holder complete (used with 61-1922)	C Group	4 4 9
61-3001	Fork Top Nut Spanner (front fork)	A, B, C and M	13 6
61-3002	Adjuster Sleeve Assembly Tool (steering head)	B, C and M	12 1
61-3003	Fork Plug Spanner (front fork)	A, B, C and M	13 6
61-3005	Oil Seal Holder Assembly Tool (front fork)	A, B, C and M	1 1 2
61-3006	Oil Seal Extractor (front fork)	A, B, C and M	15 1
61-3007	Oil Seal Assembly Tool (front fork)	A, B, C and M	6 0
61-3008	Adjuster Sleeve Assembly Tool (steering head)	A7/10, S7/8	12 1
61-3049	Cylinder Head Spanner	M20/21	10 6
61-3052	Cylinder Base Nut Spanner	M20/21	1 1 2
61-3055	Clutch Testing Tool	M to 1948	15 1
61-3060	Steering Head Ballrace Extractor	For 3/16" Balls	8 3
61-3061	Piston Ring Slipper (2 per set)	A7 to 1950	7 6
61-3063	Steering Head Ballrace Extractor	For 1/4" Balls	8 3
61-3064	Pinion Sleeve Extractor	B, C and M	2 11 5
61-3069	Inlet Tappet Guide Extractor	A7 to 1950	7 7
61-3159	Camshaft Bush Extractor	A7, A10	12 8
61-3167	Camshaft Bush Reamer (used with 61-3275/81)	A Group	3 0 6
61-3185	Gearbox Bush Extractor	M Group	15 9
61-3188	Flywheel Magneto Removal Tool (Wico Pacy)	D1, D3 and D5	6 8
61-3191	Clutch Plate Circlip Removal Tool	D1, D3 and D5	1 10 3
61-3199	Gearbox Bush Line Reaming Plate (used with 61-3205)	D1, D3 and D5	2 1 6
61-3205	Layshaft Bush Reamer only (used with 61-3199)	D1, D3 and D5	2 1 11
61-3206	Flywheel Dismantling and Assembly Tool	D1, D3 and D5	3 15 6

Comprising:—
    61-3207   Jig Body
    61-3208(2) Dismantling Bar
    61-3209   Dismantling Punch
    61-3210   Assembly Bridge
(*Note:*— Press as illustrated is not included).

Part No.	Description	Used on Model	Per Unit Retail Price
61-3212	Ballrace Pilot for large engine bearing	D1, D3 and D5	7 7
61-3213	Ballrace Pilot for small engine bearing	D1, D3 and D5	6 8
61-3214	Ballrace Pilot for gearbox pinion bearing	D1, D3 and D5	7 7
61-3215	Ballrace Pilot for gearbox mainshaft bearing	D1, D3 and D5	6 8
61-3217	Spanner for rear wheel sprocket	A7, A10	11 3
61-3220	Tube Spanner for cush drive nut	A, B, C and M	3 6
61-3222	Rear Suspension Strip and Assembly Tool	A, B and M	13 6
61-3228	Crankpin Nut Socket (used with 61-1817)	B32/4 G/S	9 1
61-3246	Reamer Gudgeon Pin Bush	D1, D3	14 6
61-3256	Extractor Set complete	All Models	1 12 7

Comprising:—
    61-351(1)   Plate
    61-776(1)   Bolt
    61-1732(2) Extractor Leg (A Group cam pinion)
    61-1733(2) Extractor Leg (engine pinion B, C and M).
    61-3187(2) Extractor Leg (crankshaft pinion A7/10).
    61-3198(2) Extractor Leg (engine sprocket etc., D, C and A).
    61-3548(2) Extractor Leg (Dandy flywheel)

BSA SERVICE TOOLS

Part No.	Description	Used on Model	Retail Price Per Unit
			£ s. d.
61-3257	Gearbox Sprocket Locknut Spanner	A, B and M	15 1
61-3258	Gearbox Sprocket Locknut Spanner	C	15 1
61-3262	Piston Ring Slipper (2 per set)	A10	6 0
61-3263	Valve Guide Punch (used on B33/34, exhaust and G/Stars with .374 dia. valve stems).		3 0
61-3264	Valve Guide Punch (comprising 61-3265/66 and 61-3307)	C10 In. and Ex.	12 8
61-3265	Valve Guide Punch (B31/32 inlet, A7/10, C11, C12 inlet and exhaust and G/Stars with .310" dia. valve stems)		6 0
61-3267	Valve Guide Punch (comprising 61-3268/9/70)	M20, M21 In. and Ex.	8 3
61-3268	Valve Guide Punch (B31/32 exhaust, B33/34 inlet and G/Stars with .348" dia. valve stems)		6 0
61-3275	Mainshaft and Camshaft Bush Reaming Jig	A7 to 1950	2 12 11
61-3281	Mainshaft and Camshaft Bush Reaming Jig	A10, AA7 onwards	2 12 11
61-3284	Reamer (mainshaft used with 61-3275/81)	A7, A10	4 6 2
61-3285	Pilot for 61-3275	A7 to 1950	15 1
61-3286	Pilot for 61-3281	A10, AA7 onwards	15 1
61-3287	Reamer Holder (used with 61-3284)	A7, A10	9 1
61-3290	Valve Seat Cutter Holder	A, B, C and M	5 3
61-3293	Valve Seat Cutter Pilot ($\frac{5}{16}$")	A, B and C	6 8
61-3294	Valve Seat Cutter Pilot (.350")	B and M	6 8
61-3295	Valve Seat Cutter Pilot (.375")	B, and M33	6 8
61-3298	Valve Seat Cutter ($1\frac{7}{16}$" dia. x 45° x 20°)	A7 and C	2 6 2
61-3299	Valve Seat Cutter ($1\frac{1}{2}$" dia. x 45° x 20°)	A10 and C	2 6 2
61-3300	Valve Seat Cutter ($1\frac{5}{8}$" dia. x 45° x 20°)	B	2 6 2
61-3301	Valve Seat Cutter ($1\frac{3}{4}$" dia. x 45° x 20°)	B and M	2 6 2
61-3302	Valve Seat Cutter ($1\frac{7}{8}$" dia. x 45° x 20°)	B and M	2 6 2
61-3305	Valve Seating Tool complete	A, B, C and M	12 16 2
61-3306	Clutch Assembly Tool	M to 1948	3 0
61-3308	Reamer for 61-3199 (comprising 61-3205 and 61-3309)	D1, and D3	2 8 1
61-3311	Crankshaft Balance Weight (18 ozs., 12 drms.)	A7 1951 onwards	15 1
61-3312	Crankshaft Balance Weight (16 ozs., 14 drms.)	A7 to 1951	15 1
61-3334	Piston Ring Slipper (2 per set)	A7 1951 onwards	6 0
61-3340	Valve Spring Compressor complete	A, B, C and M	1 1 2
61-3350	Front Fork Dismantling and Assembly Tool	A, B, C, M and S7/8	15 1
61-3362	Clutch Extractor Tool	A, B, C and M 1949 onwards	6 8
61-3366	Gudgeon Pin Bush Reamer (.750")	B, M and A10	1 1 10
61-3367	Gudgeon Pin Bush Reamer (.625")	C only	1 2 8
61-3487	Valve Guide Assembly Punch	S7 and S8	15 1
61-3497	Crankshaft Balance Weight (19 ozs. 8 drms.)	A10R/R and S/R	13 9
61-3499	Bench Die Holder (used with 61-3483)	A, B, C and M	2 18 6
61-3503	Rear Suspension Dismantling Tool	A and B S/A	1 17 10
61-3513	Rear Suspension Dismantling Tool	C12 and D3 S/A	1 14 4
61-3536	Flywheel Assembly Tool	Dandy	5 6
61-3540	Flywheel Removal Tool	Dandy	6 3
61-3542	Wheel Bearing Nut Peg Spanner	A and B, S/A	10 4
61-3548	Flywheel Removal Tool (2) (used with 61-3256)	Dandy	4 7
61-3551	Flywheel Locking Tool	Dandy	1 2
61-3552	Starter Ratchet Circlip Assembly Tool	Dandy	5 3
61-3553	Clutch Back Plate Locking Tool	Dandy	9 2
61-3554	Gearbox Sprocket Locking Tool	Dandy	5 5
61-3556	Gudgeon Pin Bush Reamer ($\frac{11}{16}$")	A7	1 17 10
61-3558	Locking Ring Spanner	8" Brake	11 10
61-3580	Gudgeon Pin Bush Reamer ($\frac{7}{16}$")	Dandy	1 0 0
61-3581	Gudgeon Pin Bush Reamer ($\frac{9}{16}$")	D5	1 6 10
65-9240	Valve Grinding Tool	A, B, C and M	1 10
65-9243	Combined "C" and Fork Top Nut spanner	A, B, C and M	1 10
67-9114	Push Rod Assembly Tool	A7/10 1951 onwards	1 5
90-297	Lucas Rotor Removal Tool	D1	1 3

BSA SERVICE TOOLS

Part No.	Description	Used on Models	Retail Price
			£ s. d.
61-3574	Tap and Die Set in wood case comprising taps and dies listed below except 61-3483	General	23 15 0
61-3575	Tap and Die Set in wood case comprising taps and dies listed below	General	32 7 0

TAPS

Part No.	Taps	Description	Retail Price
			£ s. d.
61-3461	3/8" x 19 T.P.I. B.S.P. R/H	Petrol Tap Hole	7 7
61-3462	3/8" x 20 T.P.I. B.S.F. L/H	Sunbeam Dynamo	7 7
61-3463	7/16" x 20 T.P.I. C.E.I. R/H	General	13 1
61-3464	1/2" x 20 T.P.I. C.E.I. R/H	General	14 6
61-3502	9/16" x 20 T.P.I. C.E.I. R/H	General	18 7
61-3465	9/16" x 20 T.P.I. C.E.I. L/H	Front Fork Spindle Hole	1 0 0
61-3466	5/8" x 20 T.P.I. C.E.I. R/H	General	17 3
61-3467	3/4" x 20 T.P.I. C.E.I. R/H	General	18 7
61-3468	3/4" x 20 T.P.I. B.S.W. R/H	General	18 7
61-3469	3/4" x 12 T.P.I. B.S.F. L/H	Sunbeam Rear Spindle Hole	1 0 0
61-3470	7/8" x 20 T.P.I. B.S.W. R/H	Rear Suspension Shaft	1 7 6
61-3471	1 1/16" x 20 T.P.I. C.E.I. R/H	Fork Shaft Top	1 5 6
61-3472	1 1/8" x 28 T.P.I. B.S.W. R/H	Fork Shaft	1 14 4
61-3473	1 1/2" x 20 T.P.I. B.S.W. R/H	Filler Cap	2 14 7
61-3531	14 mm. x 1.25 mm. R/H	Spark Plug	1 0 7
61-3533	1.250" x 20 T.P.I. B.S.W. R/H	D1 Fork Tube	1 11 0

DIES

Part No.	Dies	Description	Retail Price
			£ s. d.
61-3474	7/16" x 20 T.P.I. C.E.I. R/H	General	11 0
61-3475	1/2" x 20 T.P.I. C.E.I. R/H	General	12 4
61-3476	9/16" x 20 T.P.I. C.E.I. R/H	Gearbox Mainshaft	13 9
61-3477	9/16" x 20 T.P.I. C.E.I. L/H	A Group Mainshaft	17 3
61-3478	5/8" x 20 T.P.I. C.E.I. R/H	General	13 9
61-3479	3/4" x 20 T.P.I. C.E.I. R/H	General	18 7
61-3480	3/4" x 12 T.P.I. B.S.F. L/H	Sunbeam Rear Spindle	1 2 0
61-3481	1" x 24 T.P.I. C.E.I. R/H	Fork Stem	1 4 1
61-3482	1.120" x 24 T.P.I. C.E.I. R/H	Fork Stem	1 13 9
61-3483	1 7/8" x 28 T.P.I. Whit. R/H (Used with holder 61-3499)	Fork Sliding Tube Top	9 9 1

B.S.A. Motor Cycles Ltd., Service Department, Birmingham 11

Printed in England. Sept. 1958

B.S.A. Service Sheet No. 711B

Supplement to No. 711 and 711A

July 1960

SERVICE TOOLS

for

MOTOR CYCLES

B.S.A. SERVICE SHEET No. 711B (contd.)

Removing the Clutch Centre with Extractor No. 61-3583 (Model C15).

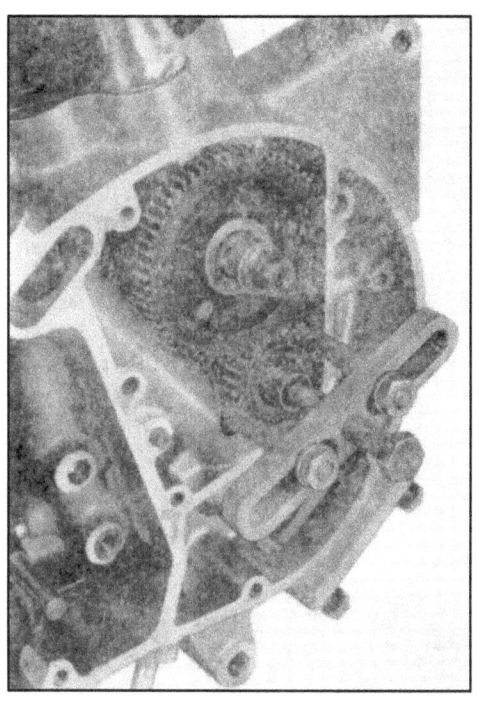

Removing the Crankshaft Pinion with Extractor No. 61-3681 using Legs No. 61-3588 (fitted with Legs 61-3585 for removing the Worm Wheel) (Model C15).

Parting the Flywheels using Bolster 61-3589, Stripping Bars 61-3590 and Punch 61-3601 (Model C15).

Assembling the Crankpin into the Gear Side Flywheel using Locating Gauge No. 61-3597 and Punch No. 61-3601 (Model C15).

B.S.A. SERVICE SHEET No. 711B (contd.)

Assembling the Drive Side Flywheel on to the Gear Side, using Bolster No. 61-3589, Bridge Piece No. 61-3591 and Punch No. 61-3601 (Model C15).

Flywheel Truing Sleeve No. 61-3592 used with Drive Side bearing on "V" blocks No. 61-692 (Model C15).

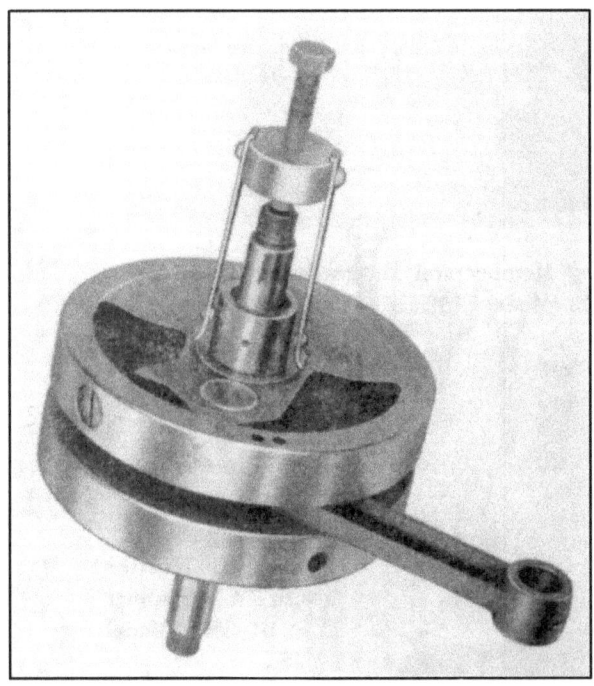

Removing the Gear Side Sleeve with Tool No. 61-3593 (Model C15).

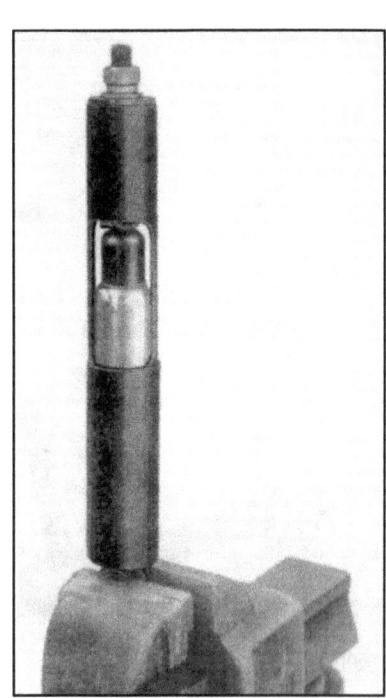

Dismantling the Rear Damper with Tool No. 61-3642 (for Models C15 and D7).

B.S.A. SERVICE SHEET No. 711B (contd.)

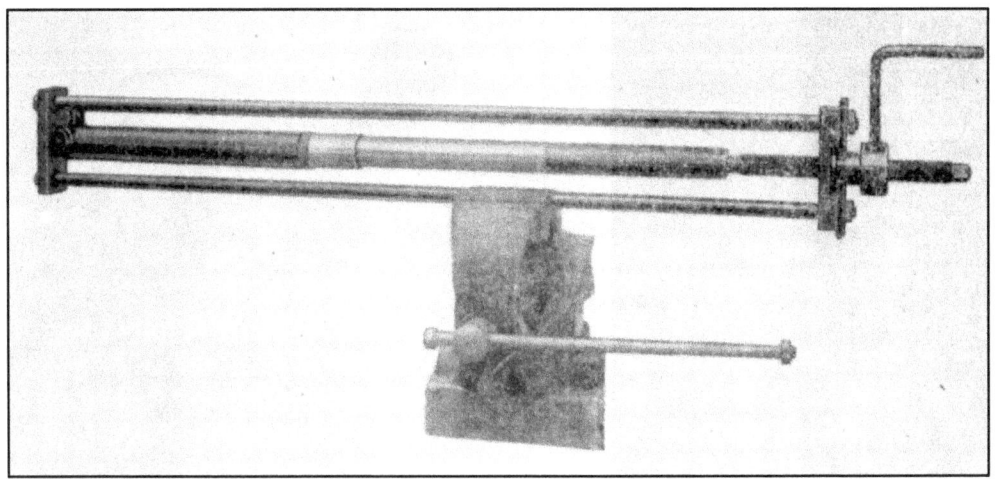

Withdrawing the Fork Main Member and Bushes from the Sliding Member using Tool No. 61-3587.

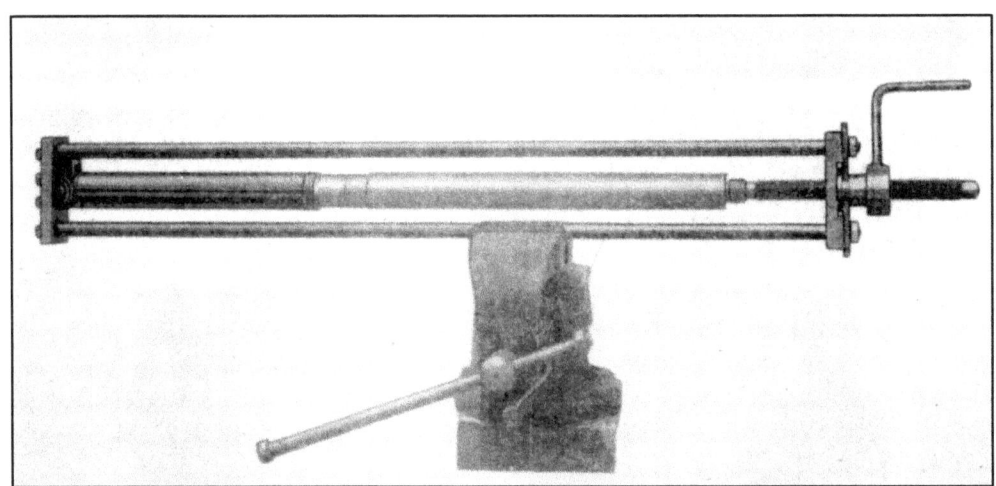

Reassembling the Fork Main Member, Sliding Member and Bushes using Tools No. 61-3587 and 61-3602 (Model C15).

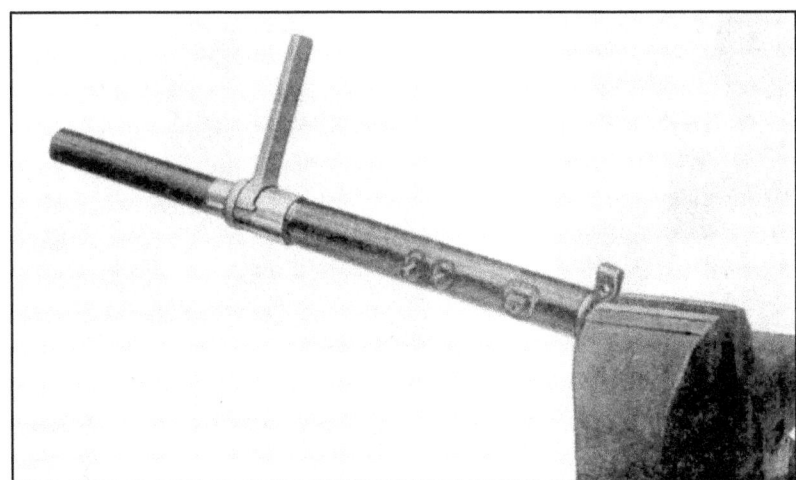

Removing the Fork Oil Seal Holder with "C" Spanner No. 61-3586 (Model C15).

B.S.A. SERVICE SHEET No. 711B (contd.)

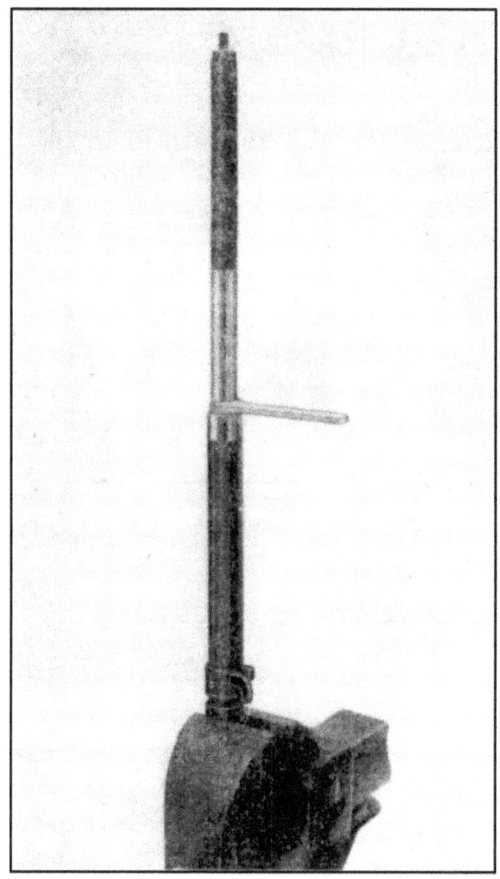

Taking off the Fork Leg Oil Seal Holder with Tool No. 3633 (Model D7).

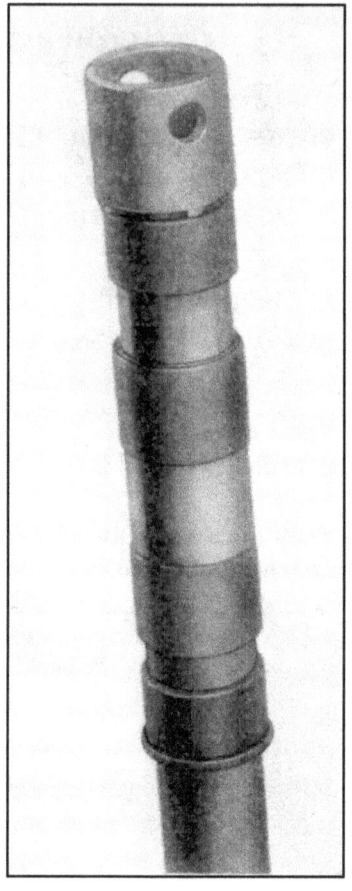

(Model C15). Removing the Fork Leg Bottom Nut with Dog Spanner No. 61-3606 (Tommy Bar not supplied).

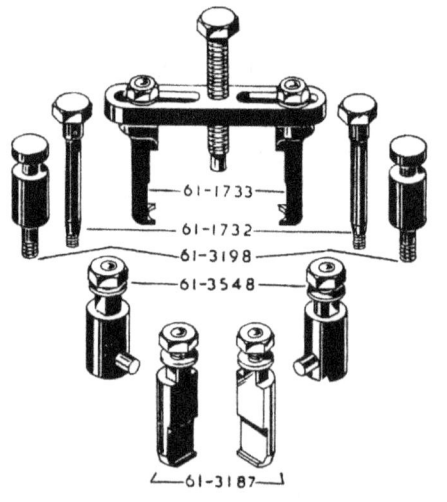

Pinion Extractor showing some of the special Legs.

PINION EXTRACTOR SETS

A Group	Part No. 61-3676
B and M Groups	Part No. 61-3677
C Group (excepting C15)	Part No. 61-3678
C15	Part No. 61-3681
D Group	Part No. 61-3679
Dandy	Part No. 61-3680
Complete Set	Part No. 61-3256

Details of comprising parts and applications are given overleaf.

B.S.A. SERVICE SHEET No. 711B (contd.)

COMPRISING PARTS OF EXTRACTOR SETS

61-3676 = 61-351 Plate, 61-776 Bolt, 61-1732 Leg (2), 61-3187 Leg (2), 61-3198 Leg (2).
61-3677 = 61-351 Plate, 61-776 Bolt, 61-1733 Leg (2).
61-3678 = 61-351 Plate, 61-776 Bolt, 61-1732 Leg (2), 61-1733 Leg (2), 61-3198 Leg (2).
61-3679 = 61-351 Plate, 61-776 Bolt, 61-3198 Leg (2).
61-3680 = 61-351 Plate, 61-776 Bolt, 61-3548 Leg (2).
61-3681 = 61-351 Plate, 61-776 Bolt, 61-3585 Leg (2), 61-3588 Leg (2).

These extractors are extremely useful for the removal of timing, worm or other gears, the legs being specially designed for the particular models.

They can also be used for other jobs of a like nature where a puller is required. All the legs are interchangeable and can be purchased separately if required.

61-358 GUDGEON PIN BUSH EXTRACTOR

is now cancelled and replaced by 61-3672.

This tool is now available for the individual models as detailed below:—

Tool No.	Model	Comprising
61-3651	—	Holder, Rod and Nut only.
61-3652	A7, A10	61-3651, and Bushes 61-3319/20.
61-3653	B Group	61-3651, and Bushes 61-3654/5.
61-3656	C10, C11, C12	61-3651, and Bushes 61-3657/8.
61-3659	C15, A7 (Steel Rod)	61-3651, and Bushes 61-3660/1.
61-3662	D1, D3	61-3651, and Bushes 61-3663/4.
61-3665	D5, D7	61-3651, and Bushes 61-3666/7.
61-3668	M20, M21	61-3651, and Bushes 61-654/5.
61-3669	Dandy	61-3651, and Bushes 61-3670/71.

B.S.A. SERVICE SHEET No. 711B (contd.)

Using a piston Ring Slipper makes replacement easier.

Piston Ring Slippers (Terry).

Now available for the following models:—

61-5004	55-60 mm. Bore	Models D1, D3.
61-5051	60-65 mm. Bore	Models C10L, C11, C12, D5, D7.
61-3682	65-70 mm. Bore	Models A Group, C15.

Additional Tools not illustrated

61-5035 valve grinding tool (Suction type). This tool is similar to 65-9240 shown on Service Sheet No. 711 but is suitable for valves with $\frac{3}{4}$ in. to 1 in. diameter heads.

61-3673 clutch nut screwdriver, designed specially for the moded C15.

BSA SERVICE SHEET No. 712X

ALL GROUPS
FLYWHEEL BALANCING (STATIC)

Revised and Reprinted October 1956.
Revised May 1958.

Flywheel balancing should not be undertaken except by an expert mechanic, who is fully equipped with the tools described in this Service Sheet.

Unless very great care is exercised, excessive engine vibration may result from any change of balance, and unless extreme care is practised in flywheel drilling, flywheels may be seriously weakened.

All flywheel assemblies are accurately balanced before leaving the Works and there should be no need to re-balance when fitting new big end assemblies unless the difference in weight between the old and new assembly is more than 1 to $1\frac{3}{4}$ozs.

When a fabricated crankshaft is employed as on the "C", "B" and "M" Group models, the method of flywheel truing is described in Service Sheet No. 607 in the case of "M" group machines and No. 305 in the case of "B" group and No. 407 - 414 - 424 - 424A for "C" group machines.

The equipment required for balancing is a drilling machine and knife edge rollers (see Fig. X10) which must be set up perfectly horizontal and sufficiently high to allow the flywheels to revolve with the Con Rod hanging.

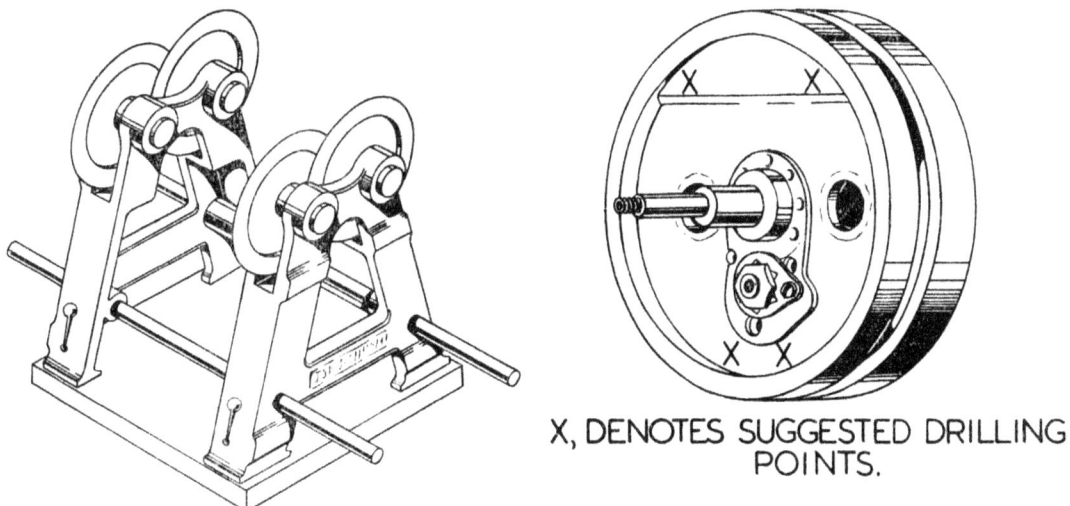

Fig. X10. Knife Edge Rollers.   Fig. X11. "B" and "M" Group Flywheels.

X, DENOTES SUGGESTED DRILLING POINTS.

For balancing purposes a small weight equivalent to part of the reciprocating weight must be attached to the small end of the Con Rod. A table of these weights is given below.

Place the assembly on the knife edges and allow to revolve till it stops, mark the lowest spot with chalk and check again two or three times.

To find the amount of the out-of-balance apply plasticine to the rim of the wheels diametrically opposite the heaviest point until the wheels remain stationary when placed in any position.

The wheels must now be drilled at the heaviest spot to remove metal equal to the weight of plasticine. Care must be taken to drill each wheel equally (see Fig. X11).

B.S.A. Service Sheet No. 712x (continued).

BALANCING "A" GROUP FLYWHEELS.

A group flywheels are treated similarly to the single cylinder models except that the Con Rods are not fitted, a balance weight being attached to each crank pin. These are available as Service Tools, 61-3310 for A7, 61-3312 for A7 after Engine No. AA7-101, 61-3311 for A10 and 61-3497 for A10 Road Rocket. New bolts and nuts must be used to secure the flywheel and the ends of the bolts peined over after locking.

Drilling is carried out on the periphery of the flywheel instead of the webs and care must be taken to keep the holes central and not too deep, the maximum depth should not be more than 3/16" (see Fig. X12). It is preferable to start with a smaller diameter hole which can be opened out if necessary, rather than a large diameter to then find that too much metal has been removed.

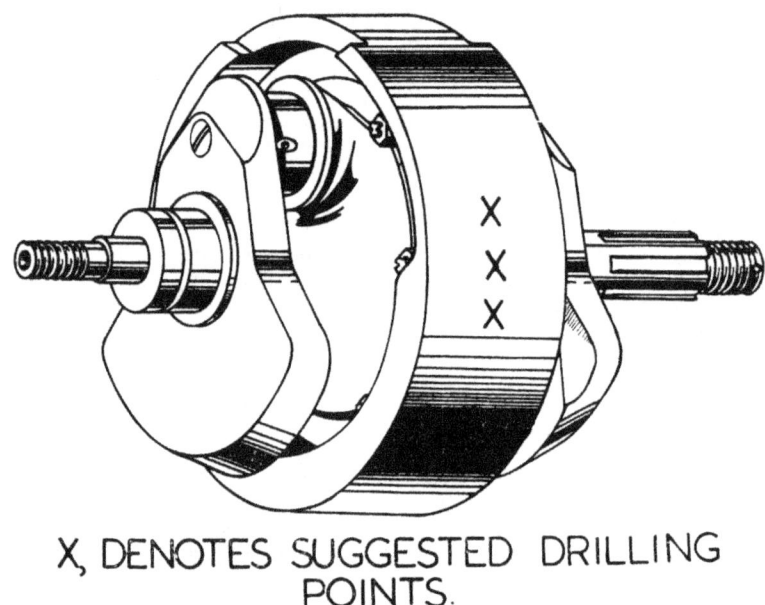

X, DENOTES SUGGESTED DRILLING POINTS.

Fig. X12. "A" Group Crankshaft.

Model	Weight attached	Model	Weight attached
A7	2 @ 19 ozs. 10 drams	B32 Competition	5 ozs. 4 drams
A7 after AA7-101	2 @ 16 ozs. 12 drams	B34 Competition	9 ozs. 9 drams
A10	2 @ 18 ozs. 10 drams	B32 Gold Star	6 ozs. 5 drams
A10 Road Rocket	2 @ 19 ozs. 8 drams	B34 Gold Star	11 ozs. 4 drams
C Group	3 ozs. 5 drams	M20	7 ozs.
B31	4 ozs. 6 drams	M21	5 ozs. 10 drams
B33 and M33	8 ozs. 8 drams		

Note :- Service Tool No. 61-3497 should be used on Crankshaft No. 67-1218 which is fitted to the Super Rocket and A10 machines after Eng. No. CA10R-4650 and DA10-101 respectively.

B.S.A. MOTOR CYCLES LIMITED, Service Dept., Birmingham, 11
(PRINTED IN ENGLAND)

BSA SERVICE SHEET No. 713

ALL MODELS EXCEPT "D" GROUP AND C15
DISMANTLING OF STEERING HEAD

Remove the headlamp from the forks after undoing the two retaining bolts, and allow it to hang in a position where it cannot be damaged. If a headlamp cowl is fitted, it should be removed complete with the headlamp.

On later models of the type shown in Fig. C31A the lamp is not removed, but it is necessary to take off the lamp front by unscrewing pin (F) and to disconnect the speedometer cable and the leads to the switch.

Detach the handlebars complete with controls, and lay them on top of the petrol tank, using a piece of rag to protect the enamel. Remove the chromium-plated top caps (A) and (B) Fig. C31. Slacken the pinch bolt (C) and remove the adjusting sleeve (D) or (E) Fig. C31A. Tap off the fork top yoke by striking it with a mallet underneath its two sides alternately.

The steering column can now be drawn downwards from the head, and the top ballrace removed. **Note.**—If the bearings are dry a means of catching the steel balls should be arranged as they will fall as the column is drawn out.

The cups which remain in the head can be withdrawn by means of extractor No. 61-3060 for "C" Group, and 61-3063 for "A", "M" and "B" Groups. This is screwed firmly into the cup, then extractor and cup are driven out from the opposite end with the aid of a suitable bar.

If the cups and cones are pitted to even a slight degree, they must be replaced, otherwise steering will be adversely affected and will rapidly become worse.

Pitting is invariably due to "hammering" of the balls in their tracks, caused by slack adjustment.

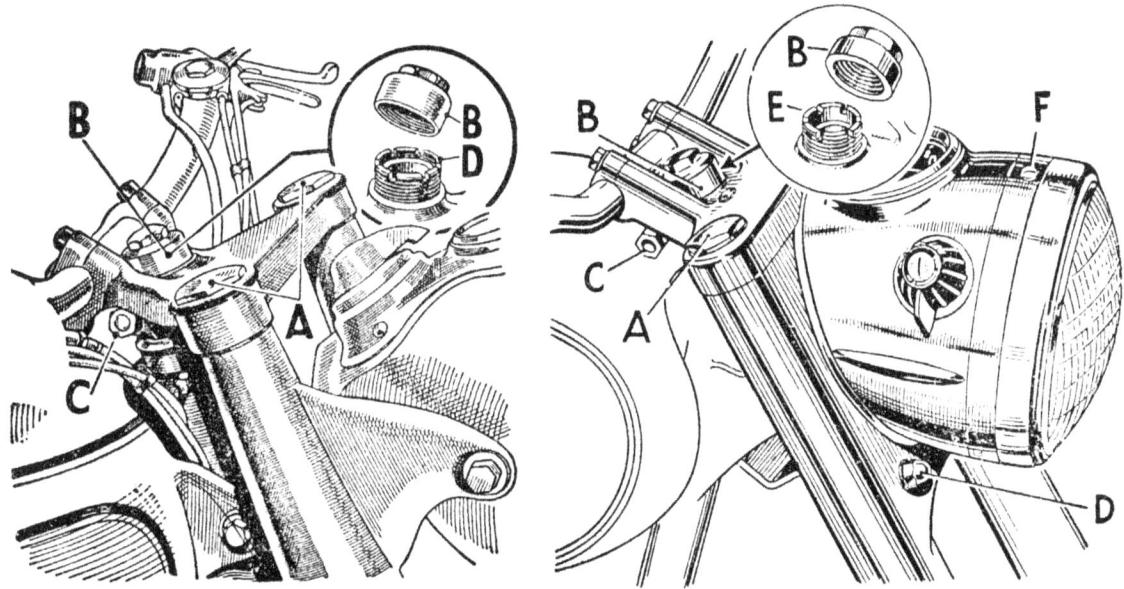

Fig. C31. The Front Fork & Steering Head.   Fig. C31A.

Reassembly of Steering Head.

When fitting new ballrace cups make sure that they are driven in squarely and that they are pressed well home. Replace the steering column balls, cone, adjusting sleeve and top-yoke. If any difficulty is experienced in retaining the balls in position, smear the tracks heavily with grease.

Adjust the column so that it turns freely without play and tighten the pinch bolt (C).

Finally replace headlamp and handlebar controls.

B.S.A. Motor Cycles Ltd., Service Dept., Armoury Road, Birmingham 11
B.S.A. Press.

BSA SERVICE SHEET No. 714

Printed September, 1956
Revised October, 1957

SPOKE SIZES.

NOTE.—All Models use Forty Spokes per Wheel except "D" Group which have Thirty-six.

YEAR	MODEL	FRONT RIM SIZE	FRONT LEFT Length	FRONT LEFT Gauge	FRONT LEFT Part Number	FRONT RIGHT Length	FRONT RIGHT Gauge	FRONT RIGHT Part Number	REAR RIM SIZE	REAR LEFT Length	REAR LEFT Gauge	REAR LEFT Part Number	REAR RIGHT Length	REAR RIGHT Gauge	REAR RIGHT Part Number
1947	C10	WM1–19	8 3/4″	10	24–7012	8 3/4″	10	24–7012	WM1–19	8 3/4″	10	24–7012	6 7/8″	10	24–7014
	C11	WM1–20	9 1/4″	10	24–6912	9 3/16″	10	29–5772	WM2–20	9 1/4″	10	24–6912	7 3/8″	10	65–5873
	B31–B33	WM2–19	8 11/16″	10	65–5872	7 1/2″	10	65–5910	WM2–19	8 9/16″	8/10	65–6072	8 3/4″	10	24–7012
	B32–B34	WM1–21	9 11/16″	10	65–5537	8 9/16″	10	90–5584	WM2–19	8 9/16″	8/10	65–6027	8 3/4″	10	24–7012
	M20–M21 Girder Fork	WM3–19	8 3/4″	10	24–7012	6 3/4″	8/10	24–6899	WM3–19	8 5/8″	8/ 3/16	15–7037	8 3/4″	8	26–6824
	A7	WM2–19	7 29/32″	10/12	67–6008	8 1/16″	10/12	67–6007	WM3–19	7 29/32″	10/12	67–6008	8 1/16″	10/12	67–6007
1948	C10	WM1–19	8 3/4″	10	24–7012	8 3/4″	10	24–7012	WM1–19	8 3/4″	10	24–7012	6 7/8″	10	24–7014
	C11	WM1–20	9 1/4″	10	24–6912	9 3/16″	10	29–5772	WM1–20	9 1/4″	10	24–6912	7 3/8″	10	65–5873
	B31	WM2–19	8 11/16″	10	65–5872	7 1/2″	10	65–5910	WM2–19	8 9/16″	8/10	65–6027	8 3/4″	10	24–7012
	B32	WM1–21	9 11/16″	10	65–5537	8 9/16″	10	29–5846	WM2–19	8 9/16″	8/10	65–6027	8 3/4″	10	24–7012
	B33	WM2–19	8 11/16″	10	65–5872	7 1/2″	10	65–5910	WM2–19	8 9/16″	8/10	65–6027	8 3/4″	10	24–7012
	B34	WM1–21	9 11/16″	10	65–5537	8 9/16″	10	90–5584	WM2–19	8 9/16″	8/10	65–6027	8 3/4″	10	24–7012
	M20–M21 Girder Fork	WM3–19	8 3/4″	10	24–7012	6 3/4″	8/10	24–6899	WM3–19	8 5/8″	8/ 3/16	15–7037	8 3/4″	8	26–6824
	M33–G.F.	WM3–19	8 3/4″	10	24–7012	6 3/4″	8/10	24–6899	WM3–19	8 5/8″	8/ 3/16	15–7037	8 3/4″	8	26–6824
	A7	WM2–19	7 29/32″	10/12	67–6008	8 1/16″	10/12	67–6007	WM3–19	7 29/32″	10/12	67–6008	8 1/16″	10/12	67–6007
1949	D1	WM1–19	8 9/16″	10	90–5584	7 1/8″	10	90–5583	WM1–19	8 5/16″	10	15–7072	8 9/16″	10	29–5846
	D1 Comp	WM1–19	8 9/16″	10	90–5584	7 1/8″	10	90–5583	WM2–19	8 5/16″	10	15–7072	8 9/16″	10	29–5846
	C10	WM1–19	8 3/4″	10	24–7012	8 3/4″	10	24–7012	WM1–19	8 3/4″	10	24–7012	6 7/8″	10	24–7014
	C11	WM1–20	9 1/4″	10	24–6912	9 3/16″	10	29–5772	WM1–20	9 1/4″	10	24–6912	7 3/8″	10	65–5873
	B32–B34 G/S Std. & Spg. Frame	WM1–21	9 11/16″	10	65–5537	8 9/16″	10	90–5584	R	8 9/16″	8/10	65–6027	8 3/4″	10	24–7012
									WM2–19S	7 29/32″	10/12	67–6008	7 29/32″	10/12	67–6008
	B31–B32 Std. & Spg Frame	WM2–19	8 11/16″	10	65–5872	7 1/2″	10	65–5910	R	8 9/16″	8/10	65–6027	8 3/4″	10	24–7012
									WM2–19S	7 29/32″	10/12	67–6008	7 29/32″	10/12	67–6008
	M20–M21–M33 Tele. Forks	WM2–19	8 11/16″	10	65–5872	7 1/2″	10	65–5910	WM2–19	8 5/8″	8/ 3/16	15–7037	8 5/8″	8	24–6896
	A7 Star Twin Std. & Spg. Frame	WM2–19	8 11/16″	10	65–5872	7 1/2″	10	65–5910	WM2–19	7 29/32″	10/12	67–6008	7 29/32″	10/12	67–6008

SPOKE SIZES—*continued.*

YEAR	MODEL	FRONT RIM SIZE	FRONT LEFT Length	FRONT LEFT Gauge	FRONT LEFT Part Number	FRONT RIGHT Length	FRONT RIGHT Gauge	FRONT RIGHT Part Number	REAR RIM SIZE	REAR LEFT Length	REAR LEFT Gauge	REAR LEFT Part Number	REAR RIGHT Length	REAR RIGHT Gauge	REAR RIGHT Part Number
1950	D1 Std. & Spg. D1 Comp. Spg.	WM1-19	8 9/16″	10	90-5584	7 1/8″	10	90-5583	WM1-19	8 5/16″	10	15-7072	8 9/16″	10	90-5584
	C10	WM1-19	8 3/4″	10	24-7012	8 3/4″	10	24-7012	WM1-19	8 3/4″	10	24-7012	6 7/8″	10	24-7014
	C11	WM1-20	9 1/4″	10	24-6912	9 3/16″	10	29-5772	WM1-20	9 1/4″	10	24-6912	7 3/8″	10	65-5873
	B31-B33 Std. & Spg. Frame	WM2-19	8 11/16″	10	65-5872	7 1/2″	10	65-5910	R	8 9/16″	8/10	65-6027	8 3/4″	10	24-7012
									WM2-19S	7 29/32″	10	65-6302	7 29/32″	10	65-6302
	B32-B34 Comp. Models	WM1-21	9 11/16″	10	65-5537	8 9/16″	10	90-5584	WM2-19	8 9/16″	8/10	65-6027	8 3/4″	10	24-7012
	350 and 500 Scramble & Grass Track Models	Varies to Spec.	9 11/16″	10	65-5537	8 9/16″	10	90-5584	Varies to Spec.	7 29/32″	10	65-6302	7 29/32″	10	65-6302
	350 & 500 O.H.V. Gold Star, Clubmans and Road Racing	Varies to Spec.	9 13/16″	10	65-5926	6 7/8″	10	24-7014	Varies to Spec.	7 29/32″	10	65-6302	7 29/32″	10	65-6302
	M20-M21-M33	WM2-19	8 11/16″	10	65-5872	7 1/2″	10	65-5910	WM3-19	8 5/8″	8/ 3/16	15-7037	8 5/8″	8	24-6896
	A7 Star Twin Rigid & Spg. Frame	WM2-19	8 11/16″	10	65-5872	7 1/2″	10	65-5910	WM3-19	7 29/32″	10	65-6302	7 29/32″	10	65-6302
	A10	WM2-19	8 7/8″	10	67-5545	5 15/16″	10	67-5544	WM3-19	7 29/32″	10	65-6302	7 29/32″	10	65-6302
1951 and 1952 (other models as 1950	C10 Spring Frame	WM1-19	8 3/4″	10	24-7012	8 3/4″	10	24-7012	WM1-19	8 3/4″	10	24-7012	6 7/8″	10	24-7014
	C11 Spring Frame	WM1-20	9 1/4″	10	24-6912	9 3/16″	10	29-5772	WM1-20	9 1/4″	10	24-6912	7 3/8″	10	65-5873
	M20-M21-M33 Spring Frame	WM1-19	8 11/16″	10	65-5872	7 1/2″	10	65-5910	WM2-19	7 27/32″	10	65-6303	7 29/32″	10	65-6302
1953 (other models as 1950/52)	B33-A7-A10 Rigid	WM2-19	8 7/8″	10	67-5545	5 15/16″	10	67-5544	WM2-19	8 3/4″	10	24-7012	8 9/16″	10	65-6027
	B33-A7-A10 Spring	WM2-19	8 7/8″	10	67-5545	5 15/16″	10	67-5544	WM2-19	7 27/32″	10	65-6303	7 29/32″	10	65-6302
	GOLD STAR Clubmans, Road Racing & Touring	WM1-19	8 7/8″	10	67-5545	5 15/16″	10	67-5544	WM2-19	7 27/32″	10	65-6303	7 29/32″	10	65-6302
		WM1-21	9 11/16″	10	67-5537	8 9/16″	10	90-5584	WM2-19	7 27/32″	10	65-6303	7 29/32″	10	65-6302
	B32-B34 Trials	WM1-21	9 11/16″	10	67-5537	8 9/16″	10	90-5584	WM3-19	7 27/32″	10	65-6303	7 29/32″	10	65-6302
	B32-B34 Scrambles	WM1-21	9 11/16″	8	42-5524	8 7/16″	8	31-6015	WM3-19	7 27/32″	10	65-6303	7 29/32″	10	65-6302

B.S.A. Service Sheet No. 714—continued

SPOKE SIZES—continued

YEAR	MODEL	RIM SIZE	FRONT LEFT Length	FRONT LEFT Gauge	FRONT Part Number	FRONT Length	FRONT RIGHT Gauge	FRONT Part Number	RIM SIZE	REAR LEFT Length	REAR LEFT Gauge	REAR Part Number	REAR Length	REAR RIGHT Gauge	REAR Part Number
1954 and 1955	D1-D3 Rigid & Spring	WM1-19	$8\frac{7}{16}"$	10	90-5584	$7\frac{1}{8}"$	10	90-5583	WM1-19	$8\frac{7}{16}"$	10	90-6042	$8\frac{7}{16}"$	10	90-5584
	D1-D3 Comp.	WM1-19	$8\frac{7}{16}"$	10	90-5584	7"	10	29-5940	WM1-19	$8\frac{7}{16}"$	10	90-6042	$8\frac{7}{16}"$	10	90-5584
	C10L	WM1-19	$8\frac{7}{16}"$	10	90-5584	7"	10	29-5940	WM1-19	$8\frac{7}{16}"$	10	90-6042	$8\frac{7}{16}"$	10	90-5584
	C11G	WM1-19	$8\frac{3}{4}"$	10	24-7012	$8\frac{3}{4}"$	10	24-7012	WM1-19	$6\frac{7}{8}"$	10	24-7014	$8\frac{3}{4}"$	10	24-7012
	C11G (1955) Rigid & Spring	WM1-19	$8\frac{1}{4}"$	10	24-7012	$7\frac{1}{2}"$	10	65-5910	WM1-19	$6\frac{7}{8}"$	10	24-7014	$8\frac{3}{4}"$	10	24-7012
	B31-B33 Rigid	WM2-19	$8\frac{7}{16}"$	10	65-5872	$7\frac{1}{2}"$	10	65-5910	WM2-19	$8\frac{7}{16}"$	Butted 8/10	65-6027	$8\frac{3}{4}"$	10	65-6302
	B31-B33 Spring	WM2-19	$8\frac{7}{16}"$	10	65-5872	$7\frac{1}{2}"$	10	65-5910	WM3-19	$7\frac{22}{32}"$	10	65-6303	$7\frac{22}{32}"$	10	65-6302
	B32-B34 Comp. Rigid	WM1-21	$9\frac{11}{16}"$	10	65-5537	$8\frac{9}{16}"$	10	90-5584	WM2-19	$7\frac{22}{32}"$	10	65-6303	$7\frac{22}{32}"$	10	65-6302
	B31 Swinging Arm	WM2-19	$8\frac{11}{16}"$	10	65-5872	$7\frac{1}{2}"$	10	65-5912	WM2-19	$7\frac{22}{32}"$	10	65-6303	$7\frac{22}{32}"$	10	65-6302
	B32-B34 Swinging Arm	WM1-21	$9\frac{11}{16}"$	10	65-5537	$8\frac{9}{16}"$	10	90-5584	WM2-19	$7\frac{22}{32}"$	10	65-6303	$7\frac{22}{32}"$	10	65-6302
	B33 1954 Swinging Arm	WM2-19	$8\frac{7}{16}"$	10	67-5545	$5\frac{13}{16}"$	10	67-5544	WM2-19	$7\frac{22}{32}"$	10	65-6303	$7\frac{22}{32}"$	10	65-6302
	B33 1955 Swinging Arm	WM2-19	$8\frac{7}{8}"$	Butted 8/10	67-5606	$5\frac{13}{32}"$	10	67-5544	WM2-19	$7\frac{22}{32}"$	10	65-6303	$7\frac{22}{32}"$	10	65-6302
	GOLD STAR Clubmans, Road Racing & Touring	WM1-19	$8\frac{7}{8}"$	10	67-5515	$5\frac{13}{32}"$	10	67-5544	WM2-19	$7\frac{22}{32}"$	10	65-6303	$7\frac{22}{32}"$	10	65-6302
		WM1-21	$9\frac{11}{16}"$	10	65-5926	$6\frac{7}{8}"$	10	24-7014	WM2-18	$7\frac{7}{16}"$	10	42-6011	$7\frac{7}{16}"$	10	42-6012
	GOLD STAR Trials	WM1-21	$9\frac{11}{16}"$	10	65-5537	$8\frac{3}{16}"$	10	90-5584	WM3-19	$7\frac{22}{32}"$	10	65-6303	$7\frac{22}{32}"$	10	65-6302
	GOLD STAR Scrambles	WM1-21	$9\frac{11}{16}"$	8	42-5524	$8\frac{3}{16}"$	8	31-6015	WM3-19	$7\frac{22}{32}"$	10	65-6303	$7\frac{22}{32}"$	10	65-6302
	M20-M21-M33 Rigid	WM2-19	$8\frac{11}{16}"$	10	65-5872	$7\frac{1}{2}"$	10	65-5910	WM2-19	$8\frac{7}{8}"$	Butted 8	15-7037	$8\frac{5}{8}"$	Butted 8	24-6896
	M20-M21-M33 Spring	WM2-19	$8\frac{11}{16}"$	10	65-5872	$7\frac{1}{2}"$	10	65-5910	WM2-19	$7\frac{22}{32}"$	10	65-6303	$7\frac{22}{32}"$	10	65-6302
	"A" GROUP Plunger & Swinging Arm 1954	WM2-19	$8\frac{7}{8}"$	10	67-5545	$5\frac{13}{16}"$	10	67-5544	WM2-19	$7\frac{22}{32}"$	10	65-6303	$7\frac{22}{32}"$	10	65-6302
	"A" GROUP Plunger & Swinging Arm 1955	WM2-19	$8\frac{7}{8}"$	Butted 8/10	67-5606	$5\frac{13}{32}"$	10	67-5544	WM2-19	$7\frac{22}{32}"$	10	65-6303	$7\frac{22}{32}"$	10	65-6302

B.S.A. Service Sheet No. 714—continued

SPOKE SIZES—continued

YEAR	MODEL	RIM SIZE	FRONT LEFT			FRONT RIGHT			RIM SIZE	REAR LEFT			REAR RIGHT		
			Length	Gauge	Part Number	Length	Gauge	Part Number		Length	Gauge	Part Number	Length	Gauge	Part Number
1956/7	D1 Plunger	WM1-19	8 3/16"	10	90-5584	7 7/8"	10	90-5584	WM1-19	8 3/16"	10	90-6042	8 3/16"	10	90-5584
	D3 Swinging Arm	WM1-19	8 3/16"	10	90-5584	7 7/8"	10	90-5584	WM1-19	8 3/16"	10	90-6042	8 3/16"	10	90-5584
	C10L	WM1-19	8 3/4"	10	24-7012	8 3/4"	10	24-7012	WM1-19	8 3/16"	10	90-6042	8 3/16"	10	90-5584
	C12	WM1-19	6 5/8"	10	29-5976	6 5/8"	10	29-5976	WM1-19	7"	10	29-5940	7"	10	29-5940
	B31 B33	WM2-19	6 1/4"	Butted 8/10	42-5635	6 1/4"	Butted 8/10	42-5635	WM2-19	6 1/4"	Butted 8/10	42-5635	6 1/4"	Butted 8/10	42-5635
	GOLD STAR Clubmans, Road Racing & Touring	WM1-19	5 7/8"	10	42-5552	5 7/8"	10	42-5552	WM2-19	7 23/32"	10	65-6303	7 23/32"	10	65-6302
	B32-B34 Comp.	WM1-21	9 11/16"	10	65-5537	8 7/8"	10	90-5584	WM3-19	7 23/32"	10	65-6303	7 23/32"	10	65-6302
	GOLD STAR Scrambles	WM1-21	9 11/16"	8	42-5524	8 7/16"	8	31-6015	WM3-19	7 23/32"	10	65-6303	7 23/32"	10	65-6302
	M21 Rigid	WM2-19	8 3/4"	Butted 8/10	67-5606	5 11/16"	Butted 8/10	66-5560	WM3-19	8 5/8"	Butted 8	15-7037	8 5/8"	Butted 8	24-6896
	M21-M33 Plunger	WM2-19	8 3/4"	Butted 8/10	67-5606	5 11/16"	Butted 8/10	66-5560	WM2-19	7 23/32"	10	65-6303	7 23/32"	10	65-6302
	A7 and Shooting Star	WM2-19	6 1/4"	Butted 8/10	42-5635	6 1/4"	Butted 8/10	42-5635	WM2-19	6 1/4"	Butted 8/10	42-5635	6 1/4"	Butted 8/10	42-5635
	A10 Plunger	WM2-19	8 3/8"	Butted 8/10	67-5606	5 11/16"	Butted 8/10	66-5561	WM2-19	7 23/32"	Butted 8/10	67-6017	7 23/32"	Butted 8/10	67-6016
	A10 and Road Rocket	WM2-19	6 1/4"	Butted 8/10	42-5635	6 1/4"	Butted 8/10	42-5635	WM2-19	6 1/4"	Butted 8/10	42-5635	6 1/4"	Butted 8/10	42-5635
	Dandy 70	WM0-15	5 5/8"	12	64-5505	5 5/8"	12	64-5505	WM0-15	5 5/8"	Butted 11/12	64-5507	5 5/8"	Butted 11/12	64-5507

BSA SERVICE SHEET No. 803

Printed August 1966

MODELS C10 AND C11
COIL IGNITION EQUIPMENT

The coil ignition equipment comprises an ignition coil and a contact breaker. The ignition is provided with an automatic timing control which automatically varies the firing point according to the requirements of the engine. A warning light is provided, which lights up when the engine is stationary or running slowly, serving as a reminder to the rider to switch off.

The contact breaker unit has a moulded base, and the shaft is carried in two porous bronze bushes.

The centrifugal automatic timing control is housed in the body of the unit beneath the contact breaker base.

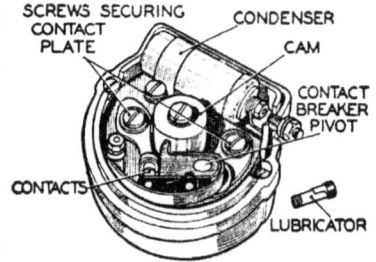

Fig. Y13.
Contact breaker, Model DKX1A

ROUTINE MAINTENANCE

Lubrication
To be carried out every 3,000 miles.

Cam.—Smear the surface of the cam very lightly with Mobilgrease No. 2 or, if this is not available, clean engine oil may be used.

Contact breaker pivot.—Place a small amount of Mobilgrease No. 2 or clean engine oil on the pivot on which the contact breaker lever works. Do not allow any grease or oil to get on to the contacts.

Shaft.—A lubricator is fitted in the shank of the unit, add a few drops of thin machine oil. Later models do not have this lubricator and no attention is required.

Automatic timing control.—Add a few drops of thin machine oil through the hole in the contact breaker base through which the cam passes.

Cleaning
To be carried out every 6,000 miles. Wipe the inside and outside of the moulding with a soft dry cloth. Examine the contact breaker. The contacts must be free from grease or oil. If they are burned or blackened, clean them with a fine carborundum stone or very fine emery cloth, afterwards wiping away any trace of dirt or metal dust with a petrol-moistened cloth. Cleaning of the contacts is made easier if the contact breaker lever carrying the moving contact is removed. To do this, unscrew the nut securing the end of the contact breaker spring, and remove the nut, spring washer and bush. Lift the contact breaker lever off its bearing. After cleaning, check the contact breaker gap setting.

Contact Breaker Gap Adjustment
Turn the engine until the contacts are seen to be fully opened, and check the gap with a gauge having a thickness of .010—.012 in. If the gap is correct, the gauge should be a sliding fit, but if the gap varies from the gauge, the setting must be adjusted.

To do this, keep the engine in the position giving maximum contact opening and

B.S.A. Service Sheet No. 803 (contd.)

slacken the two screws securing the fixed contact plate. Adjust the position of the plate until the gap is set to the thickness of the gauge and tighten the two locking screws.

High-tension Cables

Examine the high-tension cables. Any which have the insulation cracked or perished, or show signs of damage in any other way, must be replaced.

SERVICING

Testing in position to locate Ignition Fault

If a failure of ignition or misfiring occurs, first make sure that the trouble is not due to defects in the engine, carburetter, petrol supply, sparking plug, etc. If necessary adjust the sparking plug gap to the setting recommended (see Service Sheet No. 404).

Examine the high-tension cable. If the rubber shows signs of deterioration or cracking, the cable should be renewed.

Test plug and high-tension cable by removing the plug and allowing it to rest on the cylinder head and observing whether a spark occurs at the points when the engine is turned It should, however, be noted that this is only a rough test, since it is possible that a spark may not take place when the plug is under compression.

Switch on the ignition, turn the engine and observe the ammeter reading. If an ammeter reading is given which rises and falls with the closing and opening of the contacts, then the low-tension wiring is in order. If the reading does not fluctuate in this way a short-circuit in the low-tension wiring is indicated, or the contacts are remaining closed. When no reading is given, a broken or loose connection in the low-tension wiring or badly adjusted or dirty contacts are indicated.

To trace a fault in the low-tension wiring, switch on the ignition, and turn the engine until the distributor contacts are opened. Refer to the appropriate wiring diagram (see Service Sheet No. 808) and with the aid of a voltmeter (0—10 volts), fitted with two insulated leads, the ends of which are provided with clips, check the circuit as follows:—

Lead (yellow and black) from the positive battery terminal to terminal (B) on ammeter. Connect voltmeter between ammeter and earth. No reading indicates faulty lead or loose connections.

Ammeter

Connect voltmeter to ammeter (white and purple lead) and earth. No reading indicates faulty ammeter.

Lead (white and purple) between ammeter and ignition switch.

Connect voltmeter to terminal (A) on ignition switch and earth. No reading indicates faulty lead or loose connections.

Ignition Switch

Connect voltmeter to terminal (IG) on ignition switch. No reading indicates fault in switch.

Lead (white) between ignition switch and ignition coil.

Connect voltmeter to ignition coil terminal (SW) and earth. No reading indicates faulty lead or loose connections.

B.S.A. Service Sheet No. 803 (contd.)

Ignition Coil

Connect voltmeter to ignition coil terminal (*CB*) and earth. No reading indicates that fault lies in the coil primary winding.

Lead between ignition coil and contact breaker.

Remove the lead from the terminal on the contact breaker, and connect voltmeter between the end of this lead and earth. No reading indicates faulty lead or loose connections. Reconnect lead.

Contact Breaker

Connect voltmeter across the contacts. If no reading is obtained, remove the condenser and test again. If a reading is now given, a new condenser must be fitted.

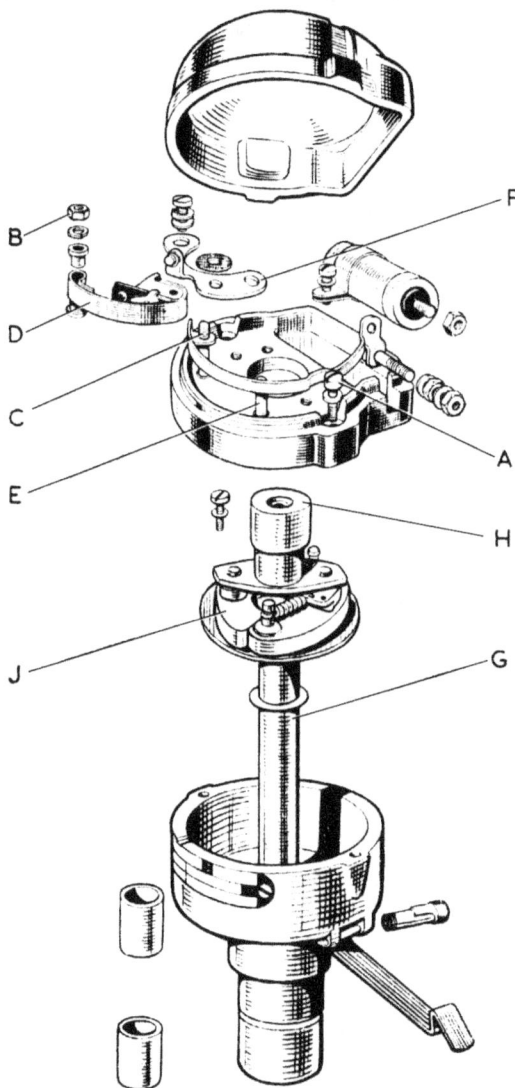

Fig. Y14. Model DKX1A Dismantled

Measure the contact breaker spring tension. This should be 20—24 ozs. measured at the contacts.

If, after carrying out these tests, the fault has not been located, remove the high-tension lead from the plug. Switch on the ignition and turn the engine until the contacts close. Flick the contact breaker lever open while the high-tension lead from the coil is held about $\frac{3}{16}$ in. away from the cylinder block. If the ignition equipment is in order a strong spark should be obtained. If no spark is given, it indicates a fault in the circuit of the secondary winding of the coil and the coil should be replaced.

To Dismantle

Spring back the securing clips and remove the moulded cap.

To remove the contact breaker base, it is only necessary to withdraw the two screws (*A*) Fig. Y14, together with the spring washers. The contact breaker base can be lifted off.

To remove the moving contact, unscrew the nut (*B*) on the pillar (*C*) and remove the nut, spring washer and bush. The contact breaker spring (*D*) can then be lifted off and the contact arm lifted from its pivot (*E*). The fixed contact is carried on a plate (*F*) secured by two screws. The condenser can be removed when its terminal nuts and single securing screw are removed.

B.S.A. Service Sheet No. 803 (contd.)

The shaft (G) carrying the cam (H) and automatic timing control (J) can be removed when the driving dog is taken off.

The automatic timing control should not be dismantled unnecessarily. If it is desired to dismantle the mechanism, carefully note the position of the various components in order that they may be refitted correctly.

Bearings

If replacement of bearings is necessary, the following points should be borne in mind. Badly worn bearings are usually indicated by the maximum opening of the contacts varying considerably as the shaft is slowly rotated by hand, while side pressure is applied to the cam.

Porous bronze bearing bushes should be inserted in the body on a highly polished mandrel, which on withdrawal will give the finished bore diameter without machining.

Before use, these bushes should be stored in a covered container, and fully covered with oil of a grade equivalent to Mobiloil Arctic or other good thin mineral oil. The minimum time of soaking should normally be 24 hours; in case of extreme urgency, this period may be shortened by heating the oil to 100°C., when the time of immersion may be reduced to 2 hours.

Reassembly

In the main, reassembly is the reverse of the operations described above. Note that an insulating washer is placed over the contact breaker pivot before the moving contact is fitted.

B.S.A. MOTOR CYCLES LTD., Service Department, Armoury Road, Birmingham 11.
B.S.A. PRESS

BSA SERVICE SHEET No. 804

C10, C11, "A", "B" AND "M" GROUP MODELS
REGULATOR UNIT–Models MCR1 and MCR2

This unit houses the generator voltage regulator unit and the cut-out. Although combined structurally, the regulator and cut-out are electrically separate.

On machines fitted with an E3L dynamo the regulator unit is type MCR2, this unit is slightly different in construction to the MCR1. The procedure for testing and adjusting is, however, unaltered.

Positive Earth Lighting System

Some machines have the battery positive terminal connected to the frame instead of the negative terminal. This does not affect the regulator adjustment except that the voltmeter connections should be reversed.

The Regulator

The regulator unit is arranged to work in conjunction with the shunt-wound generators described in Service Sheet No. 809. The regulator is set to maintain a pre-determined generator voltage at all speeds, the field strength being controlled by the automatic insertion of a resistance in the generator field circuit, and a current or series winding on the same regulator compensates this voltage figure in accordance with the output current, to ensure that the battery does no receive an excessive charging current when in a discharged condition. Hence the charging current depends upon the difference between the controlled generator voltage and the battery terminal voltage and is therefore at a maximum when the battery is discharged, automatically tapering off to a minimum as the battery becomes charged and its voltage rises. In addition, a form of temperature compensation ensures that the voltage characteristics of the regulator are matched to those of the battery for large variations in working temperature.

Normally, during day-time running, when the battery is in good condition, the generator gives only a trickle charge, so that the ammeter reading will seldom exceed 1—2 amperes.

The Cut-out

The cut-out is an automatic switch which is connected between the dynamo and battery. It consists of a pair of contacts held open by a spring and closed magnetically. When the engine is running fast enough to cause the voltage of the generator to exceed that of the battery, the contacts close and the battery is charged by the generator. On the other hand, when the speed is low or the engine is stationary, the contacts open, thus disconnecting the generator from the battery and preventing current flowing from the battery through the windings.

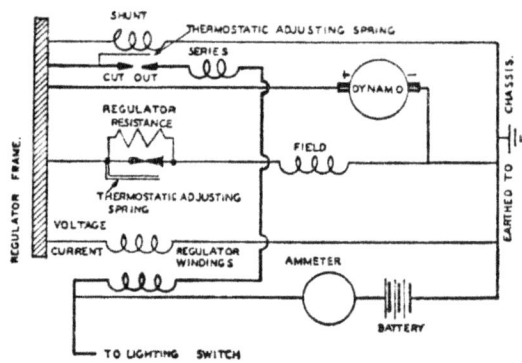

Fig. Y15. *Circuit diagram of Charging System.*

B.S.A. Service Sheet No. 804 (contd.)

Test Data

Cut-out	MCR.1	MCR.2
Cut-in voltage	6.2—6.6 volts	6.3—6.7 volts
Drop-off voltage	3.5—5.3 volts	4.5—5.0 volts
Reverse current	0.7—2.5 amperes	3.0—5.0 amperes

Regulator

SETTING IN OPEN CIRCUIT

		MCR.1	MCR.2
10°C.	50°F.	8.0—8.4 volts	7.7—8.1 volts
20°C.	68°F.	7.8—8.2 volts	7.6—8.0 volts
30°C.	86°F.	7.6—8.0 volts	7.5—7.9 volts
40°C.	104°F.	7.4—7.9 volts	7.4—7.8 volts

Servicing

TESTING IN POSITION TO LOCATE FAULT IN CHARGING CIRCUIT

If the procedure given in Service Sheet No. 809 shows the generator to be in order, proceed to check further as follows:—

First ensure that the wiring between regulator and battery is in order. To do this disconnect the wire from the (A) terminal of the regulator (Fig. Y16). It may be necessary in some cases to remove the regulator from the motorcycle.

Connect the end of the wire removed to the positive terminal of a voltmeter, and connect the negative voltmeter terminal to an earthing point on the machine.

If a voltmeter reading is given, the wiring is in order and the regulator must be examined If there is no reading, examine the wiring for broken wires or loose connections.

Regulator Adjustment

Remove the cover of the regulator unit, insert a piece of paper between the cut-out contacts, and proceed as follows:—

Connect the positive terminal of the moving coil voltmeter (0—10 volts) to the (D) terminal on the regulator and connect the other lead of the voltmeter to an earthing point on the engine.

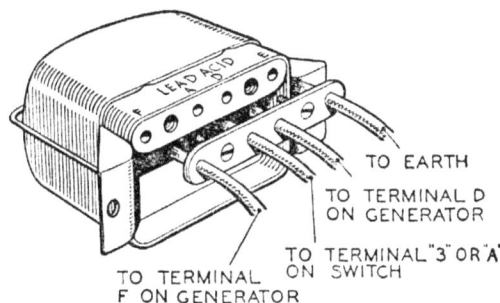

Fig. Y16. *Connections to Regulator Unit.*

Start the engine and slowly increase the speed until the voltmeter needle "flicks" and then steadies; this should occur at a voltmeter reading between the limits for the particular atmospheric temperature.

If the voltage at which the reading becomes steady is outside these limits, the regulator must be adjusted.

Shut off the engine, release the locknut (A) Fig. Y17, on the regulator adjusting screw (B) and turn the screw in a clockwise direction to raise the setting, or in an anti-clockwise direction to lower the setting. Turn the screw a fraction of a turn at a time and then tighten the locknut.

B.S.A. Service Sheet No. 804 (contd.)

When adjusting, do not run the engine up to more than half-throttle, as while the dynamo is on open circuit, it will build up to a high voltage if run at a high speed and so a false voltmeter reading would be obtained.

Remove paper from between cut-out contacts.

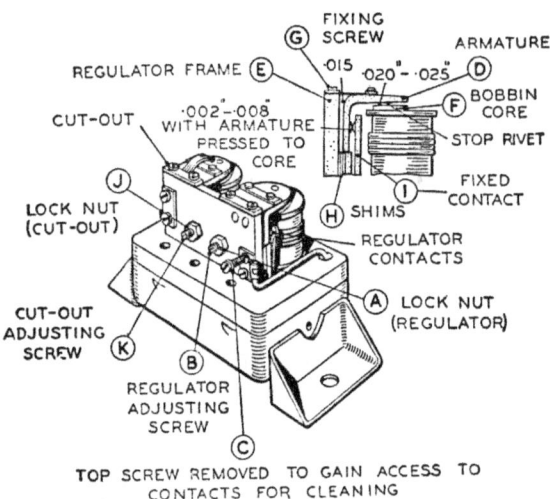

Fig. Y17. *Regulator and Cut-out Adjustment and Setting.*

Cleaning the Regulator Contacts

After long periods of service it may be found necessary to clean the vibrating contacts of the regulator. These are accessible if the top screw (C) securing the fixed contact is removed and the bottom screw slackened to permit the fixed contact to be swung outwards. The contacts can then be polished with fine emery cloth.

Mechanical Setting of Regulator

The armature carrying the moving contact of the regulator is accurately set and should no be removed. If, however, it does become necessary to re-set the contacts, slacken the two fixing screws (G) Fig. Y17, and proceed as follows:—

Insert a .015 in. (0.20 in.) feeler gauge between the back of the armature (D) and the regulator frame (E).

Press back the armature against the frame and down on to the top of the bobbin core with the gauge in position, and lock the armature by tightening the two fixing screws (G). Check the air gap between the top of the bobbin core (F) and the underside of the armature (D)—not under the stop rivet. Adjust if necessary to .025 in. (.012—.020 in.), by removing shims (H) at the back of the fixed contact on an MCR1 regulator or by bending the fixed contact breaker on an MCR2 regulator. The gap between the regulator contacts when the armature is pressed down should now be .002—.008 in. (.006—.017 in.). Finally check, and if necessary re-set, the electrical adjustment of the regulator.

The figures in brackets refer to the MCR2 regulator.

B.S.A. Service Sheet No. 804 (contd.)

Electrical Setting of Cut-out

If the regulator setting is within the correct limits, but the battery is still not receiving current from the dynamo, the cut-out may be out of adjustment or there may be an open circuit in the wiring of the cut-out and regulator unit.

Remove the cable from the terminal on the regulator marked (A). Remove the voltmeter lead from the (D) terminal of the regulator unit and connect it to terminal (A). Run the engine as before: at a fairly low engine speed, the cut-out should operate, when a voltmeter reading should be given of the same value as that when the voltmeter was connected to terminal (D). If there is no reading, the setting of the cut-out may be badly out of adjustment and the contacts not closing.

To check the voltage at which the cut-out operates, the voltmeter must be connected between the (D) terminal and earth. Start the engine and slowly increase its speed until the cut-out contacts are seen to close, noting the voltage at which this occurs. This should be 6.2—6.6 volts.

If operation of the cut-out is outside these limits, it will be necessary to adjust. To do this slacken the locknut (J) Fig. Y17, on the cut-out adjustment screw (K) and turn the screw in a clockwise direction to raise the voltage setting or in an anti-clockwise direction to reduce the setting, testing after each adjustment by increasing the engine speed until the cut-out is seen to operate, and noting the corresponding reading.

Tighten the locknut after making the adjustment. If the cut-out contacts appear burnt or dirty, place a strip of fine glasspaper between the contacts then, with the contacts closed by hand, draw the paper through. This should be done two or three times with the rough side towards each contact.

Mechanical Setting of Cut-out

If, for any reason, the armature has to be removed from the cut-out frame, care must be taken to obtain the correct air-gap settings on reassembly. These can be obtained as follows:—

Slacken the two armature fixing screws, adjusting screw (K) and the screw securing the fixed contact. Insert a .014 in. gauge between the back of the armature and the cut-out frame. (The air-gap between the core face and the armature shim should now measure .011—.015 in. If it does not, fit a armature assembly). Press the armature back against the gauge and tighten the fixing screws. With the gauge still in position, set the gap between the armature and the stop plate arm to .030—.034 in. be carefully bending the arm. Remove the gauge and tighten the screw securing the fixed contact.

Insert a .025 in. gauge between the core face and the armature. Press the armature down on to the gauge. The gap between the contacts should now measure .002—.006 in, and the drop-off voltage should be between the limits given in the test data. If necessary, adjust the gap by carefully bending the fixed contact breaker.

B.S.A. MOTOR CYCLES LTD., Service Department, Armoury Road, Birmingham 11.
Printed in England
B.S.A. Press

BSA SERVICE SHEET No. 805

Reprinted June, 1960

All Models

BATTERY — LEAD-ACID TYPES

The range of Lucas batteries listed here covers those models fitted to B.S.A. motor cycles in recent years.

PU5E and LVW5E Small capacity batteries for light-weight machines.

PU7E .. .. Standard battery for cradle mount-ting.

GU11E .. .. Larger capacity battery for sidecar machines.

SC7E .. .. Large capacity lightweight battery for machines fitted with starting motors or two-way radio equipment, e.g. police machines.

All current Lucas motor cycle batteries are 'dry charged', and do not require initial charging. Except that these batteries have porous rubber separators, they are identical with earlier models supplied wet or uncharged and require the same routine maintenance when in service.

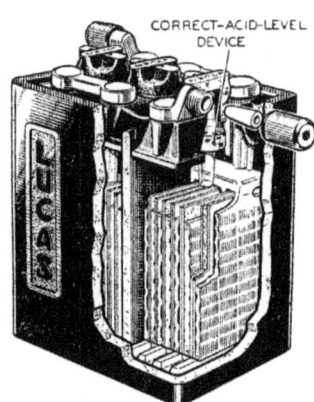

Fig. Y18. Sectioned battery, model PU7E/9

STORAGE

Used batteries must be fully charged before storing. In temperate climates they should be examined fortnightly, or weekly in the case of model LVW5E and all models when stored in the tropics. If necessary, give them a short refreshing charge.

After a long period of storage, the condition of the battery will often improve if it is put through a 'cycle', as described on page 4.

MAINTENANCE

Every fortnight, or more frequently in hot climates, examine the condition of the battery. Examine five-plate batteries every week.

Never use a naked light when examining the condition of the cells, as there is a **danger** of igniting the gas coming from the active materials.

Cleaning

Remove the battery cover and clean the cell tops. Examine the connections. If they are loose or dirty, remove them and scrape the contact surfaces clean. Coat them with petroleum jelly before replacing.

Remove the filler plugs and check that the vent holes are clear and that the rubber washer fitted under some plugs is in good condition.

Topping-up

During charging, water is lost by gassing and evaporation. Examine the electrolyte level in each cell and, if necessary, add distilled water to raise the electrolyte level with the top edges of the separators.

SC7E batteries have a woven glass pad fitted in each cell to reduce splashing when the battery is gassing during charging. When 'topping-up' this type of battery it is useful to note that the correct electrolyte level is reached when moisture appears through the porous glass pad.

B.S.A. Service Sheet No. 805 (continued)

The Lucas Battery Filler

The use of a Lucas motor cycle Battery Filler will be found helpful in this 'topping-up' process, as it ensures that the correct electrolyte level is automatically attained and also prevents distilled water from being spilled over the battery top.

Correct-Acid-Level-Devices

The correct-acid-level-device fitted to some Lucas batteries consists of a central tube with a perforated flange which rests on a ledge in the filling orifice.

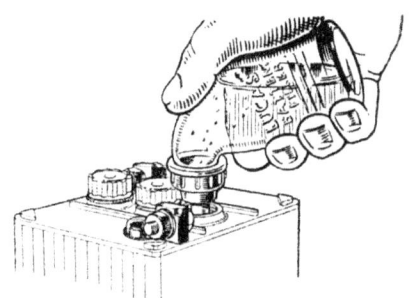

Fig Y19. The Lucas battery filler

When 'topping-up' a battery fitted with these devices, pour distilled water round the flange (not down the tube) until no more drains through into the cell. This will happen when the electrolyte level reaches the bottom of the central tube and prevents further escape of air displaced by the 'topping-up' water. Lift the tube slightly to allow the small amount of water in the flange to drain into the cell. The electrolyte level will then be correct.

If a battery requires 'topping-up' too frequently, the voltage regulator (on machines fitted with d.c. generators) may be out of adjustment, i.e. set too high, and should be checked. Conversely, a persistently low state of charge may be due to a regulator being set too low.

If one cell in particular needs 'topping-up' more than another, it is likely the container is cracked, in which event replace the battery and clean the carrier, using a solution of ammonia or bi-carbonate of soda in water. After cleaning and drying, paint the battery carrier and other surfaces affected by the electrolyte with anti-sulphuric paint.

TABLES OF SPECIFIC GRAVITIES AND CHARGING RATES

Battery	Plates per cell	Amp. Hr. Capacity		Electrolyte to fill one two-volt cell		Home Trade and Climates Ordinarily below 90°F. (32°C.) Specific Gravity of Acid (corrected to 60°F.)		Climates frequently over 90°F. (32°C.) Specific Gravity of Acid (corrected to 60°F.)		Initial Charge Current	Re-charge Current
		At 10 hour rate	At 20 hour rate	Pint	c.c.	Filling	Fully Charged	Filling	Fully Charged	Amp.	Amp.
1	2	3		4		5	6	7	8	9	10
LVW5E	5	5	5.7	1/8	71	1.270	1.270–1.290	1.210	1.210–1.230	0.3	0.5
PU5E	5	8	9	1/6	94	1.270	1.270–1.290	1.210	1.210–1.230	0.6	1.0
PU7E	7	12	13.5	1/5	113	1.270	1.270–1.290	1.210	1.210–1.230	0.8	1.5
GU11E	11	20	22.8	1/3	189	1.270	1.270–1.290	1.210	1.210–1.230	1.3	2.2
SC7E	7	22.5	26	—	250	1.270	1.270–1.290	1.210	1.210–1.230	1.5	2.5

The maximum permissible electrolyte temperature during charging is given below. Should the temperature of the electrolyte exceed this value interrupt the charge and allow the battery temperature to fall at least 10°F. (5.5°C.) before charging is resumed.

Climates normally below 80°F. (27°C.)	Climates between 80°–100°F. (27°–38°C.)	Climates frequently above 100°F. (38°C.)
100°F. (38°C.)	110°F. (43°C.)	120°F. (49°C.)

The specific gravity of the electrolyte varies with temperature. For convenience in comparing specific gravities, they are always corrected to 60°F., which is adopted as the reference temperature. The method of correction is as follows:

For every 5°F. *below* 60°F., *deduct* 0.002 from the observed reading to obtain the true specific gravity at 60°F. For every 5°F. *above* 60°F., *add* 0.002 to the observed reading to obtain the true specific gravity at 60°F.

The temperature must be that indicated by a thermometer having its bulb actually immersed in the electrolyte, and not the ambient temperature.

B.S.A. Service Sheet No. 805 (continued)

SERVICING
Battery Persists in Low State of Charge

First consider the conditions under which the battery is used. If the battery is subject to continuous discharge, e.g. long periods of night parking with lights on without suitable opportunities for recharging, a low state of charge is inevitable.

A fault in the dynamo or regulator, or neglect during a period out of commission, may also be responsible.

Vent Plugs

See that the ventilating holes in each vent plug are clear, and that the rubber washer fitted under the plug is in good condition.

Level of Electrolyte

The surface of the electrolyte should be level with the tops of the separators. If necessary, top-up with distilled water. Any loss of acid from spilling or spraying (as opposed to normal loss of *water* by evaporation) should be made good by dilute acid of the same specific gravity as that already in the cell.

Cleanliness

See that the top of the battery is free from dirt or moisture which might provide a discharge path. Check that the battery connections are clean and tight.

Hydrometer Tests

The space between each separator is not wide enough to permit the nozzle of an hydrometer to be inserted. Before taking a sample, tilt the battery to bring sufficient electrolyte above the separators. If the level of the electrolyte is so low that an hydrometer reading cannot be taken, no attempt should be made to take a reading after adding distilled water until the battery has been on charge for at least 30 minutes.

Measure the specific gravity of the acid in each cell in turn. The reading given by each cell should be approximately the same; if one cell differs appreciably from the others, an internal fault in that cell is indicated.

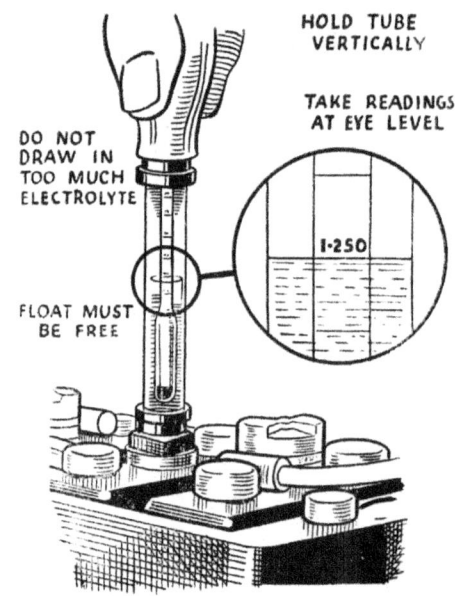

Fig Y20. Taking hydrometer readings

Specific gravity readings and their indications are as follows:

Climates under 90°F.				Climates over 90°F.
1.270—1.290	..	Cell fully charged	..	1.210—1.230
1.190—1.210	..	Cell about half discharged	..	1.130—1.150
1.110—1.130	..	Cell fully discharged	..	1.050—1.070

The appearance of the electrolyte drawn into the hydrometer when taking a reading gives a useful indication of the state of the plates: if it is very dirty, or contains small particles in suspension, it is possible that the plates are in a bad condition.

Discharge Test

Motor-cycle batteries must *not* be subjected to the heavy discharge test, as recommended for motor-car and commercial vehicle batteries.

RECHARGING FROM AN EXTERNAL SUPPLY

If the hydrometer test indicates that the battery is merely discharged, and is otherwise in a good condition, it should be recharged, either on the motor-cycle by a period of daytime running, or on the bench from an external supply.

B.S.A. Service Sheet No. 805 (continued)

If the latter, the battery should be charged at the rate given in the table until the specific gravity and voltage show no increase over three successive hourly readings. During the charge the electrolyte must be kept level with the tops of the separators by the addition of distilled water.

A battery that shows a general falling-off in efficiency, common to all cells, will often respond to the process known as 'cycling'. This process consists of fully charging the battery by passing through it from an external source the appropriate re-charge current given in the table. The battery is then discharged by connecting to a lamp board, or other load, taking a current equal to the normal re-charge current. The battery should be capable of providing this current for at least 7 hours before it is fully discharged, as indicated by the voltage of each cell falling to 1.8. If the battery discharges in a shorter time, repeat the 'cycle' of charge and discharge.

PREPARING BATTERIES FOR SERVICE

All new batteries are supplied without electrolyte but with the plates in a charged condition. When they are required for service it is only necessary to fill each cell with sulphuric acid of the correct specific gravity. No initial charging is required.

Preparation of Electrolyte

The electrolyte is prepared by mixing together distilled water and concentrated sulphuric acid. The mixing must be carried out either in a lead-lined tank or in suitable glass or earthenware vessels. Slowly add the acid to the water, stirring with a glass rod. *Never add water to acid*, as the resulting chemical reaction causes violent and dangerous spurting of the concentrated acid. The specific gravity of the filling electrolyte depends on the climate in which the battery is to be used.

The approximate proportions of acid and water are indicated in the following table:

To obtain Specific Gravity (corrected to 60°F.) of	Add 1 vol. of acid 1.835 S.G. (corrected to 60°F.) to
1.270	2.8 vols. of water
1.210	4.0 vols. of water

Heat is produced by the mixture of acid and water, and the electrolyte should be allowed to cool before pouring it into the battery.

The total volume of electrolyte required can be estimated from the figures quoted in the table on page 2.

Filling the Battery

Carefully break the seals in the cell filling holes and fill each cell with electrolyte to the top of the separators, *in one operation*. The temperature of the filling room, battery and electrolyte should be maintained between 60°F. and 100°F. If the battery has been stored in a cool place, it should be allowed to warm up to room temperature before filling.

Putting into Use

Batteries filled in this way are 90 per cent charged. If time permits, however, a freshening charge of four hours at the normal recharge rate given in the table would be beneficial.

During the charge the electrolyte must be kept level with the top edge of the separators by the addition of distilled water. Check the specific gravity of the acid at the end of the charge; if 1.270 acid was used to fill the battery, the specific gravity should now be between 1.270 and 1.290; if 1.210, between 1.210 and 1.230.

Maintenance in Service

After filling, the battery needs only the recommended attention.

B.S.A. MOTOR CYCLES LTD.
Service Dept., Waverley Works,
Birmingham, 10.

JU/B5029

Printed in England.

BSA SERVICE SHEET No. 806

Reprinted April, 1960

All Models

LAMPS

LUCAS LIGHTING

Headlamps

Although the headlamps fitted to individual models may vary in detail, they remain similar with regard to the general features described below. All headlamps are fitted with a double filament main bulb and a pilot bulb. One of the double filaments provides the main riding beam while the second, brought into operation by means of the dipper switch, provides the dipped beam.

On some models the headlamp incorporates a panel containing the ammeter and lighting switch but if a cowl is fitted then it carries these components externally to the headlamp shell.

Other headlamps contain wire wound resistances for the purpose of reducing the charging rates under certain conditions and these are described under the appropriate lighting circuit.

Setting and Focusing

The best way of checking the setting of the lamp is to park the motor cycle in front of a light coloured wall at a distance of about 25 feet. If necessary, slacken the bolts securing the headlamp and move the lamp until, with the main driving light switched on, the beam is projected straight ahead and parallel with the ground. With the lamp in this position, the height of the beam centre from the ground should be the same as the height of the centre of the headlamp from the ground.

Fig. Y.22 Headlamp Focusing.

The headlamp must be focused so that, when the main driving light is switched on, a uniform beam without any dark centre is given. If the bulb needs adjusting, remove the lamp front and reflector, as described below, and slacken the bulb holder clamping clip at the back of the reflector. Move the bulb holder backwards and forwards until the correct position is obtained, and then tighten the clamping clip.

More sealed beam light units are fitted with the pre-focus type of bulb and therefore no focusing is necessary.

Removal of Front and Reflector, pre-1948 models

Press back the fixing clip at the bottom of the lamp. The front and reflector can now be taken off. The bulb holder is secured to the reflector by means of two fixing springs. When replacing the front, locate the top of the rim first, then press on at the bottom and secure with the fixing clip.

B.S.A. Service Sheet No. 806 (cont.)

1948 Models (Fig. Y.23)

Press back the fixing clip at the bottom of the lamp, and remove the lamp front. The reflector is secured to the lamp body by means of a rubber bead. When refitting the rubber bead, locate its thinner lip between the reflector rim and the edge of the lamp body. To replace the front, locate the metal tongue in the slot at the top of the lamp, press the front on, and secure by means of the fixing catch.

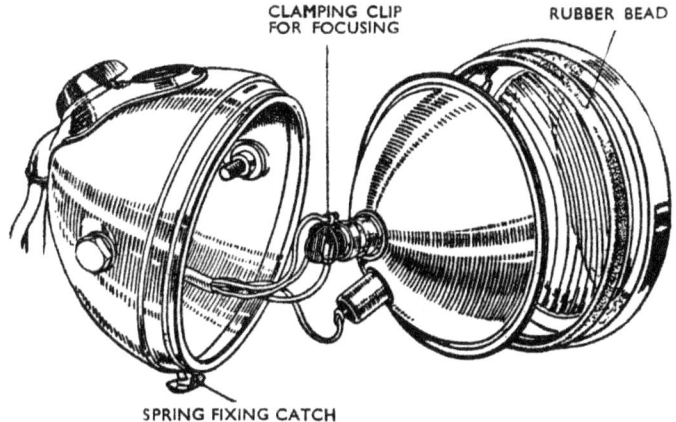

Fig. Y.23.

Sealed Beam Headlamps

Later models are fitted with a sealed light unit having the reflector and glass sealed together. After slackening the securing screw on the top of the headlamp, the rim, complete with light unit, may be removed. To replace, locate the rim on the lip at the bottom of the lamp body, press the light unit assembly and rim into position and tighten the securing screw. The main headlamp bulb in some of these headlamps is of the pre-focus type and is held in position by a cap with bayonet type fitting. In all cases access to the main or pilot bulbs is obtained by removal of the light unit assembly.

Breakage of the headlamp glass with this type of unit involves replacement of the glass and reflector complete. The light unit may be removed from the headlamp rim after prising out the retaining clips.

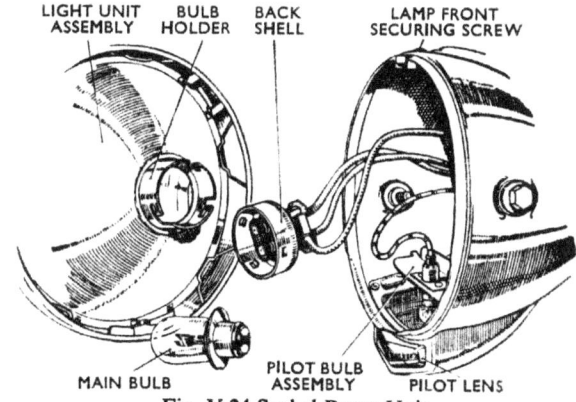

Fig. Y.24 Sealed Beam Unit.

Replacement of Bulbs

When the replacement of a bulb is necessary, it is important not only that the same size bulb is fitted, but that it has a high efficiency and will focus in the reflector. Cheap and inferior replacement bulbs often have the filament of such a shape that it is impossible to focus correctly; for example, the filament may be to the one side of the axis of the bulb resulting in loss of range and light efficiency.

Lucas Genuine Spare Bulbs are specially tested to check that the filament is in the correct position to give the best results with Lucas lamps. To assist in identification, Lucas bulbs are marked on the metal cap with a number. When fitting a replacement, see that it has the same number as the original bulb.

B.S.A. Service Sheet No. 806 (cont.)

When fitting a main headlamp bulb, care must be taken to insert it the correct way round, i.e. with the dipped beam filament above the centre filament.

The pre-focus type bulb is located by a flange and there is a notch which engages on a raised portion of the bulb holder to ensure correct positioning.

Where the pilot bulb is contained in an underslung cowl, the metal strip on which the bulb is mounted should be pushed to the rear and lifted away in order to provide access to the bulb.

Tail Lamps

Where the tail lamp is of the metal type the body or back should be removed by pushing it in, rotating to the left, and pulling away, thus providing access to the bulb. The moulded plastic type of rear lamp can be dismantled by unscrewing the two screws in the cover.

When a stop lamp is fitted, a two-filament type of bulb is employed with offset bayonet type fixing pins to ensure that it can only be fitted correctly.

MAIN BULBS

Models A7, A10, B31, 32, 33, 34, C12, C15 and M20, M21.

Lucas No. 168, 6v. 24/24w. (with E3H Dynamo). Lucas No. 169, 6v. 30/30w. (with E3L Dynamo). Lucas No. 312, 6v. 30/24w. (Pre-focus type Bulb).

Models C10 and C11.

Lucas No. 180, 6v., 18/18w. (with E3H Dynamo). Lucas No. 168, 6v. 24/24w. (with E3L Dynamo).

Models C11G and D1 (early) Lucas

Lucas No. 312, 6v. 30/24w. (Pre-focus type Bulb).

PILOT

Lucas No. 200, 6v. 3w. Lucas No. 988, 6v. 3w. (with Sealed Beam Light Unit).

TAIL

Lucas No. 205, 6v. 6w.
Lucas No. 384, 6v. 6/18w. (Stop/Tail Lamp).

B.S.A. MOTOR CYCLES LTD.
Service Dept., Waverley Works,
Birmingham, 10
Printed in England.

JU/B4780

BSA SERVICE SHEET No. 807

Reprinted June 1960

All Models

ELECTRIC HORN—HIGH FREQUENCY MODELS

General
Electric horns are adjusted to give their best performance before leaving the Works, and will give long periods of service without any attention.

Servicing
If the horn becomes uncertain in action or does not vibrate, it does not follow that the horn has broken down. The trouble may be due to a discharged battery or a loose or broken connection in the horn wiring.

The performance of the horn may be upset by the fixing bolt working loose, or by the vibration of some part adjacent to the horn. To check this, remove the horn from its mounting, hold it firmly in the hand by its bracket and press the push. If the note is still unsatisfactory, the horn may require adjustment, but this should only be necessary after a very long period of service.

Method of Adjusting
The adjustment of a horn does not alter the characteristics of the note but merely takes up wear of vibrating parts.

If the horn is used repeatedly when badly out of adjustment, due usually to unsuccessful attempts at adjustment, the horn may become damaged, due to the excessive current which it will take. When testing, do not continue to operate the push if the horn does not sound. If, when the push is operated, the horn does not take any current (indicated by an ammeter connected in series with the horn) it is possible that the horn has been adjusted so that its contact breaker is permanently open.

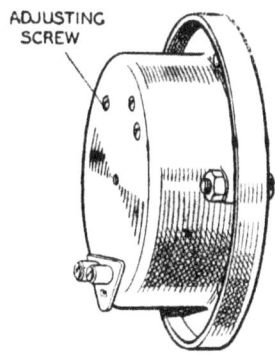

Fig. Y26.
Typical electric horn, showing adjustment screw.

After adjusting, note the current consumption, which must not exceed 3—4 amperes. A horn may give a good note, yet be out of adjustment and taking an excessive current. When adjusting do not attempt to unscrew the nut securing the tone disc or any other screw in the horn.

The adjustment is made by turning the adjustment screw, usually in a clockwise direction. The underside of the screw is serrated, and the screw must not be turned for more than 2 or 3 notches before re-testing. If the adjustment screw is turned too far in a clockwise direction, a point will occur at which the armature pulls in but does not separate the contacts.

B.S.A. Service Sheet No. 807 (contd.)

Some models have no adjustment screw at the back of the horn. Adjustment is carried out by means of the grub screw and locking collar which are revealed upon removal of the large domed nut on the front of the horn. Take care that the large nut securing the sounding disc is not disturbed. The locking collar requires a special tool, or a large screwdriver with the blade ground so as to leave two projecting prongs, in order that it may be undone. No attempt should be made to loosen the collar without a proper tool as it is very tight and may become damaged so that it cannot be removed. The adjustment should be carried out in a similar manner to that described for the other type of horn, but the locking collar should be firmly tightened after each adjustment as this affects the note.

B.S.A. MOTOR CYCLES LTD.,
Service Dept., Waverley Works,
Birmingham, 10.
Printed in England.

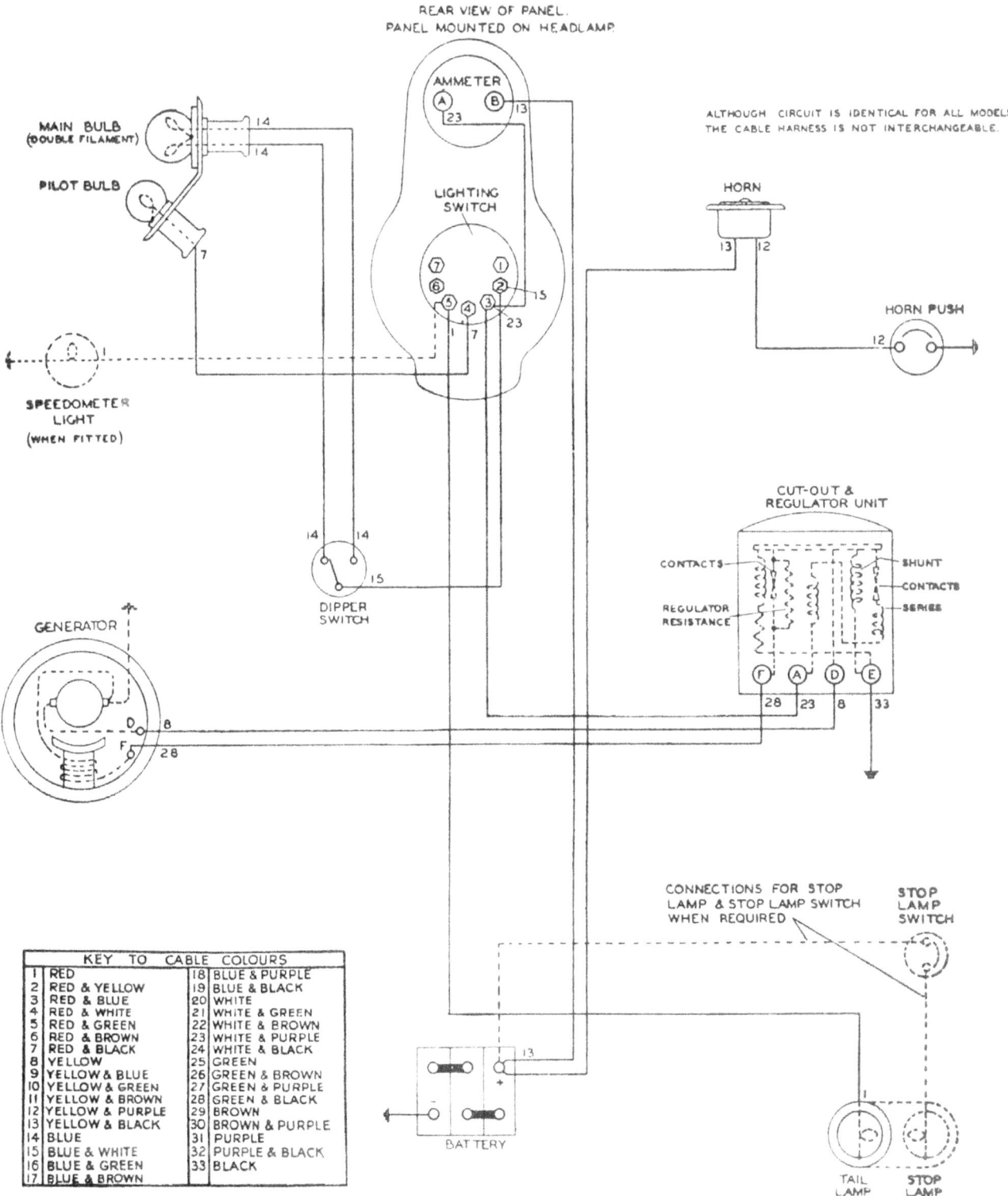

B.S.A. Service Sheet No. 808 (cont.)

C10 and C11 Models
WIRING DIAGRAM
(NEGATIVE EARTH)

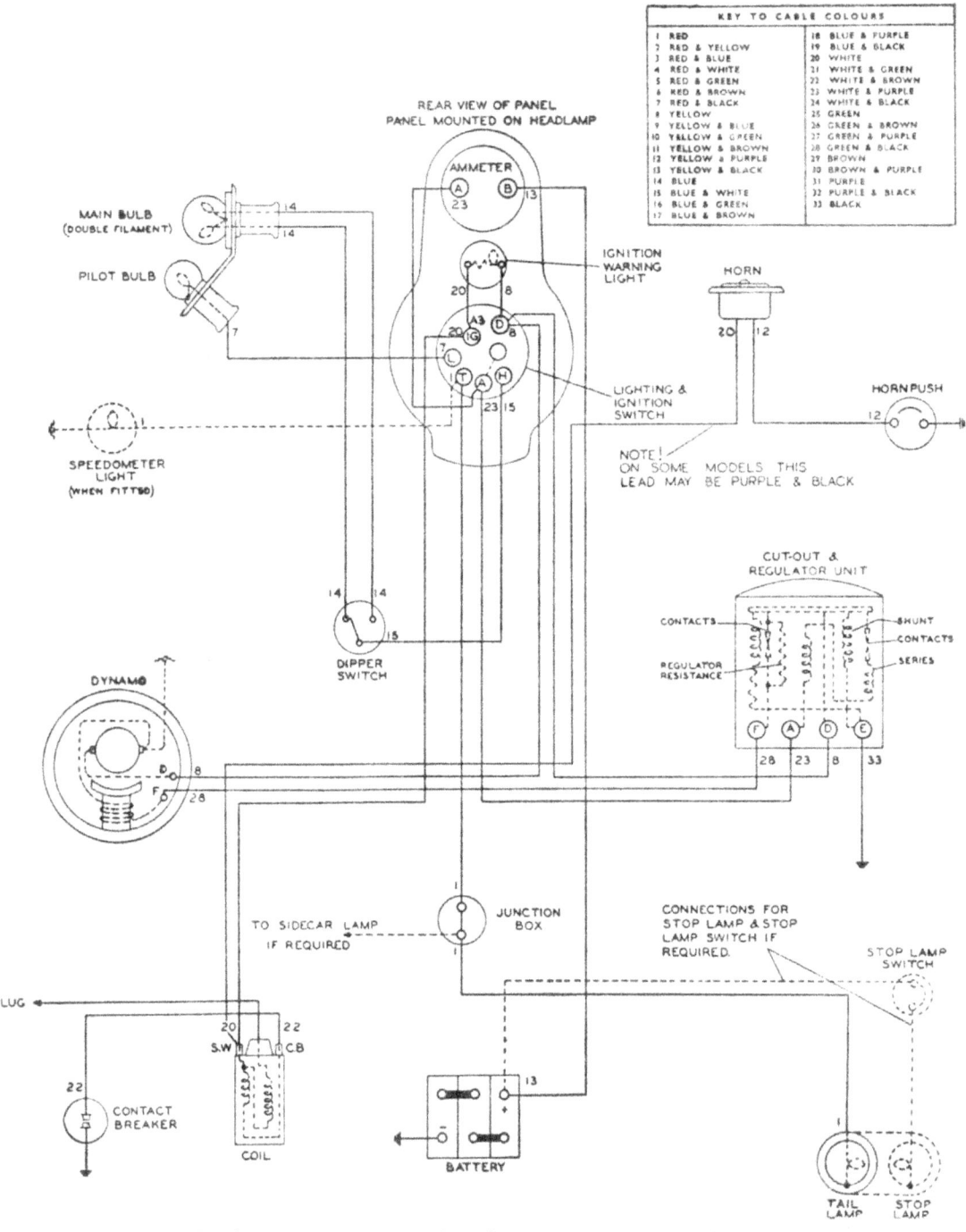

Numbers indicate cable identification colours. See key.

B.S.A. MOTOR CYCLES LTD.
Service Dept., Armoury Road,
Birmingham, 11

Printed in England.

BSA SERVICE SHEET No. 808A

A, (except A50/A65) B and M Group Models
WIRING DIAGRAM
(Positive Earth System)

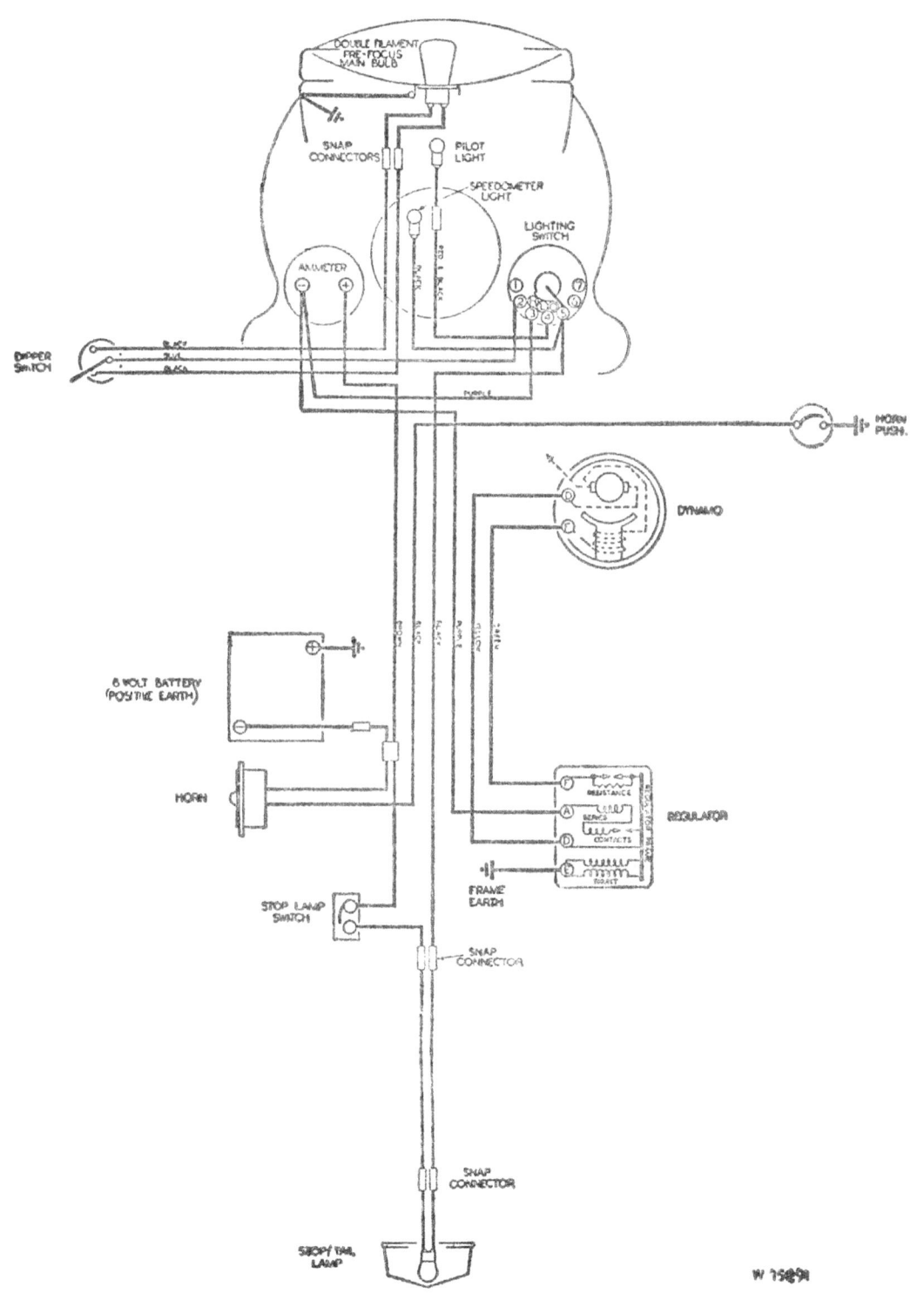

B.S.A. Service Sheet No. 808A (contd.)

C Group Models
WIRING DIAGRAM
(Positive Earth System)

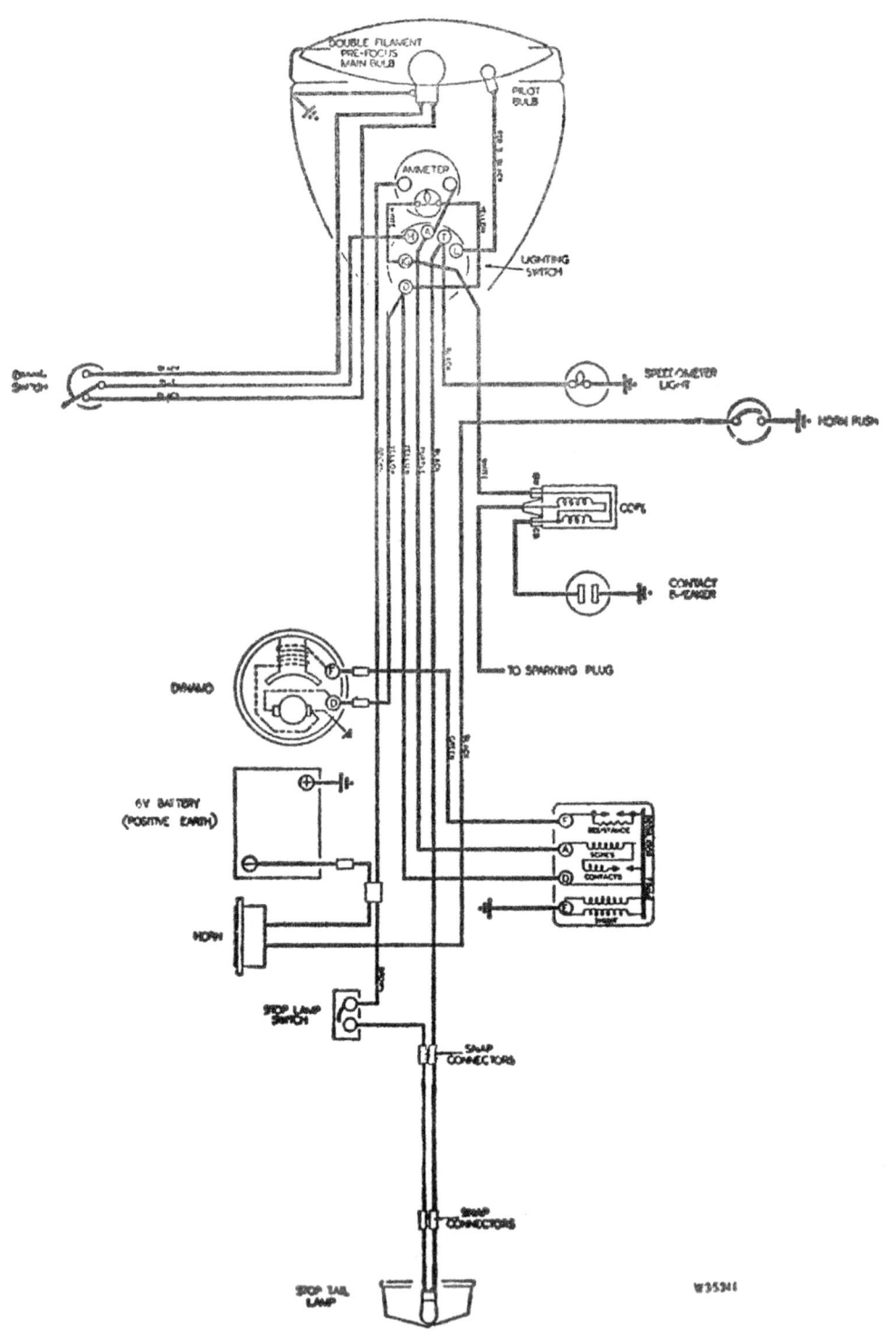

Printed in England.

B.S.A. MOTOR CYCLES LTD.
Service Dept., Armoury Road, Birmingham 11,

BSA SERVICE SHEET No. 808C
WIRING DIAGRAMS
Model C10L
(Wipac Lighting)

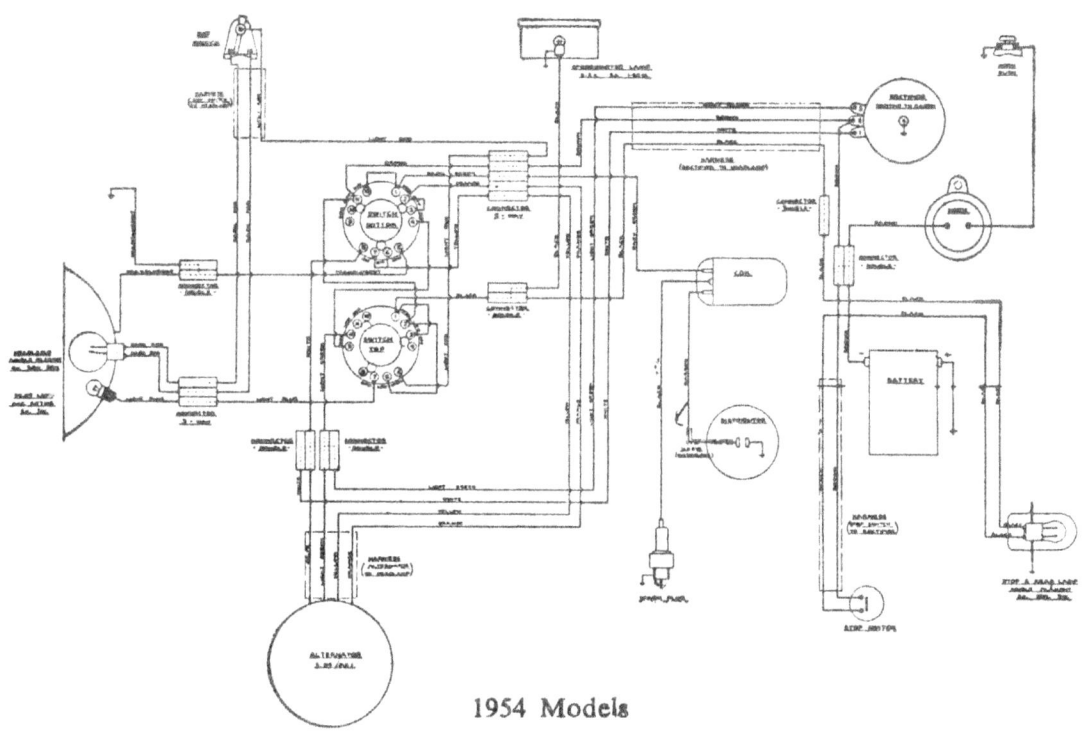

1954 Models

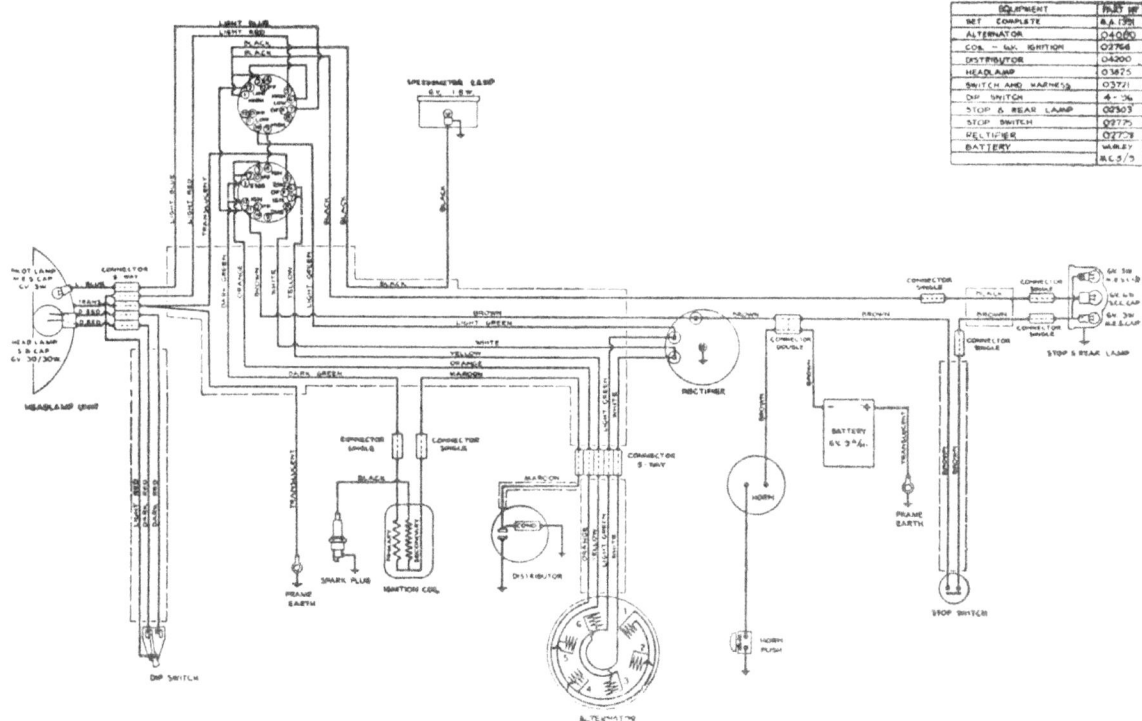

1955 Models

EQUIPMENT	PART N°
SET COMPLETE	BA1391
ALTERNATOR	04080
COIL - SW. IGNITION	02766
DISTRIBUTOR	04200
HEADLAMP	03875
SWITCH AND HARNESS	03771
DIP SWITCH	4-34
STOP & REAR LAMP	03503
STOP SWITCH	02775
RECTIFIER	02779
BATTERY	VARLEY BCS/3

B.S.A. Service Sheet No. 808C (cont.)

Model C11G
(Lucas Lighting)

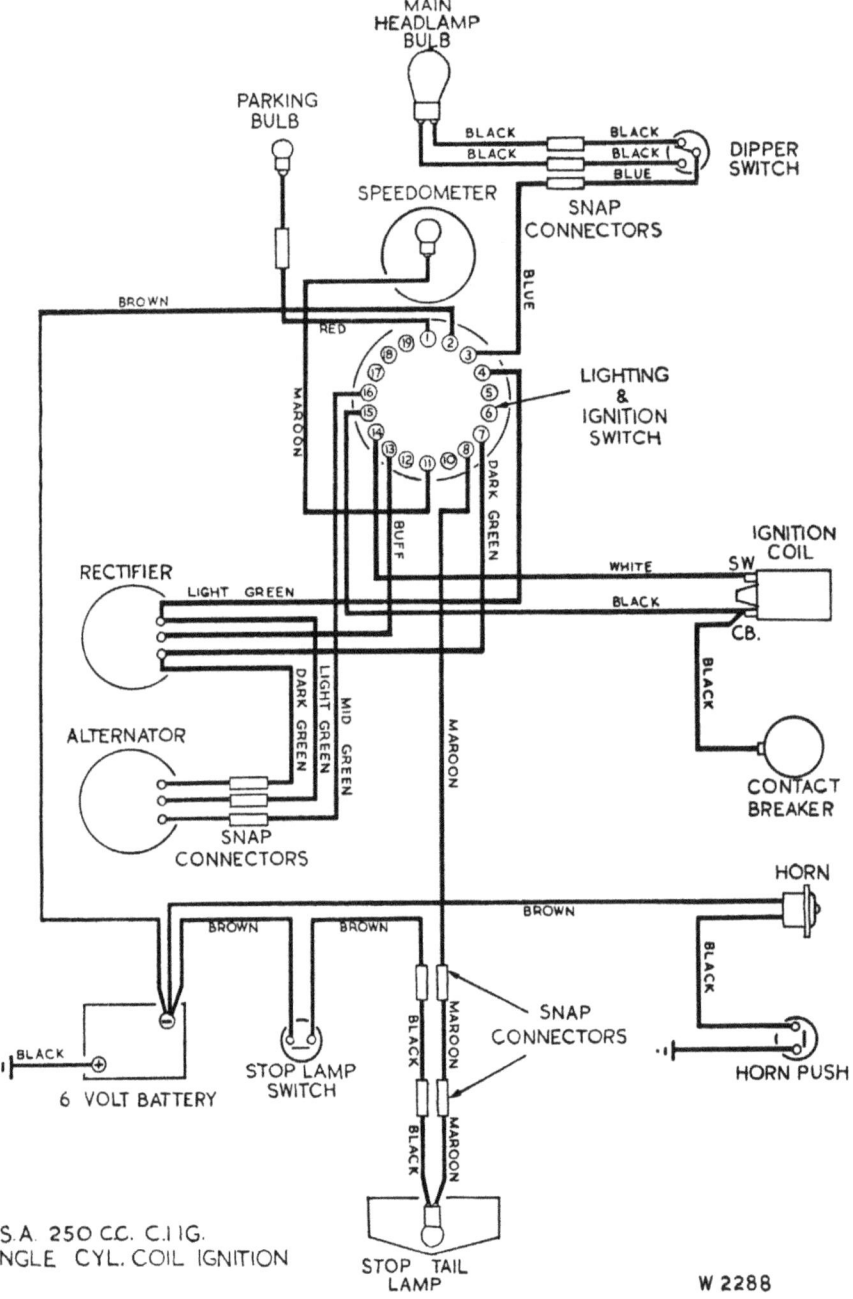

B.S.A. 250 C.C. C.11G.
SINGLE CYL. COIL IGNITION

W 2288

B.S.A. MOTOR CYCLES LTD.
Service Dept., Birmingham 11
Printed in England.

BSA SERVICE SHEET No. 808D

Reprinted February, 1964

1956 C Group Models

WIRING DIAGRAMS

C12

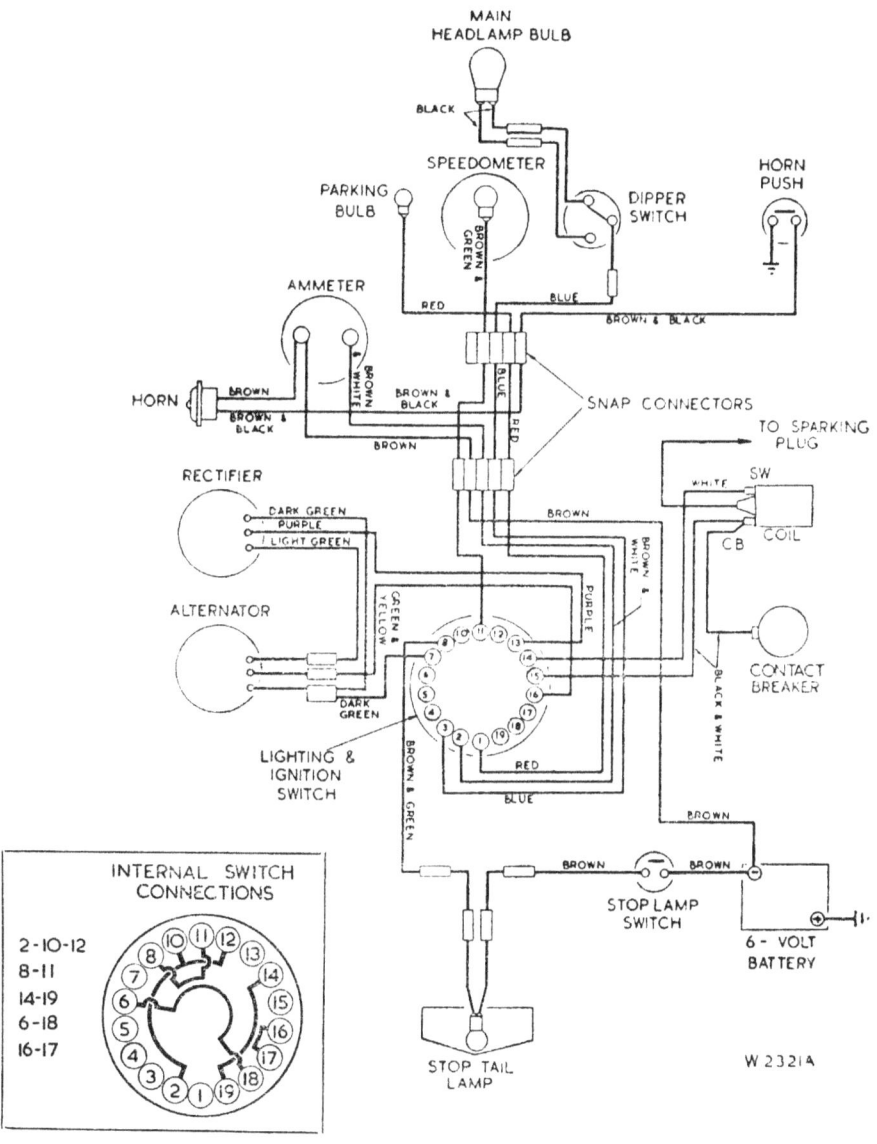

C10L (1956)

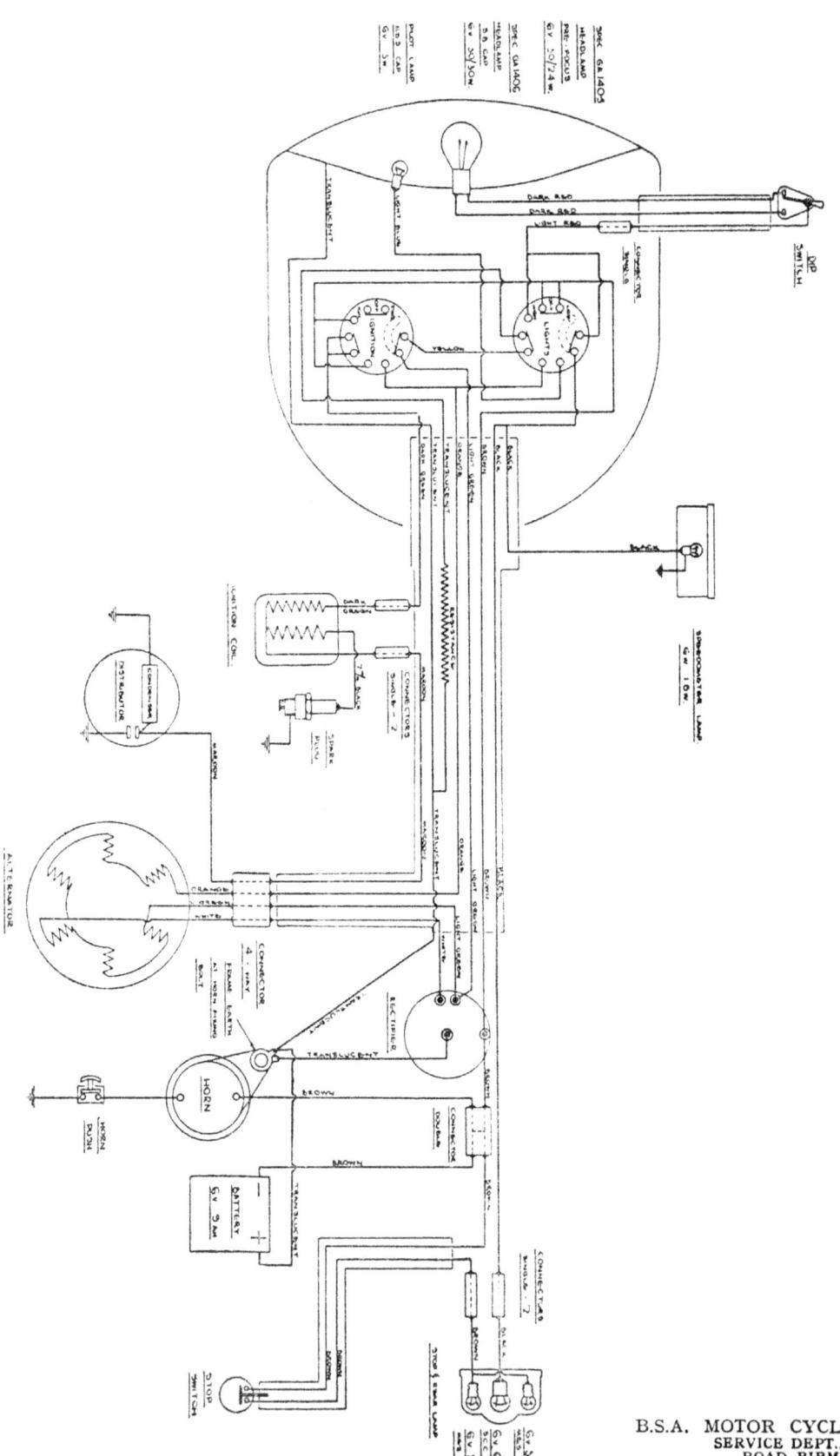

BSA SERVICE SHEET No. 809

All Models except D1, C10L, C11G, C12, C15 and "B" Group fitted with Alternators

GENERATORS–MODELS E3H and E3HM

The generator is a shunt-wound two pole machine, arranged to work in conjunction with a regulator unit to give an output which is dependent on the state of charge of the battery and the loading of the electrical equipment in use. When the battery is in a low state of charge, the generator gives a high output, whereas if the battery is fully charged the generator gives only a trickle charge to keep the battery in a good condition without overcharging. In addition, an increase of output is given to balance the current taken by the lamps when in use.

Models E3H and E3HM are similar in construction. The former will be found on motor cycles having separate magneto or coil ignition, while model E3HM is the generator portion of the combined unit known as the "magdyno".

ROUTINE MAINTENANCE

Lubrication
The lubricator at the commutator end bracket must be given a few drops of good grade thin machine oil every 1,000—2,000 miles. The bearing at the driving end is packed with H.M.P. grease and will last until the machine is taken down for a general overhaul, when the bearing should be repacked.

Inspection of Commutator and Brush Gear
About once every six months remove the cover band for inspection of commutator and brushes. The brushes are held in contact with the commutator by means of springs. Move each brush to see that it is free to slide in its holder; if it sticks, remove it and clean with a

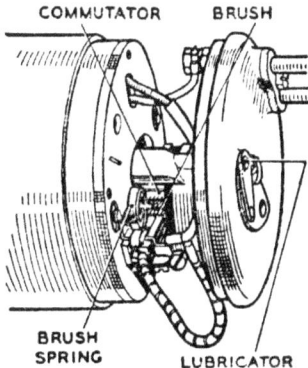

Fig. Y30. *Commutator and Bracket Assembly.*

cloth moistened with petrol. Care must be taken to replace the brushes in their original positions, otherwise they will not "bed" properly on the commutator. If, after long service, the brushes have become worn to such an extent that the brush flexible is exposed on the

B.S.A. Service Sheet No. 809 (contd.)

running face, or if the brushes do not make good contact with the commutator, they must be replaced by genuine Lucas brushes. The commutator should be free from any trace of oil or dirt and should have a highly polished appearance. Clean a dirty or blackened commutator by pressing a fine dry cloth against it while the engine is slowly turned over by means of the kickstarter crank. (It is an advantage to remove the sparking plug before doing this). If the commutator is very dirty, moisten the cloth with petrol.

Test Data

Cutting-in speed: 1,250—1,500 r.p.m. at 7 generator volts.
  Output: 6.5 amps at 1,900—2,200 r.p.m. at 7 generator volts, taken on 1.1 ohm resistance load. Resistance to be capable of carrying 10 amps without overheating.
  Field resistance: 3.2 ohms.

SERVICING

Testing in position to locate fault in Charging Circuit

In the event of a fault in the charging circuit, adopt the following procedure to locate the cause of trouble.

  Check that the generator and regulator unit are connected correctly. The generator terminal (D) should be connected to the regulator unit terminal (D) and generator terminal (F) to regulator unit terminal (F).

  Remove the cables from the generator terminals (D) and (F) and connect the two terminals with a short length of wire. Start the engine and set to run at normal idling speed.

  Connect the positive lead of a moving coil voltmeter, calibrated 0—10 volts, to one of the generator terminals and connect the negative lead to a good earthing point on the generator yoke or engine.

Fig. Y31. *Testing Brush Spring Tension.*

  Gradually increase the engine speed, when the voltmeter reading should rise rapidly and without fluctuation. Do not allow the voltmeter reading to rise above 10 volts, and do not race the engine in an attempt to increase the voltage. It is sufficient to run the generator up to a speed of 1,000 r.p.m. If there is no reading, check the brush gear as

B.S.A. Service Sheet No. 809 (contd.)

described below. If there is a low reading of approximately ½ volt, the field winding may be at fault. If there is a reading of approximately 1½ to 2 volts, the armature winding may be at fault.

Remove the cover band and examine the brushes and commutator. Hold back each of the brush springs and move the brush by pulling gently on its flexible connector. If the movement is sluggish, remove the brush from its holder and ease the sides by lightly polishing on a smooth file. Always replace brushes in their original positions. If the brushes are worn so that they do not bear on the commutator, or if the brush flexible is exposed on the running face, new brushes must be fitted.

Test the brush spring tension with a spring scale. The correct tension is 10—15 oz. and new springs must be fitted if the tension is low.

If the commutator is blackened or dirty, clean it by holding a petrol-moistened cloth against it while the engine is turned slowly by means of the kickstart (with sparking plug removed).

Re-test the generator as above. If there is still no reading on the voltmeter, there is an internal fault and the complete unit, if a spare is available, should be replaced. Otherwise the unit must be dismantled for internal examination.

If the generator is in good order, restore the original connections. Connect regulator unit terminal (D) to generator terminal (D) and regulator terminal (F) to generator terminal (F). Proceed to test the regulator unit as described in Service Sheet No. 804.

To Dismantle

Remove the generator from the motor cycle. To remove the generator from the magdynos unscrew the hexagon-headed nut from the driving end cover and slacken the two screws securing the band clip. Proceed to dismantle, as follows:—

On E3HM machines, bend back the tag on the washer (B) Fig. Y33, locking the screw (A) securing the driving gear (C) and remove the screw. On E3H machines, withdraw the cotter pin (A) and remove the nut (B) from the armature shaft. Withdraw the gear from

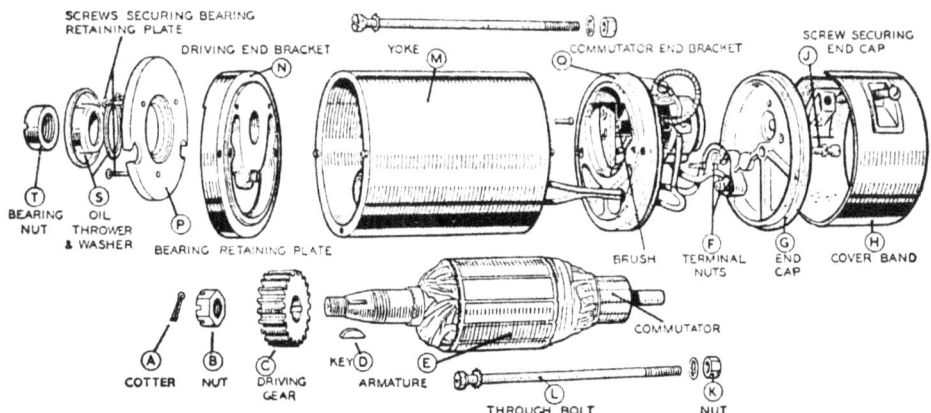

Fig. Y32. *Generator, model E3H (with oil seal).*

B.S.A. Service Sheet No. 809 (contd.)

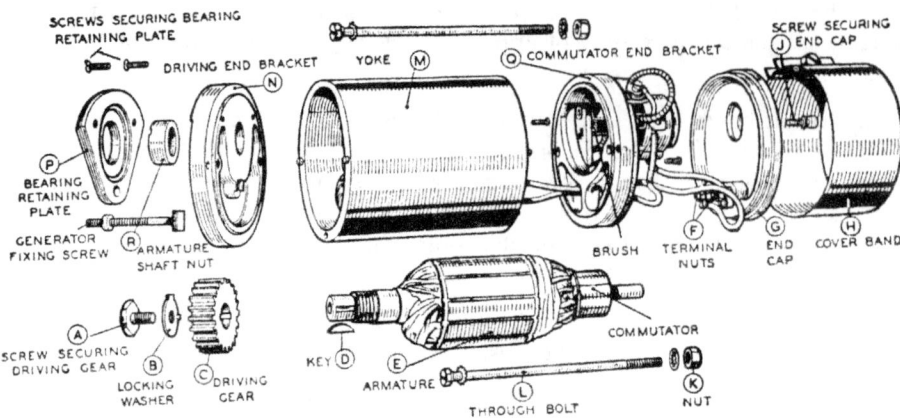

Fig. Y33. *Generator, model E3HM.*

the shaft by carefully levering it off or by means of an extractor. Remove the key(s) (D), from the shaft.

Remove the cover band (H), hold back the brush springs and lift the brushes from their holders.

Take out the screw (J), with spring washer, from the centre of the black moulded end cap (G). Draw the cap away from the end bracket, take off terminal nuts (F), and spring washers, and lift the connections off the terminals.

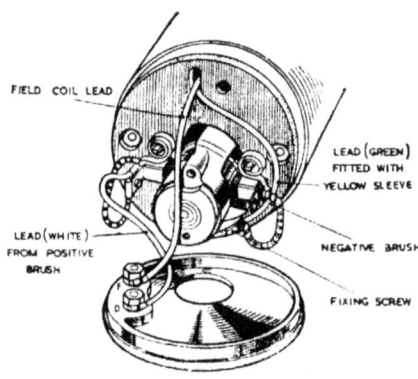

Fig. Y34. *Generator Connections.*
Note:- On later machines, the white lead is omitted, the brush flexible lead being connected direct to terminal "D"

Unscrew and remove from the driving end bracket the two through bolts (L) securing the driving end bracket (N) and commutator end bracket (Q) to the yoke (M). Hold the nuts (K) at the commutator end while unscrewing the bolts, and take care not to lose the nuts.

On E3HM Machines.—Remove the bearing retaining plate (P) from the driving end bracket secured by two screws and a long threaded bolt. Unscrew the nut (R) from the end of the armature shaft and the armature can then be removed from the driving end bracket (N) by means of a hand press.

B.S.A. Service Sheet No. 809 (contd.)

On E3H Machines.—Remove the bearing nut (T) and the oil thrower and washer (S). Withdraw the three screws securing the retaining plate (P). The armature can then be removed from the driving end bracket (N) by means of a hand press.

Take out the screw securing the green field coil lead with the yellow sleeve to commutator end bracket and remove the end bracket (Q), withdrawing the connectors through the slot in the insulating plate.

Unscrew the three screws securing the insulating plate to the commutator end bracket and remove the plate complete with brush gear.

Commutator

Examine the commutator. If it is in good condition, it will be smooth and free from pits or burned spots. Clean with a petrol-moistened cloth. If this is ineffective, carefully polish with a strip of very fine glasspaper while rotating the armature. To remedy a badly worn commutator, mount the armature with or without the drive end bracket in a lathe, rotate at high speed and take a light cut with a very sharp tool. Do not remove more metal than is necessary. Polish the commutator with very fine glasspaper.

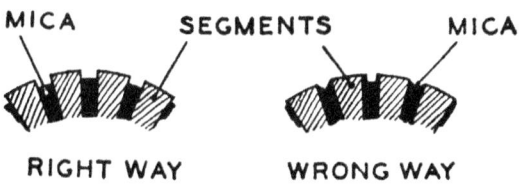

Fig. Y35. *Method of Undercutting Commutator Insulation.*

Undercut the mica insulation between the segments to a depth of $\frac{1}{32}$ in. with a hacksaw blade ground down until it is only slightly thicker than the mica.

Field Coil

Measure the resistance of the field winding by means of an ohm meter. If this is not available, connect a 6-volt D.C. supply with an ammeter in series across the coil. The ammeter reading should be approximately 1.9 amperes. No reading on the ammeter indicates an open circuit in the field winding.

To check for earthed coil, connect a mains test lamp between one end of the coil and the yoke. If the bulb lights, there is an earth between coil and yoke.

In either case, unless a replacement generator is available, the field coil must be replaced but this should only be attempted if a wheel-operated screwdriver and pole shoe expander are at hand, the latter being especially necessary to ensure that there will not be any airgap between the pole shoe and the inner face of the yoke.

To replace the field coil, proceed as follows:—

Unscrew the pole shoe retaining screw (Fig. Y36) by means of the wheel-operated screwdriver.

Draw the pole shoe and field coil out of the yoke and lift off the coil.

B.S.A. Service Sheet No. 809 (contd.)

Fit the new field coil over the pole shoe and place it in position inside the yoke. Take care to ensure that the taping of the field coil is not trapped between the pole shoe and the yoke.

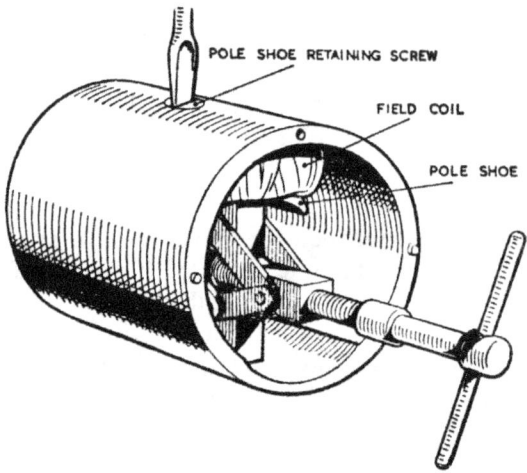

Fig. Y36. *Pole Shoe and Field Coil Assembly.*

Locate the pole shoe and field coil by lightly tightening the fixing screw. Insert the pole shoe expander, open to its fullest extent and tighten the screw. Remove the expander and give the screw a final tightening with the wheel-operated screwdriver. Lock the screw in position by caulking, that is, by tapping some of the metal of the yoke into the slot in the head of the screw.

Armature

The testing of the armature winding requires the use of a voltdrop test or growler. If these are not avilable, the armature should be checked by substitution. No attempt should be made to machine the armature core or to true a distorted armature shaft.

Bearings

A ball bearing is fitted at the driving end and a plain porous bronze bearing bush at the commutator end.

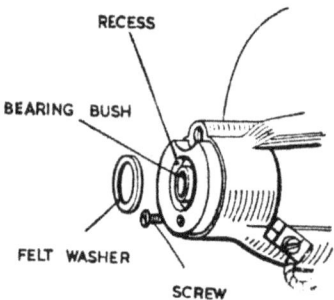

Fig. Y37. *Commutator End Bracket with Bearing Bush.*

Bearings which are worn to such an extent that they will allow side movement of the armature shaft must be replaced. To replace the bearing bush at the commutator end, proceed as follows:—

B.S.A. Service Sheet No. 809 (contd.)

Remove the screw, press the bearing bush out of the commutator end bracket and remove the felt washer (see Fig. Y37).

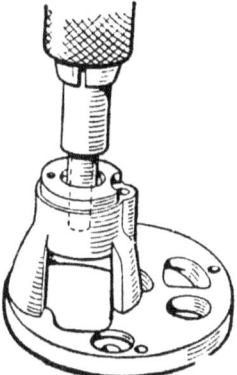

Fig. Y38. *Fitting Bearing Bush using a shouldered Mandrel.*

Press the new bearing bush into the end bracket using a shouldered mandrel (Fig. Y38) of the same diameter as the shaft which is to fit in the bearing. (NOTE:—Before use, new bearing bushes should be stored in a covered container and fully covered with oil of a grade equivalent to Mobiloil Arctic, or other good thin mineral oil. The minimum time of soaking should normally be 24 hours, but in cases of extreme urgency this period may be shortened by heating the oil to 100°C., when the time of immersion may be reduced to 2 hours). The bush should be pressed in until it is flush with the face of the end bracket. Fit the felt washer in the space between the bearing and the wall of the bearing housing.

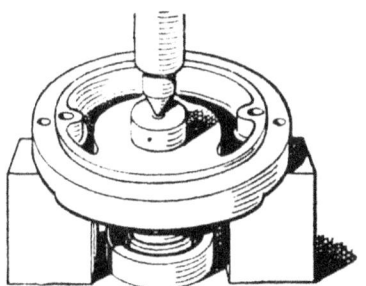

Fig. Y39. *Removing the Ball Race.*

The ball bearing at the driving end is replaced as follows:—

Remove bearing retaining plate from driving end bracket as previously described.

Press the bearing out of the end bracket, using a metal drift locating on the inner journal of the bearing (Fig. Y39).

Wipe out the bearing housing and pack the new bearing with H.M.P. grease.

Position the bearing in its housing and press it squarely home, applying pressure on the outer journal of the bearing (Fig. Y40).

B.S.A. Service Sheet No. 809 (contd.)

Reassembly

In the main, the reassembly of the generator is a reversal of the operations described in the paragraph on dismantling, bearing in mind the following points.

The field coil lead fitted with the short length of yellow tubing must be connected together with eyelet of the negative brush to the commutator end bracket by means of the screw provided.

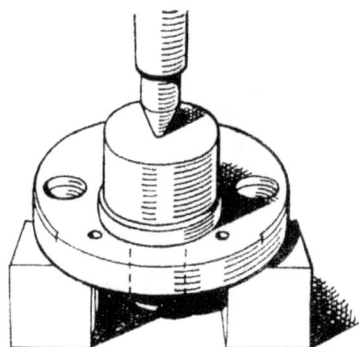

Fig. Y40. *Fitting the Ball Race.*

The second field coil lead must be connected to terminal (F) on the mouled end cap

The lead (coloured white) from the terminal on the positive brush box must be connected to terminal (D) on the mouled end cap.

(NOTE:—On later machines, the brush flexible lead is connected direct to terminal (D) and the white lead is omitted).

Take care to refit cover band in original position and make sure that the securing screw, when of flush-fitting pattern, does not short on brush gear.

E3L Dynamo

On some models an E3L dynamo is fitted. This is a higher output machine and the test figures are as follows. Cutting in speed 1,050—1,200 r.p.m. at 6.5 dynamo volts. Output 8.5 amps at 1,850—2,000 r.p.m. at 7 dynamo volts taken on .8 ohm resistance load. Resistance to be capable of carrying 10 amps without overheating. Field resistance 2.8 ohms. The dismantling and testing instructions are similar to those given for the E3H dynamo except for the following:—

1. Ball bearing fitted at commutator end.
2. Brush spring tension, 13—20 ozs.
3. Testing field coils, the ammeter reading will be 2.1 amperes.

B.S.A. MOTOR CYCLES LTD., Service Department, Armoury Road, Birmingham 11

BSA SERVICE SHEET No. 811

Models D1, D3, D5, D7 and C10L
LAMPS
(Wipac Lighting)

Headlamp.

Two types of headlamp have been employed but they differ only with regard to the headlamp switch. Early models have the body of the switch mounted inside the headlamp shell but remotely controlled through a cable and a lever mounted on the handlebars. Later models have a switch mounted in the top of the headlamp so that it can be reached from the normal riding position

The reflector and bulb holder assembly are housed in the front rim and to obtain access to the bulbs, loosen the screw situated at the bottom of the lamp rim and lift the rim outwards and upwards. To remove the bulb holder, bend down the small tab which projects from the base of the reflector. The holder can then be removed, after turning it anti-clockwise, making the main and parking bulbs easily accessible. When replacing the main bulb be sure that the word "TOP" on the bulb is uppermost.

If the bulb is not marked, assemble as illustrated:—

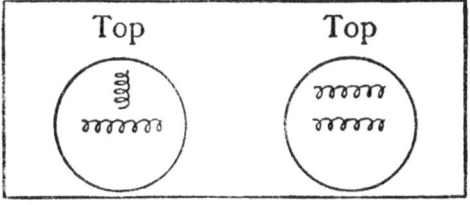

Correct way to fit double-filament bulbs.

The correct focus has been incorporated in the design of the headlamp and therefore no provision for adjustment has been necessary.

Tail Lamp.

To remove the rim of the lamp, undo the small 6BA screw and turn the rim slightly to the left, it can then be easily withdrawn. On later models a bayonet fitting is employed and it is merely necessary to push the lamp cover in, twist it to the left and then pull it away.

B.S.A. Service Sheet No. 811 (continued).

The bulb holder is of the bayonet pattern and the bulb is removed by the usual push and turn method. When a stop light is fitted a double filament bulb is used. Ensure that the bulb is the right way up. The portion marked "TOP" should be uppermost when the bulb is inserted, but if the bulb is not marked, check that it is located correctly by operating the foot brake and ensuring that the brighter filament is illuminated.

Switching.

No adjustment of the later type switch is necessary but it may occasionally be required to synchronise the earlier type of switch with the handlebar lever. This can be easily carried out after slackening the locknut on the adjuster which connects the Bowden cable to the lever assembly. Screw the adjuster in or out until the switch positions are synchronised with the lever positions, then tighten the locknut. Four positions are provided on the lever and these correspond to Parking, Head Dipped, Head Full On and Off.

Parking Battery.

Where D.C. lighting is employed a Varley accumulator is fitted. On models employing A.C. lighting a dry battery is fitted inside the headlamp shell. This is a 3-volt bicycle battery, type 800. To fit a new battery, hold it so that the vertical contact strip faces towards the lamp, the battery should then be positioned in the holding bracket in such a manner that the vertical contact connects with the metal battery holder at the rear of the lamp, while the horizontal contact fits inside its corresponding contact.

Replacement Bulbs.

Headlamp (main)	...	D1, D3, D5 and D7	24/24 watt, double filament, 6/7 volt.
		C10L	30/30 watt, double filament, 6/7 volt.
Headlamp (parking) ...	A.C. lighting	...	.25 amp. 2.5 volt M.E.S.
	D.C. lighting	...	6/7 volt, 3 watt, M.E.S.
Tail lamp (single filament) ...	...	...	6/7 volt, 3 watt S.B.C.
(with combined stop light)		...	6/7 volt. 18/3 watt, S.B.C.
(with separate twin stop lights)		...	6/7 volt, 3 watt, M.E.S.
Speedometer ...	... ...	...	6.5 volt, .3 amp.

B.S.A. MOTOR CYCLES LTD., Service Department, Armoury Road, Birmingham 11.
B.S.A. Press.

BSA SERVICE SHEET No. 813

"C" AND "B" GROUP MODELS (EXCEPT C15 COMPETITION)

FITTED WITH CRANKSHAFT MOUNTED ALTERNATORS

LUCAS LIGHTING

The electrical system used on these models provides D.C. for the battery, ignition coil and lights, by passing the A.C. output of the generator through a bridge type rectifier.

The alternator is connected to a section of the headlamp switch so that the output is automatically matched to the demands of the lighting circuit and the characteristics of the alternator prevent overcharging.

"C" Group except C15
Cable Colours
Light Green
Dark Green
Middle Green or Green/Yellow

"B" Group & C15
Cable Colours
Green/Black or Dark Green
Green/Yellow
Green/White or Light Green

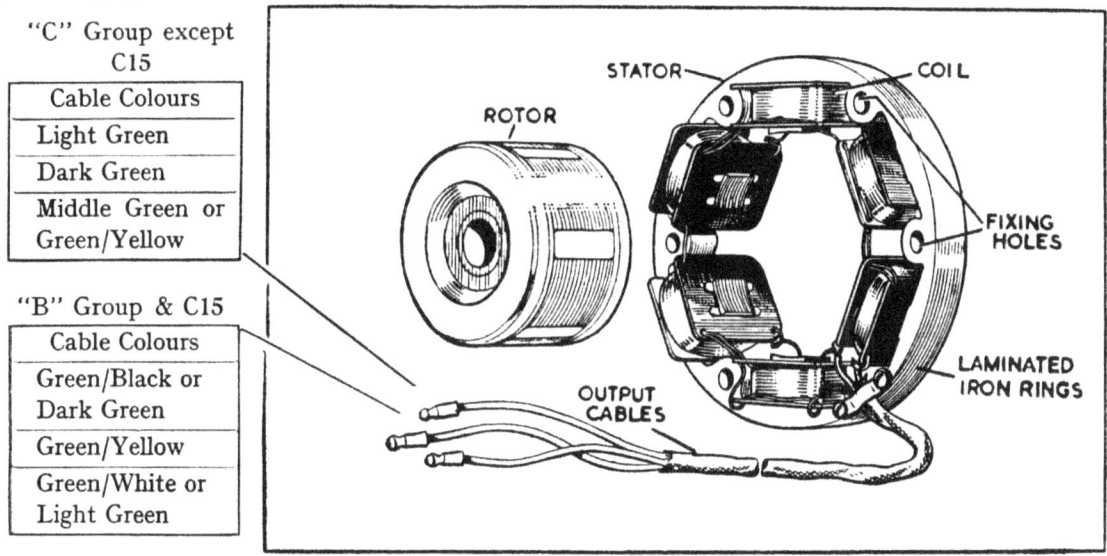

Stator and Rotor of Lucas Motor Cycle Alternator
(RM 13 on C11G and C15, RM 13/15 on C12, and RM 15 on new series "B" group machines)

Output Control

The standard circuit has the output wires from the generator connected by their snap connectors to similarly coloured wires on the wiring harness and provides the following output control.

Lighting Switch in "OFF" Position

The output is taken from one pair of coils by means of the Light Green and Dark Green wires, and the remaining coils (Light Green and Middle Green wires) (Light Green and Green/Yellow on "B" group) are open-circuited.

Lighting Switch in "PILOT" Position

Output taken from one pair of coils by Light Green and Dark Green wires as before and the remaining coils are on open-circuit.

B.S.A. SERVICE SHEET No. 813 (contd.)

Lighting Switch in "HEAD" Position

All three pairs of coils are connected in parallel and the maximum output is obtained. Note.—To provide an increased charging rate with the lighting switch in the "OFF" position, some models will be found to have the wire joining terminals 5 and 6 of the headlamp switch removed. This means that no coils are shorted out in this switch position and the charging rate is slightly increased.

In circumstances where a considerable amount of low speed running is necessary or there are long periods of parking with the lights on, it is possible to increase the charging rate with the lighting switch in the "OFF" and "PILOT" positions by connecting the Medium Green alternator cable (Green/Yellow for C15) by its snap connector to the Dark Green harness cable and the Dark Green alternator cable to the Medium Green harness cable (Green/Yellow for C15).

The Light Green cables should not be disturbed. These alternative connections considerably increase the charging rate in these switch positions, and the connections should be returned to standard for normal conditions of use or long runs.

Owing to the effects of the above modifications it is essential that the wiring circuit is returned to standard before checking the charging rates during fault finding.

Emergency Starting

With the ignition switch in the "EMG" position, the battery is not isolated from the alternator and will, in fact, receive a charge whilst the machine is being run.

This arrangement is also a safeguard against continuous running in the "EMG" position. The back pressure of the battery will increase as it is charged, until it is sufficiently strong to affect the working of the ignition system. When this happens misfiring will occur, resulting in poor engine performance. In view of this, always check that the machine is not being run with the ignition switch continually in the "EMG" position, before testing the system for other faults.

Motor Cycle Trials Events, etc.

When using the machine for trials riding, the alternator can be used continuously in the "EMG" position without a battery, providing the lead from the main harness to the battery negative terminal is earthed to the machine, but contact breaker points are liable to become badly burned.

Test Procedure

As the lights and other equipment are operated on a normal D.C. circuit they can be checked by normal continuity tests with a battery and bulb.

The following equipment is required to satisfactorily test the charging circuit. The meters used should be accurate moving coil instruments.

A.C voltmeter scale 0–15 volts.
D.C. ammeter scale 0–15 amps.
D.C. voltmeter scale 0–15 volts.

1 ohm. load resistance.
12 volt battery and 36 watt bulbs.

When checking the alternator output the engine should be run at approximately 3,000 r.p.m.

If the performance of the alternator has proved unsatisfactory, it is advisable to first check the wiring to make sure that good contact is being made at the various connections and that none of the wiring of alternator coils are shorting to the frame.

B.S.A. SERVICE SHEET No. 813 (contd.)

CHECKING D.C. INPUT TO BATTERY

Test 1. Ammeter connected in series with main lead and battery.

Test 2. Disconnect main lead from battery. Connect 1 ohm resistor in place of battery. Feed ignition coil separately from battery. Turn ignition switch to IGN position.

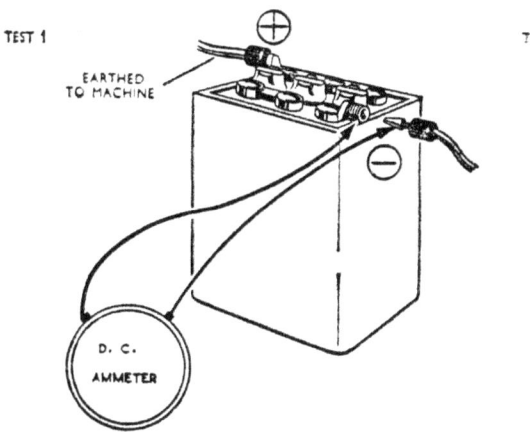
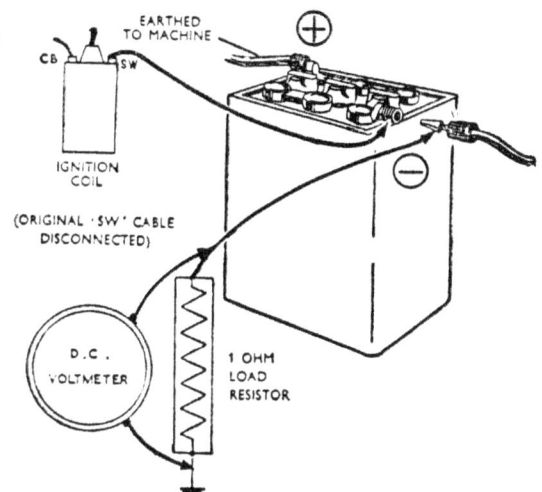

If the battery is in poor condition or low state of charge use Test 2.

Test	Switch Position	Reading Amps. at 3,000 r.p.m.		
		RM13	RM13/15	RM15
1	OFF	1.5 (min.)	1.75 (min.)	2.5 (min.)
	PILOT	0.5 (min.)	0.75 (min.)	1.5 (min.)
	HEAD	0.25 (min.)	0.5 (min.)	2.5 (min.)

Test	Switch Position	Reading Volts at 3,000 r.p.m.		
		RM13	RM13/15	RM15
2	OFF	1.5 (min.)	1.75 (min.)	2.5 (min.)
	PILOT	1.5 (min.)	1.75 (min.)	2.0 (min.)
	HEAD	3.0 (min.)	3.25 (min.)	3.0 (min.)

Conclusion from these Tests

Test 1. If meter readings are as stated, the charging circuit and alternator are satisfactory.
No reading; check the generator.
A low reading can be caused by a faulty battery.
Proceed with Test 2. If readings still low check battery with hydrometer and discharge tester.

Test 2. If meter readings are lower or higher than values stated, check the generator.
No reading on meter; check the rectifier.

Important

Inaccurate readings can be due to faulty wiring, bad connections at the snap connectors or poor earths. Make a quick visual check of all connections before proceeding with the tests.

Remember it is no use carrying out Test 1 if the battery is faulty or in a low state of charge; if in doubt proceed with Test 2.

B.S.A. SERVICE SHEET No. 813 (contd.)

Testing the RM13 Alternator on the Machine, using an A.C. Voltmeter and 1 Ohm Load Resistor

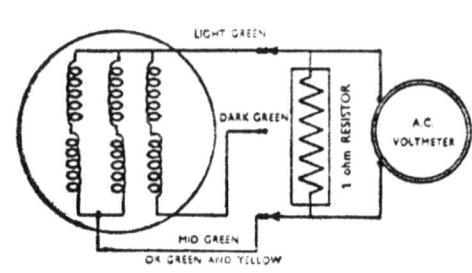

Test	Voltmeter and Resistor Connected Across	Reading Volts at 3,000 r.p.m.		
		RM13	RM13/15	RM15
1	Dark Green and Light Green	3.0 (min.)	3.25 (min.)	4.25 (min.)
2	Light Green and Mid Green or Green/Yellow	6.0 (min.)	6.25 (min.)	6.75 (min.)
3	Dark Green and Light Green (with Mid Green or Green/Yellow connected to Dark Green).	8.5 (min.)	8.75 (min.)	9.25 (min.)
4	Any one lead and Generator Stator (Earth)	No Reading	No Reading	No Reading

Conclusions from these Tests.

Low reading on any group of coils indicates shorted turns.

Zero reading will indicate open circuit coil.

If all coils read low, partial de-magnetisation of rotor may have occured as a result of faulty rectifier. Check rectifier, and battery earth polarity before replacing rotor.

A reading between any one lead and the generator stator indicates an earthed coil. Replace stator or locate earth by isolating and testing individual coils.

Note.

With the engine running at 3,000 r.p.m. (approx.) the output voltages are steady, and even if the engine is running a few r.p.m. faster or slower the values stated will be obtained from a good generator.

B.S.A. SERVICE SHEET No. 813 (contd.)

Rectifier—Bench Testing

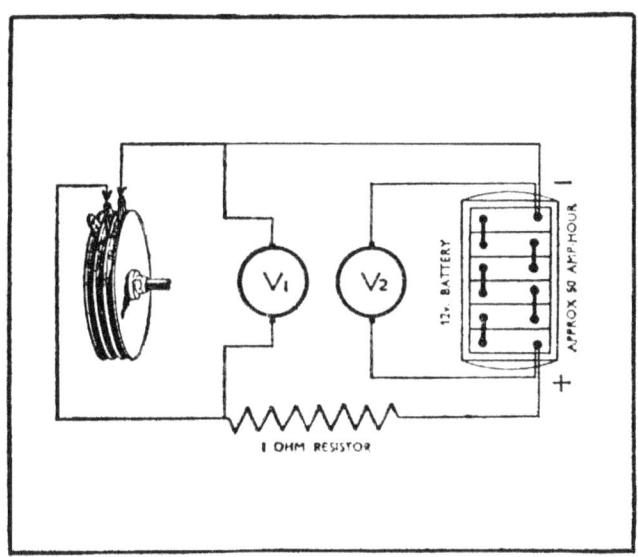
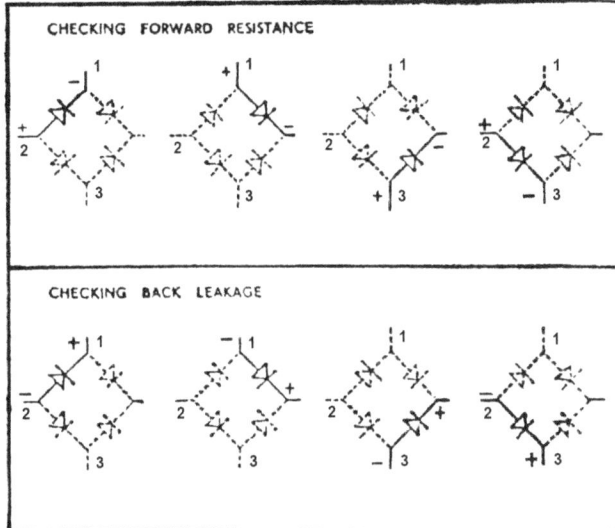

V1—will measure the volt drop across the rectifier plate.

V2—must be checked when testing the rectifier plate, to make certain the supply voltage is the recommended 12 volts on load.

It is essential that the supply is kept at 12 volts for these Tests.

Forward Resistance Test

Test 1. Connect test leads in turn to terminals 2 and 1, bolt and 1, bolt and 3, 2 and 3. Reading in all positions should not be greater than 2.5 volts. Keep the testing time as short as possible to avoid overheating the rectifier cell. Note.—If the later type of rectifier, which has no terminal markings, is fitted, the same test procedure is followed. The same voltage values also apply.

Back Leakage Test

Test 2. Proceed as for Test 1, and test each cell in turn, but reverse the test leads. Reading on V1 should not be less than 2 volts below the open-circuit reading on voltmeter No. 2, i.e., 10 volts.

Conclusion from these Tests

Test 1. If the voltage reading on V1 is more than 2.5 volts, on any cell, it is aged and the rectifier should be replaced.

Test 2. If the voltage reading on V1 is less than 10 volts, on any cell, the rectifier is shorted and should be replaced.

Important

Before fitting a replacement rectifier check the following points:—

1. Check that battery is correctly connected, **Positive to Earth.**
2. Check rectifier visually for signs of damage.

Never disturb the tension of the nut which holds the elements together on the through bolt. The efficiency of the rectifier depends upon the correct tension of the plates. The tension of the nut is set before leaving the works, and cannot be adjusted correctly in service.

B.S.A. SERVICE SHEET No. 813 (contd.)

Checking Rectifier in Position on Machine

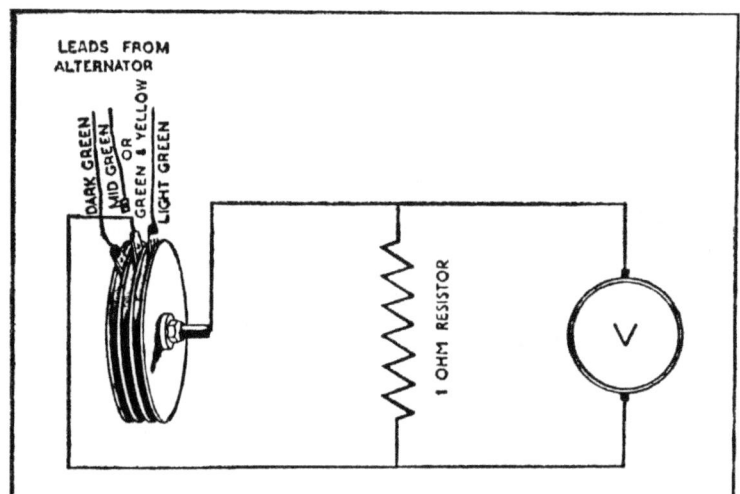
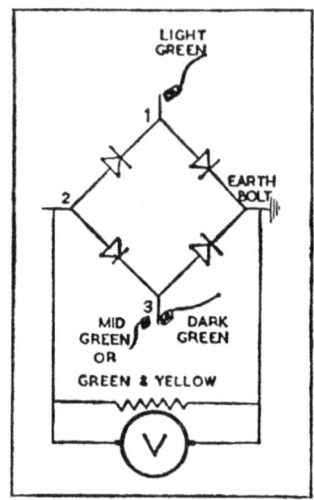

Voltmeter and Resistor Connected Across	Reading with Leads Connected as Shown
Terminal No. 2 (or centre terminal on latest type) and frame of machine	6.5 (min.) RM13 7.0 (min.) RM13/15 7.75 (min.) RM15

Procedure

Connect the alternator leads as detailed direct to the rectifier terminals No. 1 and No. 3.

(Note.—On the latest type rectifiers the terminals are not numbered, so connect the alternator leads to the outer cranked terminals).

Connect the test leads which must have a D.C. voltmeter with 1 ohm load shunted across, between earth (frame of machine) and terminal No. 2 (centre terminal on latest type rectifier) when the values stated should be obtained with engine running at 3,000 r.p.m.

Conclusions from these Tests

If the alternator passes its individual test, but it fails on this test it indicates that either the rectifier is faulty or it is not properly earthed.

Connecting the test leads to the centre bolt will eliminate the possibility of faulty earth connection

B.S.A. SERVICE SHEET No. 813 (contd.)

Testing the External Wiring Circuit

Using D.C. Voltmeter only
1. All cables, including battery, to be connected as normal.
2. Connect voltmeter Red test lead to earth.

Testing Charging Circuit through Ignition Switch
3. Connect Black test lead to No. 2 terminal on rectifier.
4. Switch ignition to IGN position.
5. Battery volts, i.e., six, should register on voltmeter.
6. If there is zero reading on voltmeter in the above condition, check circuit back through ignition switch, ammeter, etc., to the battery.

Testing Emergency Start Circuit (Single Cylinder Machine)
7. Connect Red test lead to earth.
8. Connect Black test lead to C.B. terminal on ignition contact breaker.
9. Open ignition contacts.
10. Switch ignition switch to EMG position.
11. Battery volts should register on voltmeter.
12. Transfer Black test lead to alternator Mid-Green lead.
13. Battery volts should register on voltmeter.

Note

These tests are to be carried out in the case of "No Charge" or "No Emergency Start" if previous tests have been carried out and all is in order.

It is important that both the ignition timing and the rotor timing is correct for efficient operation of Emergency Start.

Testing the 'Low,' 'Medium' and 'High' Charge Positions

Using D.C. Voltmeter only
1. Connect Red test lead to earth.
2. The set, including battery connected as normal, with the exception of the alternator Middle Green cable which should be disconnected at the snap connector under the saddle
3. Connect Black test lead to Mid-Green cable coming from headlamp (i.e., not coming from alternator).
4. With ignition switch in IGN position and lighting switch OFF.
5. A low voltage (i.e., 1—2) should register on voltmeter.
6. With lighting switch in PILOT, zero voltage should register on voltmeter.
7. With lighting switch in HEAD position a low voltage should register on voltmeter.

Note

Incorrect switching of these cables will cause incorrect charging rates, i.e., failure of Mid-Green and Dark Green linking together in HEAD position will result in a low charge rate with headlight switched on.

In the case of incorrect switching it is necessary to check the wiring and the switch for correct connections, etc.

B.S.A. SERVICE SHEET No. 813 (contd.)

Headlamp Switch

If both the rectifier and alternator appear satisfactory the wiring and switch contacts must be checked most carefully to eliminate any possible faults. The correct headlamp switch connections are shown in Service Sheets.

No. 808D ...	... C12
No. 808C ...	... C11G
No. 808H ...	... "B" models
No. 808J ...	... C15

Alternator Romoval and Replacement

The procedure for removing and replacing the alternator is described in Service Sheets No. 314 for "B" group machines and 409 for C11G and C12, and No. 422 for C15. Note that the stator should be assembled with the clip retaining the output cables on the side of the stator next to the engine on C11G and C12 but on C15 and "B" group machines the clip should be on the side away from the engine

B.S.A. MOTOR CYCLES LTD.,
Service Department, Armoury Road, Birmingham, 11
Printed in England.

BSA SERVICE SHEET No. 813A

C12, A Group and M21 Models

ADJUSTING THE CHARGING RATE OF LUCAS ALTERNATORS ON RADIO EQUIPPED MACHINES

GENERAL

The running conditions of radio equipped machines vary from long distance daylight patrol work with occasional use of the radio, to slow running convoy or short distance local work involving considerable use of the radio and possibly of the lights as well. There is a heavy load on the battery while transmitting, and the receiver may be left switched on for long periods representing a constant drain on the battery.

Obviously, the charging rates necessary to balance these varying loads must differ widely. Lucas alternators are designed to provide three alternative charge-rates which are selected by inter-changing the wiring connections.

The adjustments are simple to perform but the responsibility for making them should rest with the Maintenance Personnel who, being familiar with the running conditions and the state of charge of the batteries, are best placed to judge when any alteration is necessary. In the event of doubt, advice should be sought from Lucas Service Organisation.

It must be emphasised that battery charging from an external source may become necessary if a large proportion of night riding with the radio in use, or transmitting for long periods with the engine stopped is involved.

The C12 is fitted with a model RM13/15 Alternator in conjunction with a PRS8 Lighting and Ignition Switch.

By connecting or removing a wire link between switch terminals 5 and 6, two intermediate charge-rates can be obtained in addition to the three already mentioned.

B.S.A. Service Sheet No. 813A—*continued*

With the link in place the switch automatically increases the alternator output in the "Pilot" and "Head" positions. When the link is removed, the output increases only in the "Head" position.

If the alternator wiring is connected as in stage 3, maximum output is developed in all switch positions.

"A" GROUP AND M21 MODELS

These machines are fitted with a model RM15 Alternator as well as the normal 60 watt, E3L dynamo, and have a model U39 Lighting Switch. This is similar to the switch fitted to standard models, but it is provided with two toggle arms to control the alternator output in the various switch positions.

As on C12, stage 3, connections give maximum alternator output in all switch positions.

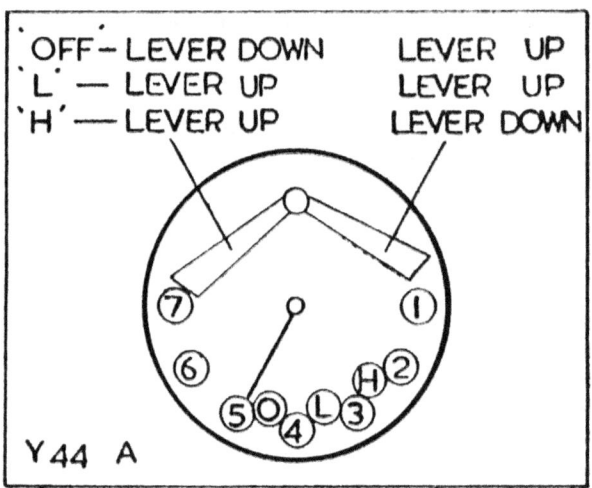

Current for all normal purposes is supplied by the alternator. This is supplemented by the dynamo as necessary when a heavy load is placed on the system. For servicing and testing purposes the two instruments should be dealt with separately, one being disconnected while testing the other.

When the radio is out of use for a prolonged period, it is important that the light green wire from the alternator is disconnected and the end taped up, otherwise the battery will become over-charged.

TESTING

As the radio is connected directly across the battery, the current taken will not be shown on the ammeter. To check whether the charging output is sufficient to balance the load, a second ammeter must be inserted in the cable between battery and radio. The reading on this ammeter must then be deducted from the charge shown on the ammeter fitted to the machine.

B.S.A. Service Sheet No. 813A—*continued*

DAYTIME CHARGING RATES

Alternator Cable Connections—Stage 1

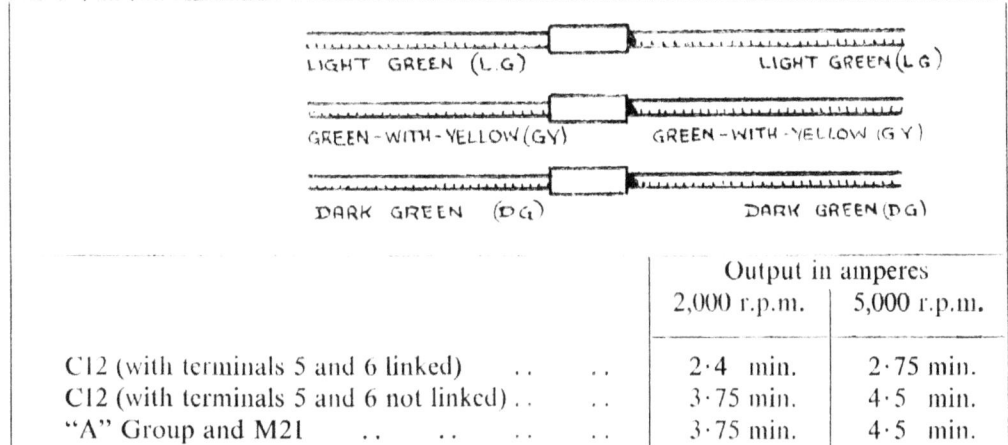

	Output in amperes	
	2,000 r.p.m.	5,000 r.p.m.
C12 (with terminals 5 and 6 linked)	2·4 min.	2·75 min.
C12 (with terminals 5 and 6 not linked)	3·75 min.	4·5 min.
"A" Group and M21	3·75 min.	4·5 min.

Alternator Cable Connections—Stage 2

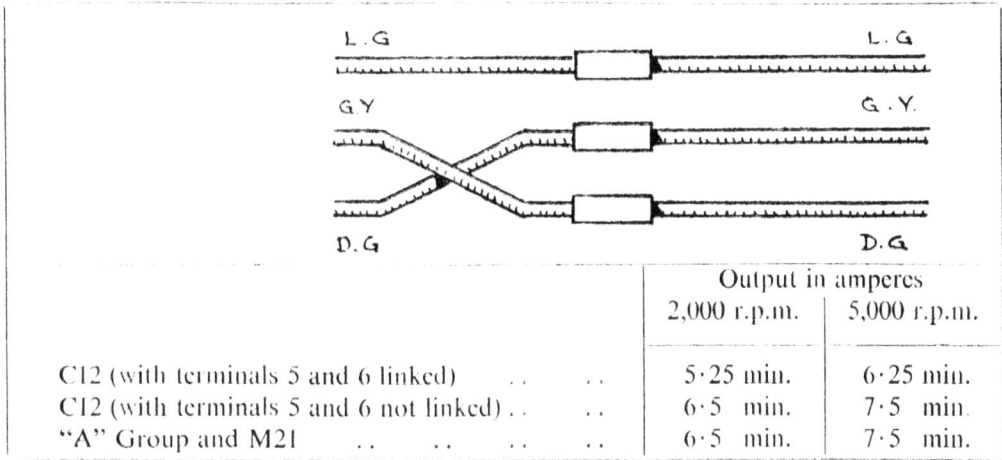

	Output in amperes	
	2,000 r.p.m.	5,000 r.p.m.
C12 (with terminals 5 and 6 linked)	5·25 min.	6·25 min.
C12 (with terminals 5 and 6 not linked)	6·5 min.	7·5 min.
"A" Group and M21	6·5 min.	7·5 min.

Alternator Cable Connections—Stage 3

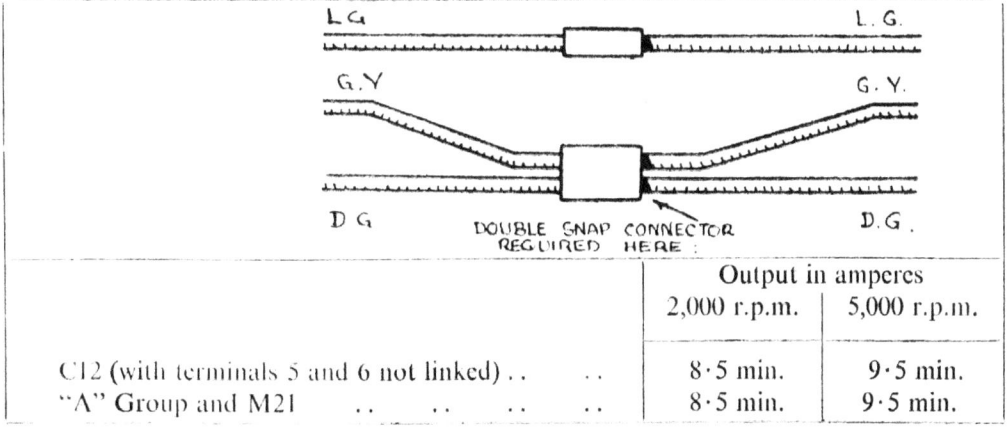

	Output in amperes	
	2,000 r.p.m.	5,000 r.p.m.
C12 (with terminals 5 and 6 not linked)	8·5 min.	9·5 min.
"A" Group and M21	8·5 min.	9·5 min.

B.S.A. Service Sheet No. 813A
continued

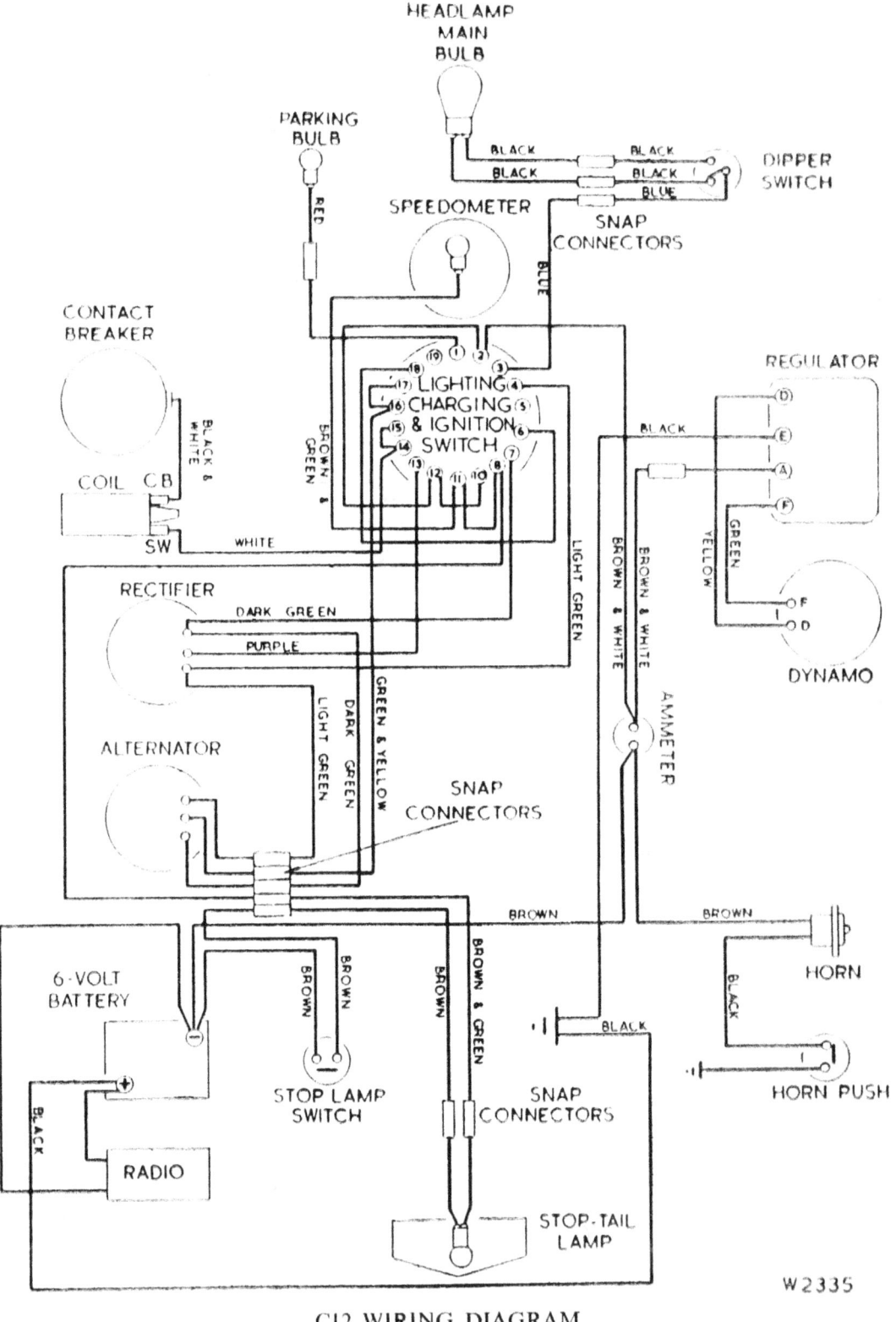

C12 WIRING DIAGRAM

B.S.A. Service Sheet No. 813A—continued

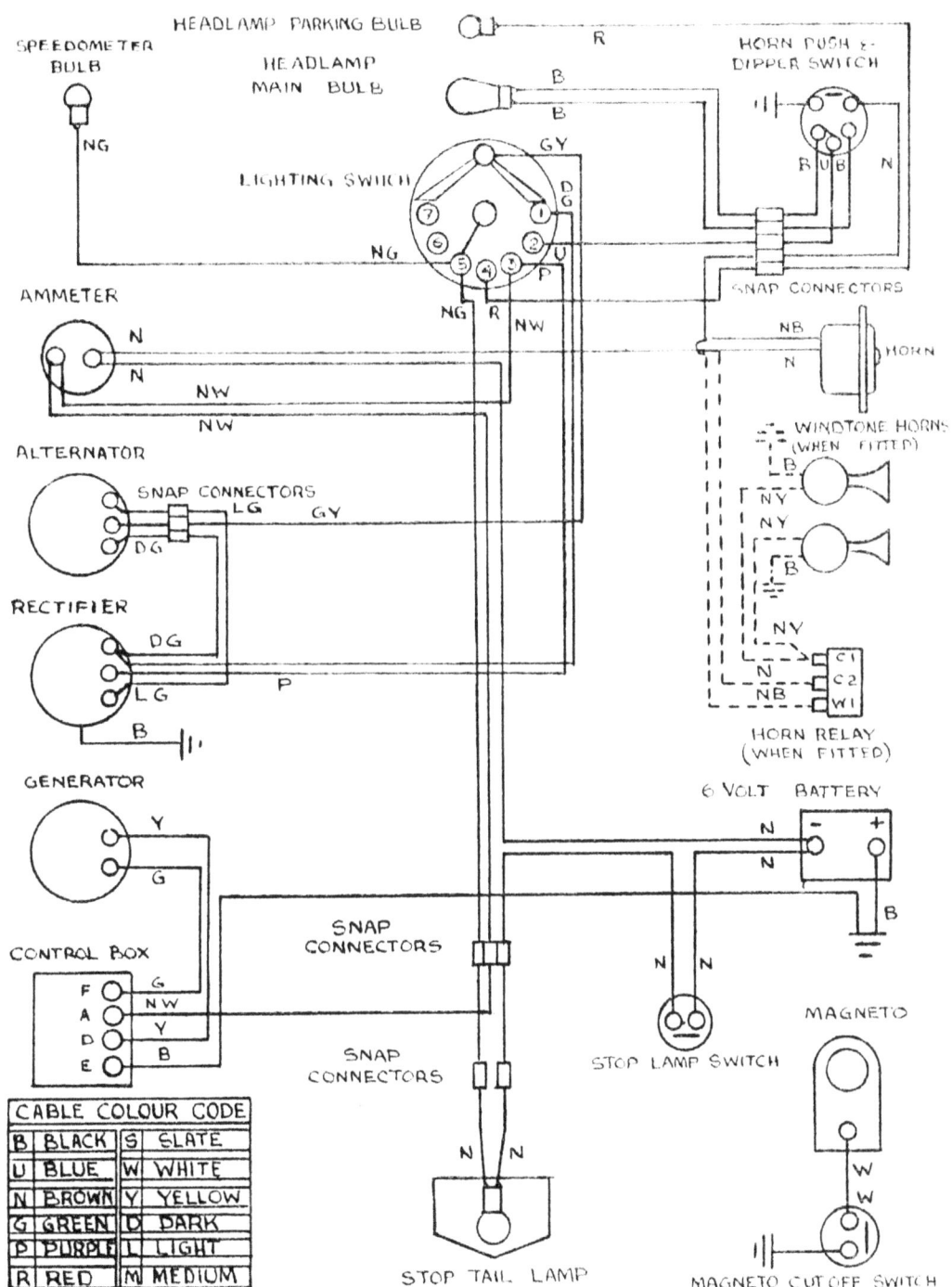

"A" GROUP WIRING DIAGRAM

B.S.A. Service Sheet No. 813A—*continued*

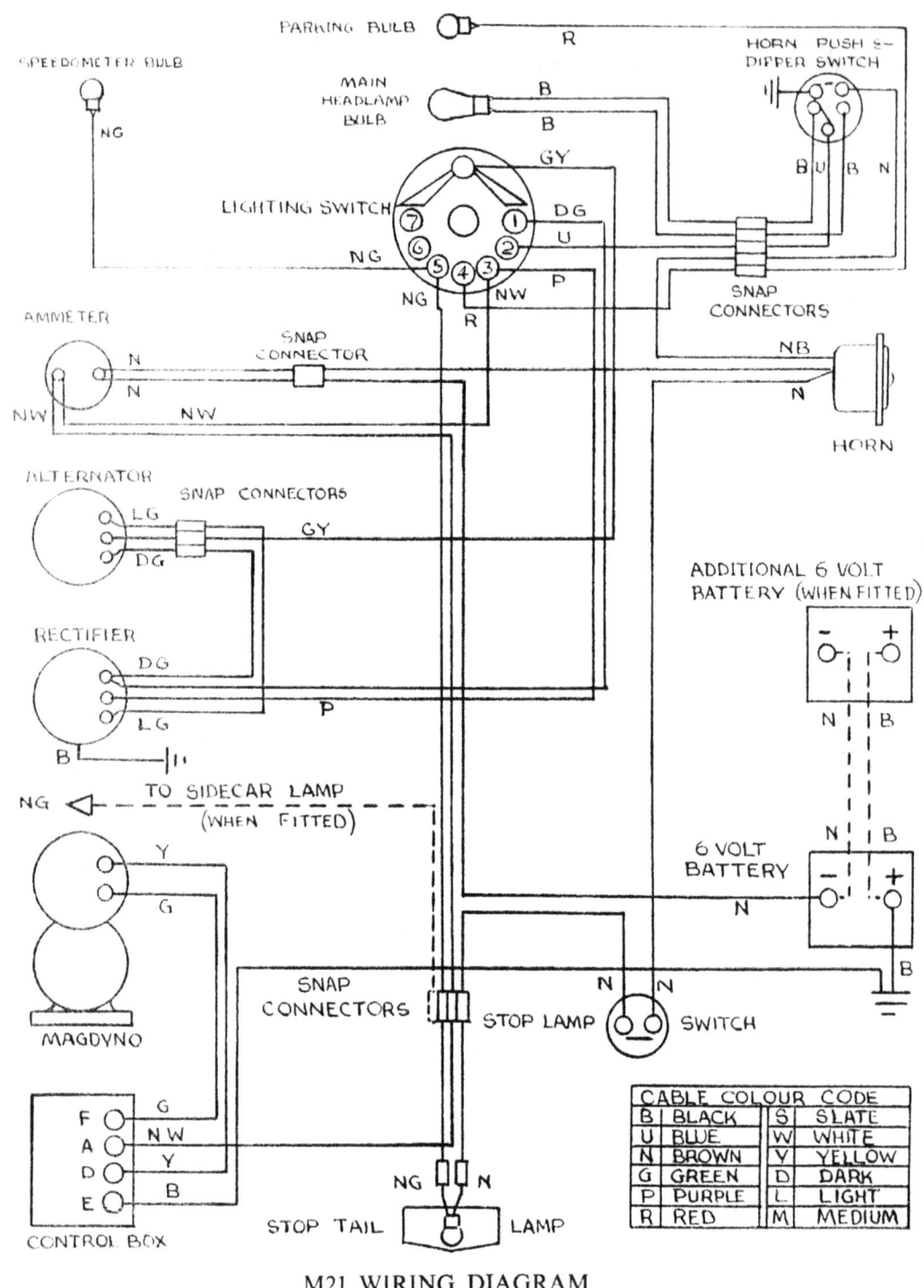

M21 WIRING DIAGRAM

B.S.A. MOTOR CYCLES LTD., Service Department, Armoury Road, Birmingham 11
Printed at The B.S.A. Press

BSA SERVICE SHEET No. 814

November, 1954

Model C1OL

WIPAC LIGHTING

The lighting circuit is supplied by an A.C. generator through a bridge type rectifier, so that, except when the headlamp switch is in the "Emergency" position, the coil, battery and lights are supplied with direct current in the normal way.

The generator output is automatically controlled by means of the headlamp switching to match the demands of the circuit and the characteristic of the generator prevents overcharging.

Alternator

The general arrangement of the alternator is as shown in Fig. Y45 and its dismantling entails removing the primary chaincase (See Service Sheet No. 409). No keeper is required for the magnets when dismantling.

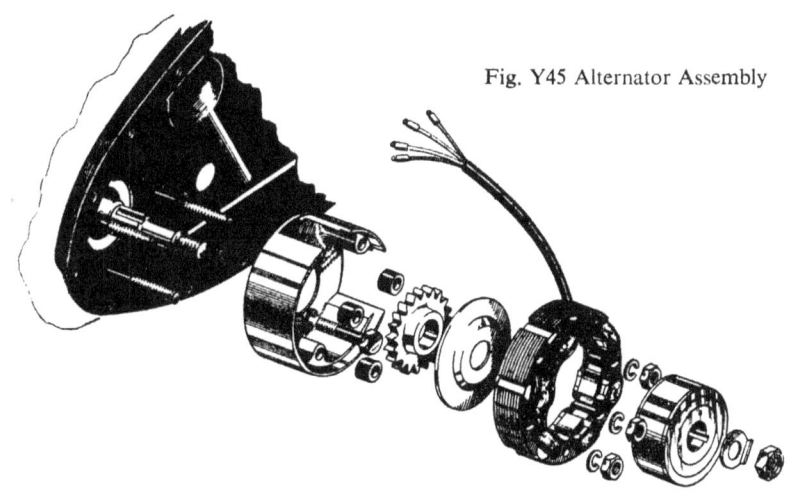

Fig. Y45 Alternator Assembly

The alternator employs six permanent magnets set in a central rotor and six output coils mounted on a surrounding stator. Two of the coils are connected in parallel within the generator and their output is brought out through the green and white leads. These two coils are permanently connected to the rectifier and supply current to the battery in all switch positions.

The remaining four coils are also connected in parallel (terminating in the orange and yellow leads) and are employed only when the headlight is on or when the headlamp switch is in the emergency start position.

Note: When replacing the stator, the bracket securing the output leads should be on the side of the stator facing away from the machine.

B.S.A. Service Sheet No. 814 (cont.)

Fault Finding

As the lighting circuit operates on the D.C. system, all bulb and electric horn connections can be checked by normal continuity tests with a D.C. Voltmeter or a spare bulb. Note that the system is positive earth.

The charging circuit can only be checked when the engine is running and for test purposes the engine speed should be not less than 2,200 r.p.m.

A suitable ammeter should be placed in series with the battery feed wire to check that the charging rate in each switch position agrees approximately with the following table.

Position 1. All Lights Off.   2.0 amps.
Position 2. Lights on Low ("L")
     (Pilot, Rear and Speedo Bulbs on)   .5 amp.
Position 3. Lights on High ("H")
     (Main, Rear and Speedo Bulbs on)   5 amp.

Failure to attain the listed rate in position 1 or 2 may indicate that the green or white lead is earthed at some point, or that one or both coils are earthed internally or are on open circuit.

Less than the correct charge in position 3 when correct charge is obtained in position 1 and 2, may indicate that the yellow or orange leads or any of the four coils are earthed, or are on open circuit.

Unsatisfactory performance in all switch positions is likely to be due to a faulty rectifier but may indicate any of the faults listed above.

Note: If a faulty rectifier is found, the tests should be repeated after replacement to ensure that the alternator has not been damaged. Alternatively, a burnt out alternator may be due to a faulty rectifier and the tests should again be repeated, taking care to ensure that the alternator is not again damaged if the rectifier or any other part of the circuit is shorting.

Checking the Rectifier

Detach the rectifier from the machine and using a 6v. battery in series with a 6v. 3 watt bulb apply the test leads to the rectifier in the following sequence. The rectifier terminals are illustrated in Fig. 46.

1. Positive lead to leg A.C.1, Negative to EARTH rectifier terminal.
1a. Reverse test leads and repeat above.
2. Positive lead to leg A.C.2, Negative to EARTH rectifier terminal.
2a. Reverse test leads and repeat above.
3. Positive lead to BATTERY rectifier terminal. Negative to leg A.C.1.
3a. Reverse test leads and repeat above.
4. Positive lead to BATTERY rectifier terminal. Negative to leg A.C.2.
4a. Reverse test leads and repeat above.

The bulb should light on the first of each pair of tests and not on the other, e.g. it should light on No. 1 test and not on 1a, and so on.

If the bulb lights in both directions on one or more of the four tests, the plate or plates have shorted.

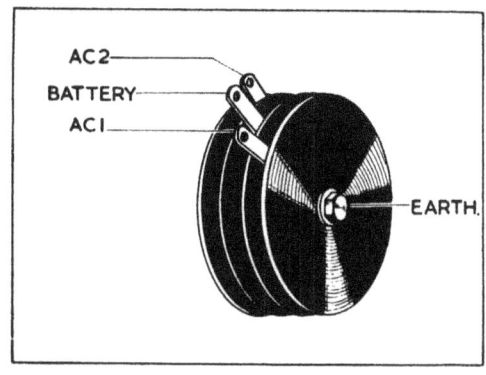 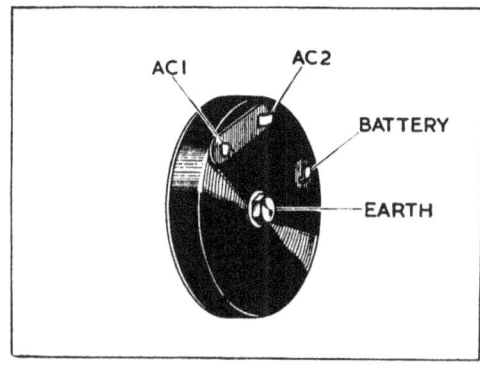

Rectifier, Finned Type   Rectifier, Pancake Type

Fig. Y46

If the bulb does not light in either direction on one or more of the four tests the plate or plates are in open circuit.

These tests will only check whether the rectifier is on open or short circuit, and will not provide any indication of a partial breakdown, which can only be detected by special equipment.

The rectifier must always be in a position where it can be adequately cooled by the air flow or a major failure may occur due to overheating.

The Headlamp Switch

In the event of trouble with this unit it should be inspected carefully for a dry soldered joint or a detached wire. Should neither of these be apparent the fault may be that the spring loaded ball contact of the switch does not make proper contact between two of the switch posts. Rapidly switching on and off several times may overcome this fault but otherwise the complete switch should be replaced.

The Emergency Start

If the machine fails to start owing to a flat battery the headlamp switch should be turned to the Emergency Start position "EMG". The machine can then be started in the normal way and when the engine is running at a reasonable speed the switch should be rapidly rotated to the normal running position.

If the battery is badly damaged or missing, the machine may be run with the switch in the "EMG" position but the live battery wire from the rectifier must be connected to earth or the rectifier will be seriously damaged.

When the machine is being run with the switch in the "EMG" position it may be found that its performance is adversely affected. This is due to the affect of phase shift and the symptons will disappear when the switch is returned to its normal position.

Ignition Coil

The ignition coil is of the oil filled type and should not require any attention whatsoever. Removal of the two slotted screws will permit the cap to be removed for inspection of the top connections and the suppressor, when fitted.

B.S.A. Service Sheet No. 814 (cont.)

Note: Burning out of bulbs is often due to an imperfect connection between the rectifier and battery or the battery and earth. Check the battery terminals regularly for corrosion, as a faulty connection at these points will cause trouble.

The double connectors used on the lighting system are internally connected so that all four plug-in sockets are interconnected.

U/5228.

B.S.A. MOTOR CYCLES LTD.
Service Dept., Birmingham 11
Printed in England.

BSA SERVICE SHEET No. 815

Models D1, D3 and C10L
VARLEY BATTERY. TYPE MC5/9.

The Varley battery differs in several ways from the conventional form of lead acid battery and the following description of its construction and the maintenance required will assist in ensuring that its maximum capacity is maintained.

The battery has the same general characteristics of the free-acid lead battery, but is unspillable and less sensitive to vibration by virtue of its construction. The acid in the battery is fully absorbed in the porous material which fills the space between the lead plates, and therefore, there is no free acid which can flow from the vents if the battery is overturned.

Maintenance

Whilst in service on the machine, the only maintenance required is to add the equivalent of a teaspoonful of distilled water to each cell at intervals of approximately once a month or six weeks. This small addition is to replace the moisture lost by evaporation and electrolysis, and it is essential that excess liquid is not added. All the added liquid should be absorbed within 20 minutes, and if any remains in the vents after this period, it must be removed by syphoning or shaking out. Topping up should not be carried out immediately before a journey.

An overflow of liquid from the Varley battery (usually indicated by a milky white substance on top of the battery) can only be caused by the addition of excess liquid and failure to remove the surplus, or by overcharging, or a combination of both.

As long as the overflow is not excessive and remains white in colour, the battery will probably remain completely unharmed. It should, therefore, be cleaned and any surplus liquid still remaining should be drained off. After spilling of this nature has taken place it may be advisable to add weak battery acid instead of distilled water when next the battery is due for topping up.

If the overflow develops a brown colour it is an indication of very heavy overcharging, and the battery has probably been damaged **beyond repair**.

In the event of the battery capacity being reduced after a considerable period of service it may prove advantageous to use weak battery acid instead of distilled water for topping up on one or two occasions.

State of Charge

The state of charge of Varley batteries should be determined by the following voltage readings. It is not possible to use a hydrometer.

Fully discharged	5.7 volts or under.
Partially discharged	6.15 volts or under.
Fully charged	6.3 volts or over.
On charge, fully charged	7.8 volts or over.

Charging the Battery from a Separate Source

All Varley batteries fitted to B.S.A. machines have already been filled and charged before despatch from the Works. A glance at the battery will show exactly when the battery was initially charged as a date code is stamped into each individual battery case.

A letter 'C' on the left-hand bottom corner of the positive side of the battery denotes that the battery has been fully charged by the manufacturer.

On the opposite bottom corner of the same side a letter and figure denote the month and year of the initial charge ('A' for January; 'B' for February; 'C' for March, etc., and '3' for 1953, '4' for 1954, '5' for 1955, and so on). As an example, a battery coded 'C' 'J4' denotes that the battery was filled with acid and initially charged by the manufacturer in October, 1954.

B.S.A. Service Sheet No. 815 (contd.)

If the battery is subsequently left idle for any length of time without being put into service then it should be given a boost charge in accordance with the table below:

Battery idle for 1—2 months	Charge at 1 amp. for 6 hours.
Battery idle for 3—6 months	Charge at 1 amp. for 12 hours.
Battery idle for more than 6 months ...	Charge at 1 amp. for 12 hours. Discharge the battery at 1—2 amps. then immediately recharge at 1 amp. for 12 hours.

Under normal conditions the battery should never be allowed to stand idle for more than a month without charging.

Charging the battery on the bench is carried out in exactly similar manner to that adopted for free acid batteries. Add distilled water as necessary and if the battery has been allowed to get abnormally dry it should be topped up before and during charging. When the voltage reading on charge reaches 7.8 volts, continue charging for a further three hours. All surplus moisture should be absorbed into the battery within half an hour of switching off the charging current. If any liquid does remain in the vents it must be removed by syphoning or shaking out.

Charging a New Battery

If a new battery is to be installed on a machine and it has not already been filled and given its initial charge, then the following procedure must be carried out.

Remove the vent stoppers and fill the battery with pure accumulator acid of a specific gravity which agrees with the table below:

Temperate Climate	1.270
Warm Climate	1.250
Tropical Climate	1.235

The acid will be steadily absorbed into the battery and acid should be added to each cell in turn until the levels remain unchanged for several minutes.

Allow the battery to stand for a period of 2—8 hours. If any of the cells are dry after this period they should again be topped up with acid. It is particularly important that the battery absorbs sufficient acid during this initial period, if it is to give a long life and satisfactory performance. The battery must be put on charge within fifteen hours of the commencement of filling.

For the initial charge the input should be 60 Ah. at a rate not exceeding 1 amp. (i.e., 60 hours at 1 amp. or 80 hours at .75 amp.). During this first charge top up with distilled water only.

The charge should be continuous and it is not advisable for the current to be switched off until completion. If, for any major reason, the charging has to be stopped, the open circuit standing time should be allowed for.

During the final stage of charge, the voltage of the battery should read at least 7.8 volts (i.e., 2.6 volts per cell) and every cell should be gassing freely.

After completion of charge any liquid remaining in the vents should be removed by syphoning or shaking out. The battery should then be cleaned and thoroughly dried. Before replacing the vent stoppers, remove the sealing tape, if any. Grease the terminals slightly with vaseline before connecting up.

B.S.A. MOTOR CYCLES LTD.,
Service Dept., Armoury Road, **Birmingham 11**.
Printed in England.

VELOCEPRESS MANUALS - MOTORCYCLE

1930'S BRITISH MOTORCYCLE CARBS & ELEC COMPONENTS (BOOK OF)
1930'S BRITISH MOTORCYCLE ENGINES (OVERHAUL & MAINTENANCE)
1930'S BRITISH MOTORCYCLE GEARBOXES & CLUTCHES (BOOK OF)
AJS 1932-1948 SINGLES & TWINS 250cc THRU 1000cc (BOOK OF)
AJS 1945-1960 SINGLES 350cc & 500cc MODELS 16 & 18 (BOOK OF)
AJS 1955-1965 SINGLES 350cc & 500cc (BOOK OF)
ARIEL UP TO 1932 (BOOK OF)
ARIEL 1932-1939 PREWAR MODELS (BOOK OF)
ARIEL 1933-1951 (WORKSHOP MANUAL)
ARIEL 1939-1960 4 STROKE SINGLES (BOOK OF)
ARIEL 1958-1964 LEADER & ARROW (BOOK OF)
BMW R26 R27 (1956-1967) FACTORY WORKSHOP MANUAL
BMW R50 R50S R60 R69S (1955-1969) FACTORY WORKSHOP MANUAL
BRIDGESTONE 90 SERIES FACTORY WSM & PARTS CATALOGUE
BRIDGESTONE 175 SERIES FACTORY WSM & PARTS CATALOGUE
BRIDGESTONE 350 SERIES FACTORY WSM & PARTS CATALOGUES
BSA BANTAM ALL MODELS FROM 1948 ONWARDS (BOOK OF)
BSA SINGLES & V-TWINS UP TO 1927 (BOOK OF)
BSA SINGLES & V-TWINS UP TO 1930 (BOOK OF)
BSA SINGLES & V-TWINS UP TO 1935 (BOOK OF)
BSA SINGLES & V-TWINS 1936-1939 (BOOK OF)
BSA C10, C11 & C12 1945-1958 FACTORY SERVICE SHEETS MANUAL
BSA OHV & SV SINGLES 250-600cc 1945-1959 (BOOK OF)
BSA C15 & B40 1958-1967 FACTORY SERVICE SHEETS MANUAL
BSA OHV & SV SINGLES 250cc (ONLY) 1954-1970 (BOOK OF)
BSA B31, B32, B33 & B34 1945-60 FACTORY SERVICE SHEETS MANUAL
BSA OHV SINGLES 350 & 500cc 1955-1967 (BOOK OF)
BSA M20, M21 & M33 1945-1963 FACTORY SERVICE SHEETS MANUAL
BSA TWINS A7 & A10 1948-1962 FACTORY SERVICE SHEETS MANUAL
BSA TWINS A7 & A10 1948-1962 (BOOK OF)
BSA TWINS A50 & A65 1962-1969 (SECOND BOOK OF)
CYCLEMOTOR (BOOK OF)
DOUGLAS 1929-1939 PREWAR ALL MODELS (BOOK OF)
DOUGLAS 1948-1957 POSTWAR ALL MODELS FACTORY SHOP MANUAL
DUCATI 160cc, 250cc & 350cc OHC MODELS FACTORY SHOP MANUAL
HONDA 50 ALL MODELS UP TO 1970 INC MONKEY & TRAIL (BOOK OF)
HONDA 90 ALL MODELS UP TO 1966 (BOOK OF)
HONDA 125-150cc TWINS C/CS/CB/CA FACTORY WORKSHOP MANUAL
HONDA 250-305 TWINS C/CS/CB FACTORY WORKSHOP MANUAL
HONDA 450 CB/CL 1965-1974 K0 TO K7 WORKSHOP MANUAL
HONDA C100 SUPER CUB FACTORY WORKSHOP MANUAL
HONDA C110 SPORT CUB 1962-1969 FACTORY WORKSHOP MANUAL
HONDA TWINS & SINGLES 50cc THRU 305cc 1960-1966 (BOOK OF)
HONDA TWINS ALL MODELS 125cc THRU 450cc UP TO 1968 (BOOK OF)
INDIAN PONYBIKE, BOY RACER & PAPOOSE ILL PARTS LIST & SALES LIT
J.A.P. ENGINES 1927-1952 & MOTORCYCLES 1934-1952 (BOOK OF)
LAMBRETTA 1947-1957 ALL 125 & 150cc MODELS (BOOK OF)
LAMBRETTA 1957-1970 LI & TV MODELS (SECOND BOOK OF)
MATCHLESS 1931-1939 ALL MODELS 250cc THRU 990cc (BOOK OF)
MATCHLESS 1945-1956 350 & 500cc SINGLES (BOOK OF)
MATCHLESS 1955-1966 350 & 500cc SINGLES (BOOK OF)
NEW IMPERIAL ALL SV & OHV FROM 1935 ONWARDS (BOOK OF)
NORTON 1932-1939 PREWAR MODELS (BOOK OF)
NORTON 1932-1947 (BOOK OF)
NORTON 1938-1956 (BOOK OF)
NORTON 1955-1963 MODELS 19, 50 & ES2 (BOOK OF)
NORTON 1955-1965 DOMINATOR TWINS (BOOK OF)
NORTON 1960-1970 TWIN CYLINDER FACTORY WORKSHOP MANUAL
NORTON 1970-1975 COMMANDO FACTORY WORKSHOP MANUAL
NORTON 1975-1978 MK 3 COMMANDO FACTORY WORKSHOP MANUAL
NSU PRIMA 1956-1964 ALL MODELS (BOOK OF)
NSU QUICKLY 1953-1963 ALL MODELS (BOOK OF)
PANTHER 1932-1958 LIGHTWEIGHT MODELS 250 & 350cc (BOOK OF)
PANTHER 1938-1966 HEAVYWEIGHT MODELS 600 & 650cc (BOOK OF)
RALEIGH MOPEDS 1960-1969 (BOOK OF)
RALEIGH MOTORCYCLES 1919-1933 (BOOK OF)
ROYAL ENFIELD 1934-1946 SINGLES & V TWINS (BOOK OF)
ROYAL ENFIELD 1937-1953 SINGLES & V TWINS (BOOK OF)
ROYAL ENFIELD 1946-1962 SINGLES (BOOK OF)
ROYAL ENFIELD 1958-1966 250cc & 350cc SINGLES (SECOND BOOK OF)
ROYAL ENFIELD 736cc INTERCEPTOR FACTORY WORKSHOP MANUAL
RUDGE 1933-1939 (BOOK OF)
SUNBEAM 1928-1939 (BOOK OF)
SUNBEAM 1946-1957 S7 & S8 (BOOK OF)
SUZUKI 50cc & 80cc UP TO 1966 (BOOK OF)
SUZUKI T10 1963-1967 FACTORY WORKSHOP MANUAL
SUZUKI T20 & T200 1965-1969 FACTORY WORKSHOP MANUAL
SUZUKI TWINS 1962 ONWARDS 125-500cc WORKSHOP MANUAL
TRIUMPH 1935-1939 PREWAR MODELS (BOOK OF)
TRIUMPH 1935-1949 (BOOK OF)
TRIUMPH 1937-1951 (WORKSHOP MANUAL)
TRIUMPH 1945-1955 FACTORY WORKSHOP MANUAL
TRIUMPH 1945-1958 TWINS (BOOK OF)
TRIUMPH 1956-1969 TWINS (BOOK OF)
VELOCETTE 1925-1970 ALL SINGLES & TWINS (BOOK OF)
VESPA 1951-1961 (BOOK OF)
VESPA 1955-1963 125 & 150cc & GS MODELS (SECOND BOOK OF)
VESPA 1955-1968 GS & SS (BOOK OF)
VESPA 1963-1972 90, 125 & 150cc (THIRD BOOK OF)
VILLIERS ENGINE UP TO 1959 INC. 3 WHEELERS (BOOK OF)
VILLIERS ENGINE UP TO 1969 (BOOK OF)
VINCENT 1935-1955 (WORKSHOP MANUAL)
YAMAHA 1961-1967 YA5 & YA6 (WORKSHOP MANUAL & ILL PARTS LIST)
YAMAHA 1971-1972 JT1& JT2 (WORKSHOP MANUAL & ILL PARTS LIST)

VELOCEPRESS TECHNICAL BOOKS – MOTORCYCLE

CATALOG OF BRITISH MOTORCYCLES (1951 MODELS)
LUCAS ELECTRONICS BRITISH M/CYCLES REPAIR & PARTS (1950-1977)
MOTORCYCLE ENGINEERING (P.E. Irving)
MOTORCYCLE ROAD TESTS 1949-1953 (Motor Cycle Magazine UK)
SPEED AND HOW TO OBTAIN IT (Motor Cycle Magazine UK)
TUNING FOR SPEED (P.E. Irving)

VELOCEPRESS MANUALS - THREE WHEELER'S

BSA THREE WHEELER (BOOK OF)
VINTAGE MORGAN THREE WHEELER (BOOK OF)

VELOCEPRESS MANUALS - AUTOMOBILE

ALFA ROMEO GIULIA WORKSHOP MANUAL 1300 TO 2000cc 1962-1975
ALFA ROMEO GIULIA TECH MANUAL CARBURETED CARS FROM 1962
ALFA ROMEO GIULIA TECH MANUAL FUEL INJECTED CARS FROM 1969
ALFA ROMEO GIULIETTA & GIULIA 750 & 101 SERIES 1955-1965 WSM
AUSTIN-HEALEY SPRITE & MG MIDGET WORKSHOP MANUAL 1958-1971
BMW 600 LIMOUSINE FACTORY WORKSHOP MANUAL
BMW 600 LIMOUSINE OWNERS HAND BOOK & SERVICE MANUAL
BMW 2000 & 2002 1966-1976 WORKSHOP MANUAL
BMW ISETTA FACTORY WORKSHOP MANUAL
CORVAIR 1960-1969 WORKSHOP MANUAL
CORVETTE V8 1955-1962 WORKSHOP MANUAL
FIAT 500 FACTORY WORKSHOP MANUAL 1957-1973
FIAT 600, 600D & MULTIPLA FACTORY WORKSHOP MANUAL 1955-1969
JAGUAR E-TYPE 3.8 & 4.2 SERIES 1 & 2 WORKSHOP MANUAL
JAGUAR MK 7, 8, 9 & XK120, 140, 150 WORKSHOP MANUAL 1948-1961
METROPOLITAN FACTORY WORKSHOP MANUAL
MGA & MGB OWNERS HANDBOOK & WORKSHOP MANUAL
MG MIDGET TC, TD, TF & TF1500 WORKSHOP MANUAL
PORSCHE 356 1948-1965 WORKSHOP MANUAL
PORSCHE 911 2.0, 2.2, 2.4 LITRE 1964-1973 WORKSHOP MANUAL
PORSCHE 911 2.7, 3.0, 3.2 LITRE 1973-1989 WORKSHOP MANUAL
PORSCHE 912 WORKSHOP MANUAL
TRIUMPH TR2, TR3, TR4 1953-1965 WORKSHOP MANUAL
VOLKSWAGEN TRANSPORTER, TRUCKS & WAGONS 1950-1979 WSM
VOLVO 1944-1968 ALL MODELS WORKSHOP MANUAL

VELOCEPRESS TECHNICAL BOOKS - AUTOMOBILE

FERRARI 250/GT SERVICE AND MAINTENANCE
FERRARI GUIDE TO PERFORMANCE
FERRARI OWNER'S HANDBOOK
FERRARI TUNING TIPS & MAINTENANCE TECHNIQUES
HOW TO BUILD A FIBERGLASS CAR
HOW TO BUILD A RACING CAR
HOW TO RESTORE THE MODEL 'A' FORD
MASERATI OWNER'S HANDBOOK
OBERT'S FIAT GUIDE
PERFORMANCE TUNING THE SUNBEAM TIGER
SOUPING THE VOLKSWAGEN
SOLEX CARBURETORS (EMPHASIS ON UK & EU AUTOMOBILES)
SU CARBURETORS (EMPHASIS ON UK AUTOMOBILES)
WEBER CARBURETORS (EMPHASIS ON ALFA & FIAT)

VELOCEPRESS BOOKS & GUIDES - AUTOMOBILE

ABARTH BUYERS GUIDE
COMPLETE CATALOG OF JAPANESE MOTOR VEHICLES
FERRARI 308 SERIES BUYER'S AND OWNER'S GUIDE
FERRARI BERLINETTA LUSSO
FERRARI BROCHURES AND SALES LITERATURE 1946-1967
FERRARI BROCHURES AND SALES LITERATURE 1968-1989
FERRARI OPP, MAINTENANCE & SERVICE H/BOOKS 1948-1963
FERRARI SERIAL NUMBERS PART I - ODD NUMBERS TO 21399
FERRARI SERIAL NUMBERS PART II - EVEN NUMBERS TO 1050
FERRARI SPYDER CALIFORNIA
HENRY'S FABULOUS MODEL "A" FORD
MASERATI BROCHURES AND SALES LITERATURE

VELOCEPRESS BOOKS – RACING

CARRERA PANAMERICANA - MEXICAN ROAD RACE (BOOK OF)
DIALED IN - THE JAN OPPERMAN STORY
IF HEMINGWAY HAD WRITTEN A RACING NOVEL
VEDA ORR'S NEW REVISED HOT ROD PICTORIAL

AUTOBOOKS WORKSHOP MANUALS & BROOKLANDS ROAD TEST PORTFOLIOS

FOR A COMPLETE LISTING OF THE AUTOBOOKS & BROOKLANDS TITLES THAT WE CURRENTLY HAVE AVAILABLE, PLEASE VISIT OUR WEBSITE.

www.VelocePress.com

Please check our website:

www.VelocePress.com

for a complete
up-to-date list of
available titles

www.ingramcontent.com/pod-product-compliance
Lightning Source LLC
Chambersburg PA
CBHW080431230426

43662CB00015B/2242